Analyzing Wagner's Operas

Alfred Lorenz (1868–1939)

Analyzing Wagner's Operas

Alfred Lorenz and
German Nationalist Ideology

Stephen McClatchie

 University of Rochester Press

First published 1998

University of Rochester Press
668 Mt. Hope Avenue
Rochester, NY 14620   USA

and at P.O. Box 9
Woodbridge, Suffolk IP12 3DF
United Kingdom

ISBN 1–58046–023–2
ISSN 1071–9989

Library of Congress Cataloging-in-Publication Data

McClatchie, Stephen, 1965–
    Analyzing Wagner's operas : Alfred Lorenz and German nationalist
ideology / Stephen McClatchie.
        p.   cm. — (Eastman studies in music)
    Includes bibliographical references (p.   ) and index.
    ISBN 1–58046–023–2 (alk. paper)
    1. Lorenz, Alfred Ottokar, 1868–1939. 2. Wagner, Richard,
1813–1883. Operas. 3. Musical form. I. Title. II. Series.
ML423.L637M33   1998
782.1´092—dc21   98–28637
                                                                              CIP
                                                                              MN

British Library Cataloguing-in-Publication Data
A catalogue record for this book is
available from the British Library

Designed and typeset by Cornerstone Composition Services
Printed in the United States of America
This publication is printed on acid-free paper

Contents

Figures

Musical Examples

Eastman Studies in Music

(ISSN 1071–9989)

The Poetic Debussy: A Collection of
His Song Texts and Selected Letters
(Revised Second Edition)
Edited by Margaret G. Cobb

Concert Music, Rock, and Jazz since 1945:
Essays and Analytical Studies
Edited by Elizabeth West Marvin and
Richard Hermann

Music and the Occult:
French Musical Philosophies, 1750–1950
Joscelyn Godwin

"Wanderjahre of a Revolutionist and
Other Essays on American Music
Arthur Farwell, edited by Thomas Stoner

French Organ Music from the Revolution
to Franck and Widor
Edited by Lawrence Archbold and
William J. Peterson

Musical Creativity in Twentieth-Century
China: Abing, His Music, and Its Changing
Meanings (includes CD)
Jonathan P.J. Stock

Elliott Carter: Collected Essays and
Lectures, 1937–1995
Edited by Jonathan W. Bernard

Music Theory in Concept and Practice
Edited by James M. Baker, David W.
Beach, and Jonathan W. Bernard

Music and Musicians in the Escorial
Liturgy under the Habsburgs, 1563–1700
Michael Noone

Analyzing Wagner's Operas: Alfred Lorenz
and German Nationalist Ideology
Stephen McClatchie

Forthcoming

The Gardano Music Printing Firms, 1569–1611
Richard J. Agee

"The Broadway Sound": The Autobiography and
Selected Essays of Robert Russell Bennett
Edited by George J. Ferencz

Theories of Fugue from the Age of Josquin to the Age of Bach
Paul Mark Walker

Preface

The long shadow of Alfred Lorenz still hangs over the field of Wagner research two decades after Joseph Kerman attempted to exorcize his influence by vainly asserting that "Lorenz has finally gone under after withstanding a fantastic plowing."[1] But Lorenz has far from "gone under." In their survey of the history of operatic analysis, Carolyn Abbate and Roger Parker speak of "the ritual slap upon Lorenz's hand" as a necessary accoutrement to any Wagnerian analysis, and present the relationship between Lorenz and the modern Wagnerian analyst in almost agonistic terms, suggesting that "if we can thus make [Lorenz's work] an artifact, we can free ourselves from anxiety about its influence."[2] However desirable this goal may be from an analytical point of view, its success is doubtful until Lorenz's work has been considered and evaluated in its entirety—an enterprise which, surprisingly, has never been attempted. Rather more to the point is Geoffrey Chew's contention that "[d]espite the familiarity of modern English-language theory with Schoenberg and Schenker, other German theory of that period is still too little known, either in the English-speaking world or elsewhere, and it too needs to be thoroughly digested by modern writers."[3]

Between 1924 and 1933 Lorenz published a four-volume study of Wagnerian form entitled *Das Geheimnis der Form bei Richard Wagner* in which he attempted to counter the charge that Wagner's music was "formless." In this study Lorenz argues that the form of a work is recognized through the perception of larger, coherent sections which are defined by such fundamental parameters as rhythm, tonality, and melody. He focuses on a little-noticed (at that time) section in *Oper und Drama* where Wagner suggests that his works are unified through a succession of *dichterisch-musikalische Periode*, each delineated by a principal key. Lorenz sets out these "poetic-musical periods" for the *Ring*, *Tristan*, *Meistersinger*, and *Parsifal*. Within these tonally determined periods, Lorenz discovers certain types of melodic patterning which seem to recur frequently in Wagner's works. Particularly important among these is a three-part A-B-A form, which Lorenz calls Bogen form (arch form), and the A-A-B form, or Bar form, employed by the medieval Meistersingers; a Bar is comprised of two Stollen and an Abgesang.

---

1. Joseph Kerman, "Viewpoint," *19th-Century Music* 2 (1978): 189.

2. Carolyn Abbate and Roger Parker, "Introduction: On Analyzing Opera," in *Analyzing Opera: Verdi and Wagner,* ed. Carolyn Abbate and Roger Parker (Berkeley and Los Angeles: University of California Press, 1989), 14–15.

3. Geoffrey Chew, "Ernst Kurth, Music as Psychic Motion, and *Tristan und Isolde*: Towards a Model for Analysing Musical Instability," *Music Analysis* 10 (1991): 190.

Recent work in literary and cultural theory has shown the value of approaching works as texts—as multivalent entities that both reflect and are reflected by society. By paying attention to how things are said, and in what context(s), a critic can often unpack latent meanings, contradictions, and so on. This approach is particularly fruitful in the case of Alfred Lorenz, for whom even such basic work as an evaluation of the aesthetic and philosophical background of his analytical methodology has not been done. Lorenz was an explicit follower of the philosophy of Arthur Schopenhauer (particularly as it relates to the arts), and as a Wagnerian, a proponent of the so-called "expressive" aesthetic position (*Ausdrucksäthetik*). The first part of the second chapter presents the expressive aesthetic as formulated in such works as Friedrich von Hausegger's *Musik als Ausdruck*, and discusses its paradoxical basis in both the idealistic philosophy of Schopenhauer and the positivistic evolutionary science of the nineteenth century. Hausegger's expressive aesthetic is contrasted with the formal aesthetic of Hanslick, and the impossibility of any viable comparison is argued on the grounds of their fundamentally different notions of what music is and does.

The second part of the second chapter surveys developments in late nineteenth- and early twentieth-century analysis of musical form. Topics covered include the alleged form/content split, organicism, and Gestalt psychology. The chapter concludes with a discussion of Wagnerian analysis before Lorenz, with particular emphasis on the influence of the expressive aesthetic on the Wagnerian camp.

The third chapter presents Lorenz's own aesthetic and philosophical position as revealed in his writings. It examines his understanding of the work of art and the entire question of "form." Lorenz's views derive from the expressive aesthetic position in all of its subjectivity: works of art are conceived in an instantaneous moment of inspiration, which must then be made concrete by the artist. This involves the temporalization (rhythmic division) of this initial inspiration. Enjoyment of a work of art, argues Lorenz, is a result of being attuned to its rhythmic divisions so that the "receiving spirit" vibrates in accord with the work. This subjective emphasis on the body and on reception derives straight from Hausegger, and is part of a general anti-positivistic movement typical of early twentieth-century thought. The chapter concludes with a discussion of Lorenz's view of the leitmotive and of the *Gesamtkunstwerk* which attempts to demonstrate its dependence upon an acceptance of the aesthetic position embodied in Schopenhauer's writings about music, and in writings of Wagnerians such as Hans von Wolzogen. With this background in place, chapter four discusses Lorenz's analytical method in detail: each type of form is presented and illustrated by examples taken from *Der Ring des Nibelungen* (Lorenz's analysis of which is summarized in appendix 1). The next chapter describes, briefly, the later volumes of *Das Geheimnis der Form* and the development of Lorenz's analytical technique, and concludes with an evaluation of Lorenz's method.

It is not an exaggeration to suggest that all Wagnerian analysis since Lorenz is in some respects a response to his work. If their view of Lorenz is favorable, writers may try to "correct" Lorenz's period divisions or refine the internal structuring of the periods; if it is negative, generally the entire approach is jettisoned in favor of a focus on individual details, whether harmonic or otherwise, without any attempt at totalization. That is, Wagnerian analysts traditionally sit in judgment upon Lorenz: is he right or is he wrong? Yet it might be suggested that "correctness" or "incorrectness" is not really the issue at hand—the important question is to try to understand why Lorenz was led to hear and analyze the music in such a way.

The issue is complicated by the fact that Lorenz was an ardent supporter of National Socialism, and has become mired in an ideological web from which he has never gotten free. Within the history of Lorenz reception (the basis of the sixth chapter) there is a move from treating Lorenz's work as text to treating Lorenz himself as text: that is, first, as a part of the ideology which produced him and subsequently as a reaction to that ideology after the war, and second, as a negative symbol within the prevailing postmodern ideology of our own times. That these ideological underpinnings are seldom made explicit only confirms the subtle, and largely unconscious "centering" role that ideology plays in each of us, in how we live out our relation to society, and renders apparently "objective" evaluations covertly subjective.[4]

Consequently, a value-neutral (non-ideological) treatment of Lorenz is an impossibility. What is needed is a balance between an objective description of his system and an evaluation of the ideologies shaping our own views of music and response to Lorenz. The aim is an evaluation of Lorenz which is at once critical of his analytic enterprise and sensitive to its historical positioning ("its" referring both to Lorenz and any author). The present work is therefore not an attempt to "redo" or "rehabilitate" Lorenz. Neither is it an exhaustive critique of his analyses in the sense of weighing the balance of their validity ("right" or "wrong"), although many of Lorenz's concepts will be examined and criticized along the way, as will many individual analyses. Rather it attempts to get "behind" the analyses and determine why they were generated.[5]

---

4. See Louis Althusser, "Ideology and Ideological State Apparatuses," in *Essays on Ideology* (London: Verso, 1984), 1–60, and Terry Eagleton, *Ideology: An Introduction* (London and New York: Verso, 1991).

5. Rose Rosengard Subotnik's essays on Adorno, criticism, and the workings of ideologies have, in many ways, strongly influenced the approach taken in the present work. See her *Developing Variations: Style and Ideology in Western Music* (Minneapolis: University of Minnesota Press, 1991).

To set the foundation for this approach, the first chapter presents, for the first time, a detailed evaluation of Lorenz's life and works, supplemented partially with archival material. It includes a discussion of Lorenz's personal and professional relationship with National Socialism, and of the close ties between Nazism and Lorenz's analytical methodology. The concluding chapter considers whether or not Lorenz should be understood as a formalist and argues that he is in fact a reactionary modernist—a position which serves to link him directly with the Nazis. The work is therefore framed by the National Socialist context in which I argue it is essential to see *Das Geheimnis der Form*.

In its original form, this work benefitted from the excellent advice and assistance of Jeffrey Stokes, Alison Stonehouse, Don Neville, Roger Parker, Pamela Potter, and William Kinderman, and my gratitude ought to be carried over into this new context. Its metamorphosis into a book has been ably overseen by Ralph Locke and Sean M. Culhane, and was, in many ways, indelibly shaped by their choice of an anonymous reader for the Press. I wish to thank Thomas S. Grey, who graciously identified himself to me as the said reader, for his thorough and thoughtful evaluation of the work, for his many useful suggestions, and for his subsequent advice and assistance with the revision. In addition to Tom, others have kindly read portions of this study or offered advice; to them, my warmest thanks: Lynn Cavanagh (my colleague at the University of Regina), Joan Evans, Benjamin Korstvedt, Pamela Potter, and Alison Stonehouse. Thank you as well to Louise Goldberg and Jürgen Thym, and to my colleague Robin Swales for assistance with the proofs. I would also like to express my thanks to the following libraries and archives: Richard Wagner Museum mit Nationalarchiv der Richard Wagner-Stiftung (Dr. Manfred Eger, Herr Günter Fischer); Berlin Document Center (Dr. Robert Marwell); Staatsarchiv, Coburg (Dr. Hambrecht); Landesbibliothek, Coburg (Dr. Jürgen Erdmann); Bundesarchiv, Koblenz (Dr. Ritter, Frau Brandes, Frau Bucher); Bayerisches Hauptstaatsarchiv (Herr Korn); Bayerische Staatsbibliothek (Dr. Robert Münster); Institut für Musikwissenschaft der Universität München (Dr. Fred Büttner); Landeshauptstadt München (Herr Hecker); Ludwig-Maximilians-Universität Archiv (Dr. Laetitia Boehm); Staatsarchiv München (Dr. Weber); Österreichsches Staatsarchiv, Haus-, Hof-, und Staatsarchiv (Dr. Gottfried Mraz). Initial research for this study was funded by the Social Sciences and Humanities Research Council of Canada.

Unless noted, all translations are by the author. With the exception of Wagner's *Gesammelte Schriften*, I have used published translations of secondary sources where they exist; in all cases, however, I have compared published translations with the original and made emendations where necessary. In quoted material, all emphases are original unless noted. Emphasis by means of boldface type or spacing (*Sperrdruck*) in the original has been rendered here in italics.

The following bibliographical abbreviations will be employed:

Geheimnis I	Lorenz, Alfred. *Das Geheimnis der Form bei Richard Wagner*. Vol. 1: *Der musikalische Aufbau des Bühnenfestspieles 'Der Ring des Nibelungen'*. Berlin: Max Hesse, 1924; reprint, Tutzing: Hans Schneider, 1966.
Geheimnis II	Lorenz, Alfred. *Das Geheimnis der Form bei Richard Wagner*. Vol. 2: *Der musikalische Aufbau von Richard Wagners 'Tristan und Isolde'*. Berlin: Max Hesse, 1926; reprint, Tutzing: Hans Schneider, 1966.
Geheimnis III	Lorenz, Alfred. *Das Geheimnis der Form bei Richard Wagner*. Vol. 3: *Der musikalische Aufbau von Richard Wagners 'Die Meistersinger von Nürnburg'*. Berlin: Max Hesse, 1930; reprint, Tutzing: Hans Schneider, 1966.
Geheimnis IV	Lorenz, Alfred. *Das Geheimnis der Form bei Richard Wagner*. Vol. 4: *Der musikalische Aufbau von Richard Wagners 'Parsifal'*. Berlin: Max Hesse, 1933; reprint, Tutzing: Hans Schneider, 1966.
GS	Wagner, Richard. *Gesammelte Schriften und Dichtungen*. 10 vols. Leipzig: Walter Tiemann, 1907.

Chapter One

Alfred Lorenz:
The Discoverer of Wagnerian Form

Lorenz's Life and Work

Shortly before his death in 1939, Alfred Lorenz was described in the *Bayreuther Blätter* as the "discoverer and revealer" of Wagnerian form.[1] Lorenz's marked personal and professional successes in his second career attest to a resiliency and tenacity of character which led him to embrace scholarship at fifty-two years of age after his forced retirement as Generalmusikdirektor in Coburg-Gotha. The history of his life reveals one man's particular response to the personal and political pressures of the Germany of Bismarck, Wilhelm II, and Adolf Hitler, as it encompasses almost exactly the duration of the Second and Third Reichs.[2]

Lorenz was born in Vienna on 11 July 1868 to the historian Dr. Ottokar Lorenz and his wife, Marie (Lott) Lorenz.[3] At Alfred's birth, Ottokar Lorenz was a professor at the University. In 1885 he accepted a call from Jena and moved his entire family—his wife and their three sons and one daughter—to Germany, where they became naturalized citizens. Lorenz remained at Jena until his death in 1904.

During the 1860s and 70s Ottokar Lorenz's academic work dealt principally with the Middle Ages in Germany. After the move to Jena, however, his attention became focused on genealogy and its potential as an historical tool. In a two-volume study, *Die Geschichtswissenschaft in Hauptrichtung und Aufgaben* (1886) and *Leopold Ranke: Die Generationenlehre und der*

---

1. Karl Grunsky, "Ein letzter Streifzug," *Bayreuther Blätter* 61 (1938): 231.

2. The following biographical information was compiled from such standard sources as the *New Grove*, *MGG*, Riemann, and the *Neue Deutsche Biographie*, as well as from Lorenz's own writings; from tributes, obituaries, and other writings about Lorenz; and from unpublished archival material. It is rather sparse in details about the earlier years. Despite extensive inquiry I have been unable to trace either a Lorenz *Nachlaß* or a living descendant.

3. Ottokar was born in 1832. Marie (Lott) Lorenz (1839–1917) was the daughter of an academic, Franz Lott, a scholar of the early nineteenth-century philosopher Johann Herbart. The Lorenzes were married in 1862. One of Alfred's brothers, Richard (1863–1929) became a chemist of some note.

Geschichtsunterricht (1891),[4] Ottokar sought to replace the traditional historical structure based on periodization with one that employed genealogy. He thus proposed that the most natural structural element was the biological interval of the generation. Each century is comprised of three generations, and three centuries (3 x 3 generations) together form a cycle in which particular ideas are conceived, reach maturity, and decline. All history, argued Lorenz, follows this biological-genealogical model. The consequence of such an approach is that attention is focused entirely on matters such as genealogy and race to the exclusion of external factors such as environment.[5] Such an approach was not without political implications for Lorenz, who was a staunch German nationalist of a particularly Prussian mien. This type of upbringing was to have important consequences for his son, Alfred. For instance, the conversion of the entire family from Catholicism to Protestantism—a decision which certainly had nationalistic overtones—surely set an example.

From 1878 to 1886 Alfred attended the *Schottengymnasium* in Vienna. He then spent five semesters (1886–88) studying law, at first in Jena, then in Leipzig and Berlin. While little is known about Lorenz's youth other than these basic details, clearly music must have played a leading role in his life, for he soon heeded its siren call, abandoned his legal studies, and devoted himself to music. For four additional semesters in Berlin (1889–91) he studied conducting with Hofkapellmeister Robert Radecke and musicology with Dr. Philipp Spitta. While in Leipzig, he had been a member of the Wagner-Verein; in Berlin he was president of the Berlin Akademischer Richard-Wagner-Verein from 1888–90. During this latter time, he presented two lectures which strongly anticipated his later work: "Die Charakteristik der Tonarten," outlining the principle of the "poetic-musical period," and "Über das Formale bei Wagner," concerning the Bar form.[6]

After satisfying his obligation for military service in the Thuringian infantry regiment no. 95 during 1891 and 1892, Lorenz commenced his musical career in 1893 as Solorepetitor in Königsberg. During the middle years of the decade, he held a variety of positions in smaller German centers such as Libau, Stendal, and Stettin. In 1896 he became second Kapellmeister in Elberfeld, and in 1897, Solorepetitor at the Hoftheater in Munich. He spent the remainder of his career in the service of the Duke of Saxe-Coburg Gotha: as second Kapellmeister (from 1898), first Kapellmeister (from 1904), and finally as Generalmusikdirektor (from 1917 to 1920). There, his duties included direction of the court opera and symphony, as well as the music and

4. Both published by W. Hertz in Berlin.
5. Hans Jaeger, "Generations in History: Reflections on a Controversial Concept," *History & Theory* 24 (1985): 273–93.
6. *Geheimnis* I: v.

oratorio societies of both Coburg and Gotha.[7] In 1902, he worked as an assistant at the Bayreuth Festival.

German-language music periodicals of the time contain favorable mention of Lorenz as a conductor and opera producer. For example, a mention in *Die Musik* records that during the run of a particularly impressive production of *Tristan und Isolde* in Gotha, Lorenz was named Hofkapellmeister for life.[8] Corroboration of Lorenz's talents as a conductor is found in two recommendations solicited by Lorenz after leaving Coburg in 1920.[9] The first, from Richard Strauss, refers to Lorenz as a "splendid conductor" and an "excellent musician"; the second, from Engelbert Humperdinck, is transcribed in its entirety:

> At the premiere of my opera *Königskinder* at the Coburg Hoftheater a few years ago, I met in Herr Generalmusikdirektor *A. Lorenz* a musician of extraordinary qualities, to whom, by virtue of a sensitive and effective interpretation of the score in all of its components, we are indebted for a *downright exemplary performance* of the opera. In view of his *enormous* abilities, I do not hesitate to place Herr Lorenz at the side of *Germany's leading operatic conductors.*[10]

The music periodicals also attest to Lorenz's activity as a composer. His one-act opera, *Helgas Erwachen*, was produced in Schwerin in 1896. Lorenz also composed several symphonic poems, among which may be numbered *Bergfahrt, Columbus, Wogen,* and *Fausts Vision* (several of these are with chorus). His piano quartet was published during his lifetime by C.F. Kahnt in Leipzig. When it was performed in 1938 in honor of Lorenz's seventieth birthday, it was praised in the *Zeitschrift für Musik* for its "sure formal sense, fresh tonal colors, romantic energy, warmth of expression, and clarity of thematic thought."[11] Two of his lieder, to texts by Otto Julius Bierbaum, were performed to acclaim in 1902, and were later published.[12] As well, a

---

7. The court, and its theater personnel, shuttled annually between Coburg and Gotha. Two extensive Personalakten (Theater Nr. 3433, 3434) in the Staatsarchiv Coburg contain correspondence revealing the legal and financial relationship between Lorenz and the court, stretching from his initial application documents to an extensive correspondence regarding his pension. StAC Theater Nr. 3434, fol. 538 contains a 1934 photograph of Lorenz.

8. *Die Musik* 10 (June 1911): 315.

9. These recommendations accompany a letter of 19 June 1933 from Lorenz to the Preußische Kultusministerium contained in Lorenz's file in the Berlin Document Center (henceforth BDC). They are dated 18 January and 11 March respectively.

10. "Bei der Ersta[u]fführung meiner Oper 'Königskinder' am Hoftheater in Koburg lernte ich vor einigen Jahren in Herrn Generalmusikdirektor *A. Lorenz* einen Musiker von außerordentlichen Qualitäten kennen, dem durch eine feinsinnige und wirkungsvolle Wiedergabe der Partitur in allen ihren Teilen eine *geradezu musterhafte Aufführung* der Oper zu verdanken ist. Ich stehe nicht an, Herrn Lorenz im Hinblick auf seine *enorme* Befähigung den *allerersten Bühnendirigenten Deutschlands* an die Seite zu stellen."

11. *Zeitschrift für Musik* 105 (December 1938): 1403.

12. *Die Musik* 2 (1902): 305. One of these is entitled "Glaube nur."

review in *Die Musik* reports that a piece by Lorenz may be found in the fourth volume of *Deutsche Männerchor* ("Kriegs- und Soldatenlieder"), published by Breitkopf und Härtel.[13]

Lorenz's interest in Wagner continued unabated throughout this time; indeed, Coburg became particularly known for its excellent productions of Wagner's works. In his later publications, Lorenz notes that it was a point of pride with him to produce Wagner's works without the then-customary cuts.[14] His efforts on behalf of Wagner extended beyond performances of the works, however, to include public lectures throughout southeastern Germany. These lectures, Lorenz asserts, "were by no means only leitmotivic illustrations, but already brought numerous explanations of the formal beauties in the architecture of the *Ring*, *Tristan*, *Parsifal*, and *Meistersinger*."[15] What seems to be his first published article—a piece presciently entitled "Parsifal als Übermensch"—appeared in *Die Musik* in 1901.

Personally, the Coburg-Gotha years marked Lorenz's marriage and the birth of his son. In Jena, on 3 June 1902, Lorenz married Marie Friederike Müller, the daughter of Wilhelm Müller, Professor of Anatomy at Jena. Their only child, christened with the rather Wagnerian name Wilhelm Alfred Frohwalt Ottokar, was born on 24 May 1905 in Coburg.[16] Lorenz later attested that at the outbreak of the First World War in 1914 he had wished to enlist of his own free will, despite his age, but was prevented from so doing because of his duties for the Duke of Saxe-Coburg Gotha.[17] In 1917 he was elevated to Generalmusikdirektor, but politics soon intruded. When the Weimar Republic was proclaimed on 9 November 1918, just before the capitulation of Germany, the fabric of German society was altered immeasurably. The November Revolution, as it came to be known, propelled the Social Democrats into power following the abdication of the Emperor. Little

13. *Die Musik* 4 (May 1915): 135. Several compositions by Lorenz are listed in Rudolf Potyra, *Die Theatermusikalien der Landesbibliothek Coburg*, mit einer Abhandlung zur Geschichte des Herzoglichen Hoftheaters Coburg-Gotha und seiner Notensammlung von Jürgen Erdmann, 2 vols. (Munich: Henle, 1995), 87, 255.

14. Lorenz frequently mentions this fact; e.g. *Geheimnis* I: v. For Lorenz's thoughts on the subjects of cuts in general, see his "Striche in genialen Meisterwerken," *Die Musik* 28 (1936): 597–600.

15. *Geheimnis* I: v. Ten such lectures, given on the *Ring* in Jena in 1900, are mentioned in the report of the Patronverein (p.7) which accompanied the final issue of the *Bayreuther Blätter* for 1901.

16. Marie Lorenz, four years younger than Alfred, survived the war and remained in Munich until her death on 21 December 1949. I have been unable to trace the younger Ottokar Lorenz after 1952 when he moved to Wuppertal-Elberfeld. It is unknown whether or not Ottokar Lorenz married; he had not done so by the late 1930s when the passport, now in his file in the Berlin Document Center, was issued. Ottokar Lorenz's life will be discussed in the second part of this chapter.

17. Karteiblatt from Reichserziehungsministerium/Universität München in Lorenz's file in the BDC.

is known about precisely how these radical changes affected Lorenz and his family, apart from the fact that Lorenz was pensioned off, at fifty-two years of age, in 1920. This forced retirement at the hands of the Social Democrats clearly rankled, and it would not be forgotten after Germany changed direction again in 1933.

At an age when many in his position would, however reluctantly, have accepted the forced retirement, Lorenz embarked upon a second career in academia. He moved with his family to Munich, and attended lectures in musicology (by Adolf Sandberger), philosophy, and history. From March to November 1921 he wrote his dissertation, entitled "Gedanken und Studien zur musikalischen Formgebung in Richard Wagners Ring des Nibelungen," and received the doctorate, *summa cum laude*, from the University of Frankfurt-am-Main on 9 February 1922. His dissertation examiner was Professor Dr. Moritz Bauer.[18] It was privately printed that same year, with the support of the Akademischen Werkstätten, Munich; King Ferdinand of Bulgaria; and Richard Löwenherz, a colleague from Coburg.[19]

Lorenz's dissertation is in fact the first volume of what was to become his life's work, *Das Geheimnis der Form bei Richard Wagner*.[20] In the dissertation, the entire *Ring des Nibelungen* is divided into "poetic-musical periods," delineated by tonality, and internally shaped according to one of four principal formal types: strophic form, Bogen form, refrain or rondo, and Bar form. Lorenz is unequivocal about the fact that his dissertation work originated in his practical experience in conducting the works in the theater. He also notes that his early Wagner lectures already covered much the same ground, and are referred to as the "seed of the work" (*Keim zu der Arbeit*) in the preface to the first volume of *Das Geheimnis*.

Already in the dissertation Lorenz announces his plan for a large-scale study of form in Wagner's music dramas. In fact, by the private printing of this work in 1923, Lorenz had completed the formal analysis of *Tristan und Isolde* which appeared in 1926 as the second volume of *Das Geheimnis der Form*. To sanction his approach, Lorenz invokes the authority of Wagner himself, speaking through his disciple Hans von Wolzogen:

---

18. Although in the introduction to his dissertation Lorenz points to Bauer's *Die Lieder Franz Schuberts* (Leipzig: Breitkopf & Härtel, 1915; reprint, Wallauf bei Wiesbaden: Martin Sändig, 1972) as the origin of his particular methodology (*Betrachtungsweise*), Bauer's work resembles Lorenz's only in the systematization of his attempt to present *all* of Schubert's lieder, and in his favoring of the tabular presentation of data. Nowhere does Bauer discuss musical form in a proto-Lorenzian fashion. (Bauer only completed this first volume of what was conceived as a multi-volume work.)

19. Lorenz's work quickly attracted attention, even in this limited circulation. The dissertation was given an extremely favorable review by Karl Grunsky, "Die Formfrage bei Richard Wagner," *Die Musik* 15 (1923): 436–40.

20. Published in 1924 by Max Hesse, Berlin. Differences between the dissertation and *Geheimnis* I are minor.

I am very glad that you wish to study and explain Wagnerian form in a serious fashion. That is what Wagner himself always wished, but could never obtain from the musicians among his followers and admirers. It is truly high time that something happens in this field.[21]

Wolzogen, while perhaps also recalling personal conversations with Wagner, refers to the well-known passage in Wagner's 1879 essay "Über die Anwendung der Musik auf das Drama" in which Wagner does in fact express this desire:

Concerning the new form of musical composition and its application to drama, I believe I have expressed myself in sufficient detail in earlier articles and essays—but sufficient only in the sense that I felt that I had shown others clearly enough the path to a just and at the same time useful assessment of the musical forms extracted from the drama by my own artistic efforts. To my knowledge, this path has not yet been followed; I can only think of one of my younger friends [Wolzogen] who has examined the characteristics of what he calls my "leitmotives," more along the lines of their dramatic significance and effectiveness than their utilization in the creation of musical structure (since the author was far from being a musician).[22]

In the fall of 1923, Lorenz was appointed by Sandberger as a Dozent at Munich University, where he was entrusted with the introductory music theory courses: harmony, counterpoint, and composition. He also taught the introduction to music history, and led the Collegium Musicum. Lorenz's first lecture was on 9 November, the day of Hitler's ill-fated putsch in Munich. This coincidence is striking, for Lorenz's career at Munich was to be markedly affected by his ties with the National Socialists.[23]

Lorenz was granted a study leave, supported by the Notgemeinschaft der deutschen Wissenschaft, to work on his Habilitationsschrift in Italy during March and April 1925. This was an archival study of sources for Alessandro Scarlatti's early operas. In it, Lorenz exhaustively documents and surveys sources for scores and libretti of some 32 operas, and includes

---

21. Letter from Hans von Wolzogen to Alfred Lorenz, 12 May 1921, cited by Lorenz in *Geheimnis* I: 9n.

22. Wagner, *GS* X: 185.

23. I have not seen Lorenz's personal file at Munich University (Universitätsarchiv—Personalakt E II Lorenz). Much of its contents is reported in Andreas Elsner, "Zur Geschichte des musikwissenschaftlichen Lehrstuhls an der Universität München" (Inaugural-Dissertation, Ludwig-Maximilians-Universität Munich, 1982); and Pamela Maxine Potter, "Trends in German Musicology, 1918–1945: The Effects of Methodological, Ideological, and Institutional Change on the Writing of Music History" (Ph.D. dissertation, Yale University, 1991). The following information is taken from the above works. Unless stated otherwise, all documents are found in Lorenz's file at Munich.

a second volume containing 400 musical examples (135 complete pieces), most of which had never before been published. The lengthy section entitled "conclusions" examines the evolution of Scarlatti's operatic style under the categories of harmony, melody, and rhythm. By this final category, Lorenz means the same large-scale rhythm—form—which he had uncovered in Wagner's works. He traces Scarlatti's use of strophic (a-a′), Bar (a-a-b), "Seicento" (a-b-b), and Bogen (a-b-a) forms. (The last named is of course more commonly referred to as the da-capo aria—a rather telling paradox, perhaps, given Lorenz's Wagnerian works.) The study was submitted for examination in December 1925, and on its merits Lorenz was named Honorarprofessor on 1 April 1926.[24]

Like his initial appointment, Lorenz's new position was unsalaried, despite frequent petitions to the state from the faculty.[25] For example, a petition of 31 July 1930 to the Kultusministerium requesting permission to divide a recently vacated special teaching position (*Lehrauftrag*) between Lorenz and another scholar was refused without reason on 10 September. A similar petition in the spring of 1932 met with the same fate. The following year, however, another petition was successful, and in a letter of 31 July 1933 Lorenz was awarded a two-hour/week *Lehrauftrag* which paid 250 RM.

Andreas Elsner's dissertation on the musicology faculty at Munich seems to suggest that Lorenz's success in obtaining this *Lehrauftrag* was based on a letter by Lorenz to the ministry (24 March 1933) in which he stressed the importance of the music theory courses to the students. Elsner publishes what appears to be the entire text of this letter.[26] This reasoning seems disingenuous given Lorenz's personal ties to the new Reich. An extraordinary letter of 19 June 1933 from Lorenz to the Preußische Kultusministerium— of which Elsner is perhaps unaware—more than confirms this suspicion.[27] It is striking not only for its glimpse of Lorenz's political views, but also for the additional information it provides about his forced departure from Coburg-Gotha. The opening and closing paragraphs of the letter follow:

---

24. It was published the following year as *Alessandro Scarlattis Jugendoper: Ein Beitrag zur Geschichte der italienischen oper*, 2 vols. (Augsburg: Benno Filser, 1927).

25. Lorenz and his family lived on his pension as Generalmusikdirektor (360 RM/month). An Honorarprofessor was an unsalaried, generally older scholar appointed to teach in a special field. It was technically a higher rank than the Extraordinarius; see Daniel Fallon, *The German University: A Heroic Ideal in Conflict with the Modern World* (Boulder: Colorado Associated University Press, 1980).

26. Elsner, "Zur Geschichte des musikwissenschaftlichen Lehrstuhls an der Universität München," 190–91.

27. This letter is not part of Lorenz's personal file in Munich, but is found rather among the Reichskanzlei papers in the BDC.

As a leading conductor and musicologist, I apply to the Theater and Music division of the Preußische Kultusministerium with a request for the resolution and restitution of an injustice done to me by the Weimar republic. On account of my nationalistic views, . . . I—who as Generalmusikdirektor to the Duke of Saxe-Coburg Gotha, brought, after 20 years' work, the ducal Hoftheater and the entire musical life of Gotha and Coburg to a hitherto unheard of height— was removed in 1920 by the Social Democrats to make room for a Jew. . . .

According to repeated statements by prominent men in government and the Professional Civil Service Restoration Act, the injustices done to outstanding men by the Weimar Republic ought to be made right, and so I ask for *rehabilitation*. As regards my work, I can offer the best service to the Third Reich either as the first Kapellmeister of an opera house or concert institute, or as a lecturer in musicology at a university or another college.[28]

The Professional Civil Service Restoration Act of 7 April 1933 was part of a series of legislative acts designed both to purge the civil service of "undesirables" and to reward long-standing loyalties.[29] It thus seems likely that the success of Lorenz's 1933 petition was based more on political grounds than on such apolitical matters as his acumen in teaching music theory courses, although the letter cited by Elsner suggests that Lorenz had adopted a number of strategies in order to achieve his goal.

In a letter of 7 May 1934, Lorenz's position was extended to four hours per week. The following summer, after Lorenz had reached 67 years of age—the age of retirement—he requested a continuation of his teaching activities (letter of 4 July 1935 to the Rektor). Pamela Potter reports that the continuation was requested on the basis of Lorenz's early party membership and the fact that he had taught courses on music and race as early as 1933; Lorenz argued that he was still able to contribute to the "young spirit" of the university despite his advanced age.[30] Lorenz's appeal was

---

28. "Als einer der ersten Dirigenten und Musikwissenschaftler wende ich mich an das Preußische Kultusministerium Abteilung Theater und Musik mit der Bitte, das durch das Novembersystem an mir verübte Unrecht wiedergutzumachen. Wegen meiner nationalen Gesinnung . . . wurde ich, der als Generalmusikdirektor des Herzogs von Sachsen-Coburg und Gotha in fast 20jähriger Arbeit das Herzogliche Hoftheater und das ganze Musikleben der Städte Gotha und Coburg auf eine nie dagewesene Höhe gebracht hatte, im Jahre 1920 durch die Sozialdemokraten beseitigt, um einem Juden Platz zu machen. . . . Nach wiederholten Äußerungen führender Regierungsmänner und dem Gesetz zur Wiederherstellung des Berufsbeamtentums soll das Unrecht das verdienten Männern durch das Novembersystem angetan wurde, wieder gut gemacht werden, und so bitte ich, mich zu *rehabilitieren*. Nach meinen Leistungen kann ich entweder als erster Kapellmeister eines Operntheaters oder Konzertinstitutes oder als Dozent für Musikwissenschaft an einer Universität oder anderen Hochschule dem dritten Reich die beste Dienste leisten." Letter from Lorenz to the Preußische Kultusministerium, 19 June 1933, BDC Lorenz file. The letter seems to indicate that Lorenz's pension was in danger, and he wished to ensure its continuation or supplementation.

29. These laws are reproduced and discussed in *Documents on Nazism, 1919–1945*, intro. and ed. Jeremy Noakes and Geoffrey Pridham (London: Jonathan Cape, 1974).

30. Potter, "Trends in German Musicology," 270–71.

supported by the assistant Dekan, R. Spindler, and by the director of the Dozentenschaft, Dr. Führer, and Lorenz was granted a one-year extension that was conveyed in a letter of 23 August.[31] A second one-year extension was granted the following year (30 May 1936). A letter of 18 May 1936 from the Dozentenschaft to the Rektor supported his request, noting that Lorenz was the only professor in the entire university who had belonged to the party before 1933.[32]

The following year, Lorenz attempted to convert his *Lehrauftrag* from music theory in general to a specific concentration on the study of musical form, particularly that of Wagner (*allgemeine musikalische Formenlehre mit besonderer Berücksichtigung des Wagnerschen Werkes*; letter to Gauleiter and Staatsminister Adolf Wagner, 9 September 1938). His petition was endorsed by Dekan Walther Wüst "on cultural-political and educational grounds" (*aus kulturpolitischen und unterrichtlichen Gründen*) and was again promoted by the Dozentenschaft with the following comment: "in these matters Lorenz is indispensable and of greatest importance for National-Socialist art policies."[33] While Potter suggests that its positive outcome was a given, Elsner seems unsure whether or not it was approved.

Throughout these years, Lorenz was extremely active professionally and published an astounding number of scholarly articles and books.[34] Succeeding volumes of *Das Geheimnis der Form* came out in 1926, 1930, and 1933. His Habilitationsschrift on Scarlatti appeared in 1927, and was followed the next year by a survey of music history, *Abendländische Musikgeschichte im Rhythmus der Generationen*, which employed his father's biological-genealogical methodology. Over fifty articles from Lorenz's pen emerged in a wide range of journals and newspapers. His final large-scale publication appeared in 1938, the year before his death: a two-volume edition of excerpts from Wagner's writings and letters.

Lorenz's writings may be grouped into three rather broad categories: those concerned with his new method of formal analysis; those presenting music historical topics, generally viewed through a Wagnerian lens; and those indebted to his father's historical methodology (*Generationslehre*).

31. The Dozentenschaft was a local organization of university teachers. By this time its leaders were identical with those of the Nationalsozialistischer Deutscher Dozentenbund (NSD-Dozentenbund), a national organization to which Lorenz belonged and which promulgated the National Socialist world view in universities and colleges through ideological and disciplinary means.

32. Potter, "Trends in German Musicology," 271. Elsner does not mention this fact. It is instructive to compare Potter's and Elsner's use of the documents in Lorenz's personal file, as the latter continually skirts around the issue of Lorenz's connections to the National Socialists.

33. "In diesen Dingen ist Lorenz schlechthin unersetzlich und für die nationalsozialistische Kunstpolitik von größter Bedeutung." Letter of 26 September 1938. Cited by Potter only, although its existence is noted by Elsner. I wish to thank Dr. Potter for providing me with the original German for this citation.

34. See the bibliography for a detailed list of Lorenz's publications.

These broad concerns may occasionally become interpenetrated, and one article may therefore fit into several groups.

Before his dissertation was published as the first volume of *Das Geheimnis der Form* in 1924, Lorenz attempted to publicize his new analytical method through articles in the *Deutsches Musikjahrbuch*, *Hellweg*, and the *Bayreuther Festspielführer*.[35] Similar introductory articles continued to appear in the *Festspielführer* until Lorenz's death in 1939.[36] These are usually tied to one of the works in the repertory and present an analysis of one or more periods in that work; the 1936 article on *Lohengrin* and the 1939 article on *Der fliegende Holländer* are unique in that their contents do not appear elsewhere in Lorenz's writings.[37] In other articles, Lorenz applies his formal method to such composers as Bach, Beethoven, Mozart, and Richard Strauss.[38] In them, Lorenz argues that he has discovered the universal principles of form, and that his method is appropriate for all music.

Lorenz's presentation of various issues in the history of music often reveals a strong pro-Wagnerian bias. For example, an article on the development in Beethoven's Third Symphony sets out to "prove" Wagner's claim to have inherited the mantle of Beethoven by demonstrating that Beethoven's development is shaped according to the same principles that Lorenz had discovered in Wagner's music dramas.[39] Similarly, when considering what is

---

35. "Musikalische Form bei Wagner," in *Deutsches Musikjahrbuch* 1, ed. Rolf Cunz (Essen: Schlingloff, 1923), 198–210; "Wotans Abschied und Feuerzauber: Eine Formuntersuchung," *Hellweg: Wochenschrift für Deutsche Kunst* (10 October 1923): 710–13; "Über die musikalische Form von Richard Wagners Meisterwerken," *Bayreuther Festspielführer* (1924): 138–49; reprinted in *Richard Wagner: Das Betroffensein der Nachwelt: Beiträge zur Wirkungsgeschichte*, ed. Dietrich Mach (Darmstadt: Wissenschaftlichte Buchgesellschaft, 1984), 75–87.

36. "Zum musikalischen Aufbau der Meistersinger von Nürnberg," *Bayreuther Festspielführer* (1925): 131–35, translated by Stewart Spencer in *Wagner* 4 (January 1983): 9–13; "Der Tannhäuser-Ouvertüre historische Sendung," *Bayreuther Festspielführer* (1930): 58–62; "Der musikalische Aufbau von Wagners 'Parsifal'," *Bayreuther Festspielführer* (1933): 161–68, translated by Stewart Spencer in *Wagner* 2 (January 1981): 21–25; "Die Orchestereinleitungen der Festspiel-Werke 1934," *Bayreuther Festspielführer* (1934): 171–76; "Der musikalische Aufbau von Wagners 'Lohengrin'," *Bayreuther Festspielführer* (1936): 189–98, translated by Stewart Spencer in *Wagner* 2 (April 1981): 40–44; "Der musikalische Aufbau von Wagners 'Tristan und Isolde'," *Bayreuther Festspielführer* (1938): 139–145, reprinted in *Hundert Jahre Tristan*, ed. Wieland Wagner (Emsdetten: Lechte, 1965), 91–96, translated by Stewart Spencer in *Wagner* 2 (July 1981): 74–77; "'Der fliegende Holländer'—Oper oder Worttondrama?," *Bayreuther Festspielführer* (1939): 102–108.

37. The essays on *Parsifal*, *Tristan*, and *Meistersinger* are taken from the appropriate volumes of *Das Geheimnis*, as are the *Ring* examples in the 1924 article cited in note 35. The *Tannhäuser* analyses are also found in the conclusions to *Geheimnis* IV.

38. For example: "Homophone Großrhythmik in Bachs Polyphonie," *Die Musik* 22 (1930): 245–53; "Worauf beruht die bekannte Wirkung der Durchführung im 1. Eroicasatze," *Neues Beethoven-Jahrbuch* 1 (1924): 159–83; "Das Finale in Mozarts Meisteropern," *Die Musik* 19 (1927): 621–32; "Der formale Schwung in Richard Strauss' 'Till Eulenspiegel'," *Die Musik* 17 (1925): 658–69.

39. Lorenz, "Worauf beruht die bekannte Wirkung der Durchführung im 1. Eroicasatze."

traditionally presented as the "dissolution" of tonality at the end of the nineteenth century, Lorenz reverses the usual argument: "the process in Wagner does not lead towards the dissolution of tonality but, on the contrary, to a hitherto unsuspected, unbelievable *intensification* of the tonal sense."[40] The only drawback about such an intensification, says Lorenz, is that many listeners are unable to follow it, and lose the thread of the work: the listeners are at fault, not the composer!

As might be expected, the history of opera is presented by Lorenz in particularly teleological terms.[41] Lorenz paints early operas such as Peri's *Euridice* as proto-*Gesamtkunstwerke* in which music and drama are perfectly blended into a unified whole. According to this view, opera then takes a wrong turn with the development of the aria and the ensuing recitative/aria division: *dramma per musica* becomes "opera" and the architectonic unity of the work is destroyed. Matters improve towards the end of the eighteenth century with the rise of the "constructive" (*konstruktiv*) element in which individual numbers become fused together to form longer sections of continuous music (in the finales of Mozart's comic operas, for example). Lorenz leaves no question, however, about the goal of these developments: "All things which marvelously thrill us in Mozart's and Weber's operas are premonitions of Wagner's music drama."[42] Wagner is presented as the culmination of music history in much the same way that Hegel's *Weltgeist* reaches its apotheosis in his own philosophical system. Lorenz writes that

> with [Wagner's] achievement the repeated experiments by nine generations to save opera from compromise were completed: the *Gesamtkunst* was discovered.[43]

Similarly, in a 1928 article, Lorenz insists on a distinction between opera composers who write their own libretti and a true "Wort-Ton-Dramatiker"

---

40. "Die Tonalität in Wagners 'Tristan und Isolde'," *Bayreuther Festspielführer* (1927): 185. See also "Tonalitäts-Spannung," *Münchener Neueste Nachrichten*, 13 November 1927, 18; "Der Begriff der 'Tonalitäts-Auflösung'," *Rheinische Musik- und Theaterzeitung* 28 (1927): 43–44.

41. See, for example, "Wort-Ton-Dramatiker und Text-Dichtende Komponisten," *Bayreuther Festspielführer* (1928): 117–22; "Die Oper als formal-konstruktives Experiment," *Musik im Leben* 5 (1929): 80–81; "Richard Wagner, ein Meister des musikalischen Aufbaues" *Die Sonne* 10 (1933): 63–69; "'Der fliegende Holländer'—Oper oder Worttondrama?," 102–108.

42. "'Der fliegende Holländer'—Oper oder Worttondrama?" 104. Lorenz of course is referring to the use of structured finales and reminiscence motives. For a discussion and critique of this Lorenzian way of reading opera, see Carolyn Abbate and Roger Parker, "Dismembering Mozart," *Cambridge Opera Journal* 2 (1990): 187–95.

43. "Die Oper als formal-konstruktives Experiment," 81. Notice that Lorenz's mention of nine generations (3 x 3) corresponds with his father's idea that three centuries (3 x 3 generations) form a complete cycle in which particular ideas arise, mature, and decline.

(read: Wagner) for whom words and music are only different expressions of one and the same creative impulse.[44]

In his works, Lorenz is always quick to defend Wagner against perceived slights. He will not tolerate any intimation that traces of the traditional operatic recitative/aria distinction are found in Wagner's music dramas, arguing instead that "all" is melody.[45] Likewise, he is suspicious of any suggestion that Wagner's music might have been influenced by that of other composers. For example, he refuses to recognize the undeniable thematic similarity between the setting of Sachs's words "Mein Freund, in holder Jugendzeit" (*Meistersinger* III, m. 544ff.) and the second theme of the *allegro vivace* (m. 138ff.) in Nicolai's overture to *Die lustigen Weiber von Windsor*. Wagner's theme, pronounces Lorenz, is unquestionably derived from the Jugendmotiv in *Meistersinger*, and this gesture bears no resemblance to Nicolai's tune; "and so enough of these low accusations by malicious pompous asses!"[46]

Lorenz is quite conservative in his musical taste, and speaks disparagingly of the "newer" composers and their continual hankering after effect.[47] Although he is admiring of those composers after Wagner who follow his intensification of tonality—Bruckner, Reger, Strauss, and Pfitzner, for example—he cannot abide atonality. (To my knowledge, Lorenz never once mentions the name of Arnold Schoenberg as a composer in his published writings.)[48] In a 1927 newspaper article, he combats what he terms the "fiction" that music has evolved to atonality, and argues that the atonalists have robbed music of its principal musical effect: the sense of tension and resolution provided by tonality.[49] The following comment is indicative of Lorenz's conservative stance:

> For where then has the unique art of music led us in the past 50 years, despite its almost tropical proliferation? To heterophony, atonality, and jazz! Can this be the right way?[50]

A similarly conservative article was published in an Austrian periodical, *Der Auftakt*, known for its championship of new music.[51] In it, Lorenz makes a parallel between atonal tendencies allegedly rampant around 1300 and those undeniably in the ascendant around 1900. He does so on the

---

44. See above, note 41. Lorenz argues that Wagner's true heir in this respect—despite isolated efforts by Siegmund von Hausegger (*Zinnober*) and Richard Strauss (*Guntram*)—is none other than his son, Siegfried Wagner.
45. *Geheimnis* I: 61–63.
46. *Geheimnis* III: 126.
47. For example, see *Geheimnis* I: 56, 62.
48. He does refer to his *Harmonielehre* on occasion.
49. See "Tonalitäts-Spannung."
50. "Wort-Ton-Dramatiker und Text-Dichtende Komponisten," 122.
51. "Atonale Strebungen in Jahre 1300," *Der Auftakt* 9 (1929): 8–11.

basis of the biological-genealogical methodology proposed by his father, which has already been discussed above.

Alfred first adopted his father's *Generationslehre* in a 1928 history of music entitled *Abendländische Musikgeschichte im Rhythmus der Generationen: Eine Anregung.*[52] It presents the history of music as the struggle between the conflicting principles of polyphony and homophony; that is, between spatial and temporal feelings, between objectivity and subjectivity, between irrational and rational *Rhythmik* (form). Beginning with 375 A.D., Lorenz divides music history into five, three-hundred-year periods defined by this opposition of polyphony and homophony. Each period in turn is divided into three generations. A complete cycle (polyphony-homophony-polyphony) occupies 600 years. This cyclic view of history is illustrated with a sine curve showing the oscillation between these two principles.[53]

A subgrouping of Lorenz's writings devoted to this historical methodology concerns an article by Arnold Schering in which he proposes understanding musical texture as an alternation between two opposing tendencies: certain periods, says Schering, reveal a desire for pure, unmixed instrumental sonorities (*Klangspaltung*) such as is typical in the baroque period; others, like the romantic period, seem to prefer a blended sound (*Klangverschmelzung*).[54] In several articles, Lorenz grafts Schering's view onto his own distinction between polyphony and homophony. Schering's complete waves are 300 years, Lorenz's are 600 years—Lorenz compares the proportion between the two to that of the first overtone and its fundamental.[55]

The parallel between Lorenz's division of Wagner's music dramas and the entire history of Western music into individual periods, each internally articulated, is particularly striking.[56] This tendency of Lorenz is also found

---

52. Berlin: Max Hesse, 1928. See also "Das Generationsproblem in der Musikgeschichte," *Allgemeine Musik-Zeitung* 55 (1928): 490–91; "Periodizität in der Musikgeschichte," *Die Musik* 21 (1929): 644–50.

53. Lorenz's diagram is reproduced in Warren Dwight Allen, *Philosophies of Music History: A Study of General Histories of Music 1600–1960* (New York: Dover Publication, 1962), 250.

54. Arnold Schering, "Historische und nationale Klangstile," *Jahrbuch der Musikbibliothek Peters* 33 (1927): 31–43.

55. "Der Wechsel der Klangstile in Arnold Scherings Betrachtungsweise," *München Neueste Nachrichten*, 9 December 1928, 13; "Arnold Scherings 'Welle der Klangstile'," *Rheinische Musik- und Theaterzeitung* 30 (1929): 325–26. In an article in a Festschrift for Schering, Lorenz suggests exploring the difference between what he terms a "Gruppenprinzip" and an "Übergangsprinzip" in instrumentation as a way of expanding Schering's distinction: "Neue Gedanken zur Klangspaltung und Klangverschmelzung," in *Festschrift Arnold Schering zum sechzigsten Geburtstag*, ed. Helmut Osthoff, Walter Serauky, and Adam Adrio (Berlin: A. Glas, 1937; reprint, Hildesheim: Georg Olms, 1973), 137–50.

56. Chapter two will discuss how this dynamic and cyclical view of historical phenomena enjoyed a general influence in the first decades of the twentieth century, both in society as a whole (as, for instance, in Oswald Spengler's enormously successful *The Decline of the West*) and music theory specifically.

in his biographical work. A 1930 article divides Bruckner's life into eight, nine-year "Lebenswellen,"[57] and the 1938 edition of Wagner's writings and letters presents the whole of Wagner's life partitioned into ten, seven-year *Lebenswellen*, each beginning with something "deep" in Wagner's inner life, and ascending creatively to a peak.[58]

Many of the issues addressed by Lorenz in his publications also formed the basis for the courses he taught at Munich. In addition to the introductory music theory and history courses for which he was responsible, Lorenz frequently gave more specialized courses related to his own research.[59] For example, during the winter semester 1933–34 Lorenz offered a seminar entitled "Der musikalische Aufbau von Richard Wagners *Ring des Nibelungen*" which drew on his Wagnerian work, and one entitled "Übersicht über die gesamte abendländische Musikgeschichte nach den Grundsätzen der Generationenlehre," which employed his father's methodology. That same semester, Lorenz also gave a course on "Einfluß der Rasse auf die Musikentwicklung," obviously intended to coincide with National Socialist concerns. It was followed next semester by "Richard Wagners Nationale Sendung," and the following winter by "Musik und Rasse." Other topics taught by Lorenz include Richard Strauss's symphonic poems, Bruckner's symphonies, and late nineteenth-century chromatic harmony.

Lorenz enjoyed great success in his second career in both the public and academic spheres. When the Deutsche Musikgesellschaft was reorganized under the *Führerprinzip* into the Deutsche Gesellschaft für Musikwissenschaft in 1933, Lorenz was named *Gruppenführer* of the opera task force.[60] During the Richard Wagner Gedenktag in February 1933, Lorenz was awarded a silver citizenship medal by the city of Bayreuth, and named the "discoverer of Richard Wagner's musical form."[61] The following year, he was given honorary membership in the Vienna Akademischer Wagner-Verein; the relevant letter was published in both the *Zeitschrift für Musik* and *Die Musik*.[62] His seventieth birthday in 1938 was greeted with glowing tributes in the

57. "Die Wellenlinie in Bruckners Schaffenskraft," *Kirchenmusikalisches Jahrbuch* 25 (1930): 122–27; "Auf und Ab in Bruckners Schaffenskraft," *Der Auftakt* 13 (1933): 128–31.

58. Richard Wagner, *Ausgewählte Schriften und Briefe*, ed. Alfred Lorenz, 2 vols. (Berlin: B. Hahnefeld, 1938), 1: 8–9. These periods are depicted in tabular form in the second volume, pp. 454–66.

59. See the bibliography for a complete list of the courses taught by Lorenz at Munich. The list was compiled from biannual listings of courses in German universities published in the *Zeitschrift für Musikwissenschaft* and continued by the *Archiv für Musikforschung*.

60. Reported in the "Satzung der Deutschen Gesellschaft für Musikwissenschaft (frührer "Deutsche Musikgesellschaft")" found among the Otto Ursprung papers (Ana 343) in the Bayerische Staatsbibliothek. Discussed by Potter, "Trends in German Musicology," 157–62.

61. Reported in the *Völkischer Beobachter* on 14 February 1933, and in *Die Musik* 25 (1933): 880.

62. *Zeitschrift für Musik* 101 (1934): 130–31; *Die Musik* 26 (1934): 605–606.

press,[63] and that same year he became the director of the music division of the Deutsche Akademie in Munich.[64] The news of his death on 20 November 1939 after a sudden heart attack produced a host of warm obituaries and remembrances.[65]

Lorenz and National Socialism

From a letter contained in the Party Correspondence collection now housed in the Berlin Document Center, it appears that Lorenz was an invited guest at the 1939 Reichsparteitag in Nuremberg. He had been recommended for the honor by the Reichsdozentenführer (whose recommendation noted that Lorenz demonstrated "exemplary National Socialist behavior"), and the office responsible for the event requested an endorsement from the Munich Gauleiter, Adolf Wagner.[66] Wagner's office provided the requested statement confirming Lorenz's party membership.[67] In fact, Lorenz had been a long-standing supporter of the Nationalsozialistische Deutsche Arbeiterpartei. Both he and his wife had joined the NSDAP on 1 December 1931 and were thus "Altparteigenossen," long-term party members, in the language

---

63. Paul Egert, "Alfred Lorenz 70 Jahre alt: zum 11. Juli 1938," *Die Musik* 30 (1938): 652–56; Max von Millenkovich-Morold, "Alfred Lorenz: Zu seinem 70. Geburtstage," *Zeitschrift für Musik* 105 (1938): 719–21; Anon., "Der Entdecker der Wagnerschen Formprinzipien: Zum 70. Geburtstag von Universitätsprofessor Alfred Lorenz," *Völkischer Beobachter*, 11 July 1938; Richard Würz, "Alfred Lorenz 70 Jahre alt," *Münchener Neueste Nachrichten*, 19 July 1938; Wilhelm Zentner, "Musiker und Musikgelehrter: Zum 70.Geburtstag von Alfred Lorenz am 11. Juli 1938," *Neues Münchener Tagblatt*, 8 July 1938.

64. The Deutsche Akademie was founded in 1925 in Munich as a private cultural organization with a particular interest in cultivating German culture and interests abroad. It remained apolitical until its upper ranks were gradually taken over by party members. In 1941 it became a "Körperschaft der öffentlichen Rechts" under Goebbel's Propaganda ministry. As there is no secondary literature on the Deutsche Akademie, I am grateful to Dr. Pamela Potter for the above information. Lorenz's article, "Die Pflege der deutschen Musik und die Entstehung der Schülerkapellen in Deutsch-Ostafrika," *Afrika-Nachrichten* 17 (1936): 229–31, seems to intersect with the concerns of the Akademie, and may have originated as a lecture under its auspices.

65. Rudolf von Ficker, "Alfred Lorenz," *Archiv für Musikforschung* 5 (1940): 64; Herbert Gerigk, "Alfred Lorenz," *Die Musik* 32 (1939): 105; Wilhelm Zentner, "Alfred Lorenz," *Zeitschrift für Musik* 106 (1939): 1171; Hans Alfred Grunsky, "Einer der uns fehlt: Dem Gedenken von Alfred Lorenz," in *Neue Wagner-Forschungen: Erste Folge*, ed. Otto Strobel (Karlsruhe: G. Braun, 1943), 35–42.

66. "vorbildliches nationalsozialistisches Verhalten." Letter of 14 July 1939. BDC Lorenz file. The recommendation also noted that "as an academic of a gratifyingly German mien, he plunged into the movement very early (party member since November 1931), and has also always brought the importance of his political convictions to his discipline by stressing the validity of the *Volk* principle. ["[a]ls Wissenschafter eine erfreuliche deutsche Erscheinung, ist er schon früh (Pg. seit Nov.1931) zur Bewegung gestossen und hat seine politische Überzeugung auch stets in seinem Fachgebiet durch Betonung des völkischen Prinzips zur Geltung gebracht."]

67. Letter of 22 July 1939. BDC Lorenz file.

of the day.[68] As we have seen, he did not hesitate to exploit his ties to the party in connection with his position at Munich.

Lorenz's connection to the National Socialist movement and its precursors stretches back much further than this, however. Two items in his file in the Berlin Document Center attest to his long-standing arch-conservative and anti-Semitic leanings.[69] He had been a supporter of the Prussian court theologian and politician, Adolf Stoecker, the founder of the anti-Semitic Christian Socialist party (later subsumed by the German Conservative Party), and an individual whose demagogic personal style has often been seen as an important forerunner of National Socialist oratory.[70] Lorenz was also a member of the extreme nationalistic and anti-Semitic Deutschbund, which he once refers to as a "spiritual predecessor [*geistiger Vorläufer*] of the National Socialists."[71]

The Nazi party proper was founded in Munich in April 1920, and Lorenz was a supporter from the very beginning. In the already-cited letter of 19 June 1933, he writes: "As soon as I got to know about the Hitler movement, I joined with it, fervently."[72] On his Karteiblatt from Munich University, Lorenz indicated that he had voted for the National Socialists since 1920. Although he did not officially join the party until 1931, he allowed his son, Ottokar, to join on 4 April 1925 (Pg. 546) while still a student. Ottokar Lorenz was also among those who took part in Hitler's abortive putsch in Munich on 9 November 1923.[73]

---

68. Lorenz was Pg. 724 866 and his wife was Pg. 724 865. "Pg." is a frequently encountered abbreviation for "Parteigenosse," party member.

69. These items are the Karteiblatt—Universität München and the above-cited letter to the Preußische Kultusministerium.

70. *Encyclopedia of the Third Reich*, ed. Christian Zentner and Friedmann Bedürstig, trans. and ed. Amy Hackett (New York: Macmillan, 1991), s.v. "Stoecker, Adolf."

71. Letter of 19 June 1933 in BDC file.

72. "Sobald ich die Hitlerbewegung kennen lernte, schloss ich mich ihr deshalb innerlich an."

73. BDC Ottokar Lorenz file. Ottokar Lorenz's participation in the Beer-Hall Putsch is referred to in Hans Alfred Grunsky's memorial to Alfred Lorenz, "Einer der uns fehlt," 38. From May 1931 to November 1932, Ottokar was Referent für Presse und Propaganda for the Wirtschaftspolitisches Amt in the "Braunes Haus," Berlin. In November 1932, he moved to the Reichsjugendführung as Abteilungsleiter of the Wirtschaftspolitischen Referat, and after 1933 became HJ-Gebietsführer in Berlin. In 1935 he was named to Walter Frank's Reichsinstitut für die Geschichte des neuen Deutschlands, but owing to his duties as HJ-Gebietsführer, Lorenz found it difficult to focus on scholarly works. He left the Jugendführung in 1939 and returned to Munich to work full time for the Reichsinstitut in the Hauptreferat für Volkswirtschaftslehre und Wirtschaftsgeschichte. On 27 November 1942, Lorenz was arrested and detained for three days at the orders of the Munich Gauleiter, Paul Geisler. A voluminous correspondence about this event survives, but its cause is never clearly stated. Geisler agreed to put the affair behind them in July 1943, but refused Lorenz's pleas to suppress the matter. Lorenz was called up for service in July 1943, and managed to survive the war. I have been unable to trace his whereabouts after 1952 (see above, note 16). Ottokar Lorenz published numerous monographs and articles on economic matters, mostly under the auspices of the party, including a volume in the infamous *Nationalsozialistische Wissenschaft* series, entitled *Wirtschaft und*

Lorenz and his wife were also active in Alfred Rosenberg's Kampfbund für deutsche Kultur, founded in 1929 to combat "degeneracy" in the cultural sphere. In April 1932, Lorenz affixed his signature to an open letter published by Rosenberg's group calling for support in its fight against cultural bolshevism.[74] A similar statement, also signed by Lorenz, appeared during the first days of the new regime:

> We, the undersigned German university and college instructors, publicly declare that we regard the calling of Adolf Hitler and the combination of national powers that would be active in the reconstruction of the German people as the right way to stop the enormous need and impoverishment of the German people. . . . We confidently expect the sorting out of our public life by the present government of the Reich under the leadership of Adolf Hitler, and thereby the salvation and resurgence of Germany. We are firmly resolved each to do his part.[75]

A 1939 party census form filled out by Lorenz lists his membership in the Reichsmusikkammer, the NSD-Dozentenbund, the NS-Lehrerbund, the NS-Volkswohlfahrt, and the Reichsluftschutzbund.[76] The transformation of the entire structure of German society after 1933 is quite astounding. Significant or insignificant, official or private, all organizations were required to be "coordinated" with National Socialist principles. Those groups and publications which had supported Hitler earlier were rewarded, and those opposed quickly fell into line or were shut down. Even the relatively isolated field of music witnessed great changes.[77] New

---

Rasse (Munich: Centralverlag der NSDAP, 1939). For additional information about the younger Lorenz's life, see Helmut Heiber, *Walter Frank und sein Reichsinstitut für Geschichte des neuen Deutschlands* (Stuttgart: Deutsche Verlags-Anstalt, 1966).

74. "An die deutschen Universitäten und Hochschulen!," 30 April 1932. It is unclear where this clipping was published; from the four surviving letters (". . . hter") of the newspaper's title visible at the top of the clipping, it was very likely the National Socialist *Völkischer Beobachter*, acquired by the Party in 1920 and published daily from 1923. The clipping accompanies Lorenz's letter of 19 June 1933. BDC Lorenz file.

75. "Wir unterzeichneten deutschen Universitäts- und Hochschullehrer erklären in aller Öffentlichkeit, daß wir in der Berufung Adolf Hitlers und dem Zusammenschluß der nationalen Kräfte, die am Wiederaufbau des deutschen Volkes mittätig sein wollen, den richtigen Weg sehen, der ungeheuren Not und Verelendung des deutschen Volkes Einhalt zu gebieten. . . . Wir erwarten zuversichtlich von der derzeitigen Reichsregierung unter Führung Adolf Hitlers die Gesundung unseres öffentlichen Lebens und damit die Rettung und den Wiederaufstieg Deutschlands und sind fest entschlossen, jeder an seinem Teil dafür zu wirken." "Elf Münchener Hochschullehrer stellen sich hinter Adolf Hitler." Among the signatories is Cosima Wagner's biographer, Richard Graf du Moulin Eckart. Undated clipping accompanying Lorenz's letter of 19 June 1933. BDC Lorenz file.

76. BDC Lorenz file. Information about these groups may be found in the *Encyclopedia of the Third Reich*. While the first three groups were professional in nature, the last two were purely voluntary: the *Volk* Welfare and the Reich Air Defense League.

77. The best survey of these developments in the field of musicology is Pamela Potter's dissertation, "Trends in German Musicology," previously referred to. See also her "The Deutsche Musikgesellschaft, 1918–1938," *Journal of Musicological Research* 11 (1991): 151–76; "Did

periodicals were founded and old ones "coordinated" or suppressed.[78] Censorship (self, or otherwise) became the rule: certain areas of research, Mendelssohn for example, were now forbidden; others, like folk music, were encouraged. Richard Wagner, obviously, fell into the category of acceptable research.

While the issue of Wagner's posthumous reception is complex and deserves a more comprehensive treatment, the general outline may be quickly sketched.[79] Under the direction of Baron Hans von Wolzogen, Wagner's house organ, the *Bayreuther Blätter*, grew more and more conservative, *völkisch*-nationalistic, and indeed anti-Semitic. In many ways, this was owing to the influence of Wagner's son-in-law, Houston Stewart Chamberlain, the author of the enormously successful (and anti-Semitic) *Grundlagen des 19. Jahrhunderts*. Chamberlain (1855–1927), born in England, published much pro-German propaganda during the war, and in fact, lived to greet Hitler as the savior of Germany during the latter's visit to Bayreuth in October 1923.[80] This visit, at the behest of Siegfried Wagner's wife, Winifred, marked the beginning of the close relationship between Hitler and Bayreuth. After 1933, both the *Bayreuther Blätter* and the *Festspielführer* frequently began with epigrams by Hitler or other party favorites, and the Bayreuth Festival itself became, in effect, a Hitler Festival.[81] The Hitler-Bayreuth relationship culminated in the foundation of the Richard-Wagner-Forschungsstätte by Adolf Hitler on Wagner's birthday, 22 May 1938, after which time the chief ar-

Himmler *Really* Like Gregorian Chant? The SS and Musicology," *Modernism/Modernity* 2.3 (1995): 45–68; and "Musicology Under Hitler: News Sources in Context," *Journal of the American Musicological Society* 49 (1996): 70–113. For music in general, see Michael H. Kater, *The Twisted Muse: Musicians and Their Music in the Third Reich* (New York: Oxford, 1997), which is a vast improvement on both Michael Meyer, *The Politics of Music in the Third Reich* (New York: Peter Lang, 1991) and Erik Levi, *Music in the Third Reich* (New York: St. Martin's, 1994).

78. See, for example, Marc-André Roberge, "Le périodique *Die Musik* (1901–1944) et sa transformation à travers trois périodes de l'histoire allemande," *Revue de musicologie* 78 (1992): 109–44. Potter also discusses this issue.

79. For the early history of this reception, see Winfried Schüler, *Der Bayreuther Kreis von seiner Entstehung bis zum Ausgang der Wilhelminischen Ära: Wagnerkult und Kulturreform im Geiste völkischer Weltanschauung* (Münster: Aschendorff, 1971). For an excellent selection of primary source material, see Hartmut Zelinsky, *Richard Wagner: Ein deutsches Thema* (Frankfurt-am-Main: Zweitausendeins, 1976). The history of Wagner reception between the wars remains to be written.

80. See Geoffrey G. Field, *Evangelist of Race: The Germanic Vision of Houston Stewart Chamberlain* (New York: Columbia University Press, 1981), 420–22.

81. By far the best source is Frederic Spotts, *Bayreuth: A History of the Wagner Festival* (New Haven & London: Yale University Press, 1995), 139-88, although his account is rather lacking in nuance; see my review of Spotts in *Cambridge Opera Journal* 7 (1995): 277-84, esp. 282-84. See also Kater, *The Twisted Muse*, 34-39, and Ernst Hanisch's chapter entitled "The Political Influence and Appropriation of Wagner," in *The Wagner Handbook*, ed. Ulrich Müller and Peter Wapnewski, trans. and ed. John Deathridge (Cambridge, MA: Harvard University Press, 1992), 186-201.

chivist, Otto Strobel, could describe Wagner research as "Dienst am Volke."[82] Lorenz was a favorite in Bayreuth in the interwar years, and published articles in both the *Blätter* and the *Festspielführer*.

Articles by Lorenz also appear in several National-Socialist periodicals not specifically devoted to music: *Die Sonne* (an older, *völkisch* journal co-opted by the Nazis), *Deutsches Wesen*, and *Wille und Macht*. This last-named periodical was the organ of the Hitler Youth Movement, and was edited by its notorious leader, Baldur von Schirach. After the coordination of the music journals, articles by Lorenz on issues such as music and race, and music and the "Jewish question" began to appear in such journals as the *Zeitschrift für Musik*; here, shortly before the outbreak of war, Lorenz published a rhapsodic paean to the new Germany, which concluded as follows:

> The essential, secret, and strong music of our time still exists outside of musical composition. It sounds in the march-step of the regiments, in the rhythm of work, in the whir of motors and propellers; it sounds at last in the *harmony of German hearts*, in the will to elevate the German people, in the will to power! *Hail our savior and* Führer!"[83]

The strongly conservative and nationalistic outlook attested to by his later political affiliations may be first glimpsed in a 1915 report of his own performances of Bach cantatas where he speaks of the need to protect "true German music" against foreign influence.[84] Doubtless such attitudes were a product of his upbringing by the staunch German-nationalist Ottokar Lorenz. Likewise, the essence of his later National-Socialist interpretation of *Parsifal* is found in a 1902 article published in *Die Musik*.

In "Parsifal als Übermensch," Lorenz argues for a new interpretation of the character of Parsifal. In his opinion, traditional views, based on a Schopenhauerian reading emphasizing the notion of *Mitleid*, presented a Parsifal who was far too weak. Lorenz sees Parsifal—more than Siegfried—as the embodiment of the Nietzschean *Übermensch*: a true leader, rather than one simply the first among equals, as was Amfortas. Lorenz elevates the Parsifal story into a type of German-nationalistic religion, and makes frequent reference to German mysticism, particularly that of Meister Eckhardt.[85] The only thing lacking is a modern parallel for Lorenz's Parsifal

---

82. Otto Strobel, "Ziele und Wege der Wagnerforschung," in *Neue Wagner-Forschungen: Erste Folge*, ed. Otto Strobel (Karlsruhe: G. Braun, 1943), 32. On the Forschungsstätte, see Strobel's preface and my review of Spotts in *Cambridge Opera Journal* (1985), 283-84.

83. "Die Tonkunst grüßt den Führer!" *Zeitschrift für Musik* 106 (1939): 355.

84. "Zum Bach-Pflege," *Neue Zeitschrift für Musik* 82 (1915): 170. Similar nationalistic statements are found elsewhere in his writings, notably in the third book of *Das Geheimnis der Form*.

85. Meister Eckhardt was a medieval German mystic (c. 1260–1327/28) who argued that there was a distinction between *Deus* (God) as found in the three persons of the Trinity, and *Deitas* (Godhead) which is the Ground of God, but is indescribable. He makes the same dis-

figure. Almost thirty years later, Lorenz republished much of this article in the *Bayreuther Festspielführer*, by which time his awaited leader had emerged in the person of Adolf Hitler.[86] Lorenz's points would be made a third time, only more openly, in the changed political circumstances of 1933.[87]

Lorenz's commitment to National Socialist ideals extended to his espousal of certain racist and anti-Semitic methodologies.[88] After 1933, Lorenz was an outspoken promoter of racial research, and as we have seen, taught courses on the subject at Munich. In a 1938 article entitled "Musikwissenschaft und Ahnenforschung," he argued for the inclusion of detailed genealogical tables—including both the paternal and maternal lines—in all biographies.[89] He himself provided one for Richard Wagner, designed to dismiss, once and for all, any lingering suspicion of Jewish lineage.[90] Lorenz also attacks what he terms the "leveling system which originated from the Jewish spirit": the belief that environment and contemporaries exert an influence on a composer.[91] Rather, in Lorenz's view, all is based on race. Wagner is great not because he emerged as a major figure from a common background shared by lesser contemporaries, but because he inherited certain superior traits. The history of art is advanced by personalities, not by "influences."[92] Such a valorization of the individual is certainly reflected in

tinction between the faculties of the soul, such as memory, and the *Grund* (ground) of the soul, which he refers to as the *Fünklein* (little spark) of the soul. In other words, Eckhardt brackets off the discursive and imaginative activities which normally characterize conscious life. By so doing, Eckhardt asserts that one may attain unity with the Godhead: the true aristocrat thus reaches beyond God to the Godhead. While Eckhardt's main motive for his doctrine is that the experience of mysticism is indescribable in terms of thoughts or images, his assertion that the divine can be found within each individual soul was regarded as heretical by church authorities. The appeal of Eckhardt's thought to many National Socialists lies in both its anticipation of the idealistic opposition of essence and appearance, and its obvious anticlericism.

86. "Das Heldische in Richard Wagners Parsifal," *Bayreuther Festspielführer* (1931): 102–109.

87. *Geheimnis* IV: preface. See also "Die Religion des Parsifal," *Die Musik* 25 (1933): 342–47; "Richard Wagners 'Parsifal' und der Nationalsozialismus," *Deutsches Wesen* (July 1933): 6–8. "Richard Wagners 'neue Religion'," *Allgemeine Musikzeitung* 66 (1939): 459–62.

88. For a survey see Potter, "Trends in German Musicology," 59–89.

89. *Zeitschrift für Musik* 105 (1938): 1372–73. See also his "Die Ahnentafel in der Musikerbiographie," *Allgemeine Musikzeitung* 65 (23 December 1938): 782, and what seems to be his last published article, "Musikwissenschaft und Erbbiologie," *Deutsche Militär-Musiker-Zeitung* 62 (1940): 165–66.

90. "Die Abstammung Richard Wagners," *Allgemeine Musikzeitung* 65 (1938): 311–13. It avoids the issue of Wagner's paternity by tabulating the ancestry of both Carl Friedrich Wagner and Ludwig Geyer, claiming that the latter (whom Nietzsche believed to be a Jew) had "rein Arische Blut" in his veins. Lorenz's bias is revealed by the culminating point in his argument: only an Aryan could write such music.

91. "Musikwissenschaft und Ahnenforschung," 1373.

92. Lorenz makes much the same point in the article referred to in note 89 and in "Musikwissenschaft im Aufbau," *Zeitschrift für Musik* 106 (April 1939): 367–70. In the latter article he calls for an investigation of the racial bases of music, and speaks disparagingly of

the two most influential philosophical systems of the era, that of Schopen-hauer and of Nietzsche, and the tendency to reduce everything to matters of race and genealogy finds its roots in such biological and genealogical theories of historical explanation as those developed by Ottokar Lorenz. The consequence of such a reduction in the case of Wagner is both a distor-tion of his position towards his musical predecessors and contemporaries and a falsification of aspects of the works themselves. Within Lorenz's work, its shape may be discerned in his reluctance to find traces of traditional operatic numbers in Wagner's works and in his deliberate obfuscation of the break in the genesis of the *Ring*.

In another article of 1938, Lorenz repeats his call for a systematic pre-sentation of the racial characteristics of music, particularly that of "Jewishness." He writes of the need for an update of Wagner's own treat-ment of the "Jewish Question," since Jewish music had changed signifi-cantly since Wagner. It is extremely important, argued Lorenz, to establish a distinction between "real" Jewish music (based in the "racial soul" of the Jew) and inferior Jewish imitations of non-Jewish music.[93] In this body of work, Lorenz reveals an interest in two aspects of the racial question: first, the use of race to elevate and mythologize German composers; and second, its opposite—the dismissal of certain composers and entire repertories on grounds of racial inferiority.[94]

Lorenz's Wagnerian publications after 1933 often contain such examples of National Socialist rhetoric as his evocations of "nordic feeling" and the "*Volksseele*" in an article in *Die Sonne*.[95] One particular theme to which he returns with obsessive frequency is that of Wagner as Hitler's spiritual pre-cursor.[96] An article that appears in an issue of *Deutsches Wesen* devoted to "Richard Wagner and the New Germany," is quite clear about this point:

> But [Wagner's] revolution moved towards a much more distant future than the democrats of those days and all of his contemporaries could have imagined. Frankly, I would like to pronounce that this prophet carried in his heart even at that time the meaning of the *National-Socialist revolution*, which has today become fact.[97]

---

research in exotic music [ethnomusicology] and musical experimental psychology: the former deals with music which is inherently bad as it is produced by inferior races, while the latter is only concerned with average talent, not genius.

93. "Musikwissenschaft und Judenfrage," *Die Musik* 31 (1938): 177–79.

94. These articles are discussed by Potter, "Trends in German Musicology," 60–61.

95. "Richard Wagner, ein Meister des musikalischen Aufbaues," *Die Sonne* 10 (1933): 63.

96. See "Die Religion des Parsifal"; "Richard Wagners 'Parsifal' und der National-sozialismus"; "Richard Wagners 'neue Religion'"; "Richard Wagner, ein Meister des musik-alischen Aufbaues," "'Der fliegende Holländer'—Oper oder Worttondrama?"; and "Richard Wagner als Musiker," *Wille und Macht* 1 (1 November 1933): 24–28. Also *Geheimnis* IV, passim.

97. "Richard Wagners 'Parsifal' und der Nationalsozialismus," 7.

Lorenz's final large-scale publication is a two-volume selection of excerpts from Wagner's writings and letters connected by editorial commentary.[98] Lorenz's aim is to present the "Master's spiritual development," culminating in the so-called regeneration writings of his later years.[99] He argues that Wagner was not just a composer, but a thinker of all-encompassing greatness, a spiritual forefather of Nazism. In his edition, Lorenz highlights "such thoughts which lie close to our times"[100] with a cursive typeface that contrasts with the *Fraktur* of the rest. Epigrams by Adolf Hitler and Alfred Rosenberg introduce each of the volumes, and Hitler is explicitly eulogized on the final page of the edition:

> This side of Wagner's spirit—to which this book is dedicated—was thus not yet consummated upon his death. It points towards a future in which a God-sent *man of action* unconsciously bears within himself the same aspirations, and halted the decline of his people *in fact* through the power of his superhuman [*übermenschlichen*] will, something for which in his art Wagner fought in *ideas*.[101]

In these post-1933 writings, Lorenz firmly denies any streak of liberalism in Wagner—despite his involvement in the Dresden revolution—the better to ally him politically with the National Socialists. He also attempts to minimize the theme of pessimism in Schopenhauer's writings.[102] While Schopenhauer's concept of the will is a central philosophical tenet of Nazism ("Since the appearance of our *Führer* we know the power of will, and admire it"),[103] it is as understood by Nietzsche that its influence is achieved: as a positive, life-affirming force, a will to power.[104]

That Lorenz was an anti-Semite is perfectly clear in many of his published writings (surveyed above) and may be inferred from others. For instance, it seems quite likely that Lorenz fully accepted the prevailing identification of Mime and Alberich as Jews when he noted that the quarrelling dwarves were incapable of creating a noble form; these few words carry with them a wealth of anti-Semitic assumptions and stereotypes.[105] With-

---

98. See note 58. Excerpts from this edition were published by Lorenz as "Worte des Sehers," *Zeitschrift für Musik* 105 (July 1938): 721–28.

99. Lorenz notes that these writings could find their proper interpretation only in the present time, i.e., in Nazi Germany (II: 2).

100. Dr. W. Gother, review of Lorenz's edition, *Zeitschrift für Musik* 105 (1938): 758.

101. Wagner, *Ausgewählte Schriften und Briefe*, ed. Lorenz, vol. 2, 452.

102. Schopenhauer's philosophy will be discussed in detail in the next chapter.

103. "Musikwissenschaft im Aufbau," *Zeitschrift für Musik* 106 (1939): 369–70.

104. Or, perhaps more correctly, as Lorenz's contemporaries understood Nietzsche. As is well known, Nietzsche's sister, Elisabeth Förster-Nietzsche, went out of her way to depict Nietzsche as a proto-Nazi in her publications of her brother's works, including (most notoriously), the posthumous collection of aphorisms, *Der Wille zur Macht*.

105. For example, his discussion of Guido Adler's Wagner lectures is uniformly laudatory. On the subject of anti-Semitic stereotyping in Wagner in general, see Marc A. Weiner, *Richard Wagner and the Anti-Semitic Imagination* (Lincoln: University of Nebraska Press, 1995).

out in any way excusing this fact, it is perhaps worth noting that, like Wagner himself, Lorenz could see the worth of individual Jews, or at least did not scruple to ask favors of well-positioned Jews.[106] In early 1901, Lorenz sent a number of his compositions (among them his opera *Helgas Erwachen*) to Gustav Mahler with a request that he evaluate his musical abilities; when he wrote back to remind Mahler of this fact, he mentioned that he had just been named leader of the Musikverein in Gotha and hoped to program Mahler's *Das klagende Lied* but has learned that the score is not yet published—could Mahler help?[107]

It is also worth noting that Lorenz's political beliefs did not always compromise his scholarly objectivity (or, put the other way, when Lorenz does make a political comment, it is clear that he has thought carefully about its inclusion). In May 1936, Lorenz was asked to referee an essay by Gustav Mohr, "Die Musikkritik eines unabhängigen Provinzblattes in der Kampfzeit," for possible publication by the Reichsinstitut der Geschichte des neuen Deutschlands.[108] The essay is largely a denunciation of activities in Freiburg, especially those of Professor Wilibald Gurlitt. In a letter of 21 May, Lorenz recommends against its publication, owing to its unscholarly nature; Mohr had placed too much emphasis on the first term of "kämpfenden Wissenschaft" and not enough on the latter. Nevertheless, Lorenz remarks that Mohr had done a service to point out the carbuncle in Freiburg; a scholarly study of the "Zeitungen der Systemzeit" could make use of Mohr's work, but individual publication is not recommended.[109]

An ambiguous passage from Alfred Rosenberg's *Der Mythus des 20. Jahrhunderts* may stand as symptomatic of the difficulties inherent in attempting to untangle the relationship between National Socialism, its antecedents, and particular figures such as Lorenz. Rosenberg, the chief ideologist cum philosopher of the party and a long-time supporter of Hitler, wrote in 1930:

---

106. See *Geheimnis* I: 308–9.

107. Hofoper Archives, Österreichisches Staatsarchiv, Abt. Haus-, Hof-, und Staatsarchiv, Z.604/1901. In his reply, Mahler wrote that the compositions were the work of "an exceptionally gifted musician."

108. Bundesarchiv Koblenz, R 1/9, s. 195–213.

109. Lorenz writes: "Certainly an enormous carbuncle [*Pestbeule*] exists there in Freiburg, and my colleague Gurlitt (whom I do not know personally) is most probably not guiltless in the swelling up of it. (His sympathy with Weimar [*Zentrumsfreundschaft*] is well known, and his Jewishness is rumored—but how could he still be in his position if he had not furnished proof of his Aryan descent?)" The letter is signed "Heil Hitler / Pg. Prof. Dr. Alfred Lorenz." Bundesarchiv Koblenz, Bestand R 1/9, s. 213–14. On Gurlitt, see Potter, "Trends in German Musicology," 255–59.

[Sicher ist dort in Freiburg eine enorme Pestbeule vorhanden, an deren Anschwellen mein Kollege Gurlitt, den ich indes persönlich nicht kenne, höchst wahrscheinlich nicht unschuldig sein dürfte. (Seine Zentrumsfreundschaft ist allgemein bekannt und über seine Judenstämmigkeit wird gemunkelt—aber wie könnte er noch im Amt sein, wenn er den Ariernachweis nicht erbracht hätte?)]

> The essentials of all Western art are thus made obvious in Richard Wagner: that the nordic soul is not contemplative, that it does not lose itself in the psychology of the individual, but rather deliberately experiences cosmic-spiritual laws and forms them according to spiritual-architectonic concepts.[110]

In his typically tortuous style, Rosenberg evokes a strong tradition of German idealism deriving principally (but not exclusively) from philosophers such as Kant, Schopenhauer, and Nietzsche. That is, the "essence" of Western art revealed in Wagner is its transcendence of the here-and-now; Schopenhauer argues that only through losing oneself in the pure experience (really, experiencing) of works of art can one silence the endless strivings of the will and hence of the ego: one is "lifted-out" of oneself. Such an experience is that which Nietzsche terms "Dionysian" in *Die Geburt der Tragödie* and argues is reawakened in Wagner's works. Rosenberg's phrase "nordic soul" has a sobering effect, however, implying as it does its Other: a non-nordic, or non-Aryan being. Indeed this apprehension is well justified, since large sections of *Der Mythus des 20. Jahrhunderts* are devoted to such concerns as "Race and the Racial Soul," "The Ideal of Racial Beauty," and "The Coming Reich."

Rosenberg's passage juxtaposes two seemingly contradictory impulses. On the one hand, there is the noble ideal of German philosophy, an influential and respected part of nineteenth-century thought which calls to mind the Germany of Weimar and Goethe, the Germany of thinkers and scholars. On the other hand, Rosenberg's "nordic soul" recalls the dark side of that very idealism: a tendency to mysticism and fuzzy speculation, and an anti-rational elevation of "experience" over thought that was to be embodied by the Germany of Nazism and Hitler. It is impossible to separate the two, just as it is impossible to forget the ultimate consequences of such thought.

According to Rosenberg, one of the attributes of the "nordic soul" revealed in Wagner's works is that it is "spiritually-architectonically shaped." The word "architectonic" is suggestive. Lorenz's central argument regarding Wagner's music dramas is also that they are architectonically shaped and that this shaping reveals the spirit of the work:

> Form is the breath of a work of art, and the method of its breathing the deepest expression of its inner life. The constructive framework of a piece of music is its spirit.[111]

---

110. Alfred Rosenberg, *Der Mythus des 20.Jahrhunderts: Eine Wertung der seelisch-geistigen Gestaltenkämpfe unserer Zeit*, 35–36th ed. (Munich: Hoheneichen, 1934), 433. Rosenberg's work is heavily indebted to Houston Stewart Chamberlain's *Grundlagen des 19. Jahrhunderts*.

111. "Betrachtungen über Beethovens Eroica-Skizzen: Ein Beitrag zur Psychologie des Schaffens," *Zeitschrift für Musikwissenschaft* 7 (1924–25): 420.

Might Rosenberg have been thinking of Lorenz's work when he wrote the passage cited above? It is difficult to know for sure, as Lorenz's name does not occur anywhere in *Der Mythus des 20. Jahrhunderts*. By 1930 when Rosenberg's book was published, much of Lorenz's work had already appeared, including two volumes of *Das Geheimnis der Form* (the *Meistersinger* volume appeared during 1930). Introductory accounts of Lorenz's method were published in both the *Bayreuther Blätter* and the *Bayreuther Festspielführer*; given both Hitler's, and hence the party's, interest in Wagner and Bayreuth, and, in turn, Bayreuth's conservative, *völkisch* ideological stance, it is not unreasonable to speculate that Rosenberg, as party philosopher, would at least be aware of Lorenz's work, particularly since Lorenz had been a longtime party supporter.

Just as his figure seems to hover between the lines in Rosenberg's text, so Lorenz is caught amongst the intertwining threads connecting the German intellectual tradition and National Socialism. He too is part of that tradition; he too has links, both personally and professionally, to Nazism. His analytical method, the focus of the present work, is rooted firmly in nineteenth-century philosophy and aesthetics, yet at the same time might be understood as an embodiment of National Socialist ideology. Far from being irrelevant, the ideological underpinning of Lorenz's thought is crucial for an understanding of that thought itself, and of its reception.

Chapter Two

Aesthetics and Analysis of Form
at the Turn of the Century

*I find it wonderful, I find it a simply priceless arrangement of things, that the
formal, the idea of form, of beautiful form, lies at the bottom of every sort of
humanistic calling.*

Thomas Mann, *Der Zauberberg*

In a recent monograph, Thomas Grey has very aptly described a central
question preoccupying many nineteenth-century writers about music as that
of "content and/or/as form."[1] Whether the dichotomy between form and
content was maintained ("and")—even if one side was privileged over the
other ("or")—or collapsed ("as") depended largely upon the aesthetic viewpoint of the writer. At mid-century, the dominant aesthetic position was the
Gefühlsästhetik, whereby a changeable content of feelings, the true essence
of music, was somehow contained and preserved in the "container" of form.
The form itself was of less consequence than the feelings contained therein.
This emphasis on the expressive content of music is a reflection of the nineteenth-century hermeneutic impulse, of the search for meaning rather than
structure.

Towards the end of the century, the traditional *Gefühlsästhetik* was re-
focused somewhat in light of the newly defined and idealistically conceived
Geisteswissenschaften (humanities), which placed a premium on understanding through lived experience. This experiential emphasis is reflected in
works of musical aesthetics such as Friedrich von Hausegger's *Die Musik
als Ausdruck* (1884) that are themselves indebted to the Wagnerian-
Schopenhauerian aesthetic position. The resulting expressive aesthetic position in turn exerted an influence on musical theory and analysis around
the turn of the century.

This chapter will examine the metamorphosis of the *Gefühlsästhetik* into
a late Romantic, indeed rather reactionary, expressive aesthetic that remained

---

1. Thomas S. Grey, *Wagner's Musical Prose: Texts and Contexts* (Cambridge: Cambridge
University Press, 1995), 18–20.

dominant among many German-speaking writers about music, especially Wagnerians, at least until the end of the Second World War. It provides the background out of which Lorenz emerged and against which he must be understood.

The Expressive Aesthetic

While the notion that expression is the essence of music is something of a commonplace throughout music history, it had rather a specific connotation for certain late nineteenth- and early twentieth-century writers about music. For such authors, musical gestures were believed to encode a specific emotional state, and to reawaken that state in the listener, who would intuit the meaning of the gesture instinctively. Music, within such an aesthetic, represents the essence of a phenomenon, Kant's "thing-in-itself" (*Ding an sich*).

Arthur Schopenhauer's principal work, *Die Welt als Wille und Vorstellung* (1818), follows in the tradition of Kantian (and ultimately Platonic) idealism which postulates two levels of reality for all things, that of "appearance" or "phenomena" and that of "essence" or "noumena."[2] Appearance is held to be deceptive, revealing only the exterior form of things, and leaving the "thing-in-itself" untouched. Schopenhauer's idealistic emphasis of noumena at the expense of phenomena places the onus on the individual within his philosophical system since the perception of the "essence" of an object cannot help but be a personal, subjective matter. This subjective orientation is clear from the first sentence of *Die Welt als Wille und Vorstellung*: "The world is my idea."[3] Through reason—active perception, ordering, and synthesizing of fragmentary bits of experience—I create my own representation or idea of the world (the German word *Vorstellung* can mean both); that is, the world exists only as I understand it. Put another way, all perceived phenomena are merely various grades of objectification of the "thing-in-itself."

Schopenhauer's main departure from Kant is his notion that the primary force in the world, the principal "thing-in-itself" is an irrational, insatiable drive known as the will. It is objectified (i.e., made visible, present) in all phenomena of the world. The ceaseless striving of the will is held to be the root of all problems and suffering in the world; life is seen as an endless, meaningless round of striving and suffering, with pleasure experienced as only a momentary release from pain. True freedom results from the resignation of life and desire: one must simply stop wanting.

---

2. This distinction is made in Kant's *Critique of Pure Reason*, 1781.

3. Arthur Schopenhauer, *The World as Will and Idea*, trans. R.B. Haldane and J. Kemp, 3 vols., (London: Routledge & Kegan Paul, 1883), 1.

Schopenhauer's treatment of music comes as the culmination of his consideration of the fine arts, each of which is said to embody various grades of the objectification of the will. All of the arts except music are understood as a reflection or copy of the "Platonic Ideas" behind all phenomena. Music, however,

> stands alone, quite cut off from all the other arts. In it we do not recognize the copy or repetition of any Idea of existence in the world. Yet, it is such a great and exceedingly noble art, its effect on the inmost nature of man is so powerful, and it is so entirely and deeply understood by him in his inmost consciousness as a perfectly universal language, the distinctness of which surpasses even that of the perceptible world itself, that we certainly have more to look for in it than the *exercitum arithmeticæ occultum nescientis se numerare animi*[4] which Leibnitz called it.[5]

Here Schopenhauer aligns himself with a ubiquitous romantic trope of music: music as the highest of all the arts, as a culmination, as the world itself.

Schopenhauer sees in music a direct copy of the will, unmediated by the Platonic Ideas. Music, essentially nonrepresentational, stands apart from the other arts, independent of the world of appearance. Instead of reflecting or objectifying the will secondhand, through ideas, it does so directly, without mediation:

> The (Platonic) Ideas are the adequate objectification of will. To excite or suggest the knowledge of these by means of the representation of particular things (for works of art themselves are always representations of particular things) is the end of all the other arts, which can only be attained by a corresponding change in the knowing subject. Thus all these arts objectify the will indirectly only by means of the Ideas; and since our world is nothing but the manifestation of the Ideas in multiplicity, through their entrance into the *principium individuationis* . . . , music also, since it passes over the Ideas, is entirely independent of the phenomenal world, ignores it altogether, could to a certain extent exist if there was no world at all, which cannot be said of the other arts. . . . Music is thus by no means like the other arts, the copy of the Ideas, but the *copy of the will itself*, whose objectivity the Ideas are. This is why the effect of music is so much more powerful and penetrating than that of the other arts, for they speak only of shadows, but it speaks of the thing itself.[6]

In the second part of *Die Welt als Wille und Vorstellung*, a commentary on and amplification of the first part, Schopenhauer asserts that this lack of mediation by the Ideas is the reason that music acts directly upon the feelings, passions, and emotions (the will) of the hearer, quickly raising or chang-

---

4. *Lebnitii epistolæ, collection Kortholti*, ep. 154 [Schopenhauer's note].

5. Schopenhauer, *World* 1: 330.

6. Ibid., 1: 332–33.

ing them.[7] Accordingly, the addition of music to any "scene, action, event, or surrounding seems to disclose to us its most secret meaning, and appears as the most accurate and distinct commentary upon it."[8]

The direct action of music upon our will, that is, upon our feelings and emotions rather than our reason, results in the arousal of feelings that are indistinct and imprecise:

> But it must never be forgotten . . . that music . . . never expresses the phenom-
> enon, but only the inner nature, the in-itself [*Ansich*] of all phenomena, the will
> itself. It does not therefore express this or that particular and definite joy, this or
> that sorrow, or pain, or horror, or delight, or merriment, or peace of mind; but
> joy, sorrow, pain, horror, delight, merriment, peace of mind *themselves*, to a
> certain extent in the abstract, their essential nature, without accessories, and
> therefore without their motives.[9]

But music itself, as will, belongs to the noumenal realm; it is "a perfectly universal language, the distinctness of which surpasses even that of the perceptual world itself."[10] It signifies through nonlinguistic (or extralinguistic) means. If words are attached to music as in song or opera, it is only out of a desire to embody music in an analogous example; the resulting construct stands in relation to the universal language of music as a random illustration to a general concept. Schopenhauer is adamant that words occupy a subordinate position to the music. The music does not express the words, but rather the universal which lies behind the words. They are "a foreign addition, of subordinate value, for the effect of the tones is incomparably more powerful, more infallible, and quicker than that of the words."[11]

In this section on music, Schopenhauer draws an analogy between different musical phenomena and the various grades of objectification of the will in the world (which he has already traced by this point.) For example, he compares the lowest tones of the bass to "the lowest grades of the objectification of the will, unorganized nature, the mass of the planet."[12] Melody is the highest degree of the will's objectification. Schopenhauer describes the process of melodic motion in terms of the will's appetite, its satisfaction and perpetual renewal, analogous to the melodic resolution of nonharmonic tones or modulation away from and back to a tonic.

Schopenhauer's depiction of music was to have a profound effect on many musicians—particularly composers—in the latter half of the century. This preoccupation begins with Richard Wagner himself, whose own con-

---

7. Ibid., 3: 232.
8. Ibid., 1: 339.
9. Ibid., 1: 338.
10. Ibid., 1: 330.
11. Ibid., 1: 223.
12. Ibid., 1: 333.

version to Schopenhauerian thought began in the mid-1850s and was complete by 1871 when he published an essay on Beethoven in which he summarizes the essence of Schopenhauer's understanding of music.[13] While Wagner must have been pleased by Schopenhauer's portrayal of music as the highest of all the arts, Schopenhauer's discussion of the function of art would have resonated at another level. A self-occupied (or preoccupied) composer like Wagner could not help but see himself and his work in Schopenhauer's discussion of music and its effect.

Schopenhauer argues that through intellect or reason, it is possible to escape the evil of endless willing and rise above the world of will. One must see things without subjectivity or personal interest, as objects of understanding as opposed to objects of desire. Contemplation of works of art provides momentary escape from the workings of the will. By seeing something as beautiful we are seeing the universal in the particular; we are catching a glimpse of the Platonic Idea of which the object of our contemplation is an instantiation. Although this capacity to recognize the Idea through the contemplation of works of art exists in all men, it does so to the highest degree in genius. Genius is the highest form of this will-less knowledge, the clear and impartial perception of the objective, the essential, and the universal.[14] Schopenhauer explicitly applies this notion of genius to composers:

> The composition of melody, the disclosure in it of all the deepest secrets of human willing and feeling, is the work of genius, whose action, which is more apparent here than anywhere else, lies far from all reflection and conscious intention, and may be called an inspiration. . . . The composer reveals the inner nature of the world, and expresses the deepest wisdom in a language which his reason does not understand. . . . Therefore in the composer, more than in any other artist, the man is entirely separated and distinct from the artist.[15]

Wagner would certainly have numbered himself among such composers.

Wagner's adoption of Schopenhauer's view seems to result in something of a retreat from that dialectically inevitable fusion of all the arts—the *Gesamtkunstwerk*—presented in *Oper und Drama*. Within such a fusion, music was to be only one of a series of component arts making up the music drama. In *Beethoven*, Wagner never recants the central thesis of the earlier work, but attempts to sidestep the difficulty by likening all of the other arts to music, enclosing them within her all-encompassing skirts:

> Music, which does not represent the Ideas inherent in the world's appearances [*Erscheinungen*], is itself a comprehensive Idea of the world; it completely includes the drama in itself, for drama again expresses the world's only idea on the

---

13. In *Mein Leben* Wagner claims to have read *Die Welt als Wille und Vorstellung* four times during the year after it was introduced to him by Georg Herwegh in 1854.

14. See Schopenhauer, *World* 1: §36, §37 and 2: chap. 31.

15. Schopenhauer, *World*, 1: 336.

same level as that of music. Just as a drama does not portray human characters, but lets them represent themselves directly, so the motives of music give us the character of all the world's appearances according to their innermost essence [*An-sich*]. The motion, formation, and evolution [*Veränderung*] of these motives is not only analogously related to the drama, but a drama representing the Idea can only be understood with perfect clarity through those moving, forming, and evolving musical motives. Accordingly we would not err were we to define music as man's *a priori* qualification for shaping drama in general.[16]

Given the influence of Schopenhauer on Wagner and the influence of Wagner on intellectuals at the end of the century, it is not surprising that to be a Wagnerian generally meant to be a disciple of Schopenhauer as well.

This is nowhere more clearly to be seen than in Friedrich Nietzsche's *Die Geburt der Tragödie aus dem Geist der Musik* (1871). Nietzsche's book, which contains a "Preface to Richard Wagner," posits an eternal opposition between what he terms the Apollinian and the Dionysian, and argues that the power of Greek tragedy lay in its cultivation of the latter principle. The Dionysian, which Nietzsche describes in terms of intoxication and rapture, is equated with Schopenhauer's will. It is irrational, extralinguistic, and emotional; in short, musical. Tragedy is "born of the womb of music, in the mysterious twilight of the Dionysian."[17] Nietzsche argued that the current age was witnessing a reawakening of the Dionysian spirit in German music (a "demon rising from unfathomable depths") and that this reawakening had first occurred in Wagner's music dramas.[18]

Nietzsche's discussion of music drama revolves around the necessity of Apollinian illusion in order to protect and "deliver us from the Dionysian flood and excess."[19] In making this point, he appeals

to those who, immediately related to music, have in it, as it were, their motherly womb, and are related to things almost exclusively through unconscious musical relations. To these genuine musicians I direct the question whether they can imagine a human being who would be able to perceive the third act of *Tristan und Isolde*, without any aid of word and image, purely as a tremendous symphonic movement, without expiring in a spasmodic unharnessing of all the wings of the soul?[20]

In other words, the essence of *Tristan* is a symphonic movement; all else is simply "stunts" or defenses.[21] Nietzsche thus presents music in the same

---

16. *GS* IX: 105–106.

17. Friedrich Nietzsche, *The Birth of Tragedy*, in *Basic Writings of Nietzsche*, ed. and trans. Walter Kaufmann (New York: Modern Library, 1968), 82.

18. Ibid., 119.

19. Ibid., 129.

20. Ibid., 126–27. This section of Nietzsche's text may also be found in Bojan Bujić, ed., *Music in European Thought 1851–1912* (Cambridge: Cambridge University Press, 1988), 99.

21. Carl Dahlhaus, *The Idea of Absolute Music*, trans. Roger Lustig (Chicago: University of Chicago Press, 1989), 33.

terms as Schopenhauer and Wagner: as an absolute, as "essence" itself (whether this be called *Ding an sich*, will, or the Dionysian).

The following extract from Nietzsche's text establishes the necessary balance between the Apollinian and the Dionysian, and offers us a glimpse of the nascent expressive aesthetic position whereby form is predetermined by and is a necessary consequence of the content.

> Thus the Apollinian tears us out of the Dionysian universality and lets us find delight in individuals; it attaches our pity to them, and by means of them it satisfies our sense of beauty which longs for great and sublime forms . . . [T]he Apollinian tears man from his orgiastic self-annihilation and blinds him to the universality of the Dionysian process, deluding him into the belief that he is seeing a single image of the world (*Tristan und Isolde*, for instance), and that *through music*, he is merely supposed to *see* it still better and more profoundly. What can the healing magic of Apollo not accomplish when it can even create the illusion that the Dionysian is really in the service of the Apollinian and capable of enhancing its effects—as if music were essentially the art of presenting an Apollinian content?[22]

Nietzsche was heavily under the influence of Wagner during the time in which he wrote *Die Geburt der Tragödie*, and indeed discussed many of the central concepts of the book with him. Unquestionably, he was familiar with Wagner's prose writings in general, and with *Beethoven* in particular, as this latter work transmits Wagner's aesthetic attitudes during the period of his initial acquaintance with Nietzsche. (They had met in 1869.) Along with *Beethoven*, then, *Die Geburt der Tragödie* is perhaps the first product of a Schopenhauerian-Wagnerian aesthetic position, and it would not be an exaggeration to suggested that the immense influence of Wagner and his works acted as a catalyst out of which the new expressive aesthetic emerged.[23]

Of course, in some senses it is perverse to insist that this Schopenhauerian-Wagnerian aesthetic is "new." In many ways, it is quite reactionary: an

---

22. Nietzsche, *Birth of Tragedy*, 128 (also Bujić, 100).

23. After his break with Wagner, Nietzsche was understandably embarrassed by aspects of the book. A "new" edition of 1886 omitted the latter half of the original title ("Out of the Spirit of Music") and included a lengthy preface entitled "An Attempt at a Self-Criticism" in which he (rather unsuccessfully) tries to assimilate this 1871 work to his later thought—in particular his rejection of Schopenhauerian pessimism.

A fragment entitled "On Music and Words" (published and discussed in Carl Dahlhaus, *Between Romanticism and Modernism: Four Studies in the Music of the Later Nineteenth Century*, trans. Mary Whittall [Berkeley and Los Angeles: University of California Press, 1980]), written contemporaneously with *Die Geburt der Tragödie*, attempts to refine Schopenhauer's notion of the will and its equation with music. During the course of this, Nietzsche unconditionally rejects what was to become the central tenet of the expressive aesthetic position: that music awakens a specific emotional response in a listener. Although this argument is nowhere reflected in the 1871 book, the existence of this fragment must necessarily militate against an unconditional understanding of Nietzsche as a predecessor of the expressive aesthetic position. Nevertheless, his espousal of an aesthetic of absolute music is incontestable.

updating of the older *Gefühlsästhetik* with modern idealistic terminology. In the hands of later practitioners such as Friedrich von Hausegger, Hans von Wolzogen, and even Lorenz himself, the expressive aesthetic was preoccupied with the inner life of music and its ability to transcend mundane concerns. It emerged roughly in tandem with what Wilhelm Dilthey later called the *Geisteswissenschaften*, or humanities, and likewise was a product of the nineteenth-century hermeneutic impulse.

Hermeneutics, formerly divided into biblical, classical, and judicial branches, was united as an intellectual discipline in the early nineteenth century by Friedrich Schleiermacher. It recognizes two primary bases for interpretation: either the (literary) text itself, or the author's psychological processes involved in producing the text. The continual oscillation between the two (that is, between objective and subjective, and between part and whole) produces the famous hermeneutic circle through which the technical understanding of a work is achieved, yet is transcended by psychological understanding. Notice that the hermeneutic approach is dynamic: it is constantly in motion.

Wilhelm Dilthey made the circular account of the relations between part and whole inherent in the hermeneutic circle the basis for what he termed the *Geisteswissenschaften* (humanities). While the positivistic natural sciences could explain (*erklären*) phenomena with some degree of objectivity, the *Geisteswissenschaften* can only elucidate (*erläutern*) them in a more subjective fashion. For Dilthey, lived-through experience (*Erlebnis*) was central: expression was the outward manifestation of lived experience. The process of understanding (*Verstehen*) illuminates these expressions and relates them as parts to a whole; thus experience produces expression which calls forth understanding. The hermeneutic task, as Dilthey and others (Lipps, Vischer) understood it, involved empathy (*Nachfühlen* or *Hineinversetzen*); it was subjective and experiential. Its basis was idealistic in that it strove for transcendence.[24]

The intellectual currents that contributed to the foundation of the *Geisteswissenschaften* are reflected in two central aesthetic texts of the latter nineteenth century: Eduard Hanslick's *Vom Musikalisch-Schönen* (1854) and Friedrich von Hausegger's *Musik als Ausdruck* (1884). The latter employs quasi-scientific methods to justify, in hermeneutic terms, the expressive aesthetic, while the former is notorious for its anti-Wagnerian stance— a stance that should suggest its complete opposition to the expressive aesthetic, but whose odd correspondence with aspects of this aesthetic serves to highlight some of its contradictions and fissures.

---

24. The above account of hermeneutics is derived from the entry on nineteenth-century hermeneutics by Tilottama Rajan in the *Johns Hopkins Guide to Literary Theory and Criticism*, ed. Michael Groden and Martin Kreiswirth (Baltimore: Johns Hopkins University Press, 1993), and from the introduction to Ian Bent, ed., *Music Analysis in the Nineteenth Century*, vol. 2: *Hermeneutic Approaches* (Cambridge: Cambridge University Press, 1994).

It might seem more logical to oppose a *geisteswissenschaftlich* approach, with its strongly idealistic aims, with Hanslick's apparently more prosaic model. As commonly understood, Hanslick stands as one of the first formalists in music, yet—despite received critical opinion—he neither advocates adherence to set formal schemes, nor denies the content of music. What he does is resist the idea that emotions or feelings play a role in understanding music. Hanslick wishes to replace what he regards as a passive, emotional reception of music, based on emotional analogies, with an active engagement of the imagination (*Phantasie*) of the listener. The goal of music, according to Hanslick, is not primarily the arousal of an emotional response in the listener, since there is no necessarily and uniquely valid causal relation between whatever emotions may be identified with the piece and the work itself. Rather, to follow music is to comprehend intellectually the ordering and structure of the purely musical content. Musical perception ought to be "disinterested" and objective—a purely aesthetic enjoyment of a work as an artistic object.

Hanslick's famous argument that "*der Inhalt der Musik sind tönend bewegte Formen*" introduces his idea of what he terms musical arabesques and kaleidoscopes. These images are intended to illuminate the nonrepresentational character of forms in music. He argues that these dynamically conceived musical forms do not represent (i.e., make present) emotional states *per se* but rather that the music *suggests* these states by means of psychological associations. In other words, it suggests the dynamic properties of some particular emotional state, such as agitation, or calmness, rather than the emotion itself. Form is thus a metaphor for the dynamic aspect of the emotions.

When discussing "form" and "content" in music, Hanslick does so on two levels. First, at the level of small-scale musical elements such as theme and motive, there can be no separation between form and content; a musical theme is an "aesthetically not further reducible unit of musical thought."

> When we talk about the content of a work of art, we can really only make sense if we attach form to it. The concepts of content and form mutually determine and complement each other. . . . [I]n music we see content and form, material and configuration, image and idea, fused in an obscure, inseparable entity. . . . In music there is not content as opposed to form, because music has no form other than the content.[25]

Second, Hanslick notes, however, that in music we use the terms "form" and "content" in an artistic as well as what he regards as the logical sense.

> Of course, in the case of whole compositions, particularly extended ones, we are accustomed to speaking of their form and content. This is not the original, logical

---

25. Eduard Hanslick, *On the Musically Beautiful: A Contribution towards the Revision of the Aesthetics of Music*, trans. and ed. Geoffrey Payzant (Indianapolis: Hackett, 1986), 80.

sense of these concepts, but a particularly musical signification. By the "form" of a [work] . . . we mean the architectonic of the combined components and groups of notes out of which the piece is made. Hence, more precisely, we mean the symmetry of these parts in their sequence, contrast, repetition, and development, in which case we understand the content to be the themes worked up into such an architectonic. Therefore there can be here no more question of a content as "subject," but solely of a *musical* content.[26]

Here is where unwary critics have misread Hanslick. He is quite clear that there are not one but two levels of content in music: the content of the self-identical musical materials themselves, and another content—form—resulting from their architectonic combination and juxtaposition. Form and content are indistinguishable when each is considered on the same level (either that of theme and motive or that of the work as a whole, seen as the combination of small-scale elements). They are distinguishable, though, when considered on different levels, i.e. when content is seen as theme or motive, and form is seen as the architecture of the entire piece. This second content might be termed "contextual content," and does—despite the logical absurdity noted by Hanslick—suggests a rigid division between content (understood as a specific emotional state) and form, at least in the musical sense, since that content, according to Hanslick, is only a *musical* content rather than a conceptual one.

Hanslick attempts to collapse the dichotomy between form and content by arguing that music is its own irreducible essence. It may suggest a parallel—a structural analogy—with the dynamic properties of feelings, but it does not awaken these feelings themselves. Unlike later formalists, Hanslick does not privilege musical structure as autonomous. Instead, *Vom Musikalisch-Schönen* partakes of the dynamic properties of the hermeneutic model in its emphasis on the active engagement of the listener. In this aspect, Hanslick's work oddly resembles that of Friedrich von Hausegger.

The influence of Wagner on Hausegger is unmistakable from the outset. In his first works—particularly in *Wagner und Schopenhauer*—Hausegger argued that Wagner's music dramas reveal for the first time the true inner essence of music;[27] Wagner therefore represented the apex of music history. Wagner and Schopenhauer are the two constants in Hausegger's work; in fact, it would not be an exaggeration to see *Die Musik als Ausdruck* as an attempt to prove scientifically a Wagnerian *Weltanschauung*. Hausegger's impact on Wagnerian circles was immense: Hans von Wolzogen referred to him as "one of *our* philosophers and aestheticians," and Lorenz himself

---

26. Ibid., 81.
27. Friedrich von Hausegger, *Wagner und Schopenhauer: Eine Darlegung der philosophischen Anschauungen R. Wagners an der Hand seiner Werke* (Leipzig: Schloemp, 1878).

saw Hausegger as something of a Wagnerian missionary in the field of aesthetics.[28]

In *Die Musik als Ausdruck*, Hausegger follows a positivistic methodology indebted to theories of evolution in an attempt to prove his theory that "the essence of music is expression—expression refined and raised to the highest power of effectiveness."[29] In so doing he aligns himself with the tradition stemming from Rousseau in which music's origins are traced back to the first vocal utterances of primitive peoples.[30] In such theories, the emission of sound is linked with a state of heightened emotion; together these mark the ultimate origin of music.[31] Music is seen as a consequence of—and dependent upon—a physical-spiritual condition (emotion); it follows speech on a hypothetical evolutionary hierarchy. In the words of the Hausegger scholar Ernst-Joachim Danz, "Music is nothing but sound [*Laut*] as a consequence of a physical-spiritual state of agitation [*Erregungszustandes*], progressively modified with communicative intention throughout the course of human history."[32]

When Hausegger discusses the relationship of the body and music, he does so in quite a literal manner. In this he differs from most of his nineteenth-century counterparts, such as Wagner and Nietzsche, who generally intended the relationship to be metaphorical.[33] Hausegger argues that the body has a causal relationship with music. For example, the twin parameters of pitch and rhythm originate directly in the body: the former from a change in feeling or emotion which causes a deviation from the normal speaking tone, and the latter from the shift of body weight from one leg to another.[34]

---

28. Wolzogen's reference occurs in an unpublished letter to Hausegger of 14 May 1897, cited in Ernst-Joachim Danz, *Die objektlose Kunst: Untersuchungen zur Musikästhetik Friedrich von Hauseggers* (Regensburg: Gustav Bosse, 1981), 270. Lorenz's remark is contained in a review of Ernst Kurth's *Musikpsychologie* in *Die Musik* 23 (1930): 186.

29. Friedrich von Hausegger, *Die Musik als Ausdruck*, 2nd ed. (Vienna: Konegen, 1887), 209. [First ed. published serially in the *Bayreuther Blätter* 7 (1884) and as a book in 1885.]

30. The source is Rousseau's *Essai sur l'origine des langues*, written about 1760 and published in Geneva in 1781.

31. See Downing A. Thomas, *Music and the Origins of Language: Theories from the French Enlightenment* (Cambridge: Cambridge University Press, 1995). Bujić, *Music in European Thought 1851–1912*, offers a selection of other writings concerned with the origins of music. During this period, the influence of positivism and evolutionary thinking in the natural sciences spills over into the social sciences and humanities. These new methodologies proved irresistible to researchers in humanistic fields as they seemed to invest their adopted disciplines with the cachet of science itself.

32. Danz, *Objektlose Kunst*, 267–68.

33. On this metaphorical relationship, see Tilottama Rajan, "Language, Music, and the Body: Nietzsche and Deconstruction," in *Intersections: Nineteenth-Century Philosophy and Contemporary Theory*, ed. Tilottama Rajan and David Clark (Albany: SUNY Press, 1995), 147–69.

34. Hausegger, *Musik als Ausdruck*, 7–14.

To Hausegger, music forms the phenomenal outside of the lived-through inside of a feeling. It is the means by which this feeling is made audible.[35] It follows that for each distinct internal emotion there is an equally distinct external manifestation. There is no difference between an emotion expressed musically and one that remains purely physical and psychological. Given such a conception of music, it is also immaterial whether or not a specific piece has words.

The nascent discipline of psychology (foreshadowed by Schopenhauer's dream theory) becomes an important secondary scientific basis for Hausegger's theory when he maintains that the physical movements under consideration also mirror spiritual processes.[36] These spiritual processes—we would say "emotions"—are the essence of music. Accordingly, the important thing about a musical work is not its structure, but rather its relationship to the emotional processes of which it is the expression. This results in an aesthetic position largely dependent on conception and reception, which Hausegger refers to as aesthetics from within (*von Innen*).

Hausegger grounds the successful communication between artist and recipient in the structural similarity of their bodies.[37] If music consists of emotion, it must therefore awaken the same physical-spiritual response in the listener as that of the creator, for it is the direct expression of that common internal state. Aesthetic reception is dependent upon this sympathetic feeling (*Mitempfindung*); at the moment of sounding, communicator and recipient, artist and public are one. It is just such an aesthetic position which Eduard Hanslick terms as "pathological" in *Vom Musikalisch-Schönen*—a point that clearly indicates an indebtedness of the new Wagnerian-Schoepenhauerian expressive aesthetic to the older *Gefühlsästhetik*.[38]

Under aesthetics from within, a work of art is understood on the basis of the mental or spiritual processes of the creator, and the question of aesthetic worth is inseparably bound up with those of impulse, inspiration, and manifestation of the artistic personality in music. Art is unconsciously created as a consequence of an aroused physical-spiritual state. In short, Hausegger's is an aesthetic with a psychological way of looking at things.

If an aesthetic from within is one which, in Hausegger's words, "seeks the artistic object not in its concrete, objective, representative processes but in its internal processes," then the objective form of a work of art is of less consequence than the subjective emotional processes of which it is the external expression.[39] The beautiful is located not in the work itself, but in the

35. Ernst-Joachim Danz expresses this nicely: "Music . . . is outwardly directed inner feeling." Danz, *Objektlose Kunst*, 168.
36. Hausegger develops this notion in his study of artistic creation, *Das Jenseits des Künstlers* (Vienna: Konegen, 1893).
37. Hausegger, *Musik als Ausdruck*, 27.
38. Hanslick, *On the Musically Beautiful*, 5, and the first two chapters in general.
39. Friedrich von Hausegger, "Aesthetik von Innen," *Bayreuther Blätter* 16 (1893): 327.

expression of the artist.[40] The work itself becomes merely a communicative channel between artist and public. Danz argues that this ontological "objectlessness" is the central concept underlying all of Hausegger's thought.[41]

It need hardly be emphasized that the Wagnerian-Schopenhauerian aesthetic of expression is diametrically opposed to much of Hanslick and the later formalists.[42] In fact the basis for comparison is narrow, as both stem from entirely different value judgements and criteria. While the formalist aesthetic is concerned with art as an absolute and autonomous entity, Hausegger's expressive aesthetic is more concerned with art as a medium of human communication and of human relationships. The formalist aesthetic is more directly concerned with the work of art itself than is the expressive aesthetic in which the work of art itself is important only as a communicative channel between the psyche of the artist and that of the recipient. For the Wagnerian camp, music's effect did not reside simply in the structure of the score, but involved both the creative and recreative (performance) processes. For Hanslick and his followers, investigation of the beautiful meant investigation of the material structure of the work, without any consideration of the creative or recreative processes. While Hanslick restricts the signifying power of music to purely musical matters (it signifies nothing but itself), it is a given in Hausegger's aesthetic that music communicates feelings. To Hausegger and his followers, Hanslick and his adherents are trapped in the world of appearance, examining only the external shell of a work and missing the core. This polarity between objectivity and subjectivity expresses itself in a series of binary oppositions that continue to exert influence even today: form/expression; conservative/modern; Brahms/Wagner; Hanslick/Hausegger. Even the idea that Hanslick presents an aesthetic of absolute music requires revision when seen through the lens of the expressive aesthetic. Carl Dahlhaus has noted the double significance of the term "absolute" in the nineteenth century: "absolute" in the sense of being divorced from a specific program or expressive intent, and "absolute"

---

40. Danz puts it in this manner: "Beauty never resides in an object in itself, but rather always resides in the subjects which confront it." Danz, *Objektlose Kunst*, 159.

41. Ibid., 316–19.

42. Hanslick's aesthetic of the "specifically musical" is also a product of the intellectual climate of the second half of the century. In many respects it is his *Vom Musikalisch-Schönen* which is an untainted manifestation of the positivistic impulse of the age. Part of the reason that Hausegger's *Musik als Ausdruck* was received so enthusiastically was that it gave Hanslick's opponents the appearance of an equally firm scientific basis from which to argue. See, for example, Arthur Seidl, *Vom Musikalisch-Erhabenen: Prolegomena zur Aesthetik der Tonkunst* (Regensburg: M. Wasner, 1887). Ottokar Hostinsky's *Das Musikalisch-Schöne und das Gesamtkunstwerk vom Standpunkte der formalen Ästhetik* (Leipzig: Breitkopf & Härtel, 1877) was an attempt to reconcile Wagnerian and Hanslickean aesthetics. Lorenz includes excerpts of Hostinsky's work in the appendix to *Geheimnis* I: 301–303.

as an intimation of the Absolute, the *Ding an sich*.[43] Wagner and his Schopenhauerian followers subscribe to the second of these, while Hanslick adheres to the first. Thus the Wagnerian Curt Mey can claim that Hanslick's aesthetic has nothing to do with absolute music.[44]

And yet there are some curious points of contact between Hanslick and the Wagnerian-Schopenhauerian aesthetic position. First of all, in both there is a move away from strictly formalist privileging of musical structure in favor of some reciprocal relationship of form and content. Thomas Grey has recently suggested that Wagner's *Beethoven* represents an "inadvertent reconciliation with Hanslick (at an abstract aesthetic level, at least)."[45] Grey argues that in *Beethoven*, Wagner shifts from the adjective-dominated musical description of his earlier writings to a verb-dominated one: one that was designed to show the parallel between the dramatic action and the processes of musical form. In other words, Wagner's conception of musical expression was, like Hanslick's, one of dynamic analogy.[46]

Both Hanslick and Hausegger understand musical form as large-scale rhythm (*Großrhythmik*).[47] For Hausegger, however, the basis of form is a physical impulse made concrete, and its reception is a physical matter, based in the body:

We want to *feel* the unity and beauty of form. In the empathetic vibration [*Mitschwingungen*] of our bodies, it becomes clear to our feelings that form originates from similar bodily vibrations [*Körperschwingungen*], which have given themselves over to the necessary consequence of an arousing [*erregenden*] impulse, and, as a result, to an inclination towards expressive movements.[48]

The form of a work then emerges as the external manifestation of this initial impulse; there is thus no division to be thought of between form and content as long as this initial impulse is properly brought to fruition.

One must understand *content* as the nature of the impulse; *form* indicates its power over the means. Where it is adequate to lend shape to all details of the impulse, where the means is serviceable enough to be grasped and formed by this impulse, there form and content are concealed.[49]

---

43. See Dahlhaus, *Idea of Absolute Music*, 40, and chapter 2, passim.

44. Curt Mey, *Die Musik als tönende Weltidee: Versuch einer Metaphysik der Musik. Erster Teil: Die metaphysichen Urgesetze der Melodik* (Leipzig: Hermann Seemann, 1901), 342.

45. Grey, *Wagner's Musical Prose*, 30–42, the quotation is from p. 40.

46. Lee Rothfarb makes the same point in comparing Karl Grunsky's *Musikästhetik* (Leipzig: G.F. Göschen, 1907) with Hanslick, and notes that Grunsky's critical attack on Hanslick was typical of antiformalist tendencies around 1900 ("Hermeneutics and Energetics: Analytical Alternatives in the Early 1900s," *Journal of Music Theory* 36.1 [1992]: 45).

47. Hanslick, *On the Musically Beautiful*, 28.

48. Hausegger, *Musik als Ausdruck*, 198.

49. Ibid.

Hausegger's conception of form presents something of a dialectic. On the one hand, he affirms form as a consequence of an externalized, unitary emotional impulse and discusses its psychological and dynamic aspects. On the other hand, he dismisses its importance as a central factor, longing instead for an *Aufhebung* of form.[50] If the form itself makes an impression— if it is the consequence of a formal schemata—then the work is lacking as an artistic product.

> It is actually incorrect to speak of form in music. . . . Form in itself has almost no significance—at least for those of us who are followers of aesthetics from within. It is a lifeless husk as soon it lacks that process which leads it to the beautiful, that is, to its own type of gratification of self.[51]

Hausegger argues that musical form is instead only a process, a consequence, and notes that its essence—as opposed to that of spatial form—resides in the temporally bounded parameter of rhythm:

> The ordering of the parts presents itself only externally as "form." These phenomena are however only *signs* and not the *essence* of the matter. In its vitality, form is *rhythm*. The expression "form" is to be taken only figuratively.[52]

As we shall see, Hausegger's (and Hanslick's) depiction of form as rhythm plays an important role in Lorenz's own analytical method.

As already noted, the expressive aesthetic position as crystalized in Hausegger's *Die Musik als Ausdruck* is similar to the notion of aesthetic empathy resulting from the hermeneutic circle: to "understand" a phenomena, we must attempt to "relive" the experience itself, to recreate (in the case of art) the artist's creative-psychic force through the outward projection of the self onto the work. The subjective emphasis on creation and reception is the same. But the expressive aesthetic, grounded as it is in idealistic philosophy, operates at the same time on a higher, more abstracted level.

In *Abstraktion und Einfühlung* (1908), the art historian Wilhelm Worringer advances the Schopenhauerian concept of an absolute artistic volition (*absolut Kunstwollen*) as the presupposition for all artistic creation.[53] In so doing he aimed to prove that the then-dominant principle of aesthetic empathy was not universally valid. This absolute artistic volition is

---

50. The German word "Aufhebung" is notoriously difficult to translate, since it connotes the simultaneous suspension/abolishment and preservation (through raising to a higher level) of something.

51. Hausegger, *Musik als Ausdruck*, 201; "Aesthetik von Innen I," 329.

52. Hausegger, *Musik als Ausdruck*, 201.

53. Wilhelm Worringer, *Abstraction and Empathy: A Contribution to the Psychology of Style*, trans. Michael Bullock (New York: International Universities Press, 1953), 9.

that latent inner demand which exists per se, entirely independent of the object and of the mode of creation, and *behaves as will to form*. It is the primary factor in all artistic creation and, in its innermost essence, every work of art is simply an objectification of this a priori.[54]

Accordingly, for Worringer, the stylistic peculiarities of past epochs are not to be explained by a lack of ability but by a differently directed volition. Art history therefore becomes a history of volition, with ability only a secondary consequence of that volition. That is, just as in Hausegger's aesthetics from within, emphasis is shifted from the work itself to its production and reception. The form of a work is a consequence of an expressive intent on the part of the creator; elsewhere Worringer writes:

> [T]rue psychology of style begins when the formal value is shown to be the accurate expression of the inner value, in such a way that duality of form and content ceases to exist.[55]

Worringer argues that this "will to form" expresses itself differently in different eras; for the visual arts with which he is concerned, Worringer sees the twin principles of abstraction and empathy as being operative. Notice that he does not deny the import of empathy for certain eras, only that it is a universal principle. Worringer therefore makes explicit what may only be inferred in Hausegger: the operation of a higher principle—the Schopenhauerian will—behind all phenomena. Such a distinction highlights the fundamental difference between the formalist and expressive aesthetic positions: the former takes as its basis the phenomenal world itself while the latter operates at one remove, at a higher level. The two are fundamentally incompatible.

Musical Form and Analysis

Within the expressive aesthetic, the fetishizing of the creative process above the "work" itself, or the work in performance, had an influence on musical analysis and led to the emergence of analytical techniques that aimed to capture something of the dynamic properties of the hermeneutic circle.[56] For the nascent discipline of musicology, the final decades of the nineteenth century witnessed the triumph of the *Geisteswissenschaft* model for the discipline and the emergence of a separate analytical study of music apart

---

54. Worringer, *Abstraction and Empathy*, 9. My emphasis.

55. Wilhelm Worringer, *Form in Gothic*, trans. and ed. Herbert Read (New York: Schocken Books, 1967), 7. [Translation of *Formprobleme der Gotik*, 1910.]

56. For a later example, see Otto Strobel, *Richard Wagner über sein Schaffen: Ein Beitrag zur "Künstlerästhetik"* (Munich: Bayerische Druckerei & Verlagsanstalt, 1924).

from composition theory. This analytical interest took two forms. On the one hand, a rather practical branch of analysis arose out of composition theory. Musicians such as A.B. Marx and Hugo Riemann wrote studies of musical form as part of a more general practical theory of music. At the turn of the century, these manuals were being written for their own sake by authors such as Ebenezer Prout and Hugo Leichtentritt: here, form was valued in its own right. At the same time as this positivistic turn in the discipline (part of a general reaction against hermeneutics), an experiential branch of musical analysis was developed by musicians such as August Halm and Ernst Kurth under the influence of models taken from psychology and other *Geisteswissenschaften.*

In 1914 Hermann Erpf correctly predicted that "in the near future, research into form ought therefore to constitute one of the most important and pressing problems of music history."[57] The issue of musical form—of form in general—was central for writers about music in the decades surrounding the turn of the century—not just for analytical or theoretical reasons, but for aesthetic ones. In 1902, Benedetto Croce wrote that "the aesthetic fact, therefore, is form and nothing but form."[58] In other words, the question of musical form is closely bound up with aesthetics. Any study of form must adopt from the outset a particular attitude toward the problem of form and content. Is the external shape of the work something apart from its meaning, its content? Do these shapes exist objectively apart from the work in question? Can a musical work even have a conceptual content? These and other issues are all questions of aesthetics; indeed, Ian Bent has recently noted that "aesthetics was considered a valid pursuit, and . . . critical judgement was one of the tools of the analyst."[59]

As already mentioned, technical analysis of form in the nineteenth century arises first within composition theory: musical form was taught as a component of counterpoint and composition, not as a separate entity. Such had long been the practice. In the eighteenth century, the composition treatises of Riepel, Koch, and (later) Reicha present sophisticated structural models for phrase formation, and, hence, musical form in general. In such treatment, successful musical form was understood as embodying the principle of unity in diversity, and conformed in general to rhetorical, syntactical, mechanical, or anatomical models. This changes in the nineteenth century.

As a rule, the nineteenth century was more interested in the interpretation of music's inner life as a means of transcending the phenomenal world

---

57. Hermann Erpf, "Der Begriff der musikalischen Form," *Zeitschrift für Ästhetik und allgemeine Kunstwissenschaft* 9 (1914): 386.

58. Benedetto Croce, *Aesthetic as Science of Expression and General Linguistic*, rev. ed., trans. Douglas Ainslie (New York: Noonday Press, 1962), 16.

59. Ian Bent, ed., *Music Analysis in the Nineteenth Century* (Cambridge: Cambridge University Press, 1994), 2:37.

than in explaining how it worked. Even within the purely practical realm of composition theory (Marx, Riemann), musical form was now conceived according to an organic model, as a whole-greater-than-the-sum-of-its-parts, and technical tools of thematic analysis were developed to describe these structures.[60]

From about the middle of the century one finds a preoccupation with standard schematic patterns for the larger forms; these patterns are generally defined by treatment of melodic-thematic material. The dominant figure in this understanding of form is A.B. Marx. Marx's view of form is architectonic: forms are constructed from a supply of pre-existing building blocks identified by melodic material (first theme, second theme, etc.) which create independent units or blocks (antecedent/consequent phrases, periods, etc.) which are then combined into a limited number of standard larger forms. The standard "sonata form" paradigm is typical of such an understanding of form. By the end of the century, these formal abstractions begin to be used as yardsticks against which actual compositions were measured and either approved or found wanting. This is a radical shift: formal patterns began to be seen as absolutes, rather than an idealized average of individual peculiarities.

The impulse to standardize and catalogue formal types arises from the desire to demonstrate the organic nature of pieces of music, and is typical of the positivistic spirit of the second half of the century. The resultant reification of formal types only exacerbated a tendency (going back to the early nineteenth century) to separate form from content in musical works. Now form could be understood as something external, something preexisting: a vessel into which the content of a work could be poured. It is just such a tendency that the Schopenhauerian-Wagnerian expressive aesthetic position resists.

The climax of such thought is found in the system of Hugo Riemann.[61] According to him, his work addressed "die Lehre vom *logischen* Aufbau der Tonstücke."[62] All is based on a single, logical formula (like a physical law of nature): the metrical sequence of light-heavy, applied at all levels of musical form—from the motive to the period to the work as a whole. Thus, for Riemann, all music begins with an upbeat and common time is the standard meter. All other beginnings and meters are alterations of this norm.

---

60. Useful surveys of nineteenth-century analysis may be found in the introductions to both volumes of Bent, ed. *Music Analysis in the Nineteenth Century*. See also Birgitte Moyer, "Concepts of Musical Form in the Nineteenth Century with Special Reference to A.B. Marx and Sonata Form" (Ph.D. dissertation, Stanford University, 1969).

61. Riemann's principal writings on form are the *Grundriß der Kompositionslehre* (1889), the *Große Kompositionslehre* (1902–13), and the *System der musikalischen Rhythmik und Harmonik* (1903). In preparing this work, I have used the *Grundriß der Kompositionslehre (Musikalische Formenlehre)*, 6th ed. (Berlin: Max Hesse, 1920).

62. Riemann, *Grundriß der Kompositionslehre*, 1.

Riemann argues that large-scale form is an extension of the heavy-light-heavy type within the measure, and therefore that an A-B-A pattern is the basic structural principle of large-scale form. He goes on to define larger and larger forms by expanding this model.

Riemann's theory is a consummate demonstration of the influence of the natural sciences on the humanities in the latter half of the nineteenth century. His search for a universal law to explain a musical phenomenon and his diligent cataloguing of musical processes and forms is the very embodiment of the positivistic tendency of the age. That all is derived from a single rhythmic cell (light-heavy) in Riemann invokes concepts of biological organicism derived from evolutionary theory. This biological model dominates not only the writings of Riemann and his followers, but also the work of those scholars reacting against them.[63]

By the end of the nineteenth century, however, an increasingly deductive view of form had emerged whereby formal principles were inferred from actual music (generally Beethoven) and then taught as abstractions. Manuals of musical form were published with increasing frequency.[64] Two somewhat contradictory reasons might be advanced for this trend. On the one hand, conservatories and schools of music were flourishing and there was a demand for practical musical education that often did not involve composition. On the other hand, however, the second half of the nineteenth century witnessed a shift in musical literacy on the part of the general public: a move away from a practical relationship with music (through amateur performance) to one more literary and theoretical—one that corresponded to a general emphasis on *Bildung* and which fed a flourishing publishing industry of music books—primarily "concert guides" and manuals of form.[65]

For many musicologists around the turn of the century, the entirely practical, objective, and abstract *Formenlehre* did not adequately reflect the

---

63. On the trope of music as an organism, see Ruth Solie, "The Living Work: Organicism and Musical Analysis," *19th-Century Music* 4 (1980): 147–56; Lotte Thaler, *Organische Form in der Musiktheorie des 19. und beginnenden 20. Jahrhunderts* (Munich and Salzburg: Emil Katzbichler, 1984).

64. For example, Ludwig Bussler, *Musikalische Formenlehre in dreiunddreissig Aufgaben mit zahlreichen . . . Muster-, Uebungs- und Erläuterungs-Beispielen, sowie Anführungen aus den Meisterwerken der Tonkunst* (Berlin: Habel, 1878); Salomon Jadassohn, *Die Formen in den Werken der Tonkunst, analysirt und in stufenweise geordnetem Lehrgang . . . dargestellt* (Leipzig: Kistner, 1885); Ebenezer Prout, *Musical Form* (London: Augener, 1895); Percy Goetschius, *Models of the Principal Musical Forms* (Boston: New England Conservatory, 1894); and Hugo Leichtentritt, *Musikalische Formenlehre* (Leipzig: Breitkopf & Härtel, 1911). A more complete list may be found in Bent, *Musical Analysis in the Nineteenth Century*, vol. 1, p. 353.

65. This shift has been chronicled by Leon Botstein, "Music and Its Public: Habits of Listening and the Crisis of Musical Modernism in Vienna, 1870–1914" (Ph.D. dissertation, Harvard University, 1985); see also Botstein, "Listening Through Reading: Musical Literacy and the Concert Audience," *19th-Century Music* 16 (1992): 129–45.

aesthetic nature of music. Nor was its essentially positivistic methodology seen as appropriate for a *geisteswissenschaftlich* discipline like *Musikwissenschaft*.[66] Instead, scholars embraced the dynamic principles of the hermeneutic model, with its emphasis on the experiential understanding of the whole and its parts.

Lee Rothfarb has argued that there were two branches of reform in music theory in the early decades of the twentieth century: one interested in the material nature of music (Schenker, Louis-Thuille, Schoenberg) and the other more interested in its dynamic properties. This latter branch took three rather distinct forms: first a purely hermeneutic one in the writings of Hermann Kretzschmar, his student Arnold Schering, and Paul Bekker; secondly, a phenomenological one, seen in August Halm; and thirdly, a psychological approach indebted to Gestalt psychology, found particularly in Ernst Kurth's work.[67] All three are notable for their emphasis on the dynamic and evolutionary nature of musical form, and each favored a rather subjective, listener-oriented understanding of form. There is a move away from seeing form as something of a static mold out of which works are cast towards presenting the idea of form as a perceptual construct produced by the listener while listening to a work. Viewed in this manner, form is indissolubly linked with content. It is only verifiable experientially by a (necessarily) subjective listener and not empirically by visual examination of a score. This is the understanding of form held by adherents of the expressive aesthetic. Instead of examining the writings of Kretzschmar or Schering,[68] I will briefly discuss Paul Bekker as a representative of the hermeneutic branch of experiential theory.[69] After then surveying Halm and Kurth (with an excursus on Gestalt psychology), I will conclude this section with an account of several other writers employing form-dynamic analysis.

Despite writing in-depth studies of the music of Wagner, Beethoven, and Mahler, Paul Bekker was not, and would not have called himself an analyst.

---

66. See Pamela M. Potter, "Trends in German Musicology, 1918–1943: The Effects of Methodological, Ideological, and Institutional Change on the Writing of Music History" (Ph.D. dissertation, Yale University, 1991), 1–17, for an account of the prevalence of the *Geisteswissenschaft* model in musicology until the 1920s.

67. Lee Rothfarb, "Beethoven's Formal Dynamics: August Halm's Phenomenological Perspective," in *Beethoven Forum 5* (Lincoln: University of Nebraska Press, 1996), 65–84; Rothfarb, "Hermeneutics and Energetics"; and Rothfarb, "Ernst Kurth in Historical Perspective: His Intellectual Inheritance and Music-Theoretical Legacy," *Schweizer Jahrbuch für Musikwissenschaft* 6–7 (1986–87): 23–42.

68. Hermann Kretzschmar, "Anregungen zur Förderung musikalischer Hermeneutik," *Jahrbuch der Musikbibliothek Peters* 9 (1902): 45–66; Kretzschmar, "Neue Anregungen zur Förderung musikalischer Hermeneutik," *Jahrbuch der Musikbibliothek Peters* 12 (1905): 75–86.

69. Rothfarb notes that despite their lip-service to dynamism and the *geistige Gehalt* of music, both Kretzschmar and Schering present form rather mechanistically, as the exterior "shell" of the work. Lee Rothfarb, "Music Analysis, Cultural Morality, and Sociology in the Writings of August Halm," *Indiana Theory Review* 16 (1995): 176.

Like Kretzschmar and Schering, his central concern was hermeneutic; he aimed for interpretation and understanding above all. For Bekker, the nineteenth century was dominated by the "will to expression": emotion was the first condition of all art; the second was that it must represent a perpetual state of "becoming." This latter principle Bekker takes as universal: music history is to be seen as "the history of sound and of sounding forms [*klingenden Luftformen*], as a history of the changes of feelings out of which men grasped sound and shaped it into artistic form."[70] History is not a series of facts and dates, but instead involves a demonstration of the forces that effect change. Likewise, musical form—particularly Wagnerian form—is not static: "the idea of perpetual evolutionary flux is the true formative principle of drama";[71] it depends on the "will to effect" which is the "inner driving force of all formal structures."[72] In Bekker's view, this dynamism colors everything: "thematic development is actually not development *of* the theme, it is the theme's development, that is, the theme develops, it *moves*."[73] As this passage reveals, Bekker's dynamic analysis depends on anthropomophosis; Bekker also writes that "in [Wagnerian] musical form, people, not notes, move about, not sounding, but conversing in tonal relations, not forming patterns, but acting."[74] Only Bekker's dynamism links him with other exponents of experiential theory; in fact, August Halm carried on an extended disagreement with him over his *Beethoven* volume.[75]

Although Halm also understood music as dynamic and kinetic, his whole approach was opposed to the hermeneuticist's anthropomophic application of this dynamism to inner life and the emotions.[76] Instead, Halm was concerned with revealing the interior formal logic of a work; musical logic is objective *Geist*, and the only way to illuminate this is through structural analysis of form:

> The remedy against this [focus on inner life and the emotions] is no secret: it is the cultivation of musical form, the consistent if also self-denying willingness to recognize the will of music and to adhere to it alone.[77]

70. Paul Bekker, *Musikgeschichte als Geschichte der musikalischen Formwandlungen* (Stuttgart, Berlin, and Leipzig: Deutsche Verlags-Anstalt, 1926, reprint Hildesheim: Georg Olms, 1976), 15. On Bekker, see Andreas Eichhorn, "Annäherung durch Distanz: Paul Bekkers Auseinandersetzung mit der Formalästhetik Hanslicks," *Archiv für Musikwissenschaft* 54 (1997): 194–209.

71. Paul Bekker, *Richard Wagner: His Life in His Work*, trans. M.M. Bozman (New York: Norton, 1931; reprint Westport: Greenwood Press, 1971), 231.

72. Bekker, *Musikgeschichte als Geschichte der musikalischen Formwandlungen*, 88.

73. Ibid., 134.

74. Bekker, *Richard Wagner*, 512.

75. See Rothfarb, "Music Analysis, Cultural Morality," 180–91.

76. This description of August Halm's approach is largely derived from Rothfarb, "Beethoven's Formal Dynamics: August Halm's Phenomenological Perspective" and Rothfarb, "Music Analysis, Cultural Morality."

77. August Halm, "Unsere Zeit und Beethoven," in *Von Form und Sinn der Musik:*

What is striking about Halm's approach is its focus on the listener's perception of music. He is interested in how an audience psychologically interprets harmonic action as "energy expended." As Lee Rothfarb puts it, for Halm, "musical logic is linked to cognition in an intentional structure that correlates ordered musical events, on the one hand, and our mode of consciousness of them, on the other."[78] For Rothfarb, this makes Halm a proto-phenomenologist. When Halm discusses form, he emphasizes its dynamic character (as he does when writing about music itself, which he describes in Schopenhauerian terms as "dynamic will"): "musical events [represent] energetic values that sum cumulatively to a teleological dynamic network, which we call 'form'."[79] This rather strongly recalls Hanslick's suggestion that music presents dynamic analogies to emotional states. Halm's focus on the listener's active participation in the interpretative process, however, through protentive and retentive hearing, partakes of empirically conceived descriptive psychology and leads us to a consideration of Gestalt psychology and its influence on music theory.

Just as Hausegger provided quasi-scientific justification of the expressive aesthetic for the Wagnerians, so did developments in psychology influence music theory and analysis as practiced by advocates of this aesthetic. It is curious how once again the figure of Wagner lurks in the background: the father of Gestalt psychology, Christian von Ehrenfels, was an ardent Wagnerian and, as we shall see, an important influence on Lorenz.[80]

While an account of the origins and development of Gestalt psychology is well beyond the scope of the present work, a summary of some of its main precepts is not out of place.[81] The essence of the theory is that a spatial shape, or Gestalt, is perceived on the basis of a complex of sensations of individual elements. We sense these elements and their spatial determinations, and at the same time we apprehend the basic shape as an object, or quality, which exists side by side with its associated elements. This basic shape is a total experience, a cognitive entity which is more than the mere sum or complex of sensory elements. It is a configured whole which is grasped

Gesammelte Aufsätze, ed., with an introductory essay, by Siegfried Schmalzriedt (Wiesbaden: Breitkopf & Härtel, 1978), 160; cited and translated by Rothfarb in "Musical Analysis, Cultural Morality," 175.

78. Rothfarb, "Beethoven's Formal Dynamics: August Halm's Phenomenological Perspective," 72.

79. Rothfarb, "Hermeneutics and Energetics, 56.

80. Ehrenfels's collected writings have recently been published: *Philosophische Schriften*, ed. Reinhard Fabian, 4 vols., (Munich: Philosophia Verlag, 1982–1990). His articles on Wagner are divided between the second and fourth volumes of this edition, and include: *Zur Klärung der Wagner-Controverse* (1896), "Die musikalische Architektonik" (1896, first published in the *Bayreuther Blätter*), *Richard Wagner und seine Apostaten* (1913), and *Wagner und seine neuen Apostaten* (1931).

81. Barry Smith, ed., *Foundations of Gestalt Theory* (Munich: Philosophia Verlag, 1988) is a useful introduction to the subject.

instantaneously. We can apprehend the same shape (i.e., the same spatial quality) in association with elements which, when taken individually, have nothing in common; for example we can grasp the shape of a head from an actual head, or from a drawing, or a shadow. The Gestalt quality exists therefore alongside but apart from any specific elements. It is a psychological category; a collection of data does not have a Gestalt, it is a Gestalt.

> [W]herever we have a relation . . . between a complex of experienced elements on the one hand and some associated unitary experience of a single invariant structure on the other, we are to conceive this latter structure as a Gestalt, *and to understand the given unitary experience as structurally analogous to the experience of a spatial shape.*[82]

Gestalt psychology notes that humans tend to see the structures of our environment as being more regular, more balanced, and more typical than they really are. That is, we reproduce these structures in our memory in a way which involves some adjustment towards a more simplified, or standardized ideal. This notion is called *Prägnanz*, which also refers to those features of an object which lead towards this tendency to regularity or lawfulness. The *Prägnanz* of an object is not an absolute, but rather a perceptual entity which may embody such different concepts of order as lawfulness, clarity, fullness, or typicality. Gestalt aesthetics is therefore concerned with the artist's maximization of different sorts of *Prägnanz* under given conditions.

One of the first works to explore such concepts was Christian von Ehrenfels's "On 'Gestalt Qualities'."[83] Ehrenfels based his theory on the perception of a melody, noting how memory-images of tones remain simultaneously present as a melody unfolds. The identity of a melody after transposition was for Ehrenfels confirmation of his belief that a Gestalt quality (here the idea of "melody") exists as a separate psychological conceptualization apart from any specific instantiation.

In its essence, Gestalt psychology is concerned with form. But these formal shapes are not merely conventions, but rather deep-seated principles of organization in the human mind. The result of the influence of Gesalt psychology in the realm of music theory is an overturning of traditional depictions of form. Whereas for Riemann the study of form proceeds from the individual detail (the motive) to the larger whole, in Gestalt-influenced *Formenlehre* the equation is reversed. The total shape of a work must be perceived first in order to make sense of the component parts; that is, a work is a whole whose parts are themselves determined as being such that

---

82. Smith, ed., *Foundations of Gestalt Theory*, 14.

83. Christian von Ehrenfels, "Über 'Gestaltsqualitäten'," *Vierteljahrsschrift für wissenschaftlichen Philosophie* 14 (1890): 249–92; reprinted in *Philosophischen Schriften*, vol. 3. English translation in Smith, ed., *Foundations of Gestalt Theory*, 82–117.

they can only be made sense of as parts of a whole of this given kind. The whole of a work is understood as more than just the sum of its parts. Ehrenfels argues that this unity of a higher order, the Gestalt-quality, disappears when we isolate its parts.[84] Such a view is the epitome of organicist thinking, whereby the organism dies when the parts are isolated (as, for example, in dissection).

The older *Formenlehre* traced the ordering and sequence of the parts but neglected to consider how and why the parts are perceived as a whole. In this newer theory of form, the emphasis is placed on the psychological perception of form, with the listener having the central role in the process. To listen to a piece of music requires an "Überhören," an ability to grasp the total shape of a work from its parts. It is a dynamic conception of form. Musical shapes are perceived as dynamic phenomena in their temporal unfolding. The analysis of musical form is therefore the description of the psychological functions of the sections as they appear, according to the natural process of hearing, and following the trajectory of music in time. In practice, this is an account of the large-scale rhythm of a work as created by musical tension and release.

Alongside the influence of Gestalt psychology on music theory and analysis is the increasing influence of reduction technique as an analytical tool.[85] As embodied, for example, in the Schenkerian graph, reduction technique is based principally on musical coherence, on the Gestalt of the musical process—it begins not with the details but first with the total shape. Schenker's *Ursatz* is a good example of a Gestalt-quality: although it is only revealed through analysis, to Schenker its presence is instinctively felt in coherent, tonal musical works. Individual details only achieve validity as contributing to a greater whole, with the middleground abstracted out of the foreground and the background out of the middle—all of course being mutually dependent and organically conditioned.[86] Ernst Kurth too em-

---

84. Smith, ed., *Foundations of Gestalt Theory*, 56.

85. See Helmut Federhofer, *Beiträge zur musikalischen Gestaltsanalyse* (Graz: Akademische Druck- und Verlagsanhalt, 1950) [= "Musikalische Form als Ganzheit," Habilitationsschrift, Graz University, 1944].

86. Recent studies by William Pastille and Severine Neff point out that many of the concepts of early twentieth-century analysis that we have been tracing stem from Goethe's scientific research. For example, his idea of archetypes (*Urphänomene*) depends on the sustained contemplation (*Anschauung*) of phenomena leading to a flash of analytical insight (*aperçu*)—a notion not dissimilar to that of empathy. The dynamic process of intensification (*Steigerung*) leading things to strive upwards (polarity) also comes from Goethe, and influences Schenker's concept of the *Ursatz* and Schoenberg's idea of the *Grundgestalt*. Like Gestalt psychology, these are holistic notions. See William Pastille, "Music and Morphology: Goethe's Influence on Schenker's Thought," in *Schenker Studies*, ed. Hedi Siegel (Cambridge: Cambridge University Press, 1990), 29–44, and Severine Neff, "Schoenberg and Goethe: Organicism and Analysis," in *Music Theory and the Exploration of the Past*, ed. Christopher Hatch and David W. Bernstein (Chicago: University of Chicago Press, 1993), 409–33.

ploys reduction technique in his discussion of what he terms linear counterpoint.[87]

The increasing influence of Gestalt psychology on discussions of musical form and analysis may be traced throughout the early decades of the twentieth century.[88] It is most prominent amongst admirers of Wagner (and adherents to the expressive aesthetic), but is also found in writings by supporters of Riemann. For example, in "Der Begriff der musikalischen Form," Riemann's student Hermann Erpf aims to formulate a clear definition of form, differentiated sharply from "content" or "expression."[89] Unlike his teacher, however, Erpf asserts that there exist no absolute formal laws: rather, form evolves out of the piece itself and is of psychological origin.[90] For Erpf, form is based on perception; it is a psychological process.

> [Formal laws] are only verbalizations of our psychic needs for form, our searchings for form, and the musical forms themselves constitute their projection into the realm of formal possibilities.[91]

The Gestalt-like formulation of Erpf's comment is notable, particularly given his rigidly formalistic orientation. Dahlhaus's argument that the aestheticians of content yielded the field to the formalists as soon as they too began to make a distinction between "musical" and "extra-musical" is not as absolute as he presents it; it is clear that the influence can work both ways.[92] Here, by suggesting that formal categories originate in the unconscious, Erpf undermines his own rigid distinction between content and form. If formal laws are of psychological origin and evolve from the piece itself, how can they be something apart from that piece?

---

87. In *Grundlagen des linearen Kontrapunkts* (1917). Lee Rothfarb discusses Kurth's use of reduction technique as such and in relation to Schenker's in the chapter on polyphonic melody in *Ernst Kurth as Theorist and Analyst* (Philadelphia: University of Pennsylvania Press, 1988), 79–102, esp. 100–102.

88. See, for example, Karl Grunsky's discussion of "Form als Folge" in *Musikästhetik*, 111–12; also Federhofer, *Beiträge zur musikalischen Gestaltsanalyse*. In his article, "Zur Frage der musikalischen Analyse" (*Die Musik* 31 [1939]: 225–31), Erich Schütze writes:

> Each living work of art constitutes an organism, which embraces numerous individual developments. Gestalt psychology [*Ganzheitspsychologie*] teaches us never to leave the internal coherence between the whole and the different, individual parts unconsidered (225).

89. Erpf, "Begriff der musikalischen Form."

90. Ibid., 360. Riemann includes only a small section on "psychologische Formen," by which he means mainly programmatic music. *Grundriß der Kompositionslehre*, 233–34.

91. Erpf, "Begriff der musikalischen Form," 360.

92. Dahlhaus, *Idea of Absolute Music*, 37. Dahlhaus's notion is suspect on other grounds as well, for the formal aestheticians and the content aestheticians have quite different understandings of what music is. Nietzsche arguing that the text of *Tristan* is somehow superfluous is an entirely different thing from Hanslick's thesis that the sole content of music is tonally-animated form.

Erpf's Gestaltist leanings are apparent even in his presentation of such formal matters as the eight-measure period.[93] He argues that its essence rests in the notion of prospective and retrospective hearing: a period is not heard as 1+1+1+1+1+1+1+1 but as 1+1+2+4. That is, periods are arranged in units of ever-increasing size. Certainly, Riemann (and others) suggests much the same thing, but not in the same terms.[94] In Erpf, the emphasis is placed on the perception of wholes, on the idea of grasping the musical gesture as a single entity. Erpf notes that the most general and absolute sense of form is this unity; things with unity have form, those without are formless.

Returning to our survey of dynamic approaches to musical form, we turn to the work of Ernst Kurth, which may be seen as a reaction to the positivism of Riemann.[95] From the outset Kurth adopts an explicitly Schopenhauerian orientation, differentiating between "real" music, which resides in psychic motion, and its mere appearance as the outer layer, the surface of music itself.

> [T]he whole aural phenomenal form in music, with which the laws of physical sound and physiological perception of tones begins, is already the conclusion of a primal process of interior *psychic* growth. . . The forces activated in us are projected from within onto the surface, where they take shape. The sonic impressions are nothing but the intermediary form in which psychological processes manifest themselves. . . . Musical activity merely expresses itself in tones, but it does not reside in them.[96]

The linear counterpoint which Kurth finds in Bach is the notion of melody as tonal stream: an indivisible stream of melody which traces the ebb and flow of psychic forces in the music. To understand music is to experience vicariously the flow of psychic energies which gave rise to the music in the first place—*Verstehen* requires empathy derived from *Erlebnis*:

> The central task of all music theory is to observe the *transformation* of certain *tension processes* into *sounds*. Only in this way is it possible to awaken, even in

---

93. Erpf, "Begriff der musikalischen Form," 362.

94. Compare Riemann's account in the first chapter of the *Grundriß der Kompositionslehre* ("Der symmetrische Aufbau achttaktiger Sätze").

95. Kurth's theories are presented in a trilogy of monographs, treating respectively melody, harmony, and form: *Grundlagen des linearen Kontrapunkts: Bachs melodische Polyphonie*, 3rd ed. (Berlin: Max Hesse, 1927; reprint, Hildesheim: Georg Olms, 1977 [first pub. 1917]); *Romantische Harmonik und ihre Krise in Wagners 'Tristan'*, 3rd ed. (Berlin: Max Hesse, 1923; reprint, Hildesheim: Georg Olms, 1968 [first pub. 1920]); and *Bruckner*, 2 vols. (Berlin: Max Hesse, 1925; reprint, Hildesheim: Georg Olms, 1971). Until recently, his work was almost totally unknown, even by theorists, despite its huge success in the interwar years. Lee Rothfarb has been instrumental in publicizing Kurth's work, with a dissertation (subsequently published in book form) and a translation-with-commentary of selections from Kurth's writings.

96. Kurth, *Grundlagen*, 3, 4, 7, cited and translated in *Ernst Kurth: Selected Writings*, Lee Rothfarb, ed. (Cambridge: Cambridge University Press, 1991), 23.

theoretical reflection, an empathy and internal sympathetic resonance with the animated creative forces, and so to restore once again the connection, long since torn asunder, between theory and art.[97]

Although Kurth does not (to my knowledge) ever refer to Hausegger in his writings, the correspondence between this comment and Hausegger's aesthetics from within is immediately apparent. Both are dependent upon the empathetic identification of composer and listener/analyst, as well as the Schopenhauerian notion of music as will. Kurth's thought is also indebted to that of August Halm, particularly the latter's rooting of dynamism in psychic energies.[98]

It is not just melody which exhibits this linear-kinetic energy noted by Kurth, but harmony as well: "harmonies are reflexes from the unconscious."[99] Kurth argues that "every chord is only an acoustically conceived image of certain energetic currents."

> The usual theory of harmony (especially since Riemann) designates the chord simply as *harmony* [*Klang*]. However, it is primarily *urge* [*Drang*].[100]

For example, the minor third of a triad embodies an inherently downward-striving energy, while the major third embodies the reverse. Kurth advances the notion of *Nebentoneinstellung* (neighbor-note interpolation) to explain dissonant or non-triadic chords. For Kurth, linear energetic forces dominate all music. Dissonant notes in a triad, for example an F♯ instead of a G in a C-major triad, are the result of the displacement of one or more triadic notes by kinetic-linear energy. Harmony itself may be either sensuous (*klangsinnlich*) or energetic (*energetisch*); these are the two fundamental properties of harmony in all periods. Sensuous harmonies are tertian sonorities in which linear forces are momentarily halted by the weight of piled thirds upon a fundamental (forming sevenths, ninths, elevenths, etc.); they have materiality. Energetic harmonies, on the other hand, are non-tertian sonorities (or non-tonal tertian sonorities) made up of multiple "leading tones" (as *Nebentoneinstellungen*) "on their way" to a tertian sonority.

The realm of form for Kurth is also concerned with the ebb and flow of psychic energy. Kurth saw form as essentially dynamic—more "forming" than form—and his formulation of the idea is clearly indebted to Gestaltist thought.

> Form is neither the pure streaming of the formation process nor the pure fulfillment of borders, but rather the transition, the active transformation of the former

---

97. Kurth, *Romantische Harmonik*, 2. Translation from Rothfarb, *Ernst Kurth as Theorist and Analyst*, 15–16.

98. See Rothfarb, "Ernst Kurth in Historical Perspective," 35–37; also Rothfarb, *Ernst Kurth as Theorist and Analyst*, 8–9.

99. Kurth, *Romantische Harmonik*, 1. This is the first sentence of the book.

100. Kurth, *Romantische Harmonik*, 11. Translation from Rothfarb, ed., *Selected Writings*, 28.

into the latter. . . In music . . . form is neither movement nor its synoptically grasped rigidity, neither flow nor outline, but rather the lively struggle to grasp something flowing by holding onto something firm.[101]

That is, the concept of form exists only in the process of its perception. It is not a static entity, but is rather a state of tension between becoming and being. Just as melody and harmony are external manifestations of the composer's creative psyche, so too is form. To trace the form of a work is to map the tensions and resolutions, the risings and sinkings of the musical course. Kurth refers to these pulsations as "waves," which range in amplitude from localized *Teilwellen* to all-encompassing *symphonische Wellen*. Form rests in the continual intensification of these waves which eventually peak in *Gipfelwellen*, which are followed by one or more *Nachwellen* and an *Entladung* (discharge).[102] Although Kurth does not make this clear, these cycles of intensification and resolution are essentially rhythmic phenomena. These risings and sinkings, when taken as a whole, serve to articulate a work, to give it its form.[103] To follow a work involves sensing this ebb and flow through the perception of a work's formal waves. Again, the estimation of sensation and perception over intellectual abstraction points clearly to the influence of the expressive aesthetic.[104]

Kurth's reaction against Riemann is all-pervasive. His entire theoretical system represents one analytical manifestation of an expressive aesthetic

---

101. Kurth, *Bruckner*, vol. 1, 239. Translation from Rothfarb, ed., *Selected Writings*, 30. It is true that the Gestaltists saw form as a "synoptically grasped rigidity," but Kurth is clearly referring to the static view of form found in standard *Formenlehre*.

102. Kurth's views on form are presented in the first two chapters of the second part of *Bruckner*, vol. 1. Most of the second chapter is translated in Rothfarb, ed. *Selected Writings*. See also Ernst Kurth, *Musikpsychologie* (Berlin: Max Hesse, 1931; reprint, Hildesheim: Georg Olms, 1969), 250–64.

103. This is similar in all but terminology to Lorenz's notion of form to be presented in the next chapter.

104. For a presentation and discussion of Kurth's "wave" theory, see Stephen J. Parkany, "Ernst Kurth's *Bruckner* and the Adagio of the Seventh Symphony," *19th-Century Music* 11 (1988): 262–81. The wave notion has obvious resonance with Lorenz's works employing his father's *Generationslehre*. In fact, this idea of the wave-like motion of things seems based in a general understanding of human psychology arising at the end of the nineteenth century and indebted to Schopenhauerian-Wagnerian thought. The socialist Viktor Adler wrote about political tactics in very similar terms:

All psychological things—even politics is actually in the first instance a result of the brain—are accomplished in wavy lines [*Wellenlinien*]. There are wave peaks; but every high water mark of a movement is followed with mechanical necessity by a retreat, a decline, which not only is a time of rest but again makes possible an escalation of agitation. A psychological agitation which is continuously at climax or which could be maintained for years at a high point, does not exist.

Victor Adler, *Aufsätze, Reden, und Briefe* (Vienna, 1922–29), vol. 1, p. 43, vol. 8, p. 236; cited by William McGrath in *Dionysian Art and Populist Politics in Austria* (New Haven: Yale University Press, 1974), 225–26.

orientation. Kurth's flexible terminology, with its Schopenhauerian emphasis on energy and motion ("Sound is dead; what lives within it is the *will to sound*")[105] is a far cry from the objective discourse of most theoretical systems and itself reveals his antipositivistic inclinations.[106] Likewise, the subjective nature of his formal paradigm, with its emphasis on the grasping of wholes, owes more to Gestalt psychology than to any empirical *Formenlehre*.[107] Kurth himself referred to his work as "music psychology," and synthesized his efforts in his final large-scale publication, *Musikpsychologie* (1931), which continued his emphasis on musical processes rather than static, context-free musical elements.[108]

The notion of dynamic form, as presented by music theorists of an experiential bent in the first decades of the twentieth century, forms the theoretical background against which Lorenz needs to be seen and evaluated: as part of a tendency to dissolve or cancel any distinction between form and content on the basis of a higher aesthetic viewpoint (in this case, the Schopenhauerian expressive aesthetic); as part of a tendency to elaborate analysis of form with historic and aesthetic considerations; and as part of a general anti-positivist tendency at the time. Such "form-dynamic" analysis is oriented to the perception of the analyst or listener himself—it has a psychological origin and makes its own subjectivity its primary virtue. Kurth himself was clear that he and Lorenz were independently developing similar ideas about musical form.[109] Lorenz also noted this close connection, writing in a review of *Musikpsychologie* that Kurth's "view of form coincides entirely with my own. I, too, refuse to see form as static in any way; it is a *dynamic* process."[110]

Even non-experiential theorists were influenced by some of these notions. For example, Schenker's idea of prolongation is essentially a dynamic phenomenon: a chord, as a harmonic concept, unfolds and extends in time. Rothfarb points out, however, that as surface events are conceptually absorbed at higher structural levels, Schenkerian analysis becomes "ever more inert at higher structural levels until energy is completely absorbed and neutralized in the static progenerative triad."[111] Nevertheless, Schenker begins his chapter on form in *Der freie Satz* with a description of its dynamic properties:

105. Kurth, *Romantische Harmonik*, 3.

106. On Kurth's language, see Rothfarb, *Ernst Kurth as Theorist and Analyst*, 108–109, and Rothfarb, ed., *Selected Writings*, xvi-xvii.

107. Rothfarb discusses the influence of Gestalt psychology on Kurth in *Ernst Kurth as Theorist and Analyst*, 100–101, and in *Selected Writings*, 20–22.

108. In "Die musikalische Analyse" (*Die Musik* 21 [1929]: 264–71), Werner Karthaus writes that "music psychology is . . . identical with the notion of musical analysis" (p. 267). See also Rothfarb, "Ernst Kurth's *Die Voraussetzungen der theoretischen Harmonik* and the Beginnings of Music Psychology," *Theoria* 4 (1989): 10–33.

109. Kurth, *Musikpsychologie*, 286.

110. Alfred Lorenz, review of Ernst Kurth, *Musikpsychologie*, *Die Musik* 23 (1930): 186.

111. Rothfarb, "Beethoven's Formal Dynamics," 80.

The phenomenon of form in the foreground can be described in an almost physical-mechanical sense as an energy transformation—a transformation of the forces which flow from the background to the foreground through the structural levels.[112]

By the 1930s, form-dynamic analysis was increasingly prevalent among those reacting to the positivistic approach of Riemann and his followers.[113] Here Halm, Kurth and Lorenz himself were central influences. Kurt Westphal's *Der Begriff der musikalischen Form in der Wiener Klassik: Versuch einer Grundlegung der musikalischen Formung* (1935) follows Kurth in his preference for the dynamic idea of "forming," rather than "form," and in its experiential approach:

> Form as an evolutionary curve cannot be traced from the anatomical structure of the work of art. . . . Rather, it acquires its reality only in the hearing process, a reality that is therefore a purely psychic reality. . . . Form arises first in the hearing process and only those forces that are efficacious for the hearing process are constitutive of form and its structure.[114]

Kurth's student, Rudolf von Tobel, devotes a third of his monograph *Die Formwelt der klassichen Instrumentalmusik* to what he calls *Formdynamik*: music as a mirror of a psychic play of energies. For Tobel, *Dynamik* lies at the root of the romantic style; it was an essential formal principle. In fact, Tobel understands *Dynamik* as an "urmusikalische Formprinzip," and the opposite of the "static nature of closed, independent, and juxtaposed formal sections."[115] This dynamic form is perceived only through what he calls "empathetic hearing," and not visually through the discovery of thematic alternation and symmetrical equivalences derived through rational score study; Tobel prefers "making the perception of form irrational."[116] That such an approach is less amenable to empirical verification is not seen as a problem. Indeed Tobel admits that "as opposed to the recording of

---

112. Significantly, this was one of the passages relegated to an appendix in the English translation. Heinrich Schenker, *Free Composition*, vol. 3: *New Musical Theories and Fantasies*, trans. and ed. Ernst Oster (New York: Longman, 1979), 162, omission "P." Its context is found on p. 128.

113. See Moyer, "Concepts of Musical Form," 222–32.

114. Kurt Westphal, *Der Begriff der musikalischen Form in der Wiener Klassik: Versuch einer Grundlegung der Theorie der musikalischen Formung*, ed. Walter Kolneder, vol. 11, Schriften zur Musik (2nd ed., Giebing: Emil Katzbichler, 1971; orig. Leipzig: Kister and Siegel, 1935), 52, 53; cited (and translated) by Rothfarb in "Beethoven's Formal Dynamics," 78 n. 30.

115. Rudolf von Tobel, *Die Formwelt der klassischen Instrumentalmusik* (Bern and Leipzig: Paul Haupt, 1935), 231, 232. Tobel's work originated as a doctoral dissertation under Kurth in Bern; it was published as part of the *Berner Veröffentlichungen zur Musikforschung* series edited by Kurth.

116. Ibid., 232.

architectonic form elements, the room for subjective views is greater," but sees this only as a virtue:

> In this manner dynamic perceptions of form sometimes acquire, to an even greater extent than those hitherto existing, the character of an interpretation, whose validity and worth depend upon the personality of the interpreter; the study of form will sometimes be strongly displaced from the viewpoint of specific knowledge to that of art, and intuition will have a larger role to play.[117]

Intuition and subjectivity in analysis is celebrated as something creative in its own right. This corresponds to the empathetic belief that through analysis one reaches the essence of a work—one somehow recreates the creative-psychic stream of the composer himself.

Some of the preoccupations of these theorists were reflected in society at large. Lee Rothfarb has linked the experiential basis of the theories of Halm and Kurth with the New Education movement in the early years of the century. This movement established a type of child-centered learning, stressing direct and personal experience over the rote memorization of facts.[118] We have already touched on the similarity of Kurth's idea of formal "waves" with the cyclical view of history developed by Lorenz's father. Such a view was all pervasive, as was the *Geisteswissenschaft* methodology behind it. In fact, a similarly dynamic view of history is found in Oswald Spengler's very influential *Der Untergang des Abendlandes: Umrisse eine Morphologie der Weltgeschichte* (notice too the centrality of morphology, the study of formal shapes, to Spengler's concerns).[119] Spengler argues that all cultures are temporal and organic, and have a natural life span. The organic morphology of a culture may be compared with other cultures—often extinct ones—and predications made about its future course. For Spengler, cultures are dynamic entities. They follow what he calls a "physiognomic" course—temporal and organic—instead of a logical series of effects and causes ("systematic"), and Spengler constructs a series of binarisms around this physiognomic/systematic axis, with the weight always on the first term: history/nature; form/law; being/waking-being; cosmic/microcosmic; blood/intellect; and incident/cause. It should be readily apparent that Spengler's emphasis on history, being, blood, and form has resonance with many of

---

117. Ibid., 232, 233.

118. Lee Rothfarb, "'The New Education' and Music Theory, 1900–1925," in *Music Theory and the Exploration of the Past*, ed. Christopher Hatch and David W. Bernstein (Chicago: University of Chicago Press, 1993), 449–71.

119. Oswald Spengler, *Der Untergang des Abendlandes: Umrisse einer Morphologie der Weltgeschichte* (Munich: C.H. Beck, 1918, 1922; repr. in 1 vol, 1963), English translation, *The Decline of the West*, 2 vols., trans. Charles Francis Atkinson (New York: Knopf, 1926, 1928). My discussion of Spengler is derived from that of Byron Almén, "Prophets of the Decline: The Worldviews of Heinrich Schenker and Oswald Spengler," *Indiana Theory Review* 17 (Spring 1996): 1–24.

the concerns of German cultural conservatives in the first decades of the twentieth century. Even Spengler's definition of artistic form corresponds with that of the expressive aesthetic position: "if an art has boundaries at all—boundaries of its soul-become-form [*formgewordenen Seele*]—they are historical and not technical or physiological."[120]

In the light of subsequent developments in Germany, such theoretical speculation—not restricted to music theory, but as part of a certain Germanic tendency to *Innigkeit*—has disturbing consequences in the political sphere, particularily in its devalorization of parts apart from wholes. Nietzsche appears to have sensed this, for one aphorism (§818) collected in *Der Wille zur Macht* notes that

> One is an artist at the cost of regarding what all non-artists call "form" as *content*, as "the thing itself." To be sure, then one belongs in a topsy-turvy world: for henceforth content becomes something merely formal—our life included.[121]

The Problem of Wagner

How then do Wagner and Wagnerian analysis fit into this context? It is an historical oddity to discover strange similarities in the positions and arguments of both Wagner's supporters and opponents at the end of the nineteenth century. For example, while it is hardly surprising to find that Eduard Hanslick and other formalists censured Wagner for his "formlessness" and "harmonic illogicality,"[122] it is curious to read the following from Alois John, one of Wagner's supporters:

> Separated from the textbook style of Italian and French opera with their hankering after empty effect [*Effektoper*], [Wagner's] music follows its own course as an elemental force, as the free daughter of nature. Obeying no law, as the storm-wind sings its airs, or, turned to a blissful breeze, fans the springtime blossoms, absolute music is its very own, self-glorifying force, a state of freedom, a breaking free of every rule and school, from every authority and conventional practice.[123]

---

120. Spengler, *Decline*, vol. 1, 221.

121. Friedrich Nietzsche, *The Will to Power*, trans. Walter Kaufmann and R.J. Hollingdale, ed. Walter Kaufmann (New York: Random, 1967), 433.

122. See, for example, "Die Meistersinger von Richard Wagner," in *Die moderne Oper: Kritiken und Studien* (Berlin: Allgemeiner Verein für Deutsche Literatur, 1885), especially 302–304. Hanslick writes that Wagner's music is "the conscious dissolution of all fixed form into a shapeless, sensuous, and intoxicating wash of sound; the replacement of obvious and periodic melodies with formless and vague 'melodizing'."

123. Alois John, *Richard Wagner-Studien: Sieben Essays über Richard Wagner's Kunst und seine Bedeutung im modernen Leben* (Bayreuth: C. Giessel, 1889), 39. Cited in *Geheimnis* I: 3.

John too seems to admit here that Wagner's music is formless and illogical—it "obeys no law," and is an elemental force likened to nature itself. However, rather than find the music lacking, John turns this very unconventionality into a virtue. It seems Wagner made an impression on friend and foe alike as a revolutionary force, as the transcender (or transgressor) of all conventions of harmony, melody, and form. This odd rapprochement makes it extremely difficult to investigate the treatment of purely musical issues in both pro- and anti-Wagner writings during this time without taking aesthetics into account. The two groups are really talking at cross-purposes, with neither one noting the differing presuppositions of the other.

This lack of dialogue between Wagner's supporters and his opponents mirrors the larger aesthetic quarrel between adherents of the expressive and formal aesthetic positions. As we have seen, it is difficult to compare the two in any sort of objective fashion, since the former proceeds on an entirely different plane from the latter, being more concerned with philosophical and perceptive issues than with any pretense of scientific objectivity. The same point may be made regarding the Wagnerians and the Wagner critics, since these two groups generally divide along the same aesthetic lines.

Amongst Wagner's most extreme followers (such as the "Bayreuthians" Hans von Wolzogen, Houston Stewart Chamberlain, Carl Friedrich Glasenapp, and others, not to mention Cosima herself) there is a tendency to stop the clock at Wagner's death in 1883. Wagner's final views, particularly those expressed in his late writings (the so-called *Regenerationslehre*) are presented as ultimate truth, cast in stone and defended staunchly against all attack. The Bayreuthians preached explicit adherence to the Master's last thoughts, whether musical, philosophical, or political. Hence, for example, the influence of the racial thought of Gobineau on the *Bayreuther Blätter*, the growing xenophobia in the Bayreuth Circle, and the central role of Schopenhauerian philosophy in Wagnerian aesthetics.

While it would perhaps be foolhardy to attribute the origins of the late-romantic expressive aesthetic solely to Wagner, his influence is undeniably central. Certainly, the general principles of the aesthetic may be found in Wagner's writings. As has been mentioned, in *Beethoven* Wagner explicitly adopts Schopenhauer's view of music as will, writing that "it was Schopenhauer who first recognized and defined with philosophic clarity the position of music among the fine arts, ascribing to it a totally different nature from that of plastic or poetic art."[124] Since all music is a direct copy of the will of its creator—the external manifestation of an internal state—it follows that to experience Wagner's music is to trace the path of Wagner's creative impulse itself. This explains the emphasis placed by Hausegger and others upon production and reception of works of art, and (as we shall see) the almost total concentration on the leitmotives.

---

124. *GS* IX: 66.

Within the expressive aesthetic, the notion of the *Aufhebung* of any distinction between form and content in music is second only to the belief that music, like the world itself, is will. Wagner is most clear about this collapsing of the categories of form and content in an open letter about Liszt's symphonic poems, published in 1857. Here he likens formal schemata to "swords without blades," and mocks those critics who treat form as something abstractly divorced from specific works of art. Wagner's cutting sarcasm deserves to be quoted at length:

> [I]f there were no form, there would certainly be no works of art; but neither, certainly, would there be any critics of art. This fact is so clear to those critics that they cry out in trepidation for form, while the carefree artist—who could no more exist without form than they—does not in the least worry himself about it in his work. . . . [T]he artist, without knowing it, is always creating forms, while the critics create neither forms nor anything else. It would seem that the artists, apart from everything they create as it is, ought to supply something more especially for these gentlemen who would otherwise be left with nothing. But in fact, this favor has only been granted to them by such artists who could achieve nothing on their own and so had to seek assistance in—forms; and we know what that means, do we not? Swords without blades! If someone then comes along who can forge his own blade . . . these other fools will only cut themselves on it, for they clumsily grab at the blade, just as before they had merely grabbed at the hilt proffered them. Of course, this annoys them greatly, for the clever smith holds the hilt in his hand, as is the proper way to handle a sword, but now they cannot even see that part which had once been offered to them by others. That, you see, is the reason for all this outcry about the absence of form! Who has ever seen a sword wielded without a hilt? Doesn't the secure manipulation of the sword prove that it has indeed a good, solid hilt? Naturally, this will only be visible and tangible to others when it is no longer being held; when the master is dead and the sword hung up in his armory, then these people see the hilt [*Griff*] and would detach it from the weapon—as a concept [*Begriff*].[125]

While ostensibly defending Liszt, it is apparent that Wagner is defending himself as well.[126] Rhetorically, his prose is authoritarian; his analogy makes it seem naive and silly to expect the form of works to follow pre-existing schemata to the letter. Just as all swords have hilts, so all musical works have form, even if this form is hard to discern because of the immediate impact of the work (its "wielding" by the composer). While Wagner's claim that form is created unconsciously by the artist is perhaps deliberate mythmaking on his part, it is clear that he does not dismiss the importance of

---

125. *GS* V: 187–88, trans. cited from Thomas Spencer Grey, "Richard Wagner and the Aesthetics of Musical Form in the Mid-Nineteenth Century (1840–1860)" (Ph.D dissertation, University of California, Berkeley, 1988), 421–22.

126. The publication of this open letter in the *Neue Zeitschrift für Musik* in 1857 certainly seems to suggest a response to Hanslick, whose *Vom Musikalisch-Schönen* had been published three years previously. See Grey, "Richard Wagner and the Aesthetics of Musical Form," 353–56.

form, only the belief that it could ever be considered as an abstract category apart from its context.

As already noted, Wagner's followers after his death tended to treat his every utterance as divine truth. Defenses of Wagner's work often resemble nothing so much as biblical commentaries, glosses of the Wagnerian scripture. The *Bayreuther Blätter* also partook of this authority, with anything in it implicitly sanctioned as "echt Wagnerisch." Hausegger's quasi-scientific justification of the expressive aesthetic, *Die Musik als Ausdruck*, was published serially in the journal in 1884, and his aesthetic elaboration, "Ästhetik von Innen," appeared in 1893 and 1895. These, and other pieces (not to mention Wagner's central role in its formulation) make it obvious that the expressive aesthetic is that of the Wagnerians, and is at the root of what passed for Wagnerian analysis at the time.

It is clear that it was Wagner's leitmotivic technique which first caught the imagination of his contemporaries and immediate followers. Several reasons may be advanced for this preoccupation. First, on a purely practical level, the leitmotives provide a foothold, a means of (relatively) easy entrance to the works. Wagner himself seems to suggest this avenue of inquiry with his talk of motives of "anticipation" and "reminiscence" in *Oper und Drama*, Part III: such motives would obtain a distinct associative meaning in conjunction with a significant dramatic moment and a specific text. While these principal themes, or fundamental motives, to which Wagner refers are actually dramatic elements, Wagner makes it clear that they each have a corresponding musical idea. These musical ideas would take on added significance in the course of the work through their use in differing (but related) dramatic contexts. In *Eine Mittheilung an meine Freunde* Wagner refers to a network of principal themes (*Gewebe der Hauptthemen*) encompassing the entire work, which he later (in "Über die Anwendung der Musik auf das Drama") explicitly identifies with what Wolzogen had recently termed "leitmotives."[127] Although not the first, Wolzogen is the most famous author of such leitmotivic guides to Wagner's works, in which the motives are named (The Sword, Renunciation, Brünnhilde's Justification, etc.) and traced throughout the works.[128] In an 1897 essay, Wolzogen quite

---

127. *GS* IV: 201, 322; X: 185. See also the whole of the essays referred to.

128. Hans von Wolzogen, *Thematischer Leitfaden durch die Musik zu Rich. Wagner's Festspiel 'Der Ring des Nibelungen'* (1876); *Richard Wagner's Tristan und Isolde: ein Leitfaden durch Sage, Dichtung, und Musik* (1880); *Thematischer Leitfaden durch die Musik zu R. Wagner's Parsifal* (1882). All published in Leipzig by Schloemp. Perhaps the first such treatment of Wagner's works is by Gottlieb Federlein, "'Das Rheingold' von Richard Wagner," *Musikalische Wochenblatt* 2 (1871): 8 installments between pp. 210 and 389. Federlein published similar commentary on *Die Walküre* the following year, but the series was completed by Wolzogen between 1875 and 1877.

For an illuminating account of the term, see Thomas Grey, "... *wie ein rother Faden*: On the Origins of 'Leitmotif' as a Critical Construct and Musical Practice," in *Music Theory in the Age of Romanticism*, ed. Ian Bent (Cambridge: Cambridge University Press, 1996), 187–210.

candidly notes that these guides were created as "a kind of 'guidebook' [*Leitfaden*] for that majority of guests for the first festival who would be little prepared."[129]

Secondly, interest in the thematic content of Wagner's works reflects the emphasis placed by Schopenhauer on melody as the highest objectification of the will. This is not simply to attach names to melodic gestures, but to focus on the music itself, where the will resides. Wolzogen himself is unequivocal about the subject: the "names" of the motives are simply external *aides-mémoires* not touching the inner essence of the music; in Schopenhauerian terms, they are "ideas" or "representations," not the "thing-in-itself."

> He who wants to discuss the motivic structure of a musical artwork must proceed in exactly the opposite way to the creative musician. For this latter, the motives are the natural, organically developing forms of the music speech which wells up from his soul; the commentator however must first excise them from the organic unity of the music, and separate them, relate them to concepts, in order to speak about them at all.[130]

Elsewhere, Wolzogen expands upon this point, accepting without reserve the Schopenhauerian understanding of music as a direct copy of the will itself:

> However, the "leading" in the term "leading motive" leads only to misunderstanding. One had to believe that these musical forms might, from without, "lead" the logical understanding of the music through an otherwise impenetrable labyrinth. Actually, the "leading" aspect belongs—entirely correctly—only to the poetic element of works of art. Strictly speaking, leitmotives are only to be found in the dramatic poem. That which corresponds to them in the music is more those recurring motives of purely musical *expression* [*der an sich rein musikalische* Ausdruck *hindurchleitenden Motive*].[131]

Wolzogen argues that "leitmotives," as concepts, are restricted solely to the world of appearance. The music, however, is made up of "expressive themes" (*Ausdrucksthema*) which directly represent (i.e., make present) the emotional intent of the composer, since music is a copy of the will itself, an "audible expression of the idea."[132] Music is, in essence, expression. It follows that the musical gestures embodying these emotional states reflect the similarity or difference of these emotional states themselves; that is, that

129. Hans von Wolzogen, "Leitmotive," *Bayreuther Blätter* 20 (1897): 313.

130. Wolzogen, *Tristan & Isolde: Ein Leitfaden durch Sage, Dichtung, und Musik*, cited in "Leitmotive," 316–17.

131. Hans von Wolzogen, *Musikalisch-dramatische Parallelen: Beiträge zur Erkenntnis von der Musik als Ausdruck* (Leipzig: Breitkopf und Härtel, 1906), 5–6. [First pub. serially in the *Bayreuther Blätter* between 1894 and 1903.]

132. Ibid., 47.

similar emotional states be captured in similar music, regardless of the specific context. In other words, motives might be applied to different dramatic contexts or situations, united only by a similar emotional context. Wolzogen refers to such instances as "parallels," and notes that their occurrence is a "stylistic law" which connects all of Wagner's works. A parallel occurs when "the expressive themes of a work appear to be expressive gestures [*Ausdrucksformen*] of music in general."[133] A leitmotive is dependent upon the poem to give it meaning, while a parallel is not; leitmotives were recognized first, says Wolzogen, because of this conceptual link. Parallels *become* leitmotives as they are applied to a specific text. Wolzogen's *Musikalisch-dramatische Parallelen* presents one hundred such parallels in Wagner's works from *Die Feen* to *Parsifal*. The subtitle of Wolzogen's work, "Beiträge zur Erkenntnis von der Musik als Ausdruck," is sufficient to reveal its origins in the expressive aesthetic position.[134]

For the Wagnerians, investigation of the thematic content of the music dramas, as found in the *Leitfäden* literature and elaborated with aesthetic considerations in works such as *Musikalisch-dramatische Parallelen*, sufficed as analysis of the works and were a reflection of the prevailing hermeneutic impulse of the nineteenth century.[135] Such analyses served at once to promulgate and to validate the expressive aesthetic position. They were for the most part, however, barren of any consideration of technical musical matters. In this they follow Wagner himself, who, generally, is tantalizingly vague about musical specifics. Where commentators do bring up musical details (like form or harmonic devices) it is more by way of an aesthetic judgement than out of any analytical insight; consider, for example, the following from Houston Stewart Chamberlain:

> Wagner is by far the greatest master of form that ever lived, for if one regards it as almost miraculous that Beethoven was able to give inner unity to an entire symphony . . . what ought we to say about a man who was able, in design and implementation, to wrap the iron bands of unfailing unity around such gigantic works as *Meistersinger*, *Tristan*, and the *Nibelungenring*?![136]

---

133. Ibid., 7.

134. Curt Mey in his *Die Musik als tönende Weltidee*, extends Wolzogen's notion of a parallel (which Wolzogen restricts to Wagner) to the whole realm of music. Mey refers to these as primordial motives (*Urmotive*) and even goes so far as to promulgate five "metaphysical laws" of melodic motion; for example ascending motives signify *Willensbejahung*, descending, *Willensverneinung*. He makes explicit his debt to Schopenhauer and his adherence to the expressive aesthetic position. See my "The Magic Wand of the Wagnerians: *Musik als Ausdruck*," *Canadian University Music Review* 13 (1993): 71–92.

135. Wolzogen's analysis of the *Parsifal* prelude appears in *Music Analysis in the Nineteenth Century*, ed. Ian Bent, vol. 2, *Hermeneutic Approaches*, 88–105.

136. Letter of 24 June 1884, published (significantly but misleadingly) as "Richard Wagner und die musikalische Form: Ein unveröffentlicher Brief H.S. Chamberlains," *Bayreuther Festspielführer* (1930): 33.

This naïveté is perhaps a consequence of the fact that many of Wagner's followers—unlike his critics—were not trained musicians. It is not an exaggeration to suggest that the undeniable impact of Wagnerism in the late nineteenth century was less a musical phenomenon than it was an aesthetic one.

On the other hand, the belief that the form of Wagner's works was that of a symphonic movement originates with Wagner himself, and stems from Wagner's desire to portray himself as the heir of Beethoven in the symphonic realm. In "Über die Anwendung der Musik auf das Drama," Wagner writes that

> Nevertheless, the new form of dramatic music must show the unity of a symphonic movement, if it, as music, is itself to constitute a work of art; this it attains by encompassing the entire drama (and intimately corresponding to it), not just individual, little, arbitrarily selected bits of it. This unity then provides the entire work with a continuous web of fundamental themes [*Grundthemen*], which are contrasted, supplemented, re-formed, separated, and linked together again, just as in a symphonic movement; only here the dramatic action as executed and performed dictate the rules of parting and combination.[137]

There has long been debate whether or not we are to take this passage as literal or metaphorical: are Wagner's music dramas really organized symphonically, or is Wagner merely trying to give them the cachet of the symphonic repertory? Wagner's early followers generally believed the former, while more recent critics tend to assert the latter.[138] Where the issue becomes confusing, however, is in the fact that even musically knowledgeable Wagnerians were proceeding from the aesthetic presuppositions presented above.[139]

This is where Lorenz enters the picture. Just after the passage cited above, Wagner makes a distinction between assessment of his motives from the point of view of their dramatic import and effect, and their examination as elements of the musical structure. Although his young friend Wolzogen had devoted some attention to the former method, Wagner remarks that, to his knowledge, no one had yet followed this latter path.[140] In the introduction to the first volume of *Das Geheimnis der Form* (originally his dissertation),

---

137. *GS* X: 185.

138. For one evaluation of Wagner's claim, see Carolyn Abbate, "Opera as Symphony: A Wagnerian Myth," in *Analyzing Opera: Verdi and Wagner*, ed. Carolyn Abbate and Roger Parker (Berkeley and Los Angeles: University of California Press, 1989), 92–124.

139. For symphonic interpretations of Wagner stemming from the period under discussion, see, for example, Karl Grunsky, "Wagner als Sinfoniker," *Richard Wagner-Jahrbuch* 1 (1906): 227–44; Ilmari Krohn, "Lohengrins Formbyggnad [formal structure]," *Svensk tidskrift för musikforskning* 4 (1922): 1–25.

140. *GS* X: 185.

Lorenz cites this passage as justification for his investigation, and validates his claim by publishing a personal letter from Wolzogen in which the latter approvingly writes that such an investigation was what "Wagner himself always wanted."[141]

By subjecting Wagner's music dramas to detailed musical analysis, Lorenz believed that he could silence critics such as Hanslick by proving analytically that the works were well structured and unified. By so doing, he could seemingly effect a reconciliation of the expressive and formalist aesthetic positions. Lorenz's strategy is clever, and reflects his own aesthetic beliefs. His first act is to distance himself from leitmotivic analysis. This he can do on two levels. By presenting such analyses as the necessary, but now outgrown, first stage in Wagner reception, Lorenz can appear to take up the discourse of the formalists by concentrating on purely musical matters.[142] This is not a difficult step to take, however, because of his own adherence to the expressive aesthetic which diminishes the importance of verbal constitutions of music. Lorenz then claims to have achieved his analytical insights entirely through his own practical experience in conducting the works. Here he implicitly devalues an intellectual approach to analysis in favor of a more subjective emphasis on empathetic understanding, and at the same time, seems to separate himself from his Wagnerian predecessors.[143] The ideological basis of Lorenz's argument should be clear: formal unity and hence *value* resides in these experientially perceived forms. The success or failure of Lorenz's aim will occupy us for the remainder of the work.

---

141. *Geheimnis* I: 9. The letter is cited in full in chapter 1 of the present work.

142. "No matter how important for the understanding of the Wagnerian work of art the discovery of the relationships between dramatic motivations [*Beweggründen*] and musical motives was, from a musical standpoint the leitmotives are nothing other than little stones, through the combination of which the wonderful structures [*Wunderbauten*] of Wagnerian music first arise." *Geheimnis* I: 9.

143. The first appendix of *Geheimnis* I consists of extracts by other authors dealing with musical form from earlier works on Wagner. Lorenz includes these in the interest of "scientific thoroughness" but claims that his method predates any acquaintance with this literature. These citations are arranged according to their relative closeness to Lorenz's own analysis; Lorenz rates most highly the work of Guido Adler, August Halm, Karl Grunsky, and Christian von Ehrenfels.

Chapter Three

Lorenz's Aesthetics

The untied threads left in the last chapter may, in some sense, be tied together by Lorenz himself. When asked to define his research area on a personnel card for Munich University, Lorenz responded that his work concerned the "aesthetics of musical form."[1] This response is a revealing characterization of Lorenz's analytical methodology, for matters aesthetic lie at the foundation of all of Lorenz's writings on the ontology of the work of art and its form. The present chapter will chronicle Lorenz's relationship to the expressive aesthetic position and its reflection in contemporary music theory and analysis as presented in the previous chapter. It will demonstrate the domination of this aesthetic outlook in Lorenz's treatment of the leitmotive, the *Gesamtkunstwerk*, and the question of musical form itself.

The Work of Art and its Form

Lorenz takes considerable pains to position himself historically in relation to his Wagnerian predecessors by arguing that one first had to come to terms with Wagner as a total artistic phenomenon.[2] This was largely achieved through study of his theoretical works and an unrelenting focus on the leitmotives at the expense of larger questions of musical form and technique. But now, asserts Lorenz, we are positioned for the next step. Having established an aesthetic foundation, the Wagnerian may now address these more pressing questions without being mistaken for a follower of Hanslick, since, to the Wagnerian, "form" means something quite different than the external shell of a piece. Lorenz once defined musical form as

> the unconscious outcome of a hidden artistic drive, the manifestation of a particular will, the external appearance of the boundless logic of inner thought.[3]

---

1. BDC Lorenz file. Lorenz also included "allgemeine Musikgeschichte" and "Rich. Wagner" among his research interests.
2. *Geheimnis* I: 1–3.
3. *Geheimnis* I: 2.

This definition is revealing of Lorenz's entire aesthetic viewpoint, and deserves commentary.

The dichotomies present in the above quotation (unconscious-conscious; hidden-visible; internal-external) link Lorenz quite clearly with idealistic philosophy. It is obviously the first of these terms which carries the value. The entire formulation recalls strongly Schopenhauer's discussion of the role of genius in the creation of musical works, particularly in its emphasis on the unconscious.[4] Musical forms are presented as the external manifestation of an inner will: they are the visible sign of a creative genius and attest to its inner power and fecundity. This results in an ambivalent view of form, however, since form is both the sign of a fruitful creative spirit and, at the same time, somehow ancillary to the essence of music. It should be noticed only in its absence (or abuse). Form comes into being only as a natural by-product of the creative process:

> Just as Nature innately creates crystals and flower blossoms—without knowing what it does and recognizing no rules—so beautiful forms must be created by artists if their artistic potency is fertile.[5]

Forms are like crystals or flowers: beautiful creations which are nevertheless secondary to the issue at hand (in the case of flowers, the reproductive process).[6] For musical works the essential issue is the communication of the expressive intent of the composer; form is only the trace of the essence of the work: "with the form we thus recognize the nature of the ideas weaving within the work of art."[7] Living form is created by inspiration, not simply by mechanically following external rules.

Lorenz's evocation of nature and the natural sciences in the above metaphor also harkens back to Schopenhauerian philosophy in its pairing of the composer and nature. Both Lorenz and Schopenhauer present the composer as a natural and creative force, as an equal to God himself. The metaphor serves to empower Lorenz by implicitly equating his analyses with a scientific inquiry, thereby investing them with its weight. This gesture is even more apparent when he explicitly compares formal analysis with anatomy:

> For works of art—at least those worthy of bearing that name—ought surely to be described as naturally evolving organisms, whose anatomy must first be completed before they will be able to undergo a physiological examination.[8]

---

4. See above, pp. 29–31.

5. *Geheimnis* I: 2.

6. Lorenz's metaphor ignores the fact that the growth of flowers is organic, while that of crystals is accretive.

7. *Geheimnis* III: 188.

8. *Geheimnis* I: 1–2.

If form is understood as the material trace of a composer's inspiration, as the byproduct of his expressive intent, it follows that any distinction between authorial intention on the one hand and inspiration on the other is essentially irrelevant.

As Schopenhauer understands it, the creative act involves two aspects, with the first, the unconscious germination of works, clearly taking precedence over the second, their transference into reality, since the former of necessity must precede the latter. Schopenhauer presents the unconscious as the repository of ultimate truth, as the essence of the world itself. Access to the unconscious—given only to geniuses, according to Schopenhauer—is thereby access to presence, to truth.[9] For the personal satisfaction of the genius, this omniscience suffices, but in order for others to share this vision it must be given concrete manifestation. Artistic creation, therefore, is the result of an intention to communicate an inspiration, with the former (the work of reason) being entirely dependent upon the latter. Such a view of creation in which the composer must simply "get it down right" conditions much late nineteenth-century thought, from Wagner's putative La Spezia vision and Walther's "Wahrtraumdeuterei" to Nottebohm's discussion of Beethoven's sketches.

As proof for such a view of the creative process, Lorenz offers a personal observation about his own (admittedly rare) creative endeavors. He testifies to having experienced occasional moments of inspiration in which he had been able to perceive entire works in an instant.

> So I can after all attest to an inspired moment in which, in a moment of the highest intensity, I can hear *simultaneously* in my mind everything that in actuality occurs successively. It is an incomprehensible, metaphysical phenomenon. What happens, I cannot say: one does not simply hear the beginning and end brought closer to one another, but literally all sounds of the entire work *simultaneously* in an inconceivably brief moment.[10]

If this happens even to an amateur composer such as himself, Lorenz asserts, imagine what this moment is like to a genius like Wagner. Lorenz "does not doubt" that Wagner had the power to conceive the entire *Ring* in a single instant.[11]

This spark of inspiration, however clear and concrete to the creator, nevertheless remains an "unaufgelöste Potenz" which must be made manifest in order to be perceived by others.[12] It must be split up and verticalized. Lorenz

---

9. Such thought is what Jacques Derrida has termed "logocentric" and condemned for its nostalgic belief in the possibility of presence and for providing the illusion of unitary meaning. Jacques Derrida, *Of Grammatology*, trans. Gayatri Chakravorty Spivak (Baltimore & London: Johns Hopkins, 1976 [first pub. 1967]).

10. *Geheimnis* I: 292.

11. Ibid.

12. Alfred Lorenz, "Kunstform—Kunstgeist," *Bayreuther Blätter* 50 (1927): 124.

notes that this act requires immense powers of memory and intellect: the former, because only that which was present at the moment of inspiration really belongs organically to the work (everything must derive from that moment if the work is to remain a unified whole); the latter in order to transform the simultaneity of the moment into a temporal sequence.[13]

This process of giving form to a work is, for Lorenz, essentially rhythmic: "one must be quite clear that form is nothing other than *rhythm writ large* [große Rhythmik]."[14] He thus speaks of the rhythmic division of the initial spark of inspiration. By this he means the process of splitting up and verticalization to which we have already referred. For Lorenz, then, the idea of rhythm is at once broader and more elemental than traditionally conceived: "rhythm is the creative womb of all artistic production."[15] Wilhelm Worringer makes much the same point when he observes that the point of departure for the impulse to artistic creation—what he calls the content of the absolute artistic volition—is the urge to create resting points or opportunities for repose.[16]

The creator must choose whether to fulfil the conception in a spatial or a temporal manner; that is, in the plastic arts or in the fine arts. In the plastic arts—drawing, painting, architecture, and sculpture—works of art are unified by their spatial placement. The distance between objects, their repetition, their contrast and juxtaposition—these create the rhythm of an artwork. The same holds true for the fine arts (poetry, music, and dance), only this unity is discerned in a temporal manner. Creating these rhythmic divisions is a primary event:

> The division of the metaphysical heart of an artwork into rhythmic sections is absolutely the primary and most essential thing in all artistic forms. In this division of the great inspired moment, the spirit of the artist reveals itself. [This division] is the spirit of the artwork in general.[17]

The rhythmic division of the original inspiration creates the form of a work, whether temporal or spatial. It follows therefore that in order to comprehend a work one must grasp its form.

> We can hardly perceive the inner essence of an ingenious art-work in any other manner than by a depiction of its form, because it is precisely this form which is the visible spirit of the work of art itself.[18]

---

13. *Geheimnis* I: 293.

14. *Geheimnis* IV: 2. This idea is found throughout Lorenz's writings in various forms. I have already pointed out its possible origin in Hanslick's *Vom Musikalisch-Schönen*.

15. Alfred Lorenz, "Wege zur Erkenntnis von Richard Wagners Kunstwerk," *Bayreuther Blätter* 56 (1933): 112.

16. Worringer, *Abstraction and Empathy*, 34–35.

17. Lorenz, "Kunstform—Kunstgeist," 125–26.

18. Ibid., 127.

In other words, really to know a work is to be able to retrace its compositional process in reverse. Performers and analysts may therefore attain such metaphysical moments as those ascribed by Lorenz to composers:

> If one learns a great work piece by piece—let us say, Beethoven's Ninth, Liszt's Faust Symphony, a work by Strauss or Reger, or an entire Wagnerian music drama—and masters all its details, there comes all at once a point in time in which one has the power to see the entire work in a second from beginning to end. Not only the beginning and end brought nearer to one another, however, but in fact all that lies in between to the smallest detail: each harmony, each instrumental entry; all at once, simultaneously. If one has experienced this moment of the most blissful powers of the imagination, then one knows the work. One has then reached the metaphysical heart of the work of art, like the creator, but by a different route. For the re-creative [*nachschaffenden*] artist this is the final point in his penetration of the material; for the creative artist it is the starting point. This moment is an incomprehensible phenomenon. Time and Space are then eliminated; it is a metaphysical event. All that sounds together at such a moment belongs together organically.[19]

These metaphysical moments are thus both the origin and goal of all artistic endeavor. Although Lorenz never mentions his name in this context, such an idealistic emphasis clearly recalls Hausegger in the weight placed upon the twin acts of conception and reception. As with Hausegger, the objective existence of the work itself—its appearance—is of less consequence than is the perception of its expressive intent: its essence.

For Lorenz, again like Hausegger, the impression of form is given a physiological basis. It is grounded in the breath and the heartbeat of the body itself. In one striking passage, Lorenz compares formal perception to the sympathetic vibration of a string:

> Just as a sounding string causes to resonate in sympathy those other strings whose frequencies [*Wellenstöße*] correspond with its own, in just such a way only music can thrill a listener. It accomplishes this by arousing in him the same rhythmic momentum [*Schwung*] that underlies its own existence. Now this consideration cannot deal so much with the primitive rhythm of brief measures; rather [it deals] with the large rhythm of the form that likewise pervades in sublime breaths the temporal course of musical works. Yes, it is form which in its wide rhythmic waves creates high points of excitement and low points of relaxation, and thereby brings about an inspiring resonance [*Mitschwingen*] in our soul.[20]

Formal understanding is based on an empathetic physical response to the increasing and decreasing tensions in a work. The listener must vibrate

---

19. Ibid., 123–24.
20. Lorenz, "Wotans Abschied und Feuerzauber," 710.

along with the work.[21] While Lorenz's valorization of the body has several further implications yet to be discussed, the idealistic basis of such thought should not pass without comment.

In a recent paper, Tilottama Rajan has discovered in Nietzsche's conceptualization of "music" and the "body" the typically Romantic trope of a locus of ultimate truth outside the play of language and apart from the world of concepts:

> Nietzsche's emphasis on the body . . . leads to a distinction between language and the body, or between language as *logos* and the language of the body. . . . [Understanding] the body as the most authentic form of cognition, Nietzsche turns . . . from unity to difference. For to grasp the world through our bodies is to feel rather than know it, to be unable to objectify what is still inside us, and thus to experience the real as excess, as that which exceeds representation. . . . Collapsing the boundary between inside and outside, the experience of the body precedes and impedes the separation between subject and object necessary to what [Julia] Kristeva calls the thetic: the faculty of judgement created by the illusion of using language propositionally.[22]

There is an unbreachable chasm—like that separating appearance and essence (*Ding an sich*)—between the language of concepts and the language of the body, with the former clearly of lesser value than the latter. Music expresses that which is inexpressible in language; or, in Rajan's terms, "that which exceeds representation." By configuring the experience of form in the body itself, Lorenz is able to bypass the conceptual world of language altogether. Like the creative act outlined above, artistic understanding is not the work of reason but of unconscious comprehension. Lorenz thus traces Schopenhauer's equation of music and the will in his own linking of the body and form. In its aim, Lorenz's theory strives for nothing less than its own negation.[23]

If a musical work is a copy of the will itself, than we must understand the form of a work—its "rhythm writ large"—as a blueprint of the activity of this will.

> In the formal waves which are thus generated, the inner proportion [*Gehalt*] of the piece of music condenses its "will." If we recognize their vibration [*Schwung*],

---

21. Lorenz makes much the same point in *Geheimnis* I: 56.

22. Tilottama Rajan, "Language, Music, and the Body: Nietzsche and Deconstruction," in *Intersections: Nineteenth-Century Philosophy and Contemporary Theory*, ed. Tilottama Rajan and David Clark (Albany: SUNY Press, 1995), 152–53. In this article Rajan attempts to refine the received notion of Nietzsche as a precursor of deconstruction by examining his differences from classical poststructuralism: the texts of Derrida, the later de Man, and the later Foucault.

23. It is true that Lorenz presents this idea with an idealistic emphasis on "soul" rather than a (proto-) postmodern emphasis on "body." My main point about a nonlinguistic locus of meaning remains unchanged, however.

then we penetrate into the deepest interior of the artwork, for true form is nothing extrinsic, but [rather] the innermost shape [of the work] made visible (in music, made audible). . . . *Musical* motives correspond exactly in this respect to the *spiritual* motives on which the drama is based, so that the symphonic flow pressing upon our ears represents an exact copy of the powers of the will at work in the action. Nowhere more clearly expressed than here is the truth of Schopenhauer's teaching about art: that music is a copy of the universal Will."[24]

Musical forms are the external manifestations of internal emotional states; they go "in tandem with the wave-like processes in the human soul."[25] Lorenz eventually will argue that only four basic shapes exist to embody these inner states, which he conceives in terms borrowed from the natural sciences: as genera rather than as individual species.

Whosoever naturally sees in "form" only the conceptual, barren model [*Typus*] instead of the colorful diversity of rhythmic accents may well find formal investigations cold. Only so much can be extracted from the average [*Typischen*] in musical form, as also from the average in nature. Would anybody who understands what is meant by the plant species *Orchis*, refuse, on that account, to get to know, at least roughly, the enchanting, diverse shapes [*Gestaltvariationen*] of the 2000 types of this colorfully blossomed family? However, in the study of musical form we are satisfied by the crudest parings of the coarsest [types]. Are then the orchid-like variations, for instance, less fascinating than sonata form? It is unfortunate that one has grown accustomed to thinking of form as something external and always setting it in opposition to "content."[26]

In a similar sense, he elsewhere refers to these formal genera as "Gestalt-qualities," and refutes any absolutist notion of proper size or length. This he calls the "principle of relativity" (*Relativitätsprinzip*).

Forms are "Gestalt-qualities" in the sense of the philosopher Christian von Ehrenfels. Just as an equilateral triangle remains essentially the same regardless of its size, so also do formal types, whether they last for a few measures or an entire evening's opera. It is the relative proportions between the different parts that create the formal impression.[27]

Lorenz's forms are perceptual categories rather than concrete molds. In practice they can assume a variety of appearances. This is a consequence of

24. Lorenz, "Die Orchestereinleitungen der Festspiel-Werke 1934," 171; Lorenz, "'Der fliegende Holländer'—Oper oder Worttondrama?" 103–104.

25. Alfred Lorenz, "Neue Formerkenntnisse, angewandt auf Richard Straußens 'Don Juan'," *Archiv für Musikforschung* 1 (1936): 453.

26. Lorenz, "Betrachtungen über Beethovens Eroica-Skizzen," 420.

27. Alfred Lorenz, "Das Relativitätsprinzip in der musikalischen Form," in *Studien zur Musikgeschichte: Festschrift für Guido Adler zum 75. Geburtstag* (Vienna: Universal Edition, 1930; reprint, Vienna: Universal Edition, 1971), 180. Lorenz makes the analogy with Gestalt psychology in other places as well.

their origin as will; such variation is a psychological necessity, for our emotional states are never precisely the same.

> Music must work with these [formal types], just as the will must work with the psychological states [*Seelenzuständen*]. The abundance of the mixtures gets to be endless, but we can be clear only if we pare off the individual processes. It should also be noted that each recurring psychological state is really always a little different; perfectly exact recurrences do not occur, only equivalences. Music can express this strikingly through its skill for *variation*, whereby a musical event recurs in another guise. Thus formal types must be recognized even if their repeated or recurring sections are melodically, harmonically, rhythmically or otherwise *varied*.[28]

Such an understanding of musical form results in the logical impossibility of any separation of form from content. Of necessity, they are one and the same.

> For, in true art, there is no distinction between content and form; an aesthetic of expression [*Ausdrucksästhetik*] and an aesthetic of form belong then together as one. Art is shaped content. It would never occur to us to separate content from form in a product of nature (be it plant or beast) because the inner essence of such a thing, as soon as it takes on physical appearance, is precisely its form. There is no artistic content without form.[29]

By conceiving of his formal types as Gestalt-qualities, Lorenz places the onus of understanding squarely on the listener himself. Works must be "felt" or "experienced" in order to be comprehended. Only through such physical knowledge, not through intellectual abstraction, can one truly know—and enjoy—a work.[30] But if certain musical passages do not please, this is not the fault of the composer (Lorenz of course means only "great" composers) but of the listener. In this context, while discussing Gurnemanz's long narrative in the first act of *Parsifal*—a time of dozing and furtive watch-checking on the part of many in the audience—Lorenz argues that any boredom means simply that the listener is not attuned to the rhythm of the work:

> All boredom during a work of art depends only on the fact that the listener's soul does not vibrate in the same rhythm as the artwork. Form is, however, nothing other than large-scale rhythm; that is why the wonderfully aroused resonance [*Mitschwingen*] of the soul immediately sets in, when one grasps the form at least instinctively.[31]

28. Lorenz, "Neue Formerkenntnisse," 454.
29. Lorenz, "Kunstform—Kunstgeist," 127.
30. Lorenz writes: "*The artistic enjoyment becomes increased in an unimagined way* when one is then able to breathe empathetically in tandem with the respiration of the artwork and its divisions." *Geheimnis* III: 7.
31. *Geheimnis* IV: 95.

Lorenz's emphasis on feeling and perception over hard fact partakes of the empathetic understanding demanded by the hermeneutic model. Lorenz, too, is part of the anti-positivist tendency of the *Geisteswissenschaften*. Lorenz remarks that "a conceptual content, however worthy it may be, may perhaps give rise to admiration, but never to rapture."[32] Insight into the true nature of music—the expression of the inexpressible—is a subjective matter, personal in its physical sense. Lorenz presents himself quite clearly as the product of such a view. He is adamant that he first arrived at his findings about Wagnerian form out of his practical *experience* in conducting the works in the theater.[33] Indeed, his entire approach is presented as the fulfillment of such an aesthetic presupposition:

> The perception of the large-scale rhythmic sections and groupings in music drama must thereby deepen the artistic impression considerably more than the mere understanding of the leitmotives. The latter leads to the rational dissection of the work, while the former, however, to that unified emotional sympathy [*Gefühlsverständnis*] upon which our Master always placed the greatest emphasis.[34]

Noteworthy, too, is the essentially *dynamic* character of his approach. Lorenz writes of formal processes, of perception, and of rhythm. At times, his description of musical form echos that of Kurth: "Musical form is *continually* in effect. Wave follows wave in this symphonic ocean."[35] Lorenz's understanding of musical form—at least as he describes it while outlining the foundations of his method—suggests a surprisingly different Lorenz from the one we have been taught to expect: Lorenz the Procrustean arch-formalist, "obsessed" with his fixed formal types.[36]

The Leitmotive

The centrality of the so-called "leitmotive" to much Wagnerian analysis has already been suggested. Lorenz further remarks that "there is no doubt that the musical unity of the gigantic creations could be provided only by this principle."[37] But Lorenz, as a follower of the expressive aesthetic, is

---

32. Lorenz, "Der musikalische Aufbau von Wagners 'Parsifal'," 162.
33. *Geheimnis* I: 10, 301.
34. Lorenz, "Zum musikalischen Aufbau der Meistersinger von Nürnberg," 135.
35. *Geheimnis* I: 297.
36. See, for example, Robert Bailey, "The Genesis of Wagner's *Tristan und Isolde* and a Study of Wagner's Sketches and Drafts for the First Act" (Ph.D. dissertation, Princeton University, 1969), 147–48, and Bailey, "The Structure of the Ring and its Evolution," *19th-Century Music* 1 (1977): 54.
37. *Geheimnis* I: 73.

quite clear about the fact that no name, no conceptual tag could ever convey the essence of a motive;[38] rather, he argues, it would be more fruitful to investigate the source of these motives in the language of music itself.[39] He is critical of the prevailing tendency, originating with Federlein and Wolzogen, of simply tracing the successive appearance of the leitmotives throughout the work as they relate to the drama.

> For is the artistry of a beautiful tapestry discerned if one determines that a certain red thread runs through it and another golden one repeats, but does not take into consideration the overall shaping of the model? The fundamental question, from the point of view of musical composition, is therefore what is finally made from the leitmotives.[40]

What would be more to the point, suggests Lorenz, would be an examination of the motives as elements of the musical structure.[41] Seen in this regard, he argues, "the leitmotives are nothing other than little stones, first through whose combination the wonderful structures of Wagner's music are created."[42]

Lorenz's choice of architectural metaphors ("musical constructions," "musical cathedrals," etc.), when coupled with the static appearance of the tables in *Das Geheimnis der Form*, had led many to regard him simply as a formalist. This view is not entirely correct, as this survey of his writings about musical form aims to suggest. The matter will be dealt with in detail in the final chapter of the present work. In some respects, however, Lorenz has been his own worst enemy in this, for he clearly does insist on divorcing any consideration of the leitmotives' connection to the poem from what he calls the "rein Beschreibung der musikalischen Gestalt."[43] To describe only the motives themselves is rather like describing the building materials (even if it be the richest marble) rather than the building itself. He thus seems to

---

38. Ibid., 6–8, esp. 8: "It may be that one does not perceive that a comprehensive name really cannot be found, because a word represents a concept, and music has nothing to do with concepts; with clear awareness of this Wolzogen himself has already said that the names can be taken only as identifying marks. . . . One might just as well use numbers, if they served the memory better." Nevertheless, Lorenz employs the "classic" Wolzogen names for the motives.

39. Here Lorenz mentions Wolzogen's *Musikalisch-dramatische Parallelen* and Curt Mey's *Die Musik als tönende Weltidee*. Lorenz makes much the same point in "Richard Wagners 'neue Religion'," 459–60, and discusses Mey's metaphysical *Urgesetze* in considerable detail.

40. *Geheimnis* I: 9. Lorenz makes the identical comment in *Geheimnis* III: 6 and IV: 5. This passage might be added to those discussed by Thomas Grey, ". . . *wie ein rother Faden*: On the Origins of 'Leitmotif' as a Critical Construct and Musical Practice," in *Music Theory in the Age of Romanticism*, ed. Ian Bent (Cambridge: Cambridge University Press, 1996), 187–210.

41. As Wagner himself suggested in the passage from "Über die Anwendung der Musik auf das Drama" cited above, p. 6.

42. *Geheimnis* I: 9.

43. *Geheimnis* IV: 10.

make a rigid distinction between the poetic function and the musical function of a motive, asserting that "the 'poetic function' of the motives is irrelevant to the investigation of the musical structure."[44] In practice, however, and following the tenets of the expressive aesthetic, Lorenz is much more flexible and does consider the poetic function of the motives; after all, Wagner himself argues that text and "drama" may serve to precondition formal possibilities. As I shall argue later, this may be the true "secret" of *Das Geheimnis der Form.*

The claim of a distinction between the poetic/dramatic and musical functions of a leitmotive may be traced back to Wagner's comment in "Über die Anwendung der Musik auf das Drama" already discussed in the last chapter.[45] Christian von Ehrenfels is particularly known for seizing upon this suggestion of Wagner's and turning it into a rigid doctrine. In "Zur Klärung der Wagnerkontroverse," Ehrenfels argues that such a distinction must be the basis for any investigation of Wagnerian form:

> This perception [of Wagnerian form] is made accessible by an investigation of the *musical function* of Wagner's *leitmotives.* I stress "the musical function" expressly, for the leitmotive has to carry out a poetic or dramatic function, which is most often considered in isolation and one-sidedly. . . . But the function of the leitmotive as a poetic device for expression and recall is, as it were, only the external cause of its deeper function as *formal elements in the musico-dramatic organism.* . . . Every true drama that would be a work of art, and more than a mere theatrical entertainment [*Theaterstück*], must . . . also appear as just such a self-contained organism with harmony and perfect proportions between the individual parts, just as perhaps an architectural work or a piece of absolute, symphonic music, for instance.[46]

While it is clear that Ehrenfels' distinction originates in the idealistic-Schopenhauerian binarism of essence/appearance (the musical function is described as "tiefer" than the poetic/dramatic), there is a significant ideological dimension to it as well that is made explicit by the final clause. Ehrenfels has a not-so-hidden desire to present Wagner as a master of absolute, symphonic music. This is even more apparent in the pages which precede the above quotation. Here Ehrenfels argues that the most pressing matter of the "Wagner controversy" is the formulation of an answer to the reproach that Wagner negated musical form. In his opinion, Wagner did no

---

44. *Geheimnis* II: 4. Lorenz describes this "double function" in *Geheimnis* I: 13.
45. GS X: 185.
46. Christian von Ehrenfels, *Zur Klärung der Wagnerkontroverse* (Vienna: Konegen, 1896); reprinted in Ehrenfels, *Philosophische Schriften: Ästhetik*, ed. Reinhard Fabian (Munich: Philosophia Verlag, 1986), 107, 108–109. The latter part of this quotation is also found in Ehrenfels, "Die musikalische Architektonik," *Bayreuther Blätter* 19 (1896): 257. This article is more often cited in the Wagner literature, but it is quite clear that Ehrenfels is quoting himself.

such thing; rather, he did away with the stereotypical formal patterns of number opera in which the work amounted only to a potpourri instead of a unified (read: symphonic) whole. He therefore calls for a redefinition of musical form in relation to opera.

Ehrenfels provides one example of the pronounced symphonic turn amongst post-Wagnerian (particularly German) writers on opera in the latter half of the nineteenth century and the first part of the twentieth. Their overt insistence on "opera as symphony" often masks a covert uneasiness about the genre. If an opera can be shown to be unified in the manner of a symphonic movement, if its themes can be shown to be used and developed symphonically, and if a large-scale tonal structure can be discerned, then indeed opera is as worthy of study as a Beethoven symphony. There is something chauvinistic about such claims; they reveal a need to colonize opera—originally an Italian genre—in the name of "heil'ge deutsche Kunst."[47]

Lorenz's—like Ehrenfels'—desire to validate Wagnerian opera as absolute music leads him to follow the latter's "double-function hypothesis" for the leitmotive.[48] His description of the musical side of this equation reveals even more clearly the ideological function of such claims:

> The purely musical function of these themes is none other than that of all musical motives in the structure of symphonic works: they are merely elements, only through the mixture of which can musical tensions be aroused.[49]

Elsewhere he makes explicit the implicit propagandistic aims of such an approach:

> Only if one thus frees oneself above all from the connection to the poetry can one hope to discover something useful for the perception of the purely *musical worth* of the music drama.[50]

Despite its undeniable ideological implications, positing a "double-function" for the leitmotive is problematic, particularly when seen in light of Lorenz's own aesthetic framework. The difficulty is this: how can Lorenz bracket off the poetic function of the leitmotives from their musical function when aesthetically the two are inseparable?[51]

---

47. See Abbate, "Opera as Symphony: A Wagnerian Myth," 92–94.

48. This understanding of the leitmotive is by no means restricted to Ehrenfels alone, but is typical of the age. I have focused on Ehrenfels because of Lorenz's own admission of indebtedness to him; see *Geheimnis* I: 73, 311–13.

49. *Geheimnis* I: 73. In *Geheimnis* II he equates the two even more explicitly, calling the leitmotives "nothing other . . . than the themes or motives of a symphonic movement" (4).

50. *Geheimnis* II: 4. My emphasis.

51. He writes: "I restrict myself entirely to my subject, which has never before been considered; namely: the clear description of the musical shape." *Geheimnis* IV: 10.

Wolzogen and other writers have traditionally treated leitmotives as signs such as those theorized by Ferdinand de Saussure in the *Course in General Linguistics* (1916). Saussure argues that "the linguistic sign unites, not a thing and a name, but a concept and a sound-image," which he terms the signified and the signifier.[52] The link between the two is purely arbitrary, and works by difference: there is no necessary connection, other than that of convention, between the letter combination c-a-t and the four-legged feline. On the surface it appears that Saussure's formulation creates a distinction like that between form and content, and essence or appearance: the essential cat—the concept "cat"—seems to be distinguished from the material form of its appearance, its sound-image c-a-t. In practice this is not true: the sign is an indissoluble whole that Saussure compares to two sides of the same piece of paper.[53]

In discussing the leitmotive, Wolzogen and his followers posit a similar double articulation. Here the musical motive is the sound-image, and its "essence" the concept. The latter connection is what poses the difficulty in music. Side-stepping the thorny question of musical signification,[54] we may note that Wolzogen never denies that the motives have a meaning, only that this meaning may be captured in language.[55] In other words, the conceptual content of a leitmotive is the emotional reaction awakened in the listener; it signifies without linguistic representation. Saussure makes a distinction between what he calls *langue* (language as a system; the underlying system of rules which makes an individual utterance possible) and *parole* (the individual utterance). Wolzogen makes a similar distinction between "parallels" and leitmotives, arguing that musical gestures exist first as parallels and only gradually become leitmotives when brought into contact with the poem.[56] Thus, for him, Wagner's music dramas (and the mid- and late-romantic styles in general) become the *langue*, while the leitmotives in the individual works are seen as the *parole*.

Although Wolzogen's first writings about the leitmotive predate Saussure's *Course in General Linguistics* by over four decades, there are many correspondences between the two in their respective treatments of the sign. Characteristic of both is an understanding of the sign (in Wolzogen's case, the leitmotive) as self-identical. The concept and the sound image form an indissoluble

---

52. Ferdinand de Saussure, *Course in General Linguistics*, trans. Wade Baskin (New York: Philosophical Library, 1959), 66.

53. "Language can also be compared with a sheet of paper: thought in the front and sound in the back; one cannot cut the front without cutting the back at the same time; likewise in language, one can neither divide sound from thought nor thought from sound." Ibid., 113.

54. For a discussion of the double-function hypothesis within the larger context of musical signification in general, see Carolyn Abbate, *Unsung Voices: Opera and Musical Narrative in the Nineteenth Century* (Princeton: Princeton University Press, 1991), chap. 2.

55. Wolzogen, *Musikalisch-dramatische Parallelen*, 5–6.

56. See above, pp. 62–63.

whole; each is inconceivable without the other: two sides of Saussure's piece of paper. Likewise, as we have seen, it is utterly foreign to the expressive aesthetic position to posit any split between form and content, signifier and signified. The form of a work is a necessary consequence of its particular content. They are mutually dependent.

In proposing a definite division between the musical and poetic function of the leitmotive, Lorenz introduces an aesthetic inconsistency into his work. It is particularly conspicuous, as he adheres to the expressive aesthetic in virtually all other matters.[57] In practice, however, more often than not Lorenz *does* consider the poetic functions of the motives, and indeed often uses these to argue for formal equivalences. In fact, these notions of formal symmetry and equivalence are dependent upon the leitmotives being signs and being able to "mean." They need this semantic or connotative content in order for Lorenz's principles to work.[58] It may be, therefore, that this tension in Lorenz's work is more at the rhetorical than at the conceptual level. The strong possibility exists that the double-function hypothesis was advanced more in the interest of promulgating the symphonic myth than out of any deeply considered conviction of its logical truth. While Lorenz's analyses may have the appearance of disregarding any links to the poem, in practice this is simply not true. The crux of the matter may be found in his presentation of the Wagnerian *Gesamtkunstwerk*.

The Gesamtkunstwerk

Wagner's notion of an ideal fusion of the arts into what he termed a "total art-work" (*Gesamtkunstwerk*), first presented in the Zurich writings of 1849–51, has long played a central role in attempts to understand the composer and his works. But this notion—as important a piece of Wagnerian lore as it is—has undergone several interpretative swerves throughout the intervening years. Whereas the term is generally understood today as the metaphorical expression of a Wagnerian ideal (which he achieved with varying degrees of success), for earlier generations the meaning was rather more literal. Lorenz, for example, writes:

> Rather, in Richard Wagner, *universal art* [*Allkunst*] is reawakened for the first time since Aeschylus and Sophocles: that single, *unified* art produced out of the

---

57. For example, he embraces Wolzogen's (and others') *langue/parole*-like distinction between what he calls "parallels" and leitmotives. For example:

> Wagner's masterworks are often not at all concerned with reminiscence motives [*Erinnerungsmotive*] . . . but rather with purely musical, will-symbolic motives, which conversely develop into their "significance." *Afterwards* they may well become reminiscence motives, so that they function within the space of the drama simultaneously as foreshadowing and reminiscence (*Geheimnis* IV: 103).

58. This point will be made more clear in the next chapter.

innermost manifestation of the shape of the drama, and which then finds *simultaneous* expression in word, sound, gesture, and staging. Everything proceeds from the moment of *intuition* in which the universal artwork is conceived.[59]

This statement is only one of a myriad of similar expressions of belief in the correctness of Wagner's formulation.

A literal interpretation of Wagner's idea of a "Gesamtkunstwerk" implies belief in a single governing creative impulse behind the work. Thus, all of the component arts (music, poetry, gesture, etc.) are only different expressions of this original artistic inspiration; in Lorenz's words: "word and sound are only different expressions of one and the same artistic feeling."[60] For Lorenz, as for others of his era, this single artistic feeling is the "metaphysical seed" of the work, its inspiration.[61]

As discussed above, in order for this atemporal inspiration to be made temporal and hence visible, it must be divided rhythmically once the form (spatial or temporal) of its appearance has been chosen by the creator. This initial act, however, is already a *musical* one, and all arts are thus, in a sense, made musical.

> The succession of artistic effects, even though these may pertain to every single other pleasing art form, is always the work of rhythm-creating music.[62]

This preliminary rhythmic division, as conceptual as it may be, still results in what is in effect the superimposition of musical form upon the other arts.[63]

> Wagner is concerned with something fundamentally different: namely, with the uniform expression of the *Gesamtkunst*, born from the inspired moment of intuition, and which in fact manifests itself in *musical form*. Through this creative act, text and music are unified to such an extent that it is impossible to detect an order of succession for the individual arts: in their manifestation as expression [*Ausdruckswerden*] both arts are cast into musical form, whose discovery therefore reveals the heart of text and music at the same time. The entire work is subject to absolute musical laws. Musical form is the sole framework for the many expressive possibilities of the different individual arts.[64]

---

59. Wagner, *Ausgewählte Schriften und Briefe*, ed. Lorenz, I: 2.
60. *Geheimnis* I: 276.
61. The terminology of others' discussion of this same notion of course varies, but the concept of organic unity remains the underlying link. For example, in some ways Schoenberg's idea of the *Grundgestalt* resembles Lorenz's "metaphysical seed," particularly as elaborated in *The Musical Idea and the Logic, Technique, and Art of Its Presentation*, ed., trans., and with a commentary by Patricia Carpenter and Severine Neff (New York: Columbia University Press, 1995).
62. *Geheimnis* II: 9.
63. Perhaps it is better to conceive of this in Worringer's terms, as the creation of points of repose. See above, p. 70.
64. *Geheimnis* IV: 192, 3.

The ideal synthesis of the arts proposed by Wagner in the term "Gesamtkunstwerk" was to occur in the service of the drama. Or, to reverse this idea, true drama, the Wagnerian goal, could only be achieved through the self-negating participation of each component art. Lorenz thus argues (following Wagner in *Beethoven*, of course) that the drama—the original creative impulse—is itself given musical form.

> So the musical sensation of form [*Formgefühl*] is distilled, then, not only in the motivic grouping, but simultaneously in the grouping of the dramatic occurrences. Certainly the rising and sinking, the *rhythmic momentum* [Schwung] *of the innermost dramatic events*, reveals itself in the music much better than in the poetry, for poetry does not say what happens between the lines—and that is quite a lot! . . . Music, however, (which proceeds uninterruptedly, and which can express everything, even that unattainable through words) embodies the complete course of the internal drama.[65]

Lorenz asserts that the true drama is to be found in the music, not in the text. By way of example, he notes that the poem alone cannot reveal that Brünnhilde greets the world twice in the final scene of *Siegfried*, once silently and once verbally ("Heil dir, Sonne!").[66] Because of this, and other instances, Lorenz argues that

> such instances prove that the musical form is not dependent upon the words of the poem, but that it is the *background of its dramatic life*, into which the words are merely inserted.[67]

Understood in this fashion, musical form is at once the most elemental aspect of Wagnerian drama, and the most comprehensive; it is continually effective.

Earlier writers on Wagnerian form tended to fall into two camps, seeing Wagner's works either as number operas in which the recitative/aria divisions were well hidden (Guido Adler, for example), or as a formless succession of illustrative leitmotives.[68] Lorenz reconciles these two viewpoints:

> A wonderful correspondence exists between these two points of view—that of the drama and that of the music—in this regard; not, however, because the mu-

---

65. *Geheimnis* I: 276, 297.

66. In other words, it is the music—as will—that communicates meaning to the listener. As this meaning of necessity is non-linguistic, it is therefore closer to absolute truth, and thus supersedes the linguistic meaning conveyed by the text.

67. *Geheimnis* I: 277.

68. The analytical reception of Wagner's works remains to be written. For a brief introduction, see John Deathridge, "A Brief History of Wagner Research," in *Wagner Handbook*, trans. and ed. John Deathridge (Cambridge, MA: Harvard University Press, 1992 [first pub. 1986]), 202–205, 212–18.

sical themes are simply stuck onto the dramatic motives or even onto the words, but because the dramatic structure itself has musical form. One must seek the drama in the music, not in the poem. . . . Musical form is the sculptor of the dramatic structure.[69]

It is in this sense that he argues that true form is simply shaped expression, and is in no way split from a conceptual content. Lorenz writes that "in the hand of an ingenious artist, the formal aesthetic and the expressive aesthetic are hardly opposed, since true form is nothing but shaped expression [*gestalteter Ausdruck*]."[70]

In Wagner's so-called revolutionary writings, the *Gesamtkunstwerk* is presented as something of a meta-artwork, as the *Aufhebung* of all the component arts. Here the idea of "drama" is used as a synonym for "*Gesamtkunstwerk*." By the time of *Beethoven* and the pre-eminence given to music, Wagner equates drama with music itself, writing that

just as a drama does not portray human characters, but lets them represent themselves directly, so the motives of music give us the character of all the world's appearances according to their innermost essence. The motion, formation, and evolution of these motives is not only analogously related to the drama, but a drama representing the Idea can only be understood with perfect clearness through those moving, forming, and evolving musical motives.[71]

He even goes so far as to tip the balance toward music ("we would not err were we to define music as man's a priori qualification for shaping drama in genera.").[72] This realignment on Wagner's part leads, as we have seen, to Nietzsche's own redefinition of absolute music with respect to *Tristan*.[73] Here Nietzsche presents music as the abyss of absolute, shattering Dionysian truth, which is then masked by Apollinian concepts such as language and individuality.

Lorenz, like Nietzsche, follows Wagner himself in the emphasis placed on music and drama. He argues that music is at once an unmediated representation of the will, and the most direct expression of the drama. The three terms—music, will, drama—are thus all metaphors for absolute presence; they all express the inexpressible, the *Ding an sich*.

It should by now be clear that the governing thought for Lorenz's entire approach is the expressive aesthetic, with its emphasis not only on art as the vessel of absolute truth, but also on the subjective—indeed instinctual—perception of form. This Lorenz makes clear in a 1938 article outlining the

---

69. *Geheimnis* I: 297, 277.
70. *Geheimnis* I: 297n.
71. *GS* IX: 105–106.
72. Ibid., 106.
73. See above, pp. 32–33.

aims and goals of musicology and indicating whom he saw as the primary obstacle for a proper understanding of music:

> Above all, our discipline could develop successfully if it would whole-heartedly accept Schopenhauer's aesthetic theory. . . . However, if we—even in musicology—have assimilated the firm feeling that music provides us with a direct copy of the will, then we—and above all the young composers—are freed from the shallow [*flachen*] Jewish and Jewish-influenced aesthetic theory that would see music only as the self-satisfaction of a superficial drive toward games [*oberflächtlichen Spieltrieb*], as a tinkling play of tones, as a kaleidoscope of sounds confusedly shaken about.[74]

Lorenz very probably is referring to Hanslick, whom he cannot even bring himself to name either here or in an earlier article.[75] (Elsewhere he attacks Hanslick's "external music aesthetic" as a product of his [Jewish?] "superficiality," "unreliability," and "doubtful character".)[76]

As far as music analysis is concerned, we have already mentioned that Lorenz regarded formal analysis as the primary task in investigating works of art. But this is understood only as the means to an end. Lorenz asserts that there is a higher goal for which to strive:

> We can only approach genuine works of art if we consider, without prejudice, how they have evolved. In the course of this, we must arrive at synthesis by analysis. Formal analysis is concerned with recognizing the rhythmic arrangement of the parts; one must dissect them into their component pieces. . . . After such an analysis, one would be pleased to hear quoted Mephistopheles' words:
>
> > "In the palm of his hand he holds all the sections,
> > Lacks nothing, except the spirit's connections."[77]
>
> If one stopped there, it would admittedly really be so. However, I have never taught that analysis alone suffices. It is only the *prerequisite* for properly perceiving the spiritual connection.[78]

The aim of analysis is the perception of a work's spiritual coherence, its essence. The uncovering of this unity is an ideological goal, as well as an aesthetic one, for Lorenz expressly sets out to counter the charge of Wagner's "formlessness."

> We come much closer to the true inner life of the *Gesamtkunstwerk* if we grasp the action from the structure of the themes than if we explicate the leitmotives

---

74. Lorenz, "Musikwissenschaft im Aufbau," 369–70.
75. "Dieser Mann—zu klein, um mit Namen in diesen Blättern genannt zu werden . . ." Lorenz, "Kunstform—Kunstgeist," 126. It is also possible that Lorenz means Schoenberg here.
76. *Geheimnis* IV: 192.
77. *Faust* I, *ll.* 1938–39, trans. Walter Kaufmann (Garden City, NY: Doubleday, 1961).
78. Lorenz, "Neue Formerkenntnisse," 453, 463.

from the action. Earlier "leitmotivic guides" [*Musikführer*] took the latter approach, and achieved only an unfortunate splintering of the work. My method reveals the felicitous synthesis of the whole.[79]

Thus the apparent emphasis given to form and other purely musical matters in Lorenz's work has quite a different implication than often thought if it is placed in its proper aesthetic and philosophical context. He is indeed concerned with the aesthetics of musical form. With this background in place, we turn now to the details of Lorenz's analytical methodology.

---

79. *Geheimnis* III: 5.

Chapter Four

Lorenz's Analytical Method: The *Ring* Analyses

Although the fundamentals of Lorenz's analytical methodology are readily available in standard writings about Wagner or analysis itself (Wagnerian or otherwise), no account adequately explains the philosophical underpinnings traced in the previous chapter.[1] In a sense, Lorenz's methodology mirrors its own philosophical foundations. While it is easy to focus on external matters such as the individual periods and their forms, the essence of the method resides in the internal foundations of these manifestations: Lorenz's aesthetic and philosophical presuppositions. These have seldom, if ever, been considered, and yet, as should be clear from the previous chapter, they are of the utmost importance for a proper understanding of Lorenz's approach.

Here ideology is central to the question: both that of Lorenz and that of his critics. Ideological bias—the need either to attack or validate Lorenz as a symbol of a certain type of approach—is apparent in all treatments of Lorenz, as will be shown in the sixth chapter. The closest that one can come to any type of "objective" consideration of Lorenz is an historically informed reading of his work, beginning with his starting premise that:

> Richard Wagner, whom his contemporaries considered as a destroyer of musical form and a proponent of musical chaos, in truth was *one of the greatest formal geniuses* [Formkünstler] *of all time*.[2]

The following account of the details of Lorenz's analytical method is presented less as a self-sufficient study (however much it may appear as such)

---

1. Much of this literature will be discussed in chapter six. Useful, but incomplete accounts in English are those of Gerald Abraham, *A Hundred Years of Music*, 3rd ed. (Chicago: Aldine, 1964); and David R. Murray, "Major Analytical Approaches to Wagner's Musical Style: A Critique," *Music Review* 39 (1978): 211–22. The most complete presentation of Lorenz's thought is found in Warren Jay Darcy, "Formal and Rhythmic Problems in Wagner's 'Ring' Cycle," (D.Mus.A. dissertation, University of Illinois at Urbana-Champaign, 1973), but Darcy concentrates only on Lorenz's formal schemes, deliberately leaving other matters unconsidered. He is adamant that his is not a complete account of all of Lorenz's theoretical concepts (7).

2. *Geheimnis* III: [v].

than as counterpoint to the main theme of the present work: the role of aesthetics and ideology on analytical methodology. It is of less consequence whether Lorenz's analyses are somehow "objectively" correct (if this could even be determined) than it is that the reasons for their presentation be understood.

After discussing Lorenz's analytical premises and relating these to their aesthetic context as outlined in the previous chapter, I will survey Lorenz's formal types. This chapter is largely based in both organization and content on the introduction to the first volume of *Das Geheimnis der Form*, and all of the examples are taken from that volume. Where necessary I have augmented Lorenz's comments there with reference to his later writings. Lorenz provides an introduction to his method in virtually all of his published analytical writings and occasionally arrives at a clearer (or more succinct) formulation of a concept in one of these accounts. The later volumes will be briefly considered in the next chapter.

For the most part in this chapter I have presented Lorenz's method without comment, although I am well aware of the problematic nature of much of his work when seen from a strictly analytical point of view. A critical evaluation of his approach has only been deferred, and these matters will be addressed in future chapters.

The Three Elements of Form

Lorenz's approach may be summed up in the belief that "'form' is not external, but is the sensation of the large rhythms in the sequence and structure of the music."[3] Rhythm is the basis of his entire methodology, and Lorenz, following Hausegger, gives it a physiological basis. He argues that the simple alternation of heavy and light which forms the essence of rhythm results in a formal feeling (*Formgefühl*) on a higher level when it is expanded and hierarchized through accent.[4] These accents he compares to the human pulse. Just as the pulse is not always even, the large-scale rhythms which create musical forms may not be completely proportional or rationally related. Rather, they reflect the inner state of the subject:

> Rhythm may be compared with the breathing cycles of humans: their lengths may vary greatly depending upon the inner excitement of the one breathing, and nevertheless produce a clear rhythmic course of life [*Ablauf des Lebens*].[5]

---

3. Lorenz, "Richard Wagner, ein Meister des musikalischen Aufbaues," 69. We have already noted the correspondence of this view with those of Hanslick and Hausegger; see above, pp. 40–41.

4. This is similar to Riemann.

5. *Geheimnis* I: 13.

As was discussed in the last chapter, Lorenz regards this large-scale rhythm as constitutive of all works of art, but it is perhaps worth emphasizing once again its dynamic character. Rudolf von Tobel clearly understood this point when he noted that Lorenz's discussion of *Rhythmik* corresponded to what he and Ernst Kurth called *Dynamik*.[6] Rhythm is the necessary requirement for the realization of all artistic conception. Musical works, existing in the temporal sphere, are given this rhythmic profile (Worringer's points of repose) through various means: tonality (the departure from and return to a tonic); rhythm and meter (use of a single meter over large stretches of music); and melody (thematic repetition and contrast). Other elements, such as timbre and texture may play a role as well.

Harmony and Tonality

While it is possible to speak of rhythm and melody in reference to other arts—literature or poetry, for example—harmony, understood in its technical sense, is unique to music; Lorenz calls it the "most musical of the three primary musical concepts."[7] In the common-practice period, musical works are generally unified through the use of a single, governing tonal center, which is then contrasted with one or more secondary tonal centers and moments of tonal ambiguity or tension. This departure from and final return to the tonic serves to define the structure of a work in the broadest sense. Works can thus be understood as expanded cadential progressions, with their basis in a simple cadence of tonic-subdominant-dominant-tonic that has been expanded through the tonicization of the middle elements.[8] That is, the subdominant and dominant function may be defined by their own subdominant and dominant, producing what Kurth calls the "'potentiation' [*Potenzierung*] of the harmonic progression."[9] Lorenz compares the originative tonic-subdominant-dominant-tonic cadence to a sine wave, the amplitude of which is expanded by this potentiation process.

In order to show best this structuring role of tonality, Lorenz employs the function symbols devised by Hugo Riemann. Riemann's notation is based on three letters (T, S, D) which signify the functions of tonic, subdominant, and dominant to which Riemann reduces all chord structures. These basic signs are modified through the addition of the letter "p" (indicating what German musicians refer to as a parallel key: the relative major

---

6. Rudolf von Tobel, *Die Formwelt der klassischen Instrumentalmusik* (Bern and Leipzig: Paul Haupt, 1935), 234.

7. *Geheimnis* I: 15.

8. *Geheimnis* I: 15–16. It might be worth noting here the similarity of Schenker's approach.

9. Ernst Kurth, *Romantische Harmonik und ihre Krise in Wagners 'Tristan'*, 3rd ed. (Berlin: Max Hesse, 1923; reprint, Hildesheim: Georg Olms, 1968), 137; cited by Lorenz, *Geheimnis* I: 16.

or minor), a plus sign for major, a degree sign (°) for minor, and either a small crescendo or decrescendo sign to indicate what Riemann calls the *Leittonwechselklang* of a major or minor triad.[10] The great advantage of Riemann's system is its ability to account for a myriad of chords foreign to a (traditionally conceived) key area. All chord progressions are understood in relation to a principal chord, the T around which the rest of the chords revolve, and from which they are reckoned.[11] It is for this ease of reference that Lorenz uses Riemann's notation.[12]

It must be admitted that Riemann's system—entirely deductive—has something of the Procrustean about it. Once a tonic has been decided upon, one can relate just about any tertian sonority to it using Riemann symbols. This is a decided boon in a late nineteenth-century style such as Wagner's, but whether such elaborate tonal webs bear any relation to the music itself as perceived cognitatively may be open to debate. What is perhaps more significant is the firm conviction of tonal unity which is symbolized by the use of Riemann's functional symbols. Lorenz's use of Riemann's notation may be seen as a signifier whose signified is both this belief in unity and an invocation of the empiricism of Riemann's method itself.

Lorenz's view of form as an expanded cadence is derived from an ambiguous passage from part three of *Oper und Drama* in which Wagner advances the concept of the "dichterisch-musikalische Period."[13] Here Wagner argues that modulation and tonal rounding off in drama must be derived from the affect of the text. The example he provides is the sentence "die Liebe bringt Lust und Leid" in which the latter word would be set as a "Leitton," leading to a contrasting tonal area which would be related to the first key in the same degree as the second emotion is to the first. Had the

---

10. The *Leittonwechselklang* ("leading-tone change chord") is a chord in which the prime is replaced by its leading tone. Riemann builds minor triads downwards, and calls what we would see as the fifth, the prime, making the "leading tone" the note a semitone *above* the fifth. Thus, the *Leittonwechselklang* of a C-major triad would be B-E-G; that of an A-minor triad, A-C-F.

11. Riemann's harmonic system is one based on subjective perception rather than objective essence. Since a chord may often be explained in several ways (for example, in C major the *Leittonwechselklang* of the tonic is the same as the parallel of the dominant: E-G-B), its function is determined entirely by how it is heard in context. Listening, as conceived by Riemann, is an active rather than a passive activity; it is an application of the logical functions of the mind in an attempt to explain the tonal connection between chords. It is dependent upon a different conception of tonality from that of Roman-numeral analysis: more of tonality-as-Gestalt than tonality-as-empirical-entity. As discussed in the previous chapter, however, this flexibility did not extend to Riemann's analysis of musical form.

12. Lorenz leaves the question of harmonic dualism to one side, even though it is at the root of Riemann's method. What, to him, is of the essence is the relationship between tonalities, and he notes that one could just as well use scale-step notation for his findings, only this renders the tonal relationships less immediately apparent than Riemann notation. *Geheimnis* I: 15n.

13. *GS* IV: 152–55. The entire passage is translated in Thomas S. Grey, *Wagner's Musical Prose: Texts and Contexts* (Cambridge: Cambridge University Press, 1995), 375–77.

sentence read "Liebe giebt Lust zum Leben," there would be no justification for leaving the initial tonal area. If the first sentence were followed by
the clause "doch in ihr Weh auch webt sie Wonnen," then the word "webt"
would become a second "Leitton" leading back to the first key for
"Wonnen." As presented by Wagner, musical modulation acts as a metaphor for the departure from and return to a given dramatic or textual point.
Such a completed cycle is what Wagner terms a "poetic-musical period,"
and about which he writes:

> In this we have described the poetic musical *period*, as it is determined by a
> single principal tonality [*Haupttonart*]. On that basis, we could provisionally
> describe the most perfect art-work, viewed as a vehicle of expression, as that in
> which many such periods are presented in rich profusion, such that each is con-
> ditioned by the next in the realization of the highest poetic intent [*dichterischen
> Absicht*], evolving into a rich overall manifestation of human nature, clearly and
> surely communicated to our feeling; this evolution proceeds so as to embrace all
> aspects of human nature, just as the principal key may be understood to em-
> brace all other possible keys. Such an art-work is the complete drama. In it, the
> all-embracing human element is communicated to our feeling in a consequen-
> tial, well-determined series of emotional components [*Gefühlsmomenten*] of such
> strength and conviction that the *action* of the drama seems to grow out of all
> this of its own accord—as the natural product of this rich set of conditions—
> into a larger, instinctively unified entity [*zu einem umfassenden Gesammtmotiv*],
> and perfectly intelligible as such.[14]

These semantically derived cadential movements Lorenz understands to
comprise recognizable entities within the whole, which he will refer to as
discrete formal sections. The problem arises, however, with Wagner's vague-
ness about the size of these periods. Nowhere does he give an actual example of such a period or indicate the exact role played by these poetic-
musical periods in his own compositional process. In other writings, Wagner
contends that modulation must occur in music drama only for dramatic or
textual reasons, and that far-ranging or unusual modulations, which would
be unacceptable in untexted music, may be justified by the drama and/or
the text.[15] Although this fundamental notion that bizarre harmonic progressions can be justified by the drama is not dissimilar to the premise of
the poetic-musical period as presented in *Oper und Drama*, he never again

---

14. *GS* IV: 154–55. Translation from Grey, *Wagner's Musical Prose*, 376–77.

15. See two essays from 1879, found in *GS* X: "Über das Opern-Dichten und Komponieren
im Besonderen," and "Über die Anwendung der Musik auf das Drama." The idea is most
succinctly expressed in a posthumously published fragment apparently written around the
time of *Tristan*: "On modulation in pure instrumental music and in drama. Fundamental difference. Swift and free transitions are in the latter often just as necessary as they are unjustified
in the former, owing to a lack of motive." See Carolyn Abbate, "Wagner, 'On Modulation',
and *Tristan*," *Cambridge Opera Journal* 1 (1989): 33–58 [translation is Abbate's].

uses the term, and so these later references lose the idea of self-containedness so crucial to Lorenz.[16]

For these reasons, Lorenz's adoption of the principle of the poetic-musical period has given rise to much controversy. Carl Dahlhaus, for example, has argued that Lorenz is entirely wrong in this regard. In Dahlhaus's opinion, Wagner understood the poetic-musical period as a short series of those single, internally modulating lines described above: a period of at most twenty to thirty-some measures, certainly not the several hundred-measure periods often posited by Lorenz.[17] Other scholars, such as Robert Bailey and Patrick McCreless, go along with the Lorenzian poetic-musical period for the works of the early and mid-1850s, but claim that Wagner then abandoned the poetic-musical period after the completion of the first act of *Tristan* at the end of December 1857.[18] Most recently, Thomas Grey has traced the frequent connection of the term "period" in the nineteenth century with *rhetorical* periods, and suggested that Wagner's 1837 review of Bellini's *Norma* offers evidence that Wagner "entertained the idea of a musical period, in an operatic context, as defined primarily by the rhetorical thrust of the text."[19] In Grey's opinion, the primary importance of the concept was that it gave Wagner the model for wandering tonality; he suggests that, in practice, the other aspects of the term were discarded.[20]

What remained, then, was the idea that Wagnerian formal structures (whether "periods" or not) should be flexible enough to be integrated within or evolve into larger contexts. Since Wagner himself only used the term once, it seems most sensible, for the present work, to allow Lorenz his own

---

16. Of course, this "self-containedness" can only be taken as figurative. Obviously, such a unit—like a fish—can not exist outside of its proper environment. The notion is crucial, however, for the interpretation of form-as-Gestalt.

17. Carl Dahlhaus, "Wagners Begriff der 'dichterisch-musikalischen Period'," in *Beiträge zur Geschichte der Musikanschauung im 19. Jahrhunderts*, ed. Walter Salmen (Regensburg: Gustav Bosse, 1965), 179–194.

18. Bailey's dissertation realigns many of Lorenz's period boundaries, finding ten periods in the first act, as opposed to Lorenz's twelve; see Robert Bailey, "The Genesis of 'Tristan und Isolde'." Patrick McCreless argues that "an insistence upon applying the theoretical ideas of the early 1850s to the later operas . . . mar[s] Lorenz's analyses; by carving the final two acts of *Tristan*, as well as *Die Meistersinger*, the later parts of the *Ring*, and *Parsifal* into short poetic-musical periods, he utterly misses the formal point of these works," *Wagner's 'Siegfried': Its Drama, History and Music* (Ann Arbor: UMI Research Press, 1982), 189. His own analysis uses "periods" for the first two acts (these are frequently as large, if not larger than Lorenz's own) but prefers the idea of "movements" for act three.

19. Grey, *Wagner's Musical Prose*, 196. Lorenz would not have known this text, as it was first published by Friedrich Lippmann, "Ein neuentdecktes Autograph Richard Wagners: Rezension der Königsberger 'Norma'-Aufführung von 1837," in *Musicæ scientiæ collectanea: Festschrift Karl Gustav Fellerer zum 70. Geburtstag am 7. Juli 1972*, ed. Heinrich Hüschen (Cologne: Volk, 1975), 373–79.

20. He correctly points out that, if as is generally argued, *Das Rheingold* represents Wagner's closest approximation of this theoretical model, he may have found it unsatisfactory. Grey, *Wagner's Musical Prose*, 185, 193.

understanding of the term, which at least has the advantage of being internally clear and consistent.

It may be that Lorenz's adoption of Wagner's poetic-musical period is simply a matter of convenience. In its use, Lorenz can evoke Wagner's authority yet be free to expand the term liberally. For Lorenz, the term implies two important concepts: first, that such a period would be unified "according to a principal tonality"; and second, that the "natural product" of adherence to this principle is an instinctively unified work in which the "action of the drama seems to grow out of all this of its own accord"—that is, that the music itself bears the drama within it. While the initial implication may be tested empirically, the second is more of an aesthetic judgment than an analytical insight. In this regard, Lorenz writes:

> However, once one has discovered these points of division, the most wonderful formal structures are revealed, usually instantaneously, and the work—formerly notorious as formless chaos—unfolds as a series of marvelous images [*Bilder*], beautifully intertwined and artistically shaped.[21]

Determination of these periods is presented in almost magical terms.

Since the internal division of a work is what gives it its form, Lorenz calls the discovery of the poetic-musical period the "key" to formal perception.[22] *Das Geheimnis der Form bei Richard Wagner* divides all of the *Ring*, *Tristan*, *Meistersinger*, and *Parsifal* into poetic-musical periods. On average, each act contains somewhere between fifteen and eighteen periods, each (generally) determined by a single key and dramatic action.[23] Several such periods may be grouped together to form even larger periods. The periods, numbered sequentially by Lorenz, are occasionally interspersed with unnumbered sections which are labeled with such terms as "introduction," "coda," or "transition." These transitional sections are *not* poetic-musical periods, and will be considered in some detail in the next chapter.

Lorenz notes that exact determination of the beginnings and endings of periods is difficult because of Wagner's love for what he called the "art of transition" [*Kunst des Überganges*].[24] Lorenz openly states that he regards

---

21. *Geheimnis* III: 2.

22. Lorenz, "Richard Wagner, ein Meister des musikalischen Aufbaues," 65.

23. In *Geheimnis* I: 23–46, Lorenz tabulates the poetic-musical periods for the entire *Ring*. See appendix 2 of the present work for a similar tabulation. The later volumes of his study are arranged chronologically instead of categorically, and no tabulations are provided. Regarding the tonality of the periods, Lorenz notes that this is not always made clear by Wagner's written key signature, and offers instances where this is the case: places where the key signature is changed only for ease of notation; places where the key is indicated by accidentals only; places where the key signature is changed some time before or after the actual modulation, etc. See *Geheimnis* I: 21–22.

24. Letter to Mathilde Wesendonck, 29 October 1859, *Richard Wagner an Mathilde Wesendonck: Tagebuchblätter und Briefe 1853–1871*, ed. Wolfgang Golther (Leipzig: Breitkopf & Härtel, 1904), 232–36.

his own work only as an initial attempt to determine these Wagnerian periods. That later analysts may wish to rethink some of his divisions does not,
to him, invalidate either his work or the poetic-musical period principle in
general.[25] One curiosity about Lorenz's period boundaries is that they frequently appear to cut off the final chord from the period to which it belongs. Reading more closely, we find that Lorenz intends no such thing:

> I implore my critics not to reproach me for always separating the cadential tone
> from the rest of the phrase. I assume that my readers will understand that the
> final note is to be added to the relevant phrase.[26]

Such an apparently unmusical division is necessitated by Wagner's technique of unending melody in which cadences generally have the double
function of conclusion (of one section) and commencement (of another).

For Lorenz, the second implication gleaned from Wagner's conception
of the poetic-musical period—that of dramatic coherence—is just as important as the first (tonal unity). This has seldom been noted in considerations
of his work, yet the two are intimately intertwined. As we have seen in
some detail, Lorenz equates music and drama with Schopenhauer's will
itself—in some sense all three are interchangeable. Wagner's own enigmatic
mention of the poetic-musical period concerned the construction of musical allegories for the drama. It follows, then, that Lorenz generally interprets the music in precisely this fashion at both the level of detail and on a
large scale. If the tonal progression of the individual poetic-musical period
traces its dramatic content in an allegorical fashion, Lorenz argues that the
tonal relationships which span the entire work can do the same thing. He
illustrates the tonal flow of the entire *Ring* with the graph which is reproduced as figure 4.1.[27] He then equates these tonal relationships with events
in the drama.

Throughout *Das Geheimnis der Form*, Lorenz discusses tonality in a
three-fold sense: as an individual instance, as a global phenomenon, and as
an articulative force. First, following Wagner's *Oper und Drama* model,
differing tonal centers are believed to signify differing dramatic events in a
systematic manner; in other words, the relative closeness or difference between two tonal areas serves as a musical metaphor for the parallel dramatic relationship. It follows then that similar emotional states or dramatic
situations would tend to be in the same key. Lorenz offers a number of
examples which, in themselves, are not entirely unconvincing:[28]

---

25. See, for example, *Geheimnis* I: 20, 289.
26. *Geheimnis* II: 10. Lorenz makes this point in the first volume as well, p. 92n.
27. *Geheimnis* I: 48.
28. Ibid., I: 49–50. Lorenz's third point is weakened by the fact that Siegfried really does
not have an associative key.

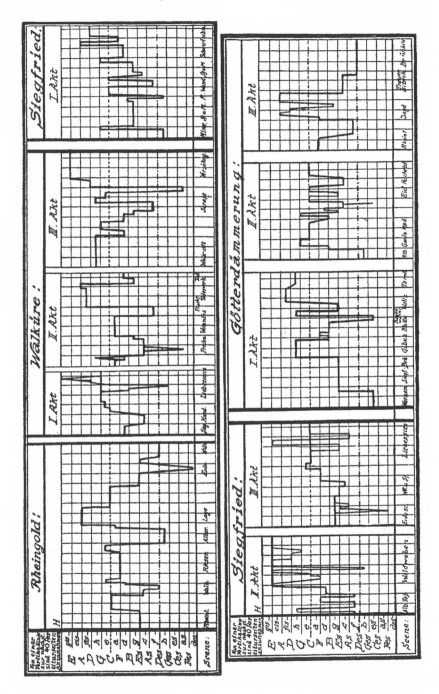

Figure 4.1. Lorenz's graph of the tonal structure of the *Ring*.

1. Siegmund and Sieglinde's love scene closes in G major, which may be seen as the dominant "seed" of the love scene between their son, Siegfried, and Brünnhilde (which is in C).
2. Siegfried forges Nothung in D major, the major variant of his father's tonality.
3. Siegfried's associative key of D major is to Hagen's associative key of B minor as Wotan's key of D-flat major is to Alberich's of B-flat minor.
4. The Waldweben, Siegfried's psychological preparation for his meeting with Brünnhilde, and the Feuerzauber, Brünnhilde's psychological preparation, are both in E major.

If this first dimension of tonality may be termed relativistic and based on the internal structure of the work, the second—based on the probable characteristics of the keys themselves—has wider implications. Lorenz argues that Wagner may choose a key for some affective reason based either on historical or psychological grounds.[29] In a sense, the relationship between the two is analogous to that between the leitmotives and the parallels: a key has both an individual and a global essence. These two dimensions enjoy a reciprocal relationship; Lorenz writes of the "continuous parallel movement of the nature of the dramatic moment and the absolute nature [*absoluten Characters*] of the relevant key."[30] There is an assumption made that the two inevitably coincide, as Lorenz writes that:

> In every measure the modulation not only shows the correct harmonic relationship to the preceding material, but also simultaneously provides the characteristic coloring for the relevant place.[31]

In addition to these two senses of the term "tonality," Lorenz refers to its role in creating form. This articulative function he deems the most important of the three. He argues that the importance of the large-scale tonal flow of a work (as illustrated by figure 4.1) for the perception of its form has been too little considered by earlier analysts.[32] According to Lorenz, the *Ring* is organized around a tonic of D-flat major; he indicates this with a

---

29. He notes that existing accounts of key characteristics in Wagner are almost uniformly dilettantish and calls for a comprehensive treatment of the subject. *Geheimnis* I: 50–51, esp. 50n where he lists and critiques seven such accounts.

30. *Geheimnis* I: 51.

31. Ibid.

32. Ibid. He suggests that this is true also for number opera, and refers to a study by Rudolf Steglich ("Händels Oper Rodelinde und ihre neue Göttinger Bühnenfassung," *Zeitschrift für Musikwissenschaft* 3 [June-July 1921]: 518–34) of the large-scale tonal structure of *Rodelinde* which aims to disprove the frequently encountered belief that baroque opera is constructed out of disparate "Arienbündel" by showing that groups of arias cohere into what Steglich calls "Szenenbilder," hence, in his estimation, proving the organic unity of the work.

dotted line in figure 4.1 (the other line, tracing C major, is included only for orientation). The first scene of *Das Rheingold*, in E-flat major, is therefore a dominant introduction to the work as a whole (as the dominant of the dominant A-flat). Along the same lines, the first two acts of *Die Walküre*—the entire Siegmund plot—are framed by D minor, which is the minor Neapolitan of the tonic key. Lorenz sees it as significant that the tonal curve usually seems to intensify in each act; by this he appears to mean that the final key is higher on the graph than the first key, although it is unclear why this is relevant.[33]

It may seem that this last form-generating category of tonality reinscribes the double-function hypothesis from the leitmotive to tonality in general, that Lorenz is arguing for some purely musical use of tonality. This is untrue. By the shaping power of tonality Lorenz means the creation of those musical allegories for the drama described above, which—of necessity—are poetic-musical periods. In practice this is always determined by the drama, which, according to Lorenz, itself has musical form.

Such large-scale tonal "plots" as those proposed by Lorenz have been much criticized in writings about operatic analysis.[34] The issue is difficult. On the one hand, Wagner's use of particular tonalities as icons associated with certain groups of characters (like B minor for the Valkyries, B-flat minor for the Nibelungs), or motives (B minor for the Curse) or other dramatic elements (like F major for Siegfried's horn call, D-flat major for Walhall) is undeniable as an essential element of his musical language.[35] It is therefore not surprising that scenes involving these characters or motives tend to be written in these keys, or in ones closely related to them. On the other hand, to elevate these correspondences into a general principle—or

---

33. In the later volumes of *Geheimnis*, Lorenz makes broader claims for such large-scale tonal progressions, arguing, for example, that *Tristan und Isolde* outlines a huge Phrygian cadence: °S (A minor)–D (B major).

34. The debate began in the late 1970s with the publication of an article by Siegmund Levarie entitled "Key Relations in Verdi's *Un Ballo in maschera*," *19th-Century Music* 2 (1978): 143–47, which provoked a number of responses: by Joseph Kerman, "Viewpoint," *19th-Century Music* 2 (1978): 186–91; by Guy A. Marco, "On Key Relations in Opera," *19th-Century Music* 3 (1979): 83–88. In the same issue as the Marco response, Levarie provides an answer to his critics, 88–89. The issue is still controversial today, as the recent exchanges between Roger Parker and Allan Atlas in *19th-Century Music* will attest; see Atlas, "Crossed Stars and Crossed Tonal Areas in Puccini's *Madama Butterfly*," *19th-Century Music* 14 (1990): 186–96; Atlas and Parker, "Counterpoint: A Key for *Chi*?: Tonal Areas in Puccini," *19th-Century Music* 15 (1992): 229–34. Atlas, at present, has had the last word: "Multivalence, Ambiguity, and Non-Ambiguity: Puccini and the Polemicists," *Journal of the Royal Musical Association* 118 (1993): 73–93. Other central texts are those of Abbate and Parker, "Introduction: On Analyzing Opera," and "Dismembering Mozart," as well as James Webster, "Mozart's Operas and the Myth of Musical Unity," *Cambridge Opera Journal* 2 (1990): 197–218. See also John Platoff, "Myths and Realities about Tonal Planning in Mozart's Operas," *Cambridge Opera Journal* 8 (1996): 3–15.

35. See Bailey, "The Structure of the Ring and Its Evolution," 51–53.

aesthetic requirement—by continually constructing elaborate relationships between characters and scenes seems to say more about the preoccupations of the analyst than about the work. Certainly, in the case of Lorenz, it stems from his need to establish quantifiable structure and unity, and hence value, in all aspects of Wagner's art. Arnold Whittall has written that

> [t]here are few today who would endorse Alfred Lorenz's argument (1924) [*recte* 1926] that the whole of *Tristan und Isolde* coheres around E major. . . . Even if it would be no less improbable to claim that the various tonal assertions and allusions in *Tristan* were totally random or accidental, the more integrated the scheme proposed, with a single "tonic" to which all other key areas are functionally subordinate, the less plausible it seems.

Nevertheless, he goes on to say that

> It would be surprising if tonal relations, as well as functional harmony, were not used as an organizing principle in through-composed opera, rather than just as an unavoidable, structurally insignificant side effect of the composer's musical language.[36]

The fundamental ambiguity of Whittall's judgment is revealing and is reflected by most, if not all, contemporary analysis of opera: both positions are readily found in the current literature—indeed, sometimes in the same work.[37] What is striking, however, is the centrality of Lorenz to this debate. Many modern analysts, such as Arnold Whittall, Carolyn Abbate, Roger Parker, James Webster, and doubtless others, locate the origin of this method of reading opera in the Wagnerian aesthetics of the early twentieth century epitomized by Lorenz's work. We will return to this point in considering the reception history of Lorenz's work.

Rhythm and Meter

Of Lorenz's three form-defining principles, small-scale rhythm (as opposed to rhythm-writ-large, which is constitutive of form) is probably the least important. Lorenz's point is basically that rhythm can differentiate sections from one another on the basis of metric pulse;[38] second, it can make sec-

---

36. *The New Grove Dictionary of Opera*, 1992, s.v. "Tonality (2)," by Arnold Whittall.

37. For example: Peter Mercer-Taylor, "Unification and Tonal Absolution in *Der Freischütz*," *Music & Letters* 78 (1997): 220–32; Harold Powers, "One Halfstep at a Time: Tonal Transposition and 'Split Association' in Italian Opera," *Cambridge Opera Journal* 7 (1995): 135–64; Arnold Whittall, "'Twisted Relations': Method and Meaning in Britten's *Billy Budd*," *Cambridge Opera Journal* 2 (1990): 145–71; Martin Chusid, "The Tonality of *Rigoletto*," in *Analyzing Opera: Verdi and Wagner*, ed. Carolyn Abbate and Roger Parker (Berkeley and Los Angeles: University of California Press, 1989), 241–61; David Lawton, "Tonal Systems in *Aida*, Act III," in *Analyzing Opera: Verdi and Wagner*, 262–75.

38. One interesting aspect of Lorenz's discussion is that he argues that Wagner takes the

tions cohere on exactly the same basis. While Lorenz's points are indisputable, their relevance is debatable. The first point seems to be included simply to prove Wagner's regularity in matters of phrasing, as in all else. Nevertheless, Lorenz does make interesting observations about Wagner's technique of phrase structure by demonstrating how he extends or compresses the four-measure phrase to suit the dramatic effect desired.

With the combining effect of rhythm and meter, Lorenz argues that a majority of the poetic-musical periods are also unified through the use of a single meter and tempo, and takes the opportunity to censure young composers for their belief that "one could produce an effect through a continually changing tempo and a rhythmic structure distorted to the point of indistinguishability."[39] In order that the listener be able to sense physically the larger rhythmic flow of a work as required by Lorenz's aesthetic project, the small scale temporal relationships (tempo and meter) must be clear and significant; only then may the communion be perceived (or achieved).

> By analogy with the phenomenon of the sympathetic vibration [*Mitschwingen*] of similarly tuned strings, a resonance [*Mittönen*] in the soul of the recipient is thus only possible if the rhythm of the piece is clear and lasts a certain amount of time, so that the rhythmic feeling of the listener may attune itself to it.[40]

In his period table for the *Ring*, Lorenz lists 209 tonally determined sections, of which 153 are in a single meter (he explicitly disregards minimal irregularities caused by minute tempo changes or conductors' whims which do not disturb the overall rhythmic flow [*großen rhythmischen Zug*] of the period).[41] Within these 153 metrically unified periods, 97 are in a single tempo as well. For the remaining 56 metrically unified periods, Lorenz advances five possible categories into which they may fall: a single tempo may emerge after an introductory tempo (this naturally does not disturb the unity in any way); there may be an acceleration during the course of a period, or toward its end; there may be an acceleration in the middle of a period, after which the original tempo returns; there may be a slowing down towards the end of a period; or there may be a slowing down in the middle. Many of these so-called variations make little or no sense when compared with the reality of the score, and testify only to Lorenz's zeal for systematization.

---

eight-measure period to be the norm, and shows that despite assertions to the contrary, Wagner does tend to compose in blocks of four. As to why this should be a virtue, Lorenz does not say. In fact, this tendency to *Vierhebigkeit* has not always been seen as a good thing; *Lohengrin*, for example, has been criticized for its almost complete reliance on duple meter (only the King's prayer in act one is in triple meter).

39. *Geheimnis* I: 56.

40. Ibid.

41. Lorenz says that he will disregard the shortest transitions in his discussion of rhythm. I have only found eight such transitions omitted.

Of the remaining 56 periods which are not in a single meter or tempo, only 18 are really a hotchpotch of these changing variables.[42] The rest have a logic about the change, which usually occurs for dramatic reasons. Within these periods there may be change of meter (occasionally with the quarter note remaining steady) alone, or accompanied by a change of tempo as well; this latter necessitates an emotional or affective change. If these changes occur only in a middle section or in a coda, the unity is not threatened. Lorenz concludes by celebrating the fact that "*scarcely an eleventh of all the music* does without the unifying effect of rhythm."[43]

The impact of such local considerations of rhythm and meter on Lorenz's methodology is less clear than that of harmony. He seems to take special pains to prove the metric unification of a majority of his periods, yet to do so he is obliged to posit so many possible variations (introductions, codas, etc.) that it is difficult to accept this as a general principle of Wagner's style. Rather, it appears more as an indication of Lorenz's own need to discover unity in all aspects of the works. In this light it is significant that in the later volumes Lorenz does not make as much of this small-scale rhythmic unity; he simply notes whether or not a period is unified metrically and/or tempowise along with the rest of the introductory matter for each period.

Melody

Lorenz understands Wagnerian "unending melody" as a collective term (*Sammelbegriff*) that encompasses three distinct elements.[44] First, the traditional recitative/aria dichotomy is abolished and everything is understood as melody. Secondly, in unending melody full closure is avoided by new cadential techniques. Thirdly, this melody is indeed "unending"—it is continually present in the symphonic web of the orchestral melody.

While Wagner saw unending melody as an essential formal principle, his critics saw it as a principle of formlessness.[45] Evaluation of such claims is first and foremost a question of aesthetics. In fact, only in Lorenz's second point is the term used in a compositional-technical sense. Instead, as Fritz Reckow has pointed out, "unending melody" is used as a type of "profound and association-rich" magic word which involves ideas of "compositional technique, aesthetics, philosophy of history, and world view" with-

---

42. That is, only $^{18}/_{209}$, or 8.6% of the work is not rhythmically "unified" in some fashion.

43. *Geheimnis* I: 60.

44. Ibid., 61–70. The term "unendliche Melodie," like "dichterisch-musikalische Periode," was a phrase employed only once by Wagner (towards the end of *Zukunftsmusik* [1860], *GS* VII: 130), although it is hinted at earlier in the essay and elsewhere in Wagner's works.

45. Thomas Grey (*Wagner's Musical Prose*, 275–77) links this with the tradition that equates melody with form and argues that, at the time, the study of musical form was identical with the study of melody.

out being bound to any single one.[46] Ernst Kurth's presentation of the term in *Romantische Harmonik* is similar to Lorenz's in its marriage of analysis and aesthetics. For Kurth, the essence of melody is free-flowing kinetic energy, which is the origin of all music. In a word: Schopenhauer's will.[47] Lorenz's use of the term in primarily an aesthetic sense is justified by both tradition and contemporary understanding.

Lorenz's adamant refusal to countenance any suggestion that a trace of the old operatic division between recitative and aria remains in Wagner's works is illustrative of his aesthetic presuppositions. His obstinance certainly strikes a modern reader as somewhat perverse in light of the sparse, declamatory sections, punctuated by chords or short motivic fragments, which occur all too frequently in that part of the *Ring* composed in the 1850s (in the initial exchange between Wotan and Fricka in *Das Rheingold*, for example, or in Wotan's narrative in *Die Walküre*). Even in Wagner's mature style there are moments which undeniably recall the genres of traditional opera;[48] performed narratives, such as Waltraute's in *Götterdämmerung* for example, are almost always written in the manner of a traditional set piece with an introductory recitative. In response to Brünnhilde's frightened question, Waltraute announces the beginning of her story with a traditional exhortation to the audience (Brünnhilde) to pay attention: "Höre mit Sinn, was ich dir sage!" This exchange is set to a notably thinner texture which is primarily chordal and which concludes with a full cadence leading to the narrative proper. The trace of a recitative/aria structure is even more apparent in Kundry's narrative in *Parsifal*; here the "aria" ("Ich sah das Kind") is unmistakable.[49]

To admit that there are places in Wagner more recitative-like than melodic would, for Lorenz, be tantamount to calling them bad music. It is the *idea* of recitative that Lorenz opposes, since, for him, it implied an accompaniment consisting solely of conventional melodic clichés, punctuated by chords, and endlessly repeated without true expressive feeling. Instead, Lorenz argues that in Wagner's works "there is no phrase, no word in this work that is not composed with the highest melodic expression."[50] This is true even if certain moments may seem like recitative on the surface, but "even in such places one is not able to detect unfeeling, conventional direction anywhere in the melody."[51] He argues that such chordal moments do

46. *Handwörterbuch der musikalischen Teminologie*, s.v. "Unendliche Melodie," by Fritz Reckow.

47. Kurth, *Romantische Harmonik*, 444–571.

48. This is not even to mention the (in)famous Conspirators' Trio at the end of the second act of *Götterdämmerung* so deplored by George Bernard Shaw.

49. See Stephen McClatchie, "Narrative Theory and Music; or, The Tale of Kundry's Tale," *Canadian University Music Review* 18 (1997): 1–18.

50. *Geheimnis* I: 62.

51. Ibid.

not result in a gap in the symphonic flow of a work, and mentions similar instances in absolute music.[52]

In Lorenz's opinion, Wagnerian melody never approaches what he sees as the lack of expression in conventional recitative. Instead, the vocal line is set with equal care for the proper expressive effect in every measure of the piece. The essence of this effect is imitation of the cadence of speech, which Lorenz sees as the foundation of all melody. Within Lorenz's cyclical view of history, Wagner thus represents a return to the ideals of the Camerata (*toskanischen Opernerfinder*), and unending melody is equated thereby with *stile rappresentativo* (which of course became recitative).[53]

With curious disregard for the historical facts of the *Ring*'s genesis (the twelve-year hiatus between the second and third acts of *Siegfried*) Lorenz advances an explanation for the obvious stylistic shift between the beginning and the end of the work:

> Naturally the symphonic work in an opera which continually intensifies over the course of ten acts must not be deployed with full intensity from the beginning (a principal failing of modern composers). Especially in *Rheingold*, long passages must thus be surmounted only by means of noble declamation without strong orchestral painting.[54]

Lorenz's unwillingness to acknowledge the change in Wagner's style is similar to his reluctance to see traditional operatic forms in Wagner's works. Both stem from his own aesthetic beliefs and blindnesses. In this latter case, to admit a stylistic discrepancy between acts in *Siegfried* would call into question his belief that Wagner conceived the entire *Ring* in a single moment of inspiration, and would seriously compromise his arguments for the organic unity not only of *Siegfried* but of the *Ring* as a whole.

If Lorenz's first element of unending melody places the emphasis upon the idea of "melody," his last two elements focus more upon its "unending" nature. The first of these points—Wagner's avoidance of closure—is given substantial emphasis in Lorenz's introduction. To him, the central issue is Wagner's abandonment of the regular cadential points ubiquitous in popular melody (or indeed any periodically conceived melodic complex). Regular cadence would almost always contradict what Lorenz refers to as the "dramatic life" of a work; its imperious, relentless flow would be negated if it were obliged to pause for cadence. This is not to say that Wagnerian melody unfolds without any caesura whatsoever, like some endless worm, as Lorenz once colorfully put it. There are clear melodic cadences,

52. In his blanket condemnation of recitative, Lorenz makes no attempt to distinguish between different types of recitative, whether by accompaniment (*semplice* or *accompagnato*), country (Italian or French), or indeed by era.

53. This portrayal of opera history was discussed in the first chapter of the present work.

54. *Geheimnis* I: 62–63.

but these are always conditioned by the logical endings of the text rather than by some abstract musical criterion such as quadratic phrase construction. That is, closure corresponds to rhetorical needs and follows the rules of grammar and punctuation. By way of example, Lorenz discusses the scene between Brünnhilde and Wotan in the third act of *Die Walküre* (mm. 666–937), which, in his estimation, has twenty-one cadential points: eleven perfect or imperfect tonic cadences and ten half cadences. With only one exception (mm. 805–806, "trautem Mahle"), these articulation points do indeed match the punctuation in the text, although there is no one-to-one matching ("all full stops are full cadences") and not every punctuation mark in the text is given musical emphasis. Still, in general, Lorenz's comments are valid.

According to Lorenz, Wagner has four primary techniques with which to mark these rhetorical caesuras without creating the effect of full closure that would destroy the progress of the drama. In the first of these, the tonic cadence marks the immediate beginning of a new motive which overlaps the melodic closure of the cadence and avoids the creation of a point of repose (ex. 4.1).

Elsewhere the voice may cadence alone, without accompaniment. The orchestra then begins a new thought on the next beat, either with the expected tonic chord, which immediately begins something new (ex. 4.2a), or not on the tonic, often in the manner of a deceptive cadence (ex. 4.2b).

A similar cadential effect is found where the tonic chord occurs in inversion rather than root position (ex. 4.3).

By far the most common manner of cadence, however, is one in which the tonic is avoided and something new begins immediately (as happens in ex. 4.2.b above, but without the beat of silence). Lorenz calls this the "most basic means to make melodies 'unending'."[55] While such avoided cadences are generally termed "deceptive," Lorenz prefers to refer to them as "linking" in function (*Verkettung des Schlusses*).

It would, however, be incorrect to label such places as "deceptive cadences" [*Trugschlüsse*],[56] for the essence of a deceptive cadence lies in the fact that it leads to (or at least indicates) a *repetition* of that cadence and the correction of the close. In this instance, however, the articulating power of the cadence takes full effect, and something *new* (merely *like* a deceptive cadence), enters simultaneously with the dissonance. This type becomes the rule to such an extent that often the melodic close of the vocal part can be omitted without altering the character of this compound in the least.[57]

---

55. Ibid., 66.

56. From Kurth, p. 260n, one sees that the deceptive cadence induces an entirely different effect than that of linking. [Lorenz's note. Certainly, however, it can and does link.]

57. *Geheimnis* I: 67. These "underthird" (*Unterterz*) cadences are discussed extensively by Kurth in *Romantische Harmonik*, 249–52.

Example 4.1. *Götterdämmerung*, Vorspiel, mm. 414–418.

Several things are worth noting here. Lorenz is quite right to emphasize the self-sufficiency of such cadences; their role in articulating divisions in the melodic flow is fulfilled, regardless of their harmonic incompleteness. He suggests that what is needed in Wagnerian analysis is a realignment of the idea of closure, just as in Wagnerian harmony a major-minor seventh chord may in fact function as a quasi-consonant sonority by acting as a chord of resolution, as is the case with the chord following the famous "Tristan" chord in the prelude to that opera.

The hierarchical positioning of the orchestral texture above the vocal lines implied by the final line of the above quotation leads us to another shading of the "unending" aspect of the concept: the placement of the *locus* of melody in the symphonic texture rather than in the vocal parts themselves. About this third aspect of "unending melody," Lorenz writes:

> The melody would not stop when the voice is silent, but would spin constantly on in the orchestra, not only during the rests, but also after the song is over, in this way forming an unending line of continual melodic flow.[58]

---

58. *Geheimnis* I, 68.

Example 4.2a. *Die Walküre* III, mm. 907–912.

Example 4.2b. *Die Walküre* III, mm. 1199–1202.

Example 4.3. *Das Rheingold*, mm. 918–922.

These melodic links are by no means "Zwischenspiele" but rather the "continual melody, which goes on—mutely, as it were—in the soul of the one singing."[59] By way of example, he offers several instances from the Waldweben in *Siegfried* (ex. 4.4).[60]

He goes on to argue that the main melodic interest resides in the orchestra even when the voice is present "if the interior of the soul, which the orchestral melody follows, is more powerful than the words, which concern rather the outward appearance."[61] From his comments it is clear that Lorenz regards this situation as the rule, rather than the exception. In places where the voices are completely silent, as in orchestral transitions, melody passes to the orchestra. He attributes to the orchestra in general the character of a symphonic melos, which he deems to be continually effective throughout the work. This melos is found not only in clearly discernible melody, but also in what Lorenz calls "latent melody," the basis of which is the

---

59. Ibid., 69.

60. These examples are reproduced from *Geheimnis* I: 68–69. The additional text underlay is added by Lorenz to prove his point that one could easily add word repetitions and lengthenings ("tasteless as these would be") to bridge the gaps in the vocal line.

61. Ibid., 68.

Example 4.4. *Siegfried* II.

totality of the symphonic motives and their use, or sometimes even individual harmonic and/or rhythmic effects. Lorenz describes this melos in terms which unmistakably reveal his philosophical debt to Schopenhauer:

> This melos, which incessantly blossoms forth from the orchestral symphony, is the soul, as it were, that permeates the entire work; in this sense, the vocal line is only a part of it.[62]

Now leaving no doubt about the relative importance of the vocal parts and the orchestra, Lorenz writes that the former is often identical with the heart of this melos, or may be contrapuntally related to it (which occurs more frequently in *Die Meistersinger* than in the *Ring*).

Lorenz, as a follower of Schopenhauer, places emphasis on melody as the highest objectification of the will, but then locates this melody, as melos, in the symphonic texture of the work. It is important to note that Lorenz speaks of melos, not melody, the former having a wider, more all-encompassing implication than the latter. This notion of melos, when described, proves to have strong Schopenhauerian foundations; indeed, according to the expressive aesthetic, it is the external manifestation of the will itself.

---

62. Ibid., 69.

Lorenz thus equates the idea of unending melody with the will, and argues that the investigation of its articulation is nothing less that the goal of his entire approach: the discovery of musical form.

> This melos finds its effect not only on the surface of the vocal melody, but also in the melodic and polyphonic structure of the symphonic motives, the web of which depicts the heart of the entire drama. The shaping of this musical web must be identical with the phases of the psychological event; it is the outward appearance of the incomprehensible dramatic will. Through its description we reach an understanding of the intellect which pervades the drama. The study of the formal design of this symphonic event is actually nothing other than the question of the structure of the unending melody that courses through the entire work and speaks to us in the sum of its motivic processes [*Motivverarbeitungen*]; it is therefore a part of the third point just discussed: the construction of form through melodic elements.[63]

In the above paragraph Lorenz justifies the central position occupied by the leitmotives in his analyses. It is the leitmotives themselves which generally articulate Lorenz's formal types. While the tonally unified poetic-musical period may be the first principle of Lorenz's method, his description of melody-as-melos makes it clear that the latter occupies a somewhat higher plane than the former. Large-scale rhythm (as articulated tonally, rhythmically, and melodically) may well form the basis of form, but melos, as a concept, clearly precedes form: it is the will itself, the unrealized initial inspiration. In philosophical terms, it seems that melody occupies the position of essence, while the other form-determining elements are stuck at the level of appearance. On the surface, melody in the sense of thematic recurrence does serve to delineate formal sections, but on the conceptual level it is superior. Nevertheless, whether this conceptual privileging of melos is reflected practically in Lorenz's analytical methodology is questionable.

In this way are harmony, rhythm, and melody treated as form-building elements, all of course subject to the all-encompassing parameter of large-scale rhythm. It may surprise some to discover that the idea of form-as-schemata—traditionally linked with Lorenz—is clearly secondary to the notions of melos and rhythm. The forms of the poetic-musical periods are presented in part two of *Das Geheimnis der Form*, significantly entitled "the symphonic web."

Creation of Large-Scale Structure

It is at this juncture in his introduction that Lorenz advances the notion of a "double function" for the leitmotive, the consequences of which we have already explored in the previous chapter. Despite the aesthetic inconsis-

---

63. Ibid., 70.

tency of such an hypothesis, Lorenz is quite right to point out that little attention had at that point been paid to the poetics of the motives themselves, to their establishment and use. Instead efforts had almost unceasingly concentrated upon tracing the appearance and disappearance of the motives in the works "like an appearing and disappearing meteor."[64] Lorenz wants to investigate the effect of the leitmotives purely as musical elements, and claims not to take into account their connection to the drama.

Although leitmotivic guides to Wagner's (and others') works are legion, few ever stop to consider *how* these referential motives are established in the first place. How does a listener, hearing a work for the first time in the theater, know that a particular musical gesture is significant and will recur? And how is a conceptual content then attached to these figures?[65] With the exception of Lorenz, this matter is rarely discussed anywhere in the vast collection of literature surrounding Wagner and his works.[66]

Lorenz argues that motives are generally established through immediate repetition, either literal or varied. Of the ninety-eight motives discussed by Lorenz, all but ten are almost immediately repeated in some manner.[67] Thirty of these are established through simple repetition and the other fifty-eight are repeated in the course of some stylized formal pattern. In Lorenz's view, an entire period is usually devoted to the establishment of a new motive, which may occur as either a principal or secondary theme, or even as an introductory or cadential theme. In other words: anywhere. While this assertion of Lorenz may make sense in the abstract, in practice it is formulated so generally as to become meaningless. If a new motive need not be the principal theme of a period but may occur anywhere, then any period may have any thematic content whatsoever. Obviously a new motive occurs in a single period, but whether this period is in any way "devoted" to it is doubtful. Lorenz himself lists instances where two or more new motives are introduced in a single period (presumably equally devoted to all).

Turning first to the motives which are immediately repeated, Lorenz lists seven which form the principal theme of a period; among these are the

---

64. Ibid., 74.

65. It is for this reason that Wolzogen's first *Leitfaden* was issued: so that visitors to Bayreuth in 1876 would be prepared for the performance. Indeed this is the primary reason behind the continued proliferation of such guides today.

66. To my knowledge, there is only one study which does so: Jeffrey L. Stokes, "Contour and Motive: A Study of 'Flight' and 'Love' in Wagner's 'Ring', 'Tristan', and 'Meistersinger'," (Ph.D. dissertation, State University of New York at Buffalo, 1984). Stokes refers to the establishment of a motive as its moment of genesis, and argues that motives best be thought of as "a particular point of dramatic culmination or intensity on a line of musical development, as a special fixing of otherwise fluid and perhaps even commonplace musical material" (64).

67. Lorenz almost always employs Wolzogen's motive names where they exist. Wolzogen had identified and numbered ninety motives used in the *Ring* in his *Thematischer Leitfaden durch die Musik zu Rich. Wagner's Festspiel 'Der Ring des Nibelungen'*. Following Lorenz, I too have chosen to use Wolzogen's labels.

Vertragsmotiv, the Freiamotiv, and the ill-named Fluchtmotiv. Three motives (Liebesfesselung, Tarnhelm, Wälsungen Liebesmotive) are secondary
themes within a period. Themes first heard in the introduction (two:
Rheingoldfanfare and Regenbogen) or coda (nine, among which are: Frohn,
Walküren, Liebeserlösung, and Welterbschaft) of a period are said to have
an intensifying function, either of the expectation of the main theme of a
period, or of the period's conclusion. Four motives are established through
immediate but varied repetition (Ring, Siegfried, Kriechmotiv, Liebesschlinge)
and a final five through sequential repetition of a short motive, either at the
same pitch level (Ritt, Rachewahn), or ascending (Schlummer, Liebeslust),[68]
or descending (Schmiede). The ascending type of sequential repetition usually climaxes in a strong harmonic or dynamic explosion, or with a significant motivic gesture.[69]

The remaining fifty-eight motives that are established through repetition
mostly do so in the course of one of four broadly defined formal patterns:
strophic repetition, Bogen form (a-b-a), rondo or refrain patterns, or Bar
form (a-a-b). These patterns, of course, also form the basis of the internal
organization of the periods themselves, and will be discussed in detail later
in the chapter. A number of these fifty-eight are established either through
what Lorenz terms "creation-before-our-ears" (Siegfrieds Herothema,
Heldenliebe, Siegesruf der Wälsungen) or through such polyphonic techniques as canon (Urelemente, Vertrage mit den Riesen, "Hagensche
Lustigkeit") or free imitation (Wellenfigur, Liebesgruß, Liebesverwirrung,
Brünnhilde, Liebesentschluß).

There are, however, ten motives discussed by Lorenz which are exceptions to the rule of repetition. He divides these into two categories. First,
there are those orchestral motives which are given emphasis through some
other means, such as a particularly significant stage action; one example of
this type is Alberich's Herrscherruf which forms the climax of his long bul-
lying speech to Mime and the Nibelungs (*Rheingold*, mm. 2289–95). Here
Wagner's stage direction indicates that Alberich is to draw the Ring from
his finger, kiss it, and elevate it threateningly. Lorenz's second category is
comprised of those motives which he feels are "non-orchestral." These are
melodically clear-cut motives which first occur in the vocal line. As they
often convey a text of particular dramatic importance, such as Alberich's
curse, it is usually dramatically inappropriate that they be immediately repeated.[70] Non-orchestral motives may also originate as the theme of a song-

---

68. Lorenz notes that the Fluchtmotiv, which forms one of the principal themes of *Rheingold*
period 6, could also be numbered among these motives.

69. This type of repetition he refers to here and throughout his works as *Tristansteigerungen*,
and credits its origins to Beethoven's Seventh Symphony (*Geheimnis* I: 81). Although Lorenz
does not name a specific passage, he is most likely referring to the transitional material in the
first movement, especially mm. 268–72 and mm. 354–64.

70. These of course are the *Erinnerungsmotive* which form the past tense of the system of

like (Liedmäßig) section such as Siegmund's "Winterstürme" or Siegfried's Forging songs. Either of these latter types, through frequent use and repetition, may achieve (*erhalten*) the character of a symphonic motive. Lorenz thus makes a distinction between recurring themes and symphonic motives which is both apt and sanctioned by operatic tradition.[71]

This section of Lorenz's work is largely unexceptionable and, indeed, in itself forms a very valuable contribution to Wagnerian scholarship, which seems never to have been noted by his erstwhile critics. It is followed by an account of what Lorenz terms the "Themenverarbeitung": the use and development of the motives whose establishment he has just traced. This forms the bulk of the remainder of the book.

Before embarking on a discussion of each and every period in the *Ring*, Lorenz spends several pages establishing certain fundamental principles of his investigation which have to do with the creation of large-scale structure. First and foremost, he makes a distinction between the ideas of development-as-label and development-as-technique, embracing the latter while rejecting the former. He notes that it would be easy to sidestep the question of Wagnerian form by calling everything "development" in the sense in which it is used in the sonata principle. From a technical sense, this would be correct: in Wagner's works, the leitmotives are transformed, fragmented, reharmonized, regrouped, and polyphonically combined in the manner of a symphonic theme.[72] Conceptually, for Lorenz, however, the label "development" implied a negation of form, rather than a component thereof. The development in a sonata movement is a negative concept, defined by what it is not. It exists solely as a divider between the formed sections of the

---

motives discussed by Wagner in part three of *Oper und Drama*. As originally conceived, they were to be a product of the "verse melody" resulting from the conjunction of a poetic text and its musical setting, and hence be associated with their original text and dramatic situation; in other words, all motives were originally to have been vocal in character. In practice this notion is increasingly ignored the farther Wagner proceeded in the composition of the *Ring*; indeed many of the motives first heard in *Das Rheingold* originate in the orchestra rather than in the vocal lines (for example, the Rheingoldfanfare and the Vertragsmotiv, both of which occur near the beginning of the work).

71. Recurring themes (also called reminiscence motives) have long played an important role in operas by composers such as Mozart, Méhul, Grétry, Spohr, and Weber. Lorenz's distinction is upheld by recent scholarship; see, for example, Arnold Whittall's article "Leitmotif" in the *New Grove Dictionary of Opera*.

72. In *Die Anwendung der Musik auf das Drama*, Wagner writes that the fundamental themes (*Grundthemen*), which make up the symphonic web of his works, "are contrasted, supplemented, re-formed, separated, and linked together again, just as in a symphonic movement." *GS* X: 185. It is essential to separate the objective and ideological threads in the argument. In an objective, technical sense, Wagner does treat the leitmotives in this way, as is seen, for example, in the development of the Walhalla motive from that of the Ring in the interlude between the first two scenes in *Das Rheingold*. We have already discussed the ideological dimension of this statement in the account of the double-function hypothesis in the preceding chapter.

work, elevated and effective solely by its formlessness. Lorenz saw this label "development" as something of an analytical dodge on the part of "embarrassed" authors who reveal the truth of the aphorism that "that which
one cannot pigeon-hole, one sees as 'development'."[73] Of course, to some
extent, this is close to Lorenz's own tactics.

To Lorenz, the most famous and effective developments in the symphonic
literature were not formless at all, but reveal a "very prominent rhythmic
momentum . . . which may be created not only by rhythm itself, but also
through melody, harmony, dynamism [*Dynamik*], and tonality."[74] An article on Beethoven's Eroica Symphony, roughly contemporary with the writing and publication of these thoughts, attempts to demonstrate this opinion.[75] Here Lorenz argues that Beethoven's famously lengthy development
falls into four major sections which together form an introduction and
Reprisenbar.[76] Although the Eroica analysis forms the bulk of Lorenz's article, he also analyzes the developments of the Fifth through Ninth Symphonies in a similar manner: each is revealed to be shaped according to one
of Lorenz's formal types (here only Bar or Bogen). He then uses these results to validate Wagner's claim to be the true successor of Beethoven.

> The cumulative mass of forms I have found in Wagnerian music drama are not
> rooted in Wagner's operatic predecessors but in *Beethoven's symphonies*, prov-
> ing the truth of Wagner's claim that the symphony had flowed into his own
> dramatic works.[77]

Lorenz's discomfort with the development label is thus more conceptual
than actual; he hints at this himself when he calls for a reconsideration of
the idea of development in classical sonata movements.[78]

For Lorenz, the perception that Wagner obeyed the laws of symphonic
development in his use of themes did not end the matter, but only served to
spark his main line of inquiry, which he conveniently sums up for us in a
long series of questions:

> Much more remains to be investigated: whether a rhythmic momentum [*Schwung*]
> manifests itself once more in these processes; whether they proceed according
> to large-scale breathing cycles [*Atemzügen*] which permit a resonance

---

73. *Geheimnis* I: 118. Lorenz encloses this statement in quotation marks, but fails to name
his source.

74. Ibid.

75. Lorenz, "Worauf beruht die bekannte Wirkung der Durchführung im I. Eroicasatze?"

76. Introduction (mm. 156–70), Stollen 1 (mm. 170–224), Stollen 2 (mm. 224–88), Abgesang
(mm. 288–402). The Abgesang is itself in two parts: development (288–342) and reprise (342–
402). The Reprisenbar form will be discussed in more detail below. Lorenz compares its structure to the sonata principle itself, and so here seems to propose that the Eroica contains within
itself a miniature symphony—a symphonic *mise en abyme*.

77. Lorenz, "Worauf beruht die bekannte Wirkung der Durchführung im I. Eroicasatze," 183.

78. *Geheimnis* I: 118. A reconsideration presumably based on his own principles!

[*Mitschwingen*] in the listener's soul; whether the thematic material is always expounded anew, in the manner of instrumental music; whether correspondences [*Entsprechungen*] exist which have the same effect in time as symmetry does in space; in short: whether it can be shown that there is a "large-scale architecture" [*große Architektonik*] throughout the whole work which generates the entire musical event by means of our three primal elements?[79]

It is soon apparent that these questions are largely rhetorical, and that all will be answered in the affirmative.

Lorenz maintains that the principal departure point for the investigation of the formal design of the periods must be that of the arrangement or ordering of the motives, since it is this element that makes the strongest impression on our ears.[80] The proportional duration of the sections and their harmonic effect also play an important role in articulating this design. (Lorenz here reminds us that tonality is the first principle for determining the boundaries of the poetic-musical period.)

As has already been remarked, Lorenz argues that the individual periods are constructed according to the same forms used in the establishment of the leitmotives. Only simple repetition is not transferred to this larger context, since "above all, ever greater becomes the extent of the self-shaping formal structure."[81] The individual sections of these forms may be multithematic, or may themselves contain a smaller form; indeed, the possibilities are virtually endless. If the forms of the sections are the same as the principal, larger form, Lorenz refers to this as formal "potentiation" (*Potenzierung*). Potentiation of the form occurs, for example, if three small Bogens together form a larger Bogen, or if each section of a Bar is itself in Bar form. More common than potentiation is a mixture of different forms in a larger, composite (*ineinandergefügte*) form. For example, the sections of a Bogen may be strophic or Bar forms, or a Bar may be made up of two strophes and a Bogen.

Lorenz makes a distinction between periods which are one large form (*einheitliche Formen*), and those which contain a succession of different forms (*aneinandergereihte Formen*). In the former case, this single form may be either simple (*einfach*) or complex (*zusammengesetzt*). If a period is short, the form tends to be simple: a single Bar, Bogen, or whatever. Longer periods are more often found in complex forms, either potentiated or composite.

In both cases of single-form periods, the form is understood as a Gestalt quality in the Ehrenfels sense; it is a unified, perceptual entity and occupies what Lorenz calls a single breathing cycle (*Atemzug*). About this he writes:

The overall form, which binds different, smaller forms into a unified whole, is the harmonizing bond which satisfactorily rounds off periods (or sections), and

---

79. Ibid., 119.
80. Ibid.
81. Ibid., 120.

which allows the *breath-filled breast to exhale again at the conclusion of the period, in order to prepare for a new rhythmic section.*[82]

Those periods without a single, governing form are instead made up of a succession of smaller forms; Lorenz refers to these as "many smaller breathing cycles which follow one another."[83] They may be partially unified, coda-like, or (even!) without unity.

Finally, Lorenz combines numbers of periods together to form what he calls "higher" (*übergeordnete*) forms or *Großperioden*. He discusses these in an almost biological manner, describing how each form is organically linked to the next: periods cohere into *Großperioden*, *Großperioden* into acts, and acts into entire works. He argues that this is Wagner's primary contribution to operatic history.

> The growth of my formal types from tiny seeds to graspable forms, and then to periods, large-scale periods and finally to entire acts, ultimately goes beyond this to effect a unified shape for the entire drama; in this, above all, lies the ingenious final step taken by Wagner in the evolution of all opera.[84]

This type of organic development Lorenz finds on all levels of his analyses. It represents the ultimate in the search for proof of a work's organic unity. The work is equated with a dividing cell wherein the parts do not develop in an additive fashion but rather in a more complex manner, which Lorenz refers to as multiplicative.

> Through the spinning out of a thought, or its combination with another, one of the formal types is again created, only of much larger size. Several of these forms together grow into a middle-sized form, several of which combine yet again to form a still larger form, and so on, until finally the entire act is generated by a kind of "multiplication of forms" (Otto Baensch's expression). Nowhere in Wagner does one find the meaningless juxtaposition (addition) of forms that satisfies other, lesser, composers.[85]

Lorenz elsewhere makes it clear that it is the presence of this "multiplication of forms" which allows one to distinguish between works of genius and hack work.[86]

Lorenz next turns to questions of formal symmetry. This he presents in no uncertain terms as a requirement of all good art.[87] Symmetry lies at the

---

82. Ibid., 253.
83. Ibid.
84. *Geheimnis* IV: 184.
85. Lorenz, "Richard Wagner, ein Meister des musikalischen Aufbaues," 64.
86. Lorenz, "Neue Anschauung auf dem Gebiete der musikalischen Formenlehre," 288.
87. "In this ingenious manner, Wagner brings to its apotheosis the desire for symmetry, which lives in all good musicians." Lorenz, "Tannhäuser-Ouvertüre historische Sendung," 60.

heart of the concept of musical form, whether it be in the framing sections surrounding a contrasting middle section in the Bogen form, or in the larger, contrasting Abgesang of a Bar, which balances the two introductory Stollen. Its essence is repetition, which is the *sine qua non* of musical form. But this symmetry is rarely exact.

> [M]usic's aim (not just that of recent music) is to lessen the identical nature of the parts; through variation to make them merely similar. . . . In Wagner's architectonic one can never establish an absolute identity of the parts—at the very least there is a variation of tonality or figuration.[88]

Indeed Lorenz presents these asymmetrical symmetries and inexact repetitions as something of a psychological necessity; given music's origin as the will itself, it is impossible to repeat an internal process of the will in a mathematically exact manner.[89] It suffices that the sections be equivalent:

> For without repetition of some type, no rhythm is imaginable, and thus no form. Such repetitions, however, need not be exact [*notengetreu*]: it suffices that they are recognized as "equivalent".[90]

In music, symmetry is generally discussed by analogy to the spatial symmetries of architecture: we speak of balanced phrases, theme areas, large-scale structures, and the like. The reversed trope of architecture as frozen music is equally common in nineteenth-century romantic aesthetics, where it is found in the writings of such authors as Goethe, Schelling, and Friedrich Schlegel.[91] But Lorenz notes that sometimes this analogy is inappropriate, especially when the symmetries are not exact:

> Often a comparison with architecture [*Baukunst*] is not suitable, and one must turn to another spatial art [*Raumkunst*] instead: painting. In paintings, there is a *symmetry of a higher order* which is not based on absolute identity of the parts, but only on their similarity.[92]

---

88. *Geheimnis* I: 121–22. Lorenz gives the example of C.P.E. Bach's "veränderten Reprisen."

89. This was discussed in chapter 3, pp. 73–74. Lorenz asserts elsewhere that Wagner's variation technique is the equal of Beethoven's, "Wotans Abschied," 713.

90. *Geheimnis* III: 2. This idea of "equivalence" is found in chapter 4 of Karl Grunsky's *Musikästhetik* (Leipzig: G.F. Göschen, 1907). Lorenz credits Grunsky with this notion.

91. The notion of architecture as "erstarrte Musik" is found in Eckerman, *Gespräche mit Goethe*, vol. 1, ed. Hans Timotheus Kroeber (Weimar: Gustav Kiepenhauer, 1918), 278 (23 March 1829), and Schelling, "Besonderer Theil der Philosophie der Kunst" (1802–1803), *Sämmtliche Werke*, vol. 5 (Stuttgart and Augsburg: J.G. Cottá, 1859), 576. Schlegel's labeling of architecture as "gefrorenen Musik," is cited (without source) by both Lorenz and Kurth (in *Bruckner*, 1: 232n). I have been unable to locate its precise source in the *Kritische Friedrich Schlegel Ausgabe*, ed. Hans Eichner (Munich, Paderborn, and Vienna: Thomas Verlag, 1967). Schopenhauer cites Goethe's comment and discusses it alongside rhythm and symmetry in *World* 3: 240.

92. *Geheimnis* I: 122. Emphasis mine.

In support of this claim he refers to painterly representations of the Ma-
donna praying, surrounded on both sides by angels. In that of Ghirlandaio,
each of the angels is identical in size and color. Over the years, in other
treatments of this motif, the surrounding angels become progressively more
and more individualized, but this, Lorenz notes, does not destroy our perception of its symmetrical Bogen structure. The surrounding motives may
be even more free than this; Lorenz refers to paintings by Rubens in which
a central figure or event is flanked by two similar but not identical events.
In the case of representations of the Last Judgment, these framing motives
are often opposites of one another since these works tend to depict a central figure of Christ surrounded on one side by the saved and on the other
by the damned.[93]

Lorenz's notions of aesthetic harmony and proportion follow those of Max
Dessoir, whose principal work, *Ästhetik und allgemeine Kunstwissenschaft*
(1906), he cites several times in his account. Turning to Dessoir, the debt is
immediately apparent; he writes:

> We should not identify symmetry and mathematically exact coincidence. . . .
> [A]symmetric forms can so often evoke aesthetic satisfaction. . . [A]greement in
> all relations of measure and form is in fact unnecessary to give the impression of
> a symmetrical pattern. Rather, the aesthetic equivalence of two halves can be
> obtained in still another way.[94]

This other way is through what Dessoir calls "isodynamia," of which absolute symmetry (complete congruence) is only the simplest type.[95] Its essence
rests in the psychological perception of balance and proportion, even in the
face of surface differences. Dessoir allows that "the halves of a spatial form
can be sensed as symmetric in spite of a very heterogeneous context"; likewise, "we assume that the right and left halves of a form, although they are
unequal, are sensed as being equivalent."[96] Dessoir's work was very influential on aesthetics in the early years of the century, perhaps since he antici-
pates Lorenz's (and other's) focus on form, writing that "the aesthetic object, for purposes of systematic study, is form."[97]

---

93. This same idea is discussed, and Lorenz cited, in the discourse section of Siegmund
Levarie and Ernst Levy, *Musical Morphology: A Discourse and a Dictionary* (Kent: Kent State
University Press, 1983), 25–28, under the general heading of the growth and limitation of
musical forms.

94. Max Dessoir, *Aesthetics and Theory of Art*, trans. Stephen A. Emery (Detroit: Wayne
State University Press, 1970), 81.

95. As Dessoir also makes the analogy with painting, Lorenz may have taken this notion
from him.

96. Dessoir, *Aesthetics*, 129, 130.

97. Ibid., 99.

Lorenz's account of musical symmetry is derived from and dependent upon these analogies from the visual arts. Central to his approach is what he calls the principle of substitution (*Stellvertretung*), which is invoked in places which correspond in mood, but have no provable equivalence.

In Wagner, with respect to parts which are very similar, indeed almost identical, we encounter stretches which are equivalent only in mood [*Stimmung*]. . . . Thus are created symmetries without demonstrable identity,[98] in which only the spiritual resonance [*geistige Niederschlag*] recurs. So here, the *principle of substitution* appears effective for melody, a principle which has long been recognized in harmony, and through which one has gained deep insights into the dominant and subdominant functions of harmony. Just as these triads may be varied through the substitution of others, so the melodies of a piece of music may be replaced by others that substitute for them without thereby eliminating the sense of equivalence or destroying the form.[99]

Lorenz gives an example from *Die Walküre* where a Fluchtmotiv which turns into a Liebesmotiv is balanced by an "actual" Liebesmotiv.[100] This type of symmetry Lorenz describes as "free symmetry." There is one further type, again the result of motivic substitution:

This "free symmetry" may be intensified into "opposite symmetry" [*Gegensatz-Symmetrie*] if . . . directly opposing motives prove by their placement to be equivalent, and thus a perfectly proportioned large-scale rhythm is perceived.[101]

Thus, for example, at the end of *Siegfried* II, Lorenz regards the motives (Schmiedemotiv, relating to Mime, and Drachenmotiv, relating to Fafner) which accompany Siegfried's disposal of Mime's and Fafner's bodies as equivalent according to this idea of opposite symmetry, since, proportionally, they occur at the same place in each half of the form. These substitute symmetries Lorenz sometimes refers to as "geistige" (spiritual) symmetries: to be felt rather than proven. In practice, when divorced from all aesthetic justifications, these notions of symmetry are very expansive and provide Lorenz with a ready escape out of almost any analytical difficulty.

It should now be apparent why Lorenz's postulation of a purely musical function for the leitmotive is problematic: it is not only illogical according to his own aesthetic beliefs but also according to the very principles of his

---

98. In a footnote, here omitted, Lorenz cites the Dessoir passage on isodynamia quoted above.

99. *Geheimnis* I: 123.

100. Further examples of this principle will be given in the following section. It might be argued that Lorenz stacks the deck here, as Wolzogen's ill-named Fluchtmotiv is simply a particular instantiation of the more general Liebesmotive. See Deryck Cooke, *I Saw the World End: A Study of Wagner's Ring* (London: Oxford University Press, 1979).

101. *Geheimnis* I: 123.

analytical methodology. A leitmotive must have a meaning—whether or not it is captured by any verbal tag, and whether it is understood logically or merely sensed—in order for the concepts of free and opposite symmetry to have any validity whatsoever. Lorenz's analyses reveal an interpenetration of (external) form and (poetic) content typical of the expressive aesthetic at their very heart: in the implicit acknowledgment of the indissolubility of the leitmotivic sign, Lorenz's claims otherwise notwithstanding.

In a later volume of *Das Geheimnis der Form* Lorenz attempts to account for this necessary reliance on the text and dramatic action despite his explicit claim to concentrate solely on musical matters by providing an aesthetic justification for an analytical necessity:

> In the tables of the present book, such places of free or opposite symmetry are more easily made clear through the words of the poetry, through statement of the situation or events than by detailed description of the music; nevertheless, one must be aware that these places also have to do with *musical* form. The *Gesamtkunstwerk* is formed *temporally*, i.e., musically, even if in its inner processes, relations are often *perceptible* only poetically. Musical form is the sole framework for the many expressive possibilities of the different individual arts.[102]

Just as Lorenz places the burden of belief on the listener for the perception of form in the first place, so too does he leave it to the reader to judge the acceptability of instances of free or opposite symmetry. What is striking is Lorenz's celebration of the role of subjectivity in his methodology.

> Of course, that is a case where the scholarly method [*Wissenschaftlichkeit*] of the investigation *can* cross over into subjective fantasy, but in spite of this, I believe that I should be able to cite my opinion in this regard, as psychological subjectivity does form an important component of aesthetics. Places of free or opposite symmetry can only *gradually* be separated from those of an identical nature, therefore a discussion of them cannot be singled out, rather it must always follow that of the actual forms [themselves]. It thus remains for the reader to decide where he will place the dividing line between exact proof, permissible substitution, and fantastic special pleading [*fantastischer Kühnheit*].[103]

It should now be clear that much of Lorenz's formal methodology is dependent upon his aesthetic suppositions. Without this background, like an arch when the keystone is removed, Lorenz's method tends to collapse into rubble. Even Lorenz's undeniable fetishization of formal coherence and quantifiable structure is based on a understanding of form-as-Gestalt derived subjectively and experientially, and notions of symmetry and balance taken from other (component) arts—indeed, Lorenz relies on these

---

102. *Geheimnis* III: 3.
103. *Geheimnis* I: 123–24.

other arts in order to prove the validity of these very notions. It is essential to keep this in mind as we turn to consideration of Lorenz's formal types.

Lorenz's Formal Types

After establishing the aesthetic foundation of his analytical method, Lorenz embarks upon an investigation of each period in the *Ring*. He does so in a categorical rather than a chronological manner, beginning with the simple forms and proceeding through the complex and successive forms to conclude with the large-scale, higher forms, always keeping in mind the fundamental aim of his investigation:

> The essence of this investigation depends specifically on proving that the organizing spirit of genius is *always and everywhere* present in the work of art, ordering it and giving it its form.[104]

This layout has the didactic intent of first accustoming the reader to the method through the simplest forms and then gradually introducing the more irregular and complex forms.

This section will follow Lorenz through his presentation of these Wagnerian formal types and will provide an example or two of each, plus some general comments as to their effectiveness.[105] It is not my intention to offer the kind of negative analysis (or analysis-by-criticism) of the *Ring* that would result from a detailed consideration of every Lorenzian period. Such an analysis would far exceed the bounds of the present work, and its worth would be doubtful in any case. Suffice it to note that Lorenz *has* been much criticized—at times with justification—on grounds which will become clear in the following chapters.

Periods in Single Forms

Simple Forms

Strophic Forms. Although the idea of strophic form needs very little introduction from Lorenz, he does spend some time reinforcing the idea that the strophes should not be exact repetitions but rather variations of a basic model: "just as it is entirely impossible for an internal process of the will [*Willensvorgang*] to repeat itself in a mathematically exact manner, so also music can never be completely identical, inasmuch as it remains a copy [*Abbild*] of the will itself."[106] At the very least, he notes, there will be some variation in tone color and intensity. More common variations include a

---

104. Ibid., 124.
105. Appendix 1 presents an overview of Lorenz's formal types.
106. *Geheimnis* I: 125.

change in pitch level and/or rhythm, a melodic alteration (through motivic substitution), or the addition of one or more additional themes. Each of these techniques is applicable for every form. Likewise, each may be enlarged by an introduction or coda.

Thirteen periods and transitions in the *Ring* are seen by Lorenz to have a strophic structure.[107] Three of these are part of the large period concluding the first act of *Die Walküre*, and provide a good indication of Lorenz's approach.[108] The second of seven sections, *Wk*.I.P.12.A.b provides a relatively straightforward instance of the strophic form. Its broad contours are immediately apparent: two strophes, one for Sieglinde (33 mm., "O fänd ich ihn heut") followed by one for Siegmund (32 mm., "Dich, selige Frau"). Lorenz's analysis is reproduced in figure 4.2.[109]

This type of presentation is typical of all of Lorenz's analyses: a list of motives (or musical description, such as "chordal punctuation") and measure counts. Its great advantage is that it makes the motivic content immediately apparent, as well as the relative proportion of the parts; the disadvantage rests in the choice of the motives listed, as occasionally Lorenz is selective as to which motives he includes. The motivic content of the above period is as Lorenz suggests: an introductory, arpeggiated motive (Schwert or Wälsungenheroenthema),[110] followed by repetitions of the Siegesruf, broken up by chordal punctuation and other figures. The variation between the strophes is immediately apparent, and both conclude with a cadence in G. The cadences are not equal, however, as Siegmund's is a full cadence to G minor, and Sieglinde's is a linking cadence of the type described last chapter (although Sieglinde's vocal line does cadence fully). Still, as far as Lorenz is concerned, both may be described as "G cadences."

Another strophic period within the act's concluding large period shows another facet of the analytical technique in practice (*Wk*.I.P.12.B.c). As before, the period comprises two vocal strophes, one each for Sieglinde ("O laß in Nähe") and Siegmund ("Im Lenzesmond / leuchtest du Hell"), and is introduced by a two-line phrase for Siegmund ("O süßeste Wonne"), which motive (Ahnensmotiv), Lorenz notes, acts as a "motto" for the entire period.[111]

---

107. See appendix 2 for a tabulation of the poetic-musical periods of the *Ring* and their formal types. The following abbreviations will be employed: *Rh.* for *Das Rheingold*; *Wk.* for *Die Walküre*; *Sf.* for *Siegfried*; *Gd.* for *Götterdämmerung*; *P.* for period. A roman numeral after the title will indicate act (with Vor. referring to the prelude to *Götterdämmerung*). Thus *Sf*.III.P.13 refers to the thirteenth period of the third act of *Siegfried*. For the reader's ease, the table in appendix 2 is keyed to the widely available Schirmer piano-vocal scores.

108. *Wk*.I.P.12 comprises seven individual periods which together form an expanded Bogen; see *Geheimnis* I: 270.

109. These figures are generally direct translations of Lorenz's own, although occasionally I have introduced simplifications. Where this occurs, it is clearly indicated in the text.

110. This is a convincing example of motivic substitution.

111. As in the manner of the baroque aria that German musicians refer to as a "Devisenarie." *Geheimnis* I: 83, 242.

I. Strophe		II. Strophe	
Schwertmotive with Kampflustrhythmus	4mm.	Wälsungenheroenthema with chord punctuation (substitution for Schwertmotive)	6 mm.
Siegesruf	2 mm.	Siegesruf	2 mm.
Figural work	12 mm.	Chordal punctuation and figural work	12 mm.
Siegesruf	2 mm.	Siegesruf	2 mm.
Figures	6 mm.	Chordal punctuation	4 mm.
Siegesruf twice	4 mm.	Siegesruf intensified melodically	2 mm.
Eighth-note figure, cadencing	3 mm.	Chords, and similar figure in sixteenths, cadencing	4 mm.
	33 mm.		32 mm.

Figure 4.2. Wk.I.P.12.A.b.

When the openings of the strophes are compared (ex. 4.5), we see that this motive—the principal one of the period—occurs in both the vocal line and the orchestra in the first strophe, and only in the orchestra in the second. This happens frequently in the analyses, and is justified by Lorenz's arguments concerning the symphonic melos of the works, of which the vocal line is only a component.[112]

The final section of P.12 (Wk.I.P.12.C.b) contains two strophes of fifty-nine and sixty-one measures respectively ("Siegmund heiß ich" and "Siegmund, den Wälsung / siehst du, Weib"). Lorenz notes that these correspond to the pair of strophes forming the second section of the large period (P.12.A.b, discussed above), but that these final strophes are not as "regular" as the earlier ones.[113] In fact, they provide a case of opposite symmetry, since the first strophe is concerned with Siegmund's "need of a sword," while the second treats of the "joys of love." Lorenz's analysis is presented as figure 4.3.

It is rather more problematic than the other two cases. Although the beginnings of the strophes are readily seen as parallel, their conclusions diverge notably. The final 41 measures of the first strophe—the (curious) recurrence

---

112. The tonality of this period is notable, as it begins in D-flat after a full cadence in that key (mm. 1218–19). It ends, however, with a full cadence in G. The initial key area was reached at the end of the preceding period section; Lorenz notes that both periods "stark in die Unterdominantsphären modulierend" but that the latter "bis G-dur zurückkehrend" (Geheimnis I: 30). As we shall see, the requirement that a poetic-musical period—which each of these periods is, remember—be in a single key proves to be somewhat flexible in Lorenz's hands. In the present case, the section under discussion is itself part of a larger period: it is the Abgesang of the Bar which forms the middle section (MS) of the Bogen that is P.12 as a whole (see Geheimnis I: 270). There is some ambiguity, then, as to the status of the sections comprising P.12: are they each poetic-musical periods, or is the true poetic-musical period the larger one? If the former is true, then why not count the parts as separate periods, and give them different numbers? This would not preclude them from together forming the larger Bogen of P.12—in fact, the majority of Lorenz's higher forms are constructed out of individually numbered periods.

113. Geheimnis I: 127.

Example 4.5a. *Wk.*I.P.12.B.c. Strophe 1 (opening), mm. 1227–1230.

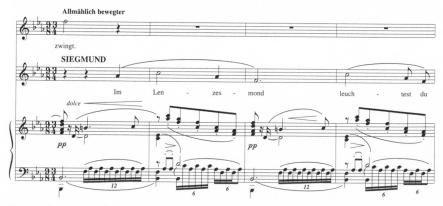

Example 4.5b. *Wk.*I.P.12.B.c. Strophe 2 (opening), mm. 1241–1244.

I. Strophe		II. Strophe	
Wälsungheroenthema w. Schwertmotive	18mm.	Schwertmotive & Wäsungheroenthema	15mm.
Entsagungsmotive w. concluding ascent	21mm.	Siegesruf, Schwertmotive, and "Winterstürme"	17mm.
Nothung baptism	20mm.	Liebesmotive 8 ⎤ Motiv der Ahnens ⎥ and chords 11 ⎥ Bogen Liebestaumel 10 ⎦	29mm.
	59mm.		61mm.

Coda: Liebesmotiv, Schwertmotiv, Fluchtmotiv, Liebesweben, Frohnmotiv   =   26mm.

Figure 4.3. *Wk.*I.P.12.C.b.

of the Entsagungsmotiv and the anticipation of the Nothung phrase ("Nothung! Nothung!")—are not paralleled in any way in the second strophe.[114] Lorenz argues for their equivalence under the banner of opposite symmetry, but the striking difference in musical weight and affect between the sections (ponderous and static as opposed to rapturous and kinetic) resists any attempt to equate them except in a completely abstract manner.[115]

In most cases, periods in strophic form are readily apparent to the listener, as is the case in the prelude to *Das Rheingold*, which is immediately understandable as a theme and four variations (plus coda). Likewise *Sf.*II.P.10, the Woodbird's song, is clearly in two strophes, although the first of these is purely orchestral as Siegfried has yet to be able to understand its song.

Bogen Forms. By the term Bogen, or arch, Lorenz means simply a ternary form. There are five types possible: simple, expanded, perfect, double, or supporting. Each of these, like the strophic forms discussed above, may be varied timbrally, rhythmically, or melodically; enlarged through the addition of introductions or codas; or enriched through free or opposite symmetry.

The simple Bogen—an A–B–A structure—forms the basis of thirteen of the thirty-seven periods which are in Bogen form. Several of these are moments of leitmotivic genesis, such as that of the Walhalla motive in *Rh.*P.4. There Fricka's anxious awakening of Wotan is framed by twin statements of the motive in question, at first only orchestrally, but supplemented on its repetition by Wotan's greeting to the castle: "Vollendet das ewige Werk!" The first occurrence of the Logemotiv (*Rh.*P.9) is similarly constructed; there it is the Walhalla motive which forms the middle section (*Mittelsatz*; here-

114. And the second strophe, like several others of Lorenz's simple forms, contains a smaller other form (here a Bogen) which, logically, would make the period's form complex rather than simple. Lorenz remarks that this may happen occasionally; see *Geheimnis* I: 160.

115. As is shown in figure 4.3, the period concludes with a 26-mm. coda which serves to balance the 29-mm. introduction to P.12 as a whole; see *Geheimnis* I: 134.

after "MS") of the period.[116] More complex is the period devoted to the establishment of the Friedensmelodie and the Weltenhortthema (*Sf*.III.P.13). The first section of the period (*Hauptsatz*; HS) begins with the E-major statement of the theme (also used in the *Siegfried Idyll*) and concludes with its restatement in E minor ("Ewig war ich"). The reprise (hereafter "Rp") begins with its transfiguring repetition in E major ("Ewig licht") and concludes with a full, linking cadence in that key. Between these two points, however, there are not one but two middle sections. The first, the MS proper, marks the first occurrence of the Weltenhortthema ("O Siegfried! / Herrlicher! / Hort der Welt!"). It is followed by what Lorenz calls a varied reprise or development of the MS. This is the passage between mm. 1515–39 where Brünnhilde compares her being to the reflection of a face in the stream. This kind of variation of, or divergence from, the norm of his formal types is typical of Lorenz's technique in practice.[117]

The expanded Bogen form is one in which the outer sections are multithematic. The themes of the HS recur in the Rp in the same order as they were first presented. In this they recall the expanded *Liedform* of the classical and romantic eras, which many writers have seen as the basis of the sonata form.[118] The expanded Bogen accounts for nine of the thirty-seven periods in Bogen form. The beginning of Sieglinde's narrative about the provenance of the sword in the tree is a good example of this formal type (*Wk*.I.P.12.A.a). After a twenty-nine measure introduction, the Bogen proper begins with the tale itself ("Der Männer Sippe"). The HS opens with recitative-like declamation over sustained chords and concludes with the E-major statement of the Walhalla motive identifying Wotan as the mysterious stranger at her wedding feast.[119] The Rp begins similarly, both musically and textually, at "[Der] Männer Alle / so kühn sie sich mühten," and ends with another E-major statement of the Walhalla motive as Sieglinde links Siegmund with the one chosen to win the Sword. Figure 4.4 shows Lorenz's analysis of the principal section of the period.

If the themes of the HS are repeated in mirrored fashion in the Rp, Lorenz refers to this as a perfect (*vollkommene*) Bogen form. This is the reverse of

---

116. This period is complicated by two transitional sections which frame the MS (mm. 1206–24 and 1237–74); see *Geheimnis* I: 94–95. This analysis is problematic, as are many of the *Rheingold* analyses.

117. And would be understood by Lorenz as an instance where the essential form (understood as a Gestalt quality) is still seen to be applicable even in the face of variations upon its appearance.

118. There has long been debate as to whether the sonata form is in essence a two- or three-part form. Lorenz is of the opinion that it is a two-part form, essentially like the Reprisenbar; see below, p. 134. For a discussion of this issue in nineteenth-century theory, see Moyer, "Concepts of Musical Form in the Nineteenth Century."

119. The 29-mm. introduction is that which parallels the coda to P.12 as a whole, which was discussed above in note 112.

Chordal accompaniment		e	8 ⎤ HS 22mm.
Walhalla motive		E-f#	14 ⎦
Melody		E	9 ⎤
Development of Schwertmotiv		E-C	14 ⎥ MS 27mm.
Melody		E	4 ⎦
Chordal accompaniment	⎡enriched by Schwertmotiv	E-a	10 ⎤ HS 18mm.
Walhalla motive	⎣		⎦

Figure 4.4. *Wk.I.P.12.A.a* (principal section).

the usual classical practice by which themes are recapitulated in the order in which they first occur. It is unclear why this form should be any more "perfect" than any other, however, apart from the fact that it is more symmetrical. Lorenz does refer to the suggestion by the art historian Jakob Burckhardt that this form (which the latter calls "pediment form" [*Giebelform*]) originated in certain Greek tragedies which contain a culminating scene in the middle. Lorenz cites Burkhardt's opinion that

> [s]uch things no eye has seen, nor ear heard, but nevertheless they are true; there are things which are not yet clear to us at present, but which reveal to us the supreme artistic ability of the poet.[120]

The perfection of this type of Bogen seems to reside more in Lorenz's fetishization of total symmetry rather than in anything inherent in the form itself. Indeed, perfect Bogen, as Lorenz himself notes, are often difficult to perceive on the part of the listener.

One such Bogen occurs at the death of Fafner in the second act of *Siegfried* (*Sf.*II.P.9). Lorenz makes the symmetry apparent by lining up the parallel sections through differing degrees of indentation (fig. 4.5).

An aspect of Lorenz's analysis which should be already apparent is the subjectivity of his motivic choices; here, the Fafner motives and the Vernichtungsrhythmus are found in both the sections numbered 1 and 3 but Lorenz chooses to make first one, then the other, the principal motive of the section in order that the "perfect" symmetry be apparent. The perfection rests more in Lorenz's description of the sections than in the actual musical content of the period.

The double and supporting Bogen forms are uncommon. The double Bogen is presented by Lorenz as a combination of the expanded and perfect Bogen forms. An internal, expanded Bogen is surrounded by two additional HS, with its themes also ordered in parallel.

---

120. Jacob Burckhardt, *Griechische Kulturgeschichte*, vol. 3, 241; cited in *Geheimnis* I: 137. [Lorenz does not specify which edition he uses; one modern edition is Burckhardt, *Griechische Kulturgeschichte* (Darmstadt: Wissenschaftliche Buchgesellschaft, 1962), vol. 3, 220.]

1. Fafner-tritone (tuba) and Fafnermotiv accompanied by
   Vernichtungsrhythmus and portion of Waldknabenruf   11 ⎤
2. Fluchmotiv, followed by Siegfriedmotiv   9 ⎬ HS 28 mm.
3. Vernichtungsrhythmus with Fafnermotiv and bit of Waldknaben   8 ⎦
   Riesenmotiv   6 ⎤
   Fafnermotiv with Ringmotiv   5 ⎬ MS 16 mm.
   Drachenmotiv with Schwertwartmotiv, cadencing in A-flat   5 ⎦
3. Vernichtungsrhythmus with Fafnermotiv and bit of Waldknaben   9 ⎤
2. Fluchmotiv, followed by Siegfriedmotiv   13 ⎬ HS 28 mm.
1. Fafner-tritone and Fafnermotiv (w/o above accompaniment; Fafner   6 ⎦
   no longer lives)

Figure 4.5. *Sf*.II.P.9.

Lorenz finds only one of these hybrid forms in the work: the first period of *Siegfried* I. Here the outer HS contain the Schmiedemotiv followed by Mime's lament "Zwangvolle Plage! Müh' ohne Zweck!" The inner HS are rather different, however, as the second contains prominent occurrences of the Ringmotiv and the motivic combination known as Nibelungentriumph. The MS is a short Bar form out of the Drachenmotiv (see figure 4.6). Certainly, each of the sections coheres as such, so that the overall form—or at least its sectional construction—is easily recognized. One curious aspect of Lorenz's analyses, and one to which we will return, is the tendency for the major division points in the form to be quite persuasive, but the contents of the sections rather more problematic. Many times the material between the formal divisions seems almost irrelevant—or at least of less consequence—to Lorenz; it is enough that it "fill up" the required number of measures in his formal scheme. This results in a strangely empty kind of formal analysis.

The supporting Bogen form is something of a misnomer, as it is in fact only the second half of a form. It is simply the repetition of the descent of another Bogen; this may occur either immediately or after some time. Lorenz likens this quasi-form to the flying buttresses of a cathedral, and suggests that it serves to strengthen the entire structure.[121] There are two such forms in the entire *Ring*, both between poetic-musical periods. The first forms the transition between *Wk*.I.P.1 and 2, and (loosely) repeats the conclusion of P.1. The other case, the *Rückleitung* to *Sf*.II.P.4., acts as a supporting Bogen to *Sf*.II.P.1. This instance is, in fact, rather convincing, both musically and

---

121. Here Lorenz takes his architectural metaphor a step too far. To my knowledge, no other writer constructs such elaborate sounding castles—even with flying buttresses!

Schmiedemotiv (hammer alone)		8 ⎤	
"Zwangvolle Plage, Müh' ohne Zweck"		2 ⎥	outer
Schmiedemotiv with vocal part, breaking off		9 ⎥	HS 22 mm.
Echo of Schmiedemotiv		3 ⎦	
Sinnensmotiv		6 ⎤	
Asc. 4th of Schwert with Riesenmotiv (third measure)		8 ⎥	
Frohnmotiv (enlivened by Schmiedemotiv)		4 ⎥	inner
Schwertmotiv w. strange conclusion (accompanied by Schmiedemotiv), breaking off		4 ⎥	HS 27 mm.
Pause		1 ⎥	
Sinnensmotiv		4 ⎦	
Drachenmotiv, augmented.	Bar form	23	MS 23 mm.
New conclusion (Abg.)	(7+6+10)		
Sinnensmotiv	together	7 ⎤	
Asc. 4th of Schwert and variant of Drachenmotiv			
Ringmotiv (inverted Frohnmotiv in bass)		5 ⎥	
Schwertmotiv, coming to a stop in the Nibelungentriumphmotiv and breaking off		9 ⎥	inner
Pause		1 ⎥	HS 25 mm.
Entsagungsmotiv forming a cadence		3 ⎦	
Schmiedemotiv (hammer alone)		8 ⎤	
"Zwangvolle Plage, Müh' ohne Zweck"		2 ⎥	outer
Schmiedemotiv with vocal part, breaking off		9 ⎥	HS 20 mm.
Pause		1 ⎦	

Figure 4.6. *Sf.*I.P.1.

dramatically. The supporting Bogen serves to round off the scene between Wotan and Alberich; here, as in the latter half of P.1, Alberich observes the movements of the Wanderer—then, his arrival, and now, his departure. Musically, the parallelism is obvious: the Rittmotiv, followed by several statements of the Fluchmotiv. Figure 4.7 presents Lorenz's analysis of *Sf.*II.P.1 (an expanded Bogen) and its supporting Bogen.

Rondo/Refrain Forms. The basis of these forms is identical: a recurring principal section (HS) whose repetitions are separated by at least two episodes (*Zwischensätzen*; ZS). The difference lies in the relative length and weight of the HS in relation to the ZS. In a refrain form, the HS is generally shorter and often of less consequence than the material in the ZS; about this relative relationship Lorenz writes:

> If the proportions of a rondo are altered so that the HS is relatively small, the form becomes that of a song with refrain; the old choruses [*Kehrreime*] were generally performed not only at the end of the verses but also at the beginning of the entire poem.[122]

---

122. *Geheimnis* I: 101.

Fafnermotiv with Fafner-tritone (tuba)		⎤ HS 16 mm.
Vernichtungsrhythmus		⎦
Chord progression "Naht schon des Wurmes Würger"	7⎤	
Rittmotiv combined with Götternot	19⎮	HS 32 mm.
Chord progression "Naht schon des Wurmes Würger"	6⎦	
Fafnermotiv with Fafner-tritone, framed by two Fluchmotive (variation)		⎤ HS 22 mm.
Vernichtungsrhythmus		⎦

Figure 4.7a. *Sf*.II.P.1.

Rittmotiv, combined with ⎡ Wandererakkorde ⎤ Substitution for Götternotmotiv 16 mm.
                      ⎣ Scheidegesang ⎦

Fluchmotiv, thrice	12 mm.
Vernichtungsrhythmus	4 mm.
Fafnermotiv and Fafner-tritone with Abg. of first Drachenmotiv variant	18 mm.

Figure 4.7b. *Sf*.II. **Rückleitung nach P.4–supporting Bogen to 6.a.**

In either of these forms, one or more of the ZS may also recur. Lorenz notes that both tend to be complex rather than simple forms (i.e., with other forms forming the ZS), as they can appear rather simplistic if the "weight" (*Große*) of the recurring motives is not impressive enough. There are therefore only two simple rondos and four simple refrain forms in the entire *Ring*.

Of the rondos, one marks the establishment of Gutrune's Gruß- and Liebesmotive (*Gd*.I.P.8) and the other occurs at Wotan's stormy arrival on the Valkyrie rock at the beginning of the third act of *Die Walküre* (P.4). The first of these is the more convincing.[123] Here the motives which accompany Gutrune's initial words and actions (her greeting and the proffered drinking horn) recur throughout the scene, punctuating Siegfried's toast to Brünnhilde, his outburst to Gutrune, and his request for her hand. A condensed version of Lorenz's analysis is presented as fig. 4.8:

A good example of a refrain form occurs as Donner dispels the mists at the end of *Das Rheingold* (P.18). Here the two-measure refrain ("Heda! Heda! Hedo!") is broken up by short (two or four measures) vocal strophes over running sixteenth-note figures. Another, more complex example is Siegmund's monologue in *Die Walküre* (I.P.11), where the Schwert motive acts as an obvious refrain throughout the section, and divides it into eight almost identical strophes. The refrain form is preceded by a long introduction (mm. 790–848), where, to the accompaniment of the Hunding motive, Siegmund tells of his promised sword.

---

123. In the second, the similarity of the HS rests more in the fact that they are all Valkyrie ensembles, while the ZS are all Wotan's responses.

Introduction—Gutrune's Gruß	4 mm.
HS Gutrune's Gruß and Liebesmotiv	15 mm.
I. ZS Siegfried's toast, concluding	17 mm.
with Zaubertrugmotiv	
HS Gutrune's Gruß and Liebesmotiv (reordered)	11 mm.
II. ZS Siegfried's passion. New theme	16 mm.
concluding with Hagenmotiv and	
Liebesschlinge	
HS Gutrune's Gruß and Liebesmotiv	10 mm.
III. ZS Siegfried's suit. Freundschaftsthema,	14 mm.
concluding with Hagenmotiv	
HS. Gutrune's Gruß and Liebesmotiv (developed)	10 mm.

Figure 4.8. *Gd.*I.P.8.

Bar Forms. While Lorenz was not the first, he is perhaps the best-known analyst to associate Bar form and Wagner's music.[124] In Lorenz's opinion, the Bar was a particularly Germanic form ("dem deutschen Empfinden besonders vertraut") since he held that it originated with the medieval Meistersingers.[125] A Bar contains two initial strophes, called Stollen, which are followed by a contrasting section known as the Abgesang.[126] It is first described by Wagner in *Die Meistersinger* as Kothner reads the Tabulatur to Walther and the assembled masters and apprentices:

---

124. Curt Mey discusses Wagner's use of Bar form in *Die Meistersinger* in his *Die Meistergesang in Geschichte und Kunst: Ausführliche Erklärung der Tabulaturen, Schulregeln, Sitten und Gebräuche der Meistersinger, sowie deren Anwendung in Richard Wagners 'Die Meistersinger von Nürnberg'* (Leipzig: Hermann Seemann, 1901), esp. 340–54, 363–75.

125. That is, the *name* originated with them. Lorenz himself notes that this tripartite form was also used by the Greeks (strophe, antistrophe, and epode) and in the Italian *ballata* (due piedi, una volta); see *Geheimnis* III: 185.

126. So Lorenz argues, following Wagner's own explication of the form in *Die Meistersinger*. Many authors (such as Curt Mey, cited above) have suggested that Wagner misread his late seventeenth-century source on the Meistersinger and their rules, J.C. Wagenseil's Nuremberg Chronicle (*Johann Christof Wagenseils Buch von der Meister-Singer holdseligen Kunst*, 1697), since to the historical Meistersinger, the Stollen-Stollen-Abgesang construction was known as a *Gesätz*, not a Bar. The term "Bar" represented the poem as a whole, which consisted of several *Gesätze*. In fact, Wagner was aware of this, as he appended to the Erstschrift of his 1861 prose draft four pages of notes on Wagenseil's book. In these notes he correctly differentiates between a Bar and a *Gesätz*; see Richard Wagner, *Entwürfe zu 'Die Meistersinger von Nürnberg', 'Tristan und Isolde', 'Parsifal'*, ed. Hans von Wolzogen (Leipzig: C.F.W. Siegel, 1907), 94–95. Whether Wagner consciously made the change, or simply got muddled on the details cannot be determined; certainly Wagner's Tabulatur, as read by Kothner, is contradictory. On the one hand, "ein jedes Meistergesanges Bar" is said to present a balance of different "Gesätze," each of which consists of two Stollen and an Abgesang. On the other hand, each "Meisterlied" is then described as containing several Bars (*mehre Baren*) each similarly balanced. When Sachs explains the form to Walther in the third act, the Stollen-Stollen-Abgesang combination is simply a Bar (Sachs: "Jetzt richtet mir noch einen zweiten Bar.") The discrepancy is never alluded to by Lorenz, who simply substitutes "Bar" for "Gesätz" without comment.

Ein Gesätz besteht aus zweenen Stollen,
die gleiche Melodei haben sollen;
der Stoll aus etlicher Vers' Gebänd,
der Vers hat seinen Reim am End.
Darauf erfolgt der Abgesang,
der sei auch etlich Verse lang,
und hab sein' besondre Melodei,
als nicht im Stollen zu finden sei.

[A section consists of two Stollen which shall have the same melody; the Stollen is a group of so many lines, the line has its rhyme at the end. Thereupon follows the Abgesang which is also to be so many lines long and have its own special melody which is not to occur in the Stollen.][127]

In the third act, Wagner (via Sachs) compares the Stollen to man and wife and then equates the Abgesang with their children:

Ob Euch gelang,
ein rechtes Paar zu finden,
das zeigt sich an den Kindern;
den Stollen ähnlich, doch nicht gleich,
an eignen Reim und Tönen reich;
daß man's recht schlank und selbstig find,
das freut die Eltern an dem Kind;
und Euren Stollen gibt's den Schluß,
daß nichts davon abfallen muß.

[If you've succeeded in finding a true pair, it will show in the children. Similar to the Stollen, but not exactly the same, rich in its own rhymes and tones; that people find it right slender and self-sufficient—that makes the parents proud of the child: and it will form a conclusion to your Stollen so that nothing shall fall out of place.]

Lorenz takes considerable trouble to introduce this form to the reader, since, to him, it was a form especially beloved by Wagner.[128] He suggests that Wagner's frequent recourse to Bar form is a direct result of the dynamic, open-ended character of the form itself, which makes it particularly appropriate for use in drama:[129]

The abundance of such shapings in Wagner is enormous; he especially loves this form since it is better suited for the dramatic momentum [*dramatischen Schwung*]

127. Translation from the booklet included in the Georg Solti/Vienna Philharmonic recording of the opera (Decca 417 497–2). The translator is not listed. I have substituted "Stollen" for "stanza" and "Abgesang" for "aftersong." All future translations will be taken from this source without comment.

128. *Geheimnis* I: 296. Of the 209 periods and transitional sections in the *Ring*, approximately 58 are in some type of Bar form: 28% of the total.

129. The form is also ambiguous in another way: it is binary in terms of contents (the Abgesang differs from the Stollen) but ternary according to structure (there are three sections).

than any other. The Abgesang always implies an intensification over the Stollen, an intensification [*Steigerung*] which appears at its conclusion; the dramatic life is thus better renewed by this form than if the intensification fell in the middle.[130]

The forward-propelling nature of the Abgesang makes the form convey a sense of continuity. Its effect is thus different from that of the Bogen, a more self-contained, closed form.

As is typical of Lorenz's approach, he defers entirely to Wagner's own "ästhetischen Vorlesung" on the Bar form, as presented in *Die Meistersinger*. Lorenz discusses each of Walther's four songs in Bar form, and extrapolates general principles from their musical settings. While "Am stillen Herd" is straightforward Bar (its sections are separated by interjections from the masters), Walther's trial song ("Fanget an!") is more complicated, as each Stollen contains two themes. In the first Stollen, the first theme occupies 40 mm. (from "Fanget an" to "süsse Lenzeslied") and the second, 19 mm. ("In einer Dornenhecken"). Beckmesser interrupts Walther in the midst of the second Stollen after the seeming close of the first theme. He is unable to perceive that Walther's Stollen are multithematic, and (in his text within the ensemble) refers to the second theme a "Flickgesang zwischen den Stollen." At Sachs' urging, Walther resumes his Bar with the second theme ("Aus finst'rer Dornenhecken") after a 214–measure interruption.[131] From this case, Lorenz concludes that it is permissible for the Stollen of a Wagnerian Bar to be multithematic.

The second Stollen of the Traumlied, composed by Walther on Sachs' prompting at the beginning of the third act, concludes in the dominant of the tonic key of C major; "Ihr schloßet nicht im gleichen Ton: / das macht den Meistern Pein," Sachs interjects. Just as he permits Walther his licence ("doch nimmt Hans Sachs die Lehr davon, / im Lenz wohl müßt es so sein") so too does Lorenz. The latter even extends the principle and allows the second Stollen to *begin* in a different key:

> That the Stollen "don't close in the same key" becomes the rule. They often do not even begin in the same key, but, on the contrary, the second Stollen often modulates right at the beginning.[132]

To back up this point, Lorenz provides examples of Wagnerian Bars in the *Ring* in which the second Stollen is found at every interval removed from the tonic except for the tritone.

---

130. *Geheimnis* I: 145.

131. In a note, Lorenz castigates the numerous writers (he cites Albert Heintz in particular) who have misunderstood Walther's song, and seen it "auf dem Standpunkt Beckmessers." *Geheimnis* I: 74n; "Fanget an!" is discussed in much greater detail in *Geheimnis* III: 73–79, where it occupies (with interruption) the entire penultimate period (P.18) of the first act.

132. *Geheimnis* I: 148.

When Walther sings his mastersong for the assembled masters and people on the Festwiese, he does not simply repeat the Traumlied from earlier in the act; Wagner rightly felt that this would have been anticlimactic for the audience as they would be unable to share the stage audience's delight in the song if they had already heard it.[133] Wagner thus extends all three sections of the Traumlied (although their beginnings remain the same) and leaves it at a single stanza. While the first Stollen remains largely in the tonic key, the second is tonally far-reaching, and passes through G major and B major before concluding in the former key. The result, as Lorenz notes, is that only the first six measures have the "gleiche Melodei" required by the rule of the Tabulatur; still, he ventures, they are "similar enough."[134] This dissimilar "similarity" becomes something of a third principle for the Lorenzian bar, even though Lorenz is less explicit in its endorsement than with the other two. His analyses—which often have quite different Stollen—implicitly attest to his belief in this notion, however. Thus Lorenz is quite liberal in what he recognizes as a Bar form: Stollen with more than a single theme, a second Stollen varied in key, and Stollen which are not absolutely identical but varied.

Lorenz's logic is circular: because Walther is a Meistersinger and sings in Bar form, what he sings, no matter how daring in its departures from the norm, is an acceptable Bar because he is a Meistersinger. Walther becomes an allegory of Wagner himself: Wagner's licences are worthy of elevation into a general principle because he is a *Meisterkomponist*. Indeed, Lorenz shows how these principles are operative in Wotan's Bar "Der Augen leuchtendes Paar,"[135] and concludes from this that Wagner instinctively wrote in Bar form long before he wrote *Die Meistersinger*. These forms are the "most beautiful blooms of his spirit."[136]

It is Lorenz's opinion that Wagner's treatment of Bar form in the *Ring* is even more free than in *Meistersinger*.[137] For example, he deems it irrelevant whether the form is based on a pure melodic line (as in the *Walküre* example) or on Wagnerian melos (which may be a combination of the vocal

---

133. Barry Millington, *Wagner*, rev. ed. (London: Dent, 1992), 249, 251.
134. *Geheimnis* I: 146.
135. This 35–mm. Bar (8+8+19) forms part of the MS of Wk.III.P.13, a complex, composite period in Bogen form. Each Stollen has two themes (Schlummermotiv, Kampflustrhythmus). The second Stollen has several melodic alterations ("strahlendes" a third higher than "leuchtendes," "geglänzt" goes up while "gekos't" descends, etc.) and ends, Lorenz states, in the dominant key area. The issue of key is debatable; here Lorenz suggests that the tonic is E minor and that the Bar thus begins in the Sp (relative major of the subdominant), but when he treats the period as a whole later, the tonic is said to be E major. It makes a difference in Riemann's notation. The analysis of the whole period (*Geheimnis* I: 210–16) was published in 1923 in *Hellweg* as "Wotans Abschied und Feuerzauber: Eine Formuntersuchung." Lorenz refers to this Bar as "one of the most regular Bars in the *Ring*," Geheimnis I: 148.
136. Ibid., 147.
137. Ibid., 148.

line and the symphonic web of motives), or just the pure orchestral speech of the symphonic web itself. Likewise, the Bars may show the same type of variation found in his other forms: enrichment, variation, and motivic substitution resulting in free, or even opposite, symmetry.[138] As a rule, Lorenz writes, the second Stollen "often results in manifold intensification and new tension instead of mere repetition."[139]

Although the Abgesang is said to have its "own special melody," it must nevertheless develop logically out of the preceding Stollen—like a child from its parents, as Sachs suggests. That is, it must have some ties with the Stollen so that the audience perceives that the two halves of a Bar are indeed connected, yet must still be powerful enough to be seen as an intensification, as the climax of the form.[140] Lorenz refers to the shaping of the Abgesang as a "musikalisches Urphänomen," and concludes that "in the shaping of such viable, tiny Abgesänge, the musical potency of the creator is revealed."[141] The intensification of the Abgesang is achieved by musical means (such as the entrance of a new motive), scenic means (a significant stage action, such as the arrival of a character), or both. Lorenz gives the example of the Abgesang of *Gd*.III.P.1 (it begins at m. 150): musically, the Abgesang is marked by the first use of the Nixenspott motive and scenically by Siegfried's entrance.

Lorenz is flexible about the proper size of the Abgesang. To him, the essence of the Bar rests in the "emotional discharge [*Gefühlsentladung*], a necessity of nature, in the Abgesang, after the two-fold appearance of the Stollen."[142] This discharge may occur quickly or slowly, so that there is no "normal" length for an Abgesang.

> Just as the change of feeling can occur after two normal strophes of average length, so it can follow in even the tiniest musical shoots. . . . It can also just as well follow a gigantic, cumulative double intensification of great expanse. The essence of the Bar does not reside in the actual length, but in the distribution of its powers. Whether the Bar occupies 3 measures or 1000 is irrelevant; it is always a regular Bar if the aforementioned essence is fulfilled: a double appearance as against a single balancing occurrence of equal weight.[143]

Occasionally this essence is not fulfilled, and the resulting Bars are misshapen creations with more than two Stollen.[144]

---

138. Lorenz notes that if the Stollen of a Bar shows opposite symmetry, the resulting form is that of the Hegelian dialectic.

139. *Geheimnis* I: 149.

140. Lorenz suggests that the essence of Bar form rests in the fact that the "seeds of the Stollen bear new fruit in the Abgesang." Ibid., 103.

141. Ibid.

142. Ibid., 149.

143. Ibid. This idea, which Lorenz elsewhere refers to as the *Relativitätsprinzip*, was discussed in chapter 3.

144. Curiously, the three instances of this cited by Lorenz all occur in the third act of *Die*

Lorenz discusses twenty-four simple Bar forms in the *Ring*, many of which are entirely plausible. *Wk*.II.P.3 is a good example. It begins with a 31–measure introduction, which functions as an accompanied recitative introduction to the Bar proper (beginning at "O was klag ich / um Ehe und Eid"). Two 16-measure Stollen (of which the second ends "nicht im gleichen Ton") are followed by a 24–measure Abgesang and a 6-measure coda. The Bar begins and ends in the same key.[145] Other equally obvious Bars are *Sf*.I.P.8 and the introduction to *Gd*.I.P.14.

If material from the Stollen is repeated in the Abgesang, this forms a special type of Bar, known as a Reprisenbar.[146] Here, the Abgesang is made up of two parts: the Abgesang proper, and a reprise (Rp) of part of the Stollen. This is a particularly good way to add to the intensification of the Abgesang. There is only one period with the form of a simple Reprisenbar: a portion of the orchestral transition between the scenes in the first act of

---

Walküre: in *Wk*.III.P.6, the Abg. ("Was sonst du war'st") occurs after six St.; the first HS of Brünnhilde's justification (P.9) has three St. ("War es so schmählich," "War es so niedrig," "War es so ehrlos") before the Abg. ("O sag': Vater"); the introduction to P.11 has two St. pairs before the Abg. He might profitably have invoked this notion in *Gd*.II.P.14.D as well, which he includes among the half-unified, successive periods; see *Geheimnis* I: 256.

145. Enharmonically, A-flat minor, Lorenz argues (*Geheimnis* I: 30n). He suggests that the resulting tonal relationship between Fricka and Wotan (A-flat minor: D-flat major, or °D:T) symbolizes their personal relationship as well: "How poorly the minor dominant relates to the major tonic is recognized by every harmony textbook."

Lorenz's analysis is confirmed in its essence by Anthony Newcomb in "The Birth of Music Out of the Spirit of Drama: An Essay in Wagnerian Formal Analysis," *19th-Century Music* 5 (1981): 55–56. Newcomb is taking issue with an analysis by Carl Dahlhaus (*Richard Wagner's Music Dramas*) but does not mention Lorenz at all here.

The Bar forming Fricka's Klage is framed by two periods also in Bar form. These periods, however, show a rare lack of formal clarity, which in Lorenz's opinion is responsible for some people finding the scene tiresome. Still, Lorenz argues that one can find the framework of a symphonic form in the most unsymphonic places "only with an author's imagination, which does not shy away from conjecture" (and he does not). See *Geheimnis* I: 157–58.

146. Lorenz notes that if one considers the Stollen together as a single part, the Reprisenbar becomes similar in essence to the sonata form. Because Lorenz saw his forms as absolute, essential entities, he seems to suggest that the sonata form *originated* in the Reprisenbar when he argues that this fact ought to dissuade conductors from omitting the exposition repeat (which would result in a Bogen form, rather than a Reprisenbar).

Interestingly, Lorenz cites Wilhelm Scherer, a literary scholar, in support of his position. In his *Geschichte der deutschen Literatur* (1883), Scherer concludes his discussion of the Meistersinger Bar with the comment that "the whole construction coincided in a remarkable manner with the form of our sonata" (*History of German Literature*, trans. Mrs. F.C. Conybeare, ed. F. Max Müller [New York: Haskell House, 1971], 209; trans. first pub., 1906). *Geheimnis* I: 107–108.

Although when he wrote *Geheimnis* I Lorenz believed that no other musician had made this comparison, Hugo Riemann had already written that "the development in a sonata movement is thus, first of all, an Abgesang," *Große Kompositionslehre*, 2 vols (Berlin and Stuttgart: Spemann, 1902), 1: 465. Lorenz rectifies this omission in a footnote in "Worauf beruht die bekannte Wirkung der Durchführung im 1. Eroicasatze," 167 n.30.

Götterdämmerung;[147] here it is Brünnhilde's motive from the Stollen which recurs halfway through the Abgesang (fig. 4.9).

Potentiated Forms

When a single form occupies a period of considerable expanse, it is necessary, according to Lorenz, that its parts be rationally ordered as well, so that the feeling not become shapeless.[148] If these parts are themselves arranged according to the same formal type as that of the whole, Lorenz refers to this as a potentiation of form. He does note, however, that these forms occur "naturally not with pedantic correctness."[149] A form may still be said to be potentiated even if occasionally another small form is included.[150] It is possible for any form to be potentiated, with the single, necessary, exception of strophic form. Twenty-six periods and transitional sections in the *Ring* demonstrate a potentiation of form.

Of these twenty-six, eight are potentiated Bogen forms. One reasonably convincing example is found in the multi-section period forming the conclusion to the first act of *Die Walküre* (fig. 4.10). Here, though, the themes are reversed in the Rp from the order in which they first appeared in the HS so that the Rp is less clear than it might be. Dramatically, as well, the return implied in a Rp is not present; rather, the drama continues its relentless forward drive. In Lorenz's defense, however, the internal Bogens he proposes are unassailable, and the entire period is one of the most regularly tonal in the entire *Ring*. It not only begins and ends in G, but also returns to this area throughout the period, often as a tonic pedal.

The smaller Bogen structures that comprise a potentiated Bogen may be of any type. Thus, the MS Bogen of *Rh*.P.1 is a perfect Bogen (Alberich's wooing of Woglinde and Wellgunde), while its framing Bogen are made up of various smaller, simple Bogen.

Curiously, the four examples of potentiated rondo or refrain forms (two of each) given by Lorenz all occur in *Siegfried*. This is perhaps due to the lighter, more conventionally melodic (song-like) texture of the third opera of the tetralogy. There is actually only one potentiated rondo, which occurs during the Riddle scene between the Wanderer and Mime (*Sf*.I.P.6/7). Lorenz divides the scene into two poetic-musical periods on the basis of tonality, but treats them as one unit in terms of form. This is a good example of the

---

147. The section from the end of Hagen's Wacht (m. 923) to the raising of the curtain on Brünnhilde's rock (m. 1020) is divided by Lorenz into a postlude to the preceding period (P.11), a transition, and prelude to the coming period. This curious articulation will be discussed in chapter 5.

148. *Geheimnis* I: 160.

149. *Geheimnis* III: 187.

150. It seems as if Lorenz would extend this dictum elsewhere; for example, when smaller forms are occasionally found in simple forms.

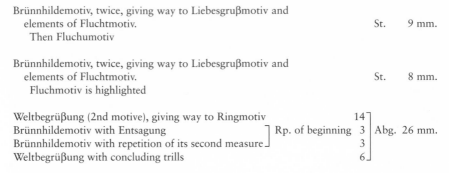

Brünnhildemotiv, twice, giving way to Liebesgruβmotiv and
   elements of Fluchtmotiv.   St.   9 mm.
      Then Fluchumotiv

Brünnhildemotiv, twice, giving way to Liebesgruβmotiv and
   elements of Fluchtmotiv.   St.   8 mm.
      Fluchmotiv is highlighted

Weltbegrüβung (2nd motive), giving way to Ringmotiv		14	
Brünnhildemotiv with Entsagung	⎤ Rp. of beginning	3	Abg. 26 mm.
Brünnhildemotiv with repetition of its second measure	⎦	3	
Weltbegrüβung with concluding trills		6	

Figure 4.9. *Gd*.I.Vorspiel zu P.12.

tension between tonal and melodic formal structure often inherent in Lorenz's analyses. To get round the necessity to have a tonal poetic-musical period, Lorenz is obliged to refer to the last outer HS, which cadences in C, as the final, "rounding-off section" of P.7. The broad outline of the rondo is illustrated in figure 4.11.

The outer HS, which is progressively shortened at each recurrence, is dominated by the Wanderer chords, although other motives also recur (particularly the chain of thirds accompanying the line "Mein Kopf ist dein").[151] The two MS are both in rondo form, articulated principally by the question and answer format of the scene. The music to which the questions are set (Schmiedemotiv, plus other motives such as Sinnen and Vertrag) recurs as an inner HS between the answers to the questions, which form the ZS of these smaller rondos.[152]

A potentiated refrain form will have an *Überrefrain* which punctuates the entire period and an *Unterrefrain* which punctuates the ZS of the larger refrain form; thus the ZS will also be in refrain form. In *Sf*.I.P.11, the *Überrefrain* is that which Lorenz refers to as the Nothungphrase ("Nothung! Nothung! / Neidliches Schwert!"), followed by a seven-beat, song-like

---

151. Lorenz argues that the Wanderer chords at the close of the I.MS recall the beginning of the scene, and thus indicate the beginning of the repetition of the outer HS as well as the conclusion of the MS; they have a double function.

152. It is instructive to compare Lorenz's analysis with the analyses of this scene offered by Reinhold Brinkmann, Patrick McCreless, and Anthony Newcomb. McCreless and Newcomb discuss the large-scale thematic recurrence found in the scene, using the concepts of "refrain" and "ritornello" respectively. If all four analyses are superimposed, it is striking how at any given time at least one is in agreement with Lorenz's. See Reinhold Brinkmann, "'Drei der Fragen stell' ich mir frei': Zur Wanderer-Szene im 1. Akt von Wagners 'Siegfried'," *Jahrbuch des Staatlichen Instituts für Musikforschung Preußischer Kulturbesitz* 5 (1972), 120–62; McCreless, *Wagner's "Siegfried"*, 126–35; Anthony Newcomb, "Those Images That Yet Fresh Images Beget," *Journal of Musicology* 2 (1983): 242–44; and Newcomb, "*Ritornello Ritornato*: A Variety of Wagnerian Refrain Form," in *Analyzing Opera: Verdi and Wagner*, 211–18.

Ahnen II	2	] shorter section	HS 10 ⌉	
Ahnen II & I	8			
Walhall			MS 10	Bogen HS 40 mm.
Ahnen II, with Freiamotiv				
Liebesweben, Ahnen I		] longer section	HS 20 ⌋	
Fluchtmotiv, 4 x			HS 7 ⌉	
Lauschakkorde			MS 6	Bogen MS 23 mm.
Fluchtmotiv, 5 x, and Liebesmotiv			HS 10 ⌋	
Walhall, introduced by Wälsungen and		] longer section	HS 21 ⌉	
Schwertmotiv				
Recall of Siegmund's Narration			MS 16	Bogen Rp 46 mm.
Ahnen II				
Walhall, introduced by Kampflustrhythmen		] shorter section	HS 9 ⌋	

Coda (figuration from Fluchtmotiv)   10 mm.

Figure 4.10. Wk.I.P.12.C.a.

phrase.[153] The *Unterrefrain* ("Hoho! Hoho! Hohei!") is alternately divided up by strophes of Siegfried's Schmelzlied and Mime's "opposing" strophes. The period becomes less and less convincing as it proceeds, and Lorenz is obliged to invoke myriad "variations" and motivic substitutions to make the form work.

A rather different case is *Sf*.III.P.5. Here the *Überrefrain*, Siegfried's "Mein Vöglein schwebte mir fort," alternates with an *Unterrefrain* (the Vaterfreude motive) which may or may not be part of the ZS. In both of these instances, the listener cannot help but be aware of the recurrence of the material which Lorenz labels as the HS of his rondos and refrains. To this extent—perhaps only on an abstract level—Lorenz is justified in his analyses.

With the potentiated Bar form, Lorenz argues that we have reached the "peak of organic-dramatic beauty."[154] Here each Stollen will itself be in Bar form, while the Abgesang may be a single Bar, or several. There is a continual process of intensification throughout the form; as Stollen give way to Abgesänge again and again "so intensification is organically piled upon intensification."[155] The smaller Bars may themselves also be in Bar form, so that a form to the third (or even fourth) power is created. In such potentiated Bars, each intensification builds on the previous one, resulting in "an organism of unbelievable beauty."[156]

---

153. This *Überrefrain* continues throughout the remainder of the act, even though the last three periods are not in refrain form.
154. *Geheimnis* I: 176.
155. Ibid., 239.
156. Ibid., 177.

P.6   Outer HS – 125 mm. (mm. 1289–1413)

                I. MS – 163 mm. (mm. 1414–1584)—Mime questions the Wanderer

        Outer HS – 58 (50) mm. (mm. 1577–1634)

P.7   II. MS – 220 mm. (mm. 1635–1854)—The Wanderer questions Mime

Abrundung   Outer HS – 30 mm. (mm. 1855–84)

Figure 4.11. The Rondo form comprising *Sf*.I.P.6, P.7, and Abrundung.

There are fourteen examples of potentiated Bar forms in the *Ring*, of which two are Reprisenbars.[157] For this latter form, Lorenz opines that the internal sections need not all be in Reprisenbar form, only the larger form must be: "the momentum of the simple Barform generally suffices to potentiate the intensifications."[158] Neither of Lorenz's examples of Reprisenbar (*Sf*.I.P.2; *Rh*.P.17) is at all convincing.

On the other hand, many examples of potentiated Bar form do have a certain logic about them. For instance, there is no question of the validity of the potentiated Bar which accompanies Brünnhilde's awakening (*Sf*.III.P.8). The first large Stollen is entirely orchestral, and the second is almost an exact repetition of the first, except for the addition of Brünnhilde's vocal line ("Heil dir, Sonne!") and some different motivic activity towards the end. The large Abgesang contains two smaller Bars (mm. 1110–16 and mm. 1132–43), the first preceded by a 2-measure introduction, and the second followed by a three-measure conclusion. Only the central fifteen measures, which recall the material of the Abgesänge of the large Stollen, are not part of a smaller Bar structure.[159]

The section of the first act of *Götterdämmerung* known as Hagen's Watch ("Hier sitz ich zur Wacht") is a similarly convincing example (P.11). Here the beginnings of the Stollen are obvious musically; each starts with Hagen's tritone and the Waldknabenruf. Only the endings of the Stollen are somewhat irregular. The first concludes with eight measures not in Bar form (the first half, Alberich's Herrscherruf, is a small Bar, however), while the second ends (after a repetition of the tiny Herrscherruf Bar) with a 5-measure perfect Bogen based on the Zaubertrug motive. Lorenz is then forced to

---

157. If one counts the potentiated Reprisenbar forming *Sf*.III.P.15.C, there are fifteen. The first two sections of the period are composite Bar forms. It seems likely that Lorenz intended these sections to be understood as Stollen and section C as the Abgesang of a large Bar form encompassing the entire period, but he never makes this clear. If this is the case, though, then all of P.15 would in fact be a potentiated Bar.

158. *Geheimnis* I: 186.

159. Such extra material which does not exactly fit into the analysis is found often in Lorenz's analyses (particularly in Abgesänge) and is rarely commented upon.

label the following measure ("mir aber bringt er den [Ring!]") as an *Übergangstakt*, although it clearly belongs, both musically and textually, to the second Stollen. The large Abgesang, however, is unexceptionable. The entire period is dominated by the Vernichtungsrhythmus, which provides another good example of Lorenz's hierarchization of the motives in his periods; here he clearly regards this almost constant rhythmic pulsation as something of a secondary phenomenon, of lesser importance than the other motives which he highlights.

The apotheosis of the potentiated Bar form is found in the Todesverkündigung scene: a Bar to the fourth power. Lorenz divides the scene into three periods (*Wk*.II.P.10–12), all in F-sharp minor, which form the Über-Stollen and Über-Abgesang of the large potentiated Bar.[160] Each of these periods is in turn a potentiated Bar form. While space precludes a detailed account of Lorenz's analysis, several points are worth mentioning. The first Stollen of P.10, like that in Brünnhilde's awakening from *Siegfried*, is entirely orchestral; its repetition is enriched by the addition of the vocal part (here Brünnhilde's call "Siegmund!" overlaps by one measure). It is a perfect example of a potentiated Bar, as may be seen by its first Stollen (ex. 4.6). This period is devoted to introductory matters, and ends with Siegmund's refusal to follow Brünnhilde to Walhalla without Sieglinde.

P.11, the second Über-Stollen, begins like the first, with repetitions of the motivic gesture known as the Schicksalsfrage. Its Stollen are less clear than those of P.10, however, as the middle forms are a combination of Bars and Bogens. It too coheres dramatically—through threats Brünnhilde attempts to convince Siegmund of his impending death, but the period ends with the two still at loggerheads. The Über-Abgesang, P.12, contains Siegmund's despair and Brünnhilde's capitulation. It provides a good example of an Abgesang intensification: here the Abgesang begins with Siegmund's attempt to kill his wife and unborn child ("Dies Schwert") and ends with the Valkyrie's promise to intervene in the battle on his behalf. In all three periods, the large Abgesänge are all significantly larger than the preceding Stollen, and all have a varied motivic content; the Abgesänge of P.10 and P.11, which ought to correspond since these periods are the Über-Stollen of the large Bar, are in fact quite different, with the former dominated by the Sterbegesang while the latter is rather a mishmash of diverse motives framed by the Schicksalsfrage. Figure 4.12 reproduces Lorenz's summation of the entire scene.[161]

It is a curiosity that each of these examples of a potentiated Bar is found at a fairly static moment in the drama: Brünnhilde's almost hieratic awak-

---

160. Although he opines that doubtless the actual tonality is G-flat minor, which would be the minor subdominant of the *Ring*. *Geheimnis* I: 179n.

161. Ibid., 184.

Example 4.6. *Wk.*II.P.10. I. Stollen, mm. 1462–1490.

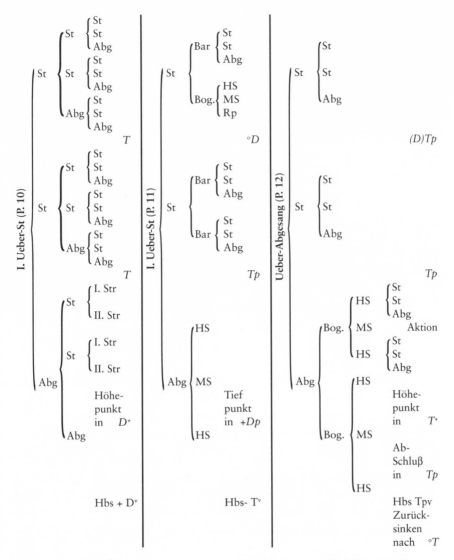

Figure 4.12. The Über-Bar of the Todesverkündigung scene (*Wk.*II.P.10–12).

ening, Hagen's unyielding malevolence (usually staged in an entirely static manner), and Brünnhilde's ritual marking of Siegmund for death. While not all of Lorenz's potentiated Bar forms are found at such moments— indeed one is found at the height of the confrontation between the Wanderer and Siegfried (*Sf.*III.P.6), certainly not a static event—it is striking that three of the more convincing examples are, for this seems to indicate that Lorenz's paradigm of the dynamic Bar, so convincingly portrayed as an essential necessity, does not always obtain in practice.

Composite Forms

By their nature, composite (*ineinandergefügte*) forms are a heterogeneous lot and resist any systematic presentation. Such forms are by far the most common type found by Lorenz; they account for 61 of the periods and transitional sections in the *Ring*. They contain a miscellany of smaller forms which are "vereinigt und ineinanderfügt" by the larger form (by which Lorenz arranges these periods). Any number of permutations are possible: "the imagination provides the full rein for an unprecedented quantity of [formal] permutations."[162] These periods all share a propensity for free (or opposite) symmetry; Lorenz writes that "the larger this is, the more difficult the equivalences are to perceive."[163] One other shared characteristic is the varying degrees of articulation of the inner forms: the parts of some composite forms are themselves in a single form, while in others the parts may contain several smaller forms. That is, the Stollen of a Bar may contain a single Bogen form, or it may contain a smaller Bar plus a Bogen. It may also contain sections which do not belong to any larger forms, but rather sit awkwardly unformed amongst the structures surrounding them.[164]

Owing to the great diversity of composite forms, it would be somewhat pointless to give examples of each type since each tends to employ the same sort of analytic sleight-of-hand when difficulties are encountered (an example of a composite Bar will follow presently). Only the large form changes. Of all the composite forms, the strophic forms are the least objectionable. That which forms the twin oaths ("Helle Wehr! / Heilige Waffe!") in the second act of *Götterdämmerung* is positively compelling (*Gd*.II.P.12). Here each strophe (one each for Siegfried and Brünnhilde) is comprised of a Bar plus a postlude which is easily discernible both musically and textually.

Bogen forms account for the majority (32) of these composite forms. Lorenz presents seven possible types, three of which are new inventions specially devised to cater to these larger forms. In addition to the expected simple, expanded, perfect, and double Bogens, Lorenz mentions three other possible types of Bogen: those with a concentrated Rp (in which the themes from the HS are heard at a faster tempo); those with shortened reprises (often considerably so); and those in which the HS and Rp show opposite symmetry to one another.

As in the potentiated types, composite rondo and refrain forms are often quite audible to the listener—at least in a superficial way—through the repetition of the HS. They thus occupy the paradoxical position of being successful in the abstract while often being quite suspect in their individual details. For example, no one would deny that the Waldweben recurs through-

---

162. Ibid., 190.
163. Ibid., 197.
164. Thus it happens that some of Lorenz's analyses appear to be simply lists of motives, one after another.

out *Sf*.II.P.7 in a rondo-like fashion, or that Siegfried's Lebenslustmotiv and Mime's Trippelmotiv permeate their lengthy encounter in *Sf*.I.P.3 (the former as the principal theme, the latter as a secondary one).[165] But can these periods in their entirety be said to be in rondo form? It is doubtful. Certain of the refrain forms are more convincing, particularly the Norn's scene in *Götterdämmerung* (Vor.P.1), where three refrains are used in an obvious manner to structure the scene: the Spinnrefrain (figuration out of Urelementemotiv and the Dämmerakkorde); the Schicksalsrefrain ("Wißt ihr noch?"; Schicksalsfragemotiv); and the Fragerefrain ("Weißt du wie das wird?"; Sterbegesang).[166]

The composite Bar which forms *Gd*.III.P.9 may serve as an example of this form in practice (fig. 4.13). Lorenz notes that this is a particularly "free" Bar. The 91–measure Bar is preceded by a 34–measure introduction, also in Bar form. In both of these Bars, the Stollen beginnings are particularly prominent (Hagen's "Hoiho!" and the Rachebund refrain in the introductory Bar, Gutrune's Schrei in the main Bar). The large Abgesang contains the confrontation between Hagen and Gunther which culminates in the latter's death. Lorenz suggests that the period ends with a 34–measure coda which concludes the Gibichung action (Gutrune's understanding and death); this coda does not begin, however, until 28 measures of the next period have elapsed, so that it thus forms an interruption of the following period.

Periods in Successive Forms

According to Lorenz's perceptual understanding of musical form, the principal form of a period—that which structures the whole—occupies a single breathing cycle (*Atemzug*). By this he does not literally mean a single inhalation/exhalation, but rather a cycle: an expanded, self-contained, complete movement, of much the same type as intended when we speak of the rhythm of a play, for example. This rhythm may be quick or measured, frantic or leisurely; more often than not it is the pacing of the scenes that is meant by the phrase.

But Lorenz admits that there are sixteen periods or transitional sections in the *Ring* that do not have this effect. Instead, they are comprised of many smaller forms (each a tiny *Atemzug* on its own) which do not cohere

---

165. Lorenz also suggests that the Waldweben music is used to create a higher rondo form which fills the entire rest of the act. *Sf*.II.P.7, P.10, P.12, and P.15+16 are HS, with the other periods understood as ZS. See *Geheimnis* I: 271.

166. A recent article by Patrick McCreless also identifies three refrains which permeate the scene (although they are not precisely those of Lorenz) and notes that Lorenz's interpretation of their structural function is similar to his own. He further writes that "Lorenz's view of the passage works perfectly well." Patrick McCreless, "Schenker and the Norns," in *Analyzing Opera: Verdi and Wagner*, 276–97.

```
Rachebund                                              2 ⎤ St.    8 ⎤
   Rachewahn                                           6 ⎦        ⎥
Rachebund                                              2 ⎤ St.   10 ⎥ Intro.      34 mm.
   Hochzeitsruf & Rachewahn, then Waldknabenruf        8 ⎦        ⎥
Sühnerecht & Entsagung                                 7 ⎤        ⎥
Waldknabenruf & Siegfried, with Ritt (bar: 2+2+3)      5 ⎥ Abg.  16 ⎦
Frohn and cadence (bar: 1+1+2)                         4 ⎦


Gutrune's Schrei                                               6 ⎤ St.        22 mm.
Cantilena ("Gutrun, holde Schwester") (bar: 4+4+3)            11 ⎥ (accusation
Rhythm of Trauermarsch, and build-up to following             5 ⎦ of Gunther)


Gutrune's Schrei                                              4 ⎤ St.        22 mm.
Cantilena ("Gutrun, holde Schwester") intensified (bar: 3+2+2) 7 ⎥ (accusation
Motivic combination: Frohn & Hagen (2 mm. x 2)        2 St.     ⎥ of Hagen)
Waldknabenruf, Gutrune's Schreit, & above     Abg.   11 ⎦
   motivic combination
      [small Reprisenbar: 2+2+5+2]


Mordwerkes: introduction to Abgesang (bar: 1+1+2)    4      ⎤
Schwurmotiv with tremolo on single pitch        HS ⎤ 8      ⎥
   Sühnerecht                                   MS ⎥ 7 Bogen ⎥
Runenphrase (its single pitch function as      HS ⎦ 8      ⎥
   substitution for Schwurmotiv)                           ⎥
                                                           ⎥
Ringmotiv descent                 1 ⎤                      ⎥ Abg.        47 mm.
   Vernichtungsrhytthmus          3 ⎥ Bogen   St.  6 ⎤     ⎥ (fight between
Ringmotiv descent                 2 ⎦               ⎥      ⎥ Hagen and Gunther)
                                                    ⎥      ⎥
Ringmotiv descent combined  ⎤ (bar: 1+1+3)  St.  5 ⎥ Reprisenbar
w. Sinnemotiv               ⎥                      ⎥
Gutrune's Gruß and chords   ⎦                      ⎥
                                                    ⎥
Fluchmotiv                        3 ⎤               ⎥
Ringmotiv (bar)                   3 ⎥ Abg.  9 ⎦     ⎥
A's Herrscherruf (bar)            3 ⎦               ⎦
```

┌───┐
│ INTERRUPTION: 28 mm. of P.10 (BRÜNNHILDE)   │
└───┘

```
Gutrune's Schrei in e, ending with drawn-out Frohnmotiv  11 ⎤ Bogen
   Brünnhilde's answer (Gutrune's Gruß + Welterbschaft)  12 ⎥ (free symmetry) Coda  34 mm.
Gutrune's Schrei, combined with Zaubertrug               11 ⎦
   –G's Liebsm.
```

Figure 4.13. *Gd*.III.P.9.

into a single, larger form. All but three of these periods Lorenz is able to provide with an illusion of unity; these he refers to as periods in which "the unity of a musical movement is apparently lacking, if one does not adopt a higher viewpoint."[167] Lorenz's willingness to adopt this "higher viewpoint" results in two of the three types of successive periods: half-unified, and coda-like (the third—"un-unified"—is not really a "type" in the strictest sense.)

Half-unified periods, of which there are five, achieve this status by virtue of being framed by the same (or similar) motives. They thus cohere into a loose type of Bogen, except that these framing sections are usually too short and unimportant to be HS in their own right; still this framing does result in a type of unity, Lorenz notes. For example, the period marking Siegfried's arrival at the hall of Gibichungs (*Gd*.I.P.6) is framed by the Fluchmotiv (first, in the orchestra alone, the second set to Hagen's words "Heil! Siegfried, theurer Held!"); these sections are 6 mm. and 15 mm. respectively. The period proper is made up of two strophes (mm. 243–53), a potentiated Bar (mm. 254–82), a potentiated Reprisenbar (mm. 283–312), a "tension-pause" (mm. 313–19), and a section of "Tristansteigerung" of the Gibichungmotiv (mm. 320–30).[168]

There are eight successive periods which occur at the conclusion of a larger dramatic action, and therefore have a coda-like character. Lorenz compares their structure to that of a classical coda in which many short coda ideas are lumped together rather loosely, and notes that this desire for repeated cadential confirmation is something of a primordial musical phenomenon. These periods, then, also have a type of unity about them:

> Seen from a higher perspective, such periods are not without unity, especially if one does not consider them in isolation, but in conjunction with what precedes them, as the conclusions of a whole scene which combines several periods into a whole.[169]

Such coda-like periods are found at the end of the first scene of *Die Walküre* (P.4), during Brünnhilde's solo scene following Wotan's long narrative (*Wk*.II.P.8), and after Waltraute's narration in *Götterdämmerung* (I.P.15). They also form the conclusions of the first acts of *Siegfried* (P.14) and *Götterdämmerung* (P.16). Siegfried's Rhine Journey (*Gd*.Vor.P.3) is a coda-like period which concludes the Vorspiel of the final opera of the *Ring*.

There remain, then, only three sections for which Lorenz is not able to discover a form: *Wk*.II.P.6; the transition to P.7, immediately following;

---

167. *Geheimnis* I: 296.

168. In later volumes of *Das Geheimnis*, Lorenz refers to these framing sections as introductory and concluding framing sections, and has no qualms about treating such periods as full periods; he drops any mention of their "half-unity."

169. *Geheimnis* I: 254.

and *Gd*.I.P.12. The last of these Lorenz analyzes as a Bar and two strophes, and notes that one could imagine this as reversal of Bar form.[170] Still, he is astounded at the apparent lack of form of these sections:

> There thus remain in the entire *Ring* only two [*sic*] [periods] which seem to have renounced the dictates of unity. Perhaps this is only owing to some error in my investigation; yes, I am convinced that the person who continues my work will discover the error—I would rather believe such a thing than think that, in a weak moment, a genius like Wagner might have lost the power to shape his statements.[171]

That Lorenz was imprisoned analytically by his aesthetic and ideological prejudices is nowhere more clear than this. Following Schopenhauer's valorization of genius, Lorenz would rather believe in his own fallibility than in Wagner's. Treading water desperately, Lorenz suggests that both of these periods form the introductions to dramatically important narrative scenes (Brünnhilde and Wotan in *Wk*.II., and Waltraute's arrival in *Gd*.), and posits some reversal of the coda impulse to explain the apparent formlessness of these periods.

Periods in Higher Forms

> Now we reach the peak of our reflections. . . . In the combination of several periods, we see *entire large* forms, which occupy scenes and half (or even whole) acts, and which—once more—belong to one of the described forms. We discover an entirely new viewpoint: that the whole dramatic structure serves as a basis for musical forms. *The musical form becomes the sculptor of the dramaturgy.* It is the motivating power [*Triebkraft*] of dramatic development.[172]

So Lorenz describes his final formal category: those forms which he labels as "higher" (*Übergeordnet*). Roughly half of the periods in the *Ring* belong to one of these higher forms, which he sometimes also refers to as large-scale periods (*Großperiode*).

A higher form may be comprised of only two periods, or of twelve—to Lorenz there is no difference. Of the periods discussed, seven have not previously been mentioned up to this point in the work; four of these are part of paired periods (*Sf*.II.P.2–3 and *Wk*.III.P.2–3);[173] one (*Sf*.III.P.4) functions as a rearranged HS for a higher form (the Erda scene); and the final two are

---

170. Lorenz adopts this form, which he refers to as "Gegenbar" form, in the final three volumes of *Geheimnis*.

171. There are really three: Lorenz omits the small transition to *Wk*.II.P.7. *Geheimnis* I: 254.

172. Ibid., 296–97.

173. As is *Sf*.I.P.6–7, the potentiated rondo discussed above.

Opera	Act	Period	Scene or action	Form
Die Walküre	I	P.1–4	First scene	Potentiated Bar
	I	P.5–10	Hunding scene	Bogen
	I	P.12 (all)	Love scene	Bogen
	II	P.7 (all)	Wotan's narrative	Bar
	II	P.10–12	Todesverkündigung scene	Bar
	III	P.1–8	First half of act	Bogen
		P.2–4	Valkyrie scene	Bogen
		P.5–8	Strafgebot scene	Bar
Siegfried	I	all		Perfect Bogen
	I	P.6–7	Riddle scene	Rondo
	I	P.11–14	Sword forging	Refrain
	II	P.2–3	Wanderer & Alberich scene	Bogen + 2 strophes [i.e., Gegenbar]
	II	P.7–16	Waldweben	Rondo
	III	P.1–4	Erda scene	Perfect Bogen
	III	P.8–15	Love scene	Rondo
Götterdämmerung	II	P.2–3	Scene 2 (Hagen, Gtrne, Sf.)	Bogen [discussed elsewhere by L.]
	II	P.7–14	Gibichungen Weddings	
		P.7–10		Bar
		P.11–13		Perfect Bogen

Figure 4.14. Lorenz's higher forms.

actually out of place.[174] The rest of the periods and transitional sections forming these higher periods have already been examined individually by Lorenz. Figure 4.14 presents an overview of his higher periods.

These higher periods represent the epitome of Lorenz's organicistic thought, particularly if the periods which comprise these larger units are themselves complex forms. If this is the case, then the resultant *Großperiod* resembles a Ukranian nesting doll: a form within a form within a form. Lorenz admits

---

174. These two periods (*Rh*.P.16 and *Gd*.II.P.9) are said to reveal "rein, geistiger Symmetrie." In other words, the form they are said to be in is entirely in Lorenz's imagination; for example, the latter period Lorenz calls a Bar, despite the fact that the two Stollen are not musically alike at all (as Lorenz admits himself)! They do both pertain to Brünnhilde, however. A large portion of this chapter is devoted to aesthetic issues—such as very free "free symmetry"—and so Lorenz discusses these periods here, although they are not higher forms at all.

Waldweben (P.7), itself a rondo	222 mm.	ca. 8 minutes
Fafner's fight and death. Ends		
with Fluchmotiv (P.8+9)	244 mm.	ca. 9–10 minutes
Waldweben (P.10) two strophes	34 mm.	ca. 1½ minutes
Siegfried wins the gold (P.11)	167 mm.	ca. 4 minutes
Waldweben (P.12) two strophes	32 mm.	ca. 1½ minutes
Mime's deception and death.		
Fluchmotiv (P.13+14)	290 mm.	ca. 9–10 minutes
Waldweben (P.15+16)	209 mm.	ca. 8 minutes

Figure 4.15. *Sf*.II. Waldweben.

that some of these higher forms are only glimpsed, "as if shimmering through a veil," by the "sensation" (*Erfühlen*) of free symmetry.[175] Figure 4.15 shows one of Lorenz's higher periods: the Waldweben in *Siegfried*.

These higher periods pose a problem in that they resist any systematic attempt to account for them. Some of the smaller *Großperiode*, such as the love scene between the Wälsungen, Wotan's narrative, and Erda's scene, undeniably do cohere as units; the correspondences which Lorenz discerns between the sections of *Wk*.I.P.12, for example, are quite convincing. Other periods, especially those which Lorenz "does not hesitate" to suggest, omit and oversimplify musical and scenic details in order to seem to make sense.[176] For example, all of *Sf*.I is said to be a perfect Bogen (fig. 4.16), as is the entirety of *Das Rheingold* (fig. 4.17).[177] Both of these analyses are so general as to be at once convincing and silly.[178] Their acceptance is based more on the reader's willingness to be convinced. On the one hand, many of Lorenz's correspondences do make a certain sense (such as Mime's negative emotions which frame the Riddle scene with the Wanderer; see figure 4.16). On the other, however, to claim, for example, that the scene in Nibelheim and the beginning of scene iv in *Das Rheingold* are equivalent (see fig. 4.17) is rather a *reductio ad absurdum* of an undeniable dramatic correspondence.

Nevertheless many of Lorenz's observations offered in the guise of these higher forms are convincing, and occasionally striking. Although his claim

---

175. *Geheimnis* I: 273.

176. Lorenz introduces each of his final three higher periods with the remark "Ich stehe nicht an. . . ." He thereby explains the entirety of *Das Rheingold* as a perfect Bogen, the action concerning Siegmund as a large Bar in D minor (St.1 = *Wk*.I; St.2 = *Wk*.II. first half; Abg. = *Wk*.II. second half), and the action concerning Siegfried as a large Bogen (HS = *Wk*.III, *Sf*.I&II; MS = *Sf*.III; HS = *Gd*.Vor.I&II).

177. The first scene is considered a dominant (V/V) introduction to the work as a whole and so is not included in the overall form.

178. Likewise with Lorenz's comment that the third act of *Götterdämmerung* ought to be understood as a supporting Bogen to all of *Das Rheingold*, since it repeats the cycle found in the earlier work (a Bogen form): Rheintöchter—Walhalla.

Mime forges a sword
  Siegfried's high spirits. Cheerful frequency of Waldknabenruf
    S.f.& Mime. Middle: two beautiful strophes. Rondo principal theme: Lebenslustmotiv
      Fahrtenlustlied
        Mime worried
          Wanderer scene. Midpoint: Walhalla motive (T of *Ring*)
        Mime in state of panic
      Fahrtenlustlied
    S.F.& Mime. Middle: two beautiful strophes. Refrain: lebenslustmotiv
  Siegfried's high spirits. Cheerful frequency of Waldknabenruf
Siegfried forges a sword

Figure 4.16. *Siegfried,* Act I.

Greeting of Walhalla
    Freia's flight
        Conflict with giants
            Freia is taken away
                Alberich's might
                    Alberich outwitted
                Alberich's helplessness (curse)
            Freia is brought back
        Conclusion of conflict with Giants
          (Erda) [interruption]
    Freia's embrace
Greeting of Walhalla

Figure 4.17. *Das Rheingold.*

that Wotan's narration in the second act of *Die Walküre* balances that of Sieglinde in the first might seem more of a dramatic analysis than a musical one, the crux of Lorenz's aesthetic position is that the two are inseparable: "the musical form is the sculptor of the dramatic structure."[179] According to his carefully articulated understanding of the creation of works of art, and of the nature of the *Gesamtkunstwerk* itself, all arts are created equal. Indeed, Lorenz devotes a considerable amount of space in his discussion to these aesthetic matters.[180] These higher forms are thus properly interpreted as allegories for the symphonic ambition which Lorenz rightly believes them to contain. In other words, they are more metaphors for Lorenz's ideological convictions than proper analyses *per se.*[181] Significantly, no higher forms at all are found in *Das Rheingold* (with the exception of its entirety), traditionally seen as the most unsymphonic of Wagner's works.

---

179. *Geheimnis* I: 277.

180. Lorenz's thoughts about the nature of the *Gesamtkunstwerk*, discussed at the end of chapter 3, are first presented in this section of the work.

181. John Deathridge is of the same opinion; see his "A Brief History of Wagner Research," *Wagner Handbook*, 214–15.

Chapter Five

The Development of
Lorenz's Analytical Method

The Later Volumes

Lorenz concluded the first volume of *Das Geheimnis der Form* with a series of questions which arose from his analyses, and which would reverberate throughout the remainder of his life's work. They were primarily historical, and concerned the origins and influence of the formal technique Lorenz believed he had discovered in Wagner. He wondered (perhaps rhetorically) whether the rest of Wagner's music dramas were similarly constructed, and, if so, whether this type of formal construction was a consequence of Wagner's theoretical thought or a matter of compositional development. To answer this question, Lorenz suggested that an examination of all of Wagner's works, both before and after the *Ring*, was needed. In fact, he had already embarked upon analyses of the last three operas, and hoped to study the pre-*Rheingold* works in a similar fashion; he also suggested the study of Wagner's predecessors and influences not only in opera, but also in the sonata, symphony, and song. Finally, he noted that one might wish to consider the development and evolution of the individual formal types found in the *Ring* within the rest of Wagner's oeuvre, as well as their influence on Wagner's successors, both operatic and symphonic.

The answers to Lorenz's first two questions are found in the remaining three volumes of *Das Geheimnis der Form bei Richard Wagner* (dealing respectively with *Tristan* [1926], *Meistersinger* [1930], and *Parsifal* [1933]) and in a series of supplemental essays which deal with the early operas.[1] He concludes that each of the post-*Lohengrin* works is indeed similarly constructed, and argues with regard to the earlier operas that "each work up to *Lohengrin* seeks more and more to unify its parts synthetically."[2] Lorenz's treatment of the pre-*Rheingold* works is not at all systematic; his essays

---

1. Most of these were published in the *Bayreuther Festspielführer* (and are listed in the bibliography of Lorenz's writings), although Lorenz briefly mentions *Tannhäuser* in the concluding pages of *Geheimnis* IV (194–95).

2. *Geheimnis* IV: 194.

typically discuss only a small section or series of sections (such as the *Tannhäuser* overture, or Lohengrin's Grail narrative), although they generally do propose a governing formal type for the acts, and often for the opera as a whole.

The books that deal with *Tristan*, *Meistersinger*, and *Parsifal* follow their predecessor in almost all respects. Like the *Ring* volume, they systematically account for every measure of the works, but unlike the latter, they are arranged chronologically instead of categorically according to formal type. While this categorical arrangement suits the expository and didactic nature of the earlier volume, it does make it impossible to follow acts and works measure by measure without flipping back and forth in the book.[3] It is thus easier to find and to follow Lorenz's discussion of particular sections in the later volumes. For readers unfamiliar with *Geheimnis* I, Lorenz includes a useful introduction to his analytical technique in the front of each of the subsequent volumes, and a tabulation of his various formal types as an appendix. Aside from these orienting sections (and advice on certain "easier" periods with which to begin), understanding of the method is taken as a given by Lorenz. This results in a more concentrated focus upon the work itself—its structure and individual details—than in the earlier volume, which was obliged to devote a lot of attention to the exposition of the method and consequently has fewer insights into the particularities of the *Ring* operas.[4] Whereas most of the periods of the *Ring* are presented in tabular form with only a minimum of prose commentary, most of the periods in *Tristan*, *Meistersinger*, and *Parsifal* are accompanied by extensive analytical discussion in addition to the expected table.

As in *Geheimnis* I, Lorenz's main focus is upon the higher forms. For the later operas, Lorenz proposes a governing form for each act as well as for the opera as whole. Thus, for example, *Parsifal* is said to be in Bogen form: acts one and three (each a Bar) both have two scenes, the second in the Castle of the Grail, while the second act (dramatically, a Bar but musically a perfect Bogen) contrasts with these in almost all respects.[5] Frequently the sections of an act cohere into *Großperiode* which make up the sections of

---

3. This arrangement is also likely the cause of the numerous errors (such as measures omitted or counted twice) in *Geheimnis* I; such errors are virtually eliminated in the later volumes.

4. Although there are many insightful comments scattered along the way, the quantity of these comments increases in later volumes.

5. Lorenz's presentation of this idea is less crude than the above description might lead one to believe, but space precludes detailed consideration of the intricacies of Lorenz's arguments. Lorenz was not without precedent in understanding entire works to be in a particular form: both Curt Mey (*Die Meistergesang in Geschichte und Kunst*) and Hans von Wolzogen ("Die Meistersinger von Nürnberg auf der Opernbühne," in *Wagneriana: Gesammelte Aufsätze über R. Wagner's Werke vom Ring bis zum Gral* [Leipzig: F. Freund, 1888], 173–92) had already argued that *Die Meistersinger* was a large Bar form.

the large form of the act itself. Thus, the first eight periods of the first act of *Parsifal* form the first Stollen, the next six periods the second Stollen, and the final eight periods the Abgesang of the Bar of the act as a whole. As proved to be the case in the *Ring*, most of the periods are determined according to dramatic and/or scenic means. In the above example, the first Stollen treats of the essence of the Grail and of Kundry (its false savior), while the second presents the foundation of the Grail community and introduces Parsifal (its true savior). The dramatic self-sufficiency of the Abgesang is immediately apparent: Amfortas's lament and the Grail scene.

In these last volumes, Lorenz is even more explicit in invoking the symphonic myth for Wagner's mature works. He argues that in both *Tristan* (Act 3) and *Meistersinger* (all acts), individual acts are constructed according to the principles of a four-movement symphony; for example, Lorenz explains the first act of the latter work as follows: the first scene is an introductory first movement, the second scene is a scherzo, and the third scene begins with an andante (assembly of Guild and Pogner's address) and concludes with the finale (Walther's scene).[6]

Since poetic-musical periods tend to cohere along dramatic or scenic lines, as well as along musical ones, it is therefore difficult to discern which is the true governing principle, despite Lorenz's claims for the latter. (These claims are perhaps belied by the fact that Lorenz gives names—"Der Nachtgesang," "Beckmessers Wut," and "Parsifals Jugend," for example—to each period.) The vast majority of the period divisions do make a certain sense dramatically, even if some may be suspect musically. The later volumes of *Das Geheimnis der Form* make much less use of the variously named transitional sections found throughout the *Ring*. Where they are found, they are without exception called transitions (*Übergänge*). The largest of these occur in dramatically transitional places similar to those in the *Ring*: before Isolde's transfiguration, between the scenes in the third act of *Die Meistersinger*, and as the Flowermaidens depart before Kundry's narration. But orchestral transitions, such as the those leading towards the Castle of the Grail in the framing acts of *Parsifal*, are more often than not designated as periods proper, as was the exception, not the rule, in the *Ring*.

Lorenz's analyses of *Tristan, Meistersinger,* and *Parsifal* uncover the same types of forms encountered in the *Ring*: simple and complex periods in simple, potentiated, composite, or successive form. As before, various permutations of Bars and Bogens make up the majority of the period forms. In these later volumes, however, Lorenz appears to have less recourse to some of his stranger formal types; there are no double or supporting Bogen forms in the later works for example. Although he ceases to regard as lesser those periods which are framed by the same motives (instead granting these full

---

6. See also *Geheimnis* III: 176.

period status without comment),[7] Lorenz adds only one new form to his arsenal. This is the reversed Bar form: the Gegenbar.

Although the idea of a reversed Bar is adumbrated twice in *Geheimnis* I by Lorenz, it was left to one of his followers to come up with a name for it.[8] In an essay on the first movement of Bruckner's Ninth Symphony, Hans Alfred Grunsky proposes the term "Gegenstollen" to complement Lorenz's own "Aufgesang," and the name "Gegenbar" for the whole.[9] In the *Tristan* volume, Lorenz adopts Grunsky's name, but still finds the form "somewhat irregular" even though it occurs five times in the work.[10] He does not include it in the appendix of forms at the back of the book until the *Meistersinger* volume in 1930. Here he suggests that the apparent increase in Gegenbar forms in Wagner's later works—they occur "ziemlich oft" in *Meistersinger*— is owing to the change in direction of the stylistic wave at the end of the century: a return to the austere seventeenth-century taste.[11] He thus equates the Gegenbar with what he called "Seicentoform" in his own work on Alessandro Scarlatti's early operas.[12] In the last two volumes of *Geheimnis der Form* Lorenz prefers the term "Nachstollen" to Grunsky's "Gegenstollen."

Towards the end of all three subsequent volumes, Lorenz offers a summary of the development of Wagner's formal structures and techniques. Thus, for example, Lorenz finds an increasing use of motivic substitution in Wagner's later works, leading to a greater occurrence of free and opposite symmetry; he speaks of a marked prevalence of free symmetry.[13] He

---

7. These periods were termed loose Bogen-structures, and counted among the half-unified, successive forms in *Geheimnis* I; see the discussion of these forms in the previous chapter. In appendix 2 of *Geheimnis* II: 190, Lorenz writes:

> If the outer sections are of less importance than the MS, one nevertheless sees a Bogen formed by these parts. However, I then no longer call these parts principal sections [HS] but framing sections (VRS = opening framing section [*Vorderer Rahmensatz*], SRS = concluding framing section [*Schließender Rahmensatz*]). In principle, it is all the same: Bogen form.

8. Lorenz posits that the conclusion of the MS of the larger MS of *Sf*.II.P.13 demonstrates a reversal of the Bar form: an Aufgesang, followed by two similar strophes (*Geheimnis* I: 221n). He also notes (somewhat indecisively) that the apparently ununified *Gd*.I.P.12 "could also be taken as proof for the rare form: Aufgesang, Stollen, Stollen," which might be conceived as a reversal of Bar form (ibid., 264). He might profitably have invoked the concept for the higher period formed by *Sf*.II.P.2 & P.3 as well.

9. Hans Alfred Grunsky, "Der erste Satz von Bruckners Neunter: ein Bild höchster Formvollendung," *Die Musik* 18 (1925): 24–25.

10. *Geheimnis* II: 32; see also 187–88.

11. *Geheimnis* III: 186. Lorenz of course is referring to his own *Abendländische Musikgeschichte im Rhythmus der Generationen* (1928), discussed in chapter 1 of the present work. Lorenz's evolutionary hypothesis may be called into question, however, because of the break in the *Ring*'s genesis—although, as we have seen, Lorenz's aesthetic presuppositions lead him to minimize, if not dismiss entirely any sense of stylistic shift between the early and later *Ring* operas.

12. *Alessandro Scarlattis Jugendopern*, vol. 2, 213–18.

13. *Geheimnis* III: 176. See also *Geheimnis* IV: 7–9.

posits that this is due to Wagner's greater reliance on that "art of transition" mentioned in the 1859 letter to Mathilde Wesendonck. But Lorenz's invocation of such conceptual symmetries is paradoxical: for Lorenz, it is testament to Wagner's genius, to his ability to vary endlessly a small number of ideal shapes (Lorenz's forms); for us, however, distanced by time and inclination from the expressive aesthetic position which is the buttress for Lorenz's thought, his reliance on this concept might be seen rather as testament to Lorenz's own analytical difficulty. Put another way: without accepting fully the entirety of Lorenz's philosophical and aesthetic foundation, it is difficult either to evaluate or to accept Lorenz's methodology.

Each volume of *Das Geheimnis der Form* has its own particular character and preoccupations which are explainable according to Lorenz's own external interests and circumstances during the time they were written. Like its immediate predecessor, the second volume is not as mystical and nationalistic as are the two later volumes. Lorenz's *Tristan* book [volume 2] is influenced most importantly by Ernst Kurth's pathbreaking study of romantic harmony in Wagner's *Tristan*, first published in 1920; Lorenz himself admits this tie, not only by dedicating the book to Kurth, but also by concluding his introduction with a long tribute to Kurth's work.[14] According to Lorenz himself, the bulk of the *Tristan* analyses were completed in the early 1920s while he was at work on his dissertation.[15] With the publication of the *Meistersinger* book [volume 3] in 1930, Lorenz's rightist and strongly nationalistic political leanings infiltrated his scholarly prose. This may only be a consequence of the subject matter at hand (the Bar form is by far the most common form in *Die Meistersinger*), but nevertheless, Lorenz writes in quite jingoistic terms of the inherent "Germanity" of the Meistersinger and their art. Sachs's final speech (particularly its conclusion: "Habt acht! / Uns dräuen üble Streich'") is presented as a call to the Germany of Lorenz's own time, a Germany "enslaved by foreigners."[16] This nationalistic turn is even more pronounced in the final volume of *Das Geheimnis der Form* (*Parsifal*, 1933), and Lorenz includes numerous "Sonderbetrachtungen" about the nationalistic and "spiritual" content of the work.[17] The volume also contains several other "Sonderbetrachtungen" which have to do with the harmonic structure of particular motives or with Wagner's systematic use of certain sonorities, such as the so-called "mystic

---

14. *Geheimnis* II: 10–11. Here Lorenz equates his own formal analysis with the "skeleton" of a human being and Kurthian harmonic analysis with the unique physical characteristics of a particular individual.

15. The preface to *Geheimnis* I refers to Lorenz's completed, but unpublished, *Tristan* analyses.

16. *Geheimnis* III: 81.

17. Examples of such "Sonderbetrachtungen" concern the medieval German mystic, Meister Eckhardt, the "Parsifal religion" founded by Wagner, and the nature of Parsifal himself. Lorenz's right-wing interpretation of *Parsifal* is discussed in chapter 1.

chord," to which Lorenz devotes over fifteen pages.[18] It thus delves into both Riemann's notation and Kurth's harmonic theories in more detail than in any of the other three volumes.

In short, there is a sense of increasing breadth and depth as successive volumes of *Das Geheimnis der Form* appear. Despite the oft-deplored "economic distress of our Fatherland" (*wirtschaftliche Not unseres Vaterlandes*) that militated against lengthy books, Lorenz pauses again and again to mention salient details—whether interpretative or analytical—which add immeasurably to our understanding of the work in question or of Wagner's musical language in general.[19] For example, in all four volumes, but to the greatest extent in the final two, Lorenz discusses Wagner's use of certain "Urmotive" as exempla of the inner consistency of the romantic musical language. The uncovering of such "Urmotive" was an important component of the "music as expression" platform, for these recurring melodic gestures were held to be the visible manifestation of the internal, unconscious strivings of the creative will.[20]

Although Wagner's works remained Lorenz's primary analytical interest throughout his career, he also published numerous essays on the works of other composers. These ancillary works (for so they must appear when compared to the totality of his writings on Wagner) employ the same analytical methodology used by Lorenz on Wagner's music dramas. Regarding this direct borrowing, Lorenz writes (here apropos of Mozart's operatic finales):

> Do not take it amiss that I apply to Mozart expressions which arose in relation to Wagner. . . . This is not a case of forcing Wagnerian principles onto eighteenth-century composers [*Klassiker*] (a damnable, entirely unhistorical enterprise which has produced many false conclusions) but rather of recognizing the *eternal laws of form*, to which Wagner, too, had to submit.[21]

Lorenz believed that he had discovered the eternal rules of form which would obtain in all works of genius from whatever century or musical style; elsewhere he offers a concise Credo to this effect:

> I discovered that all music is based on only a few formal types (Strophic, Bogen, Bar, and Gegenbar) which may be discovered in all sizes from the most extensive

---

18. This "mystische Akkord" is none other than the half-diminished seventh chord (or minor triad with added sixth), which, when built on F, is the sonority of the Tristan chord.

19. *Geheimnis* III: preface, 154; *Geheimnis* IV: preface.

20. Only by becoming familiar with the "metaphysical, primal musical laws," as promulgated by Curt Mey (*Die Musik als tönende Weltidee*, 1901) can one understand Lorenz's sometimes enigmatic references to Notmotive, Tatmotive, and the like. For a discussion of Mey's work, see my "The Magic Wand of the Wagnerians: *Musik als Ausdruck*," 85–89. Hans von Wolzogen's *Musikalisch-dramatische Parallelen*, discussed in chapter 2, also traces the Urmotive in Wagner's music dramas.

21. Lorenz, "Das Finale in Mozarts Meisteropern," 622n.

pieces of music to the shortest themes, and which, in their similar psychological effectiveness, provide the work with the same rhythmic momentum which is communicated to the listener and thereby awakens his enthusiasm [*Begeisterung*]. All of these formal types . . . are found in all classical, pre-classical, and post-classical music, and even in primitive and exotic music. Therefore they form the basis for an new typology of musical forms, understood [even] as it is created.[22]

Lorenz's non-Wagnerian analyses include works by Bach, Alessandro Scarlatti, Mozart, Beethoven, and Richard Strauss.[23] It is interesting to note Lorenz's choice of music by Scarlatti, Mozart, and Strauss, for in all three cases, Lorenz has a similar conceptual content (either text or program) as in Wagner with which to orient his analyses. His analyses of Bach and Beethoven are not noticeably different, however, and are often equally persuasive—at least in their elucidation of the large-scale formal divisions in a work.

At his death in 1939, Lorenz left behind drafts for a fifth volume of *Das Geheimnis der Form* which was to trace the evolution of this formal technique in Wagner's earlier operas, as well as the development of his four formal types throughout the course of music history. It was to be a codification of the "neue musikalische Formenlehre" that Lorenz believed he had discovered. Although he claimed to have abandoned the idea of a fifth volume in the conclusion to *Geheimnis* IV, his writings of the later 1930s seem to suggest the opposite, and a posthumous tribute to Lorenz mentions two complete chapters plus a first draft of the rest of the work.[24] Despite extensive inquiry, I have been unable to find any trace of this material. It remained for several of Lorenz's contemporaries to extend and develop his analytical methodology, the history of which forms the first section of the reception history of *Das Geheimnis der Form* in the next chapter.

Evaluating Lorenz

If one properly considers its aesthetic and philosophical underpinnings, Lorenz's analytical method resists any attempt at totalization. It seems foolhardy to

---

22. Lorenz, "Wege zur Erkenntnis von Richard Wagners Kunstwerk," 113; *Geheimnis* III: 188.

23. Many of these have already been cited: "Homophone Großrhythmik in Bachs Polyphonie"; *Alessandro Scarlattis Jugendoper*; "Das Finale in Mozarts Meisteropern"; "Worauf beruht die bekannte Wirkung der Durchführung im 1. Eroicasatze"; "Betrachtungen über Beethovens Eroica-Skizzen"; "Der formale Schwung in Richard Strauss' 'Till Eulenspiegel'"; "Neue Formerkenntnisse, angewandt auf Richard Straußens 'Don Juan'."

24. *Geheimnis* IV: 196; Hans Alfred Grunsky, "Einer der uns fehlt," 39. In "Neue Anschauungen auf dem Gebiete der musikalischen Formenlehre" (1933), Lorenz himself admits that he is currently "collecting" his diverse writings on musical form for a comprehensive book about his new formal system.

draw firm conclusions, to make either firm endorsements or firm dismissals. While it may be true that "[a]ny critic whose appetite for ridicule is keen will find Lorenz's writings a rich source,"[25] to dismiss Lorenz entirely on account of his inconsistencies, contradictions, and blindnesses is perhaps to misunderstand him. Nevertheless, in the interest of a painstaking examination of the issue, it is not inappropriate to offer certain observations and reservations about Lorenz's methodology and its application (again, the examples will be taken from the *Ring* analyses only). It is not the intent of the following discussion to demonstrate fatal flaws in Lorenz's work, nor is it meant to supersede the primary lines of inquiry: the effect of aesthetics and ideology on analytical methodology. Rather, it should be considered exegetical in intent: an attempt to synthesize aspects of Lorenz's analyses seldom considered all together. (Too often individual analyses by Lorenz are held up for inspection and found wanting; like blooms cut off from their stems, they soon wither and die.) Lorenz is very free in the application of his principles to the actual music, and it is impossible to account for every variation, every hybrid form.

Despite Lorenz's own idealistic equation of music and drama as essential absolutes, critics have rarely considered the appropriateness of many of Lorenz's forms for the dramatic instances they accompany. For example, the scene of Siegfried's death (*Gd*.III.P.6) is analyzed by Lorenz as a Bogen, with the MS in which the deed is done (beginning with Gunther's "Was hör' ich?") surrounded by twin HS in which Siegfried rhapsodizes about Brünnhilde.[26] This is certainly how the scene is perceived in the theater. Similarly, Lorenz attributes the lack of formal clarity in the scene between Alberich and Mime in the second act of *Siegfried* to their inability to create a proper, "noble" form.[27] In the Norns' scene in *Götterdämmerung*, where Lorenz argues that the tonal end of the period occurs after the second round of questioning rather than at the end of the scene, this "loss" of the tonic symbolizes the Norns' loss of wisdom and their inability to predict the future.[28]

Lorenz is also not insensitive to the use and effect of interruption in drama and acknowledges this practice several times within his analyses. We have already mentioned the case at the end of *Götterdämmerung* where the

---

25. Abbate and Parker, "Introduction: On Analyzing Opera," 14.

26. William Kinderman is entirely correct, however, to censure Lorenz for obscuring the large-scale recapitulation of Brünnhilde's Awakening scene (*Sf*.III.P.8) in the second HS of this period; see his "Dramatic Recapitulation in Wagner's *Götterdämmerung*," 101. It seems likely that Lorenz was not unaware of this fact, only that he did not see fit to mention it.

27. "The two quarreling dwarves are manifestly incapable of producing a large, noble form." *Geheimnis* I: 257.

28. A more recent analysis of this scene by Patrick McCreless concurs with Lorenz's point. McCreless, however, sees the scene as a microcosmic reflection of the large-scale tonal move of the entire act from E-flat to B. (Unlike Lorenz, he does not consider the Vorspiel apart from the act as a whole.) See McCreless, "Schenker and the Norns," 282–83.

conclusion of the last period pertaining to the Gibichungs (P.9) comes in the middle of P.10, Brünnhilde's final apostrophe. Dramatically there is no question that the short exchange between Gutrune and Brünnhilde functions as an interruption within the latter's eulogy upon the dead Siegfried; whether or not it is still appropriate today to speak of discrete "periods" in Wagner's music is another matter, but Lorenz's analysis is certainly able to convey the dramatic impact of the scene. In a similar vein, Lorenz considers Loge's aside "Ihrem Ende eilen sie zu" and the two trios of the Rhinemaidens to be interruptions within *Rh*.P.19, the Entry of the Gods into Valhalla.[29] Many other instances of Lorenz's sensitivity to Wagner's musical symbolization of the drama could be added to these examples, which ought to give pause to critics who have believed Lorenz's own claim that he was ignoring all but the "reine Beschreibung der musikalischen Gestalt."[30]

In accounts of Lorenz's analyses, it is his determination of the bounds of the periods which is most often attacked. I want to focus now on these boundaries, as well as on the unnumbered transitional sections which separate many of them, and draw some conclusions about Lorenz's principles. Despite Lorenz's statement that the periods are determined on musical grounds alone, it is readily apparent that the vast majority of them cohere along dramatic lines; they seem to follow the outlines of the text and dramatic action rather than any abstract musical principles. Thus many, if not most, of Lorenz's proposed divisions have a certain logic about them. They almost always coincide with a change in scene, and rarely occur in the middle of a character's speech, unless there is some compelling rhetorical shift in the text.[31] Each scene typically contains several periods, each of which usually coheres rhetorically and/or dramatically. Thomas Grey has recently noted that, despite his claims to the contrary, Lorenz "by no means ignored the text or stage action."[32] In the course of his discussion, too,

---

29. Although to be consistent he ought to have treated Loge's address to the Rhinemaidens ("Ihr da im Wasser!") as part of the interruption as well; he does not.

30. *Geheimnis* IV: 10. In light of recent calls by scholars such as Carolyn Abbate and Roger Parker to celebrate the forces of disjunction in operatic analysis, it is instructive to note that in *Gd*.II.P.4 Lorenz argues that the individual form-giving elements do not coincide, but rather create a type of "formal syncopation" (170).

31. As happens, for example, between *Rh*.P.11 & P.12. P.11 ends with the beginning of Loge's description of the giants' departure ("Über Stock und Stein zu Tal / stapfen sie hin"); the next period begins as he turns his attention to the gods' own plight ("Den seligen Göttern wie geht's!"). His line "Was sinnt nun Wotan so wild?" bridges the division. This type of rhetorical bridging is similar to Wagner's linking cadence.

There are only a handful of places where a character's speech is split without this dramatic justification. Fasolt's "Die ihr durch Schönheit herrscht" (discussed by Dahlhaus in "Formprinzipien" as an appropriate Wagnerian unit) contains the division between P.7 and P.8, which occurs, without any apparent justification whatsoever, at the turn to major at "Ein Weib zu gewinnen."

32. Grey, *Wagner's Musical Prose*, 13 n. 21.

Grey will frequently allow that many of Lorenz's periods do cohere as recognizable units.[33]

The scenic determination of the poetic-musical periods is not an absolute, however. Where a musical change precedes or overlaps the dramatic or rhetorical conclusion of a section, Lorenz follows the musical cue rather than the textual. For example, *Sf*.II.P.16, the Woodbird's song, begins musically in m. 1793 with the arrival in E major, but Siegfried's line "Nun sing! Ich lausche dem Gesang" belongs with the conclusion of the previous period in which he asks for the bird's help.

That Lorenz resorted more often to the drama rather than the music in the determination of his periods may be the true "Geheimnis" of *Das Geheimnis der Form*. In this light it is suggestive that with only three exceptions (*Wk*.III, *Gd*.Vor., *Gd*.II) Lorenz refers to the orchestral introductions to acts as the "Vorspiel" rather than the first period—if he were really proceeding on musical grounds alone and ignoring the drama, why not number the "Vorspiel" period as well?[34] The issue is fraught with difficulty, as the question of the primacy of music or drama for Lorenz is ultimately unanswerable. In Wagner's works, these scene changes and rhetorical shifts are almost always articulated musically as well (generally with a linking-type cadence), so it is not surprising that Lorenz's period divisions would coincide with the dramatic sense. Still, where Lorenz's choices may be arguable from a musical point of view, they are most often justified dramatically.

Lorenz's loud insistence on the purely musical aspect of the determination of his periods may be attributed to his own need to prove Wagner a master of absolute music and not of "theater music."[35] To have recognized the close connection between the musical and the dramatic sense would have undermined his claim for the self-sufficiency of Wagner's musical logic. Yet the reason that the majority of Lorenz's period divisions can be justified is on dramatic or rhetorical grounds. This is part of the subjective appeal to the listener's perception which underpins Lorenz's method as a whole. Scenes, narratives, dramatic actions, and the like are readily sensed as wholes—as Gestalts—on the part of the properly attuned listener.[36]

It must be admitted, however, that Lorenz is sometimes inconsistent in his treatment of the period. There are several instances where neighboring

---

33. Ibid., 230, 232 n. 43, for example.

34. The first period begins variously at the raising of the curtain or at the first words of the act, depending on the type of conclusion that the prelude has. In *Gd*.III, P.1 begins in the middle of the prelude.

35. He devoted an entire article to countering Nietzsche's claim in *Der Fall Wagner* that Wagner was, at heart, an "actor" (*histrio*): "Theatermusik oder dramatische Sinfonie?" in *Deutsches Musikjahrbuch* 2/3, ed. Rolf Cunz (Essen: Th. Reismann-Grone, 1925), 186–93.

36. It is not surprising, then, that most of the obvious set-pieces of the *Ring*, such as the Entry of the Gods into Valhalla, Wotan's narrative, Wotan's Farewell, Siegfried's Forging Songs, and Waltraute's narrative, are all single periods.

periods are said to be in a single key, and together form a *Großperiod* (the Todesverkündigung scene and the first four periods of *Wk*.I are two examples), and yet are considered as separate poetic-musical periods. In the latter example, as well as in the first four periods of *Gd*.I, the periods are all extremely short. Why not simply call the whole unit the period? Contradictorily, there are four instances where Lorenz partitions a large period into sections (A,B,C, etc.) yet counts the whole as the period for dramatic reasons.[37] It makes no sense to do both. As well, some of Lorenz's periods, particularly those in the final two scenes of *Das Rheingold*, are simply too large, with too much action and too much motivic and tonal activity, ever to be perceived as a single unit, whether musical or dramatic. Yet these are the exceptions, rather than the rule.

The poetic-musical periods are frequently linked together by unnumbered transitional sections which Lorenz calls (variously) *Übergänge, Überleitungen, Nachspiele, Abrundungen, Rückkehren, Einleitungen,* and in one instance, *Verwandlungsmusik* (transitions, connections, postludes, "roundings-off," returns, introductions, and scene-change music). These thirty-seven transitional sections range in length from three to sixty-three measures and are distributed approximately equally amongst the four works (allowing for the relative shortness of *Das Rheingold*). In about two-thirds of them Lorenz finds formal organization, which he then discusses either separately, or alongside the neighboring period; others are simply listed in the table of poetic-musical periods near the beginning of the work and never mentioned again. These transitional sections are entities unto themselves and quite distinct from the often similarly named portions of the periods proper. That is, a transition between two periods has an entirely different formal weight from an introductory section within a period, even if both are labeled as "introductions."

By definition, these transitional sections are not poetic-musical periods since they are not "nach einer Haupttonart bestimmt." Lorenz indicates this fact by his verbal tags for them—they do not rate a number. They are not always transitional in the accepted musical sense, however. Although they may be unstable or modulatory, they are not necessarily so. They may not always lead to a more stable section either. In fact, their use by Lorenz is so diverse as to make it difficult to generalize.[38]

---

37. These periods are as follows: *Wk*.I.P.12 (the love scene between Siegmund and Sieglinde); *Wk*.I.P.7 (Wotan's narrative); *Sf*.III.P.15 (Brünnhilde's capitulation to Siegfried's wooing; final duet); and *Gd*.II.P.14 ("Conspirator's scene," Brünnhilde, Hagen, and Gunther).

38. An article by Robbert van der Lek, "Zum Begriff Übergang und zu seiner Anwendung durch Alfred Lorenz auf die Musik von Wagners 'Ring'," *Die Musikforschung* 35 (1982): 129–47, is strongly critical of Lorenz's use of the term, but is not quite fair in its attacks. Van der Lek begins by noting that the concept of transition is difficult and has never been adequately defined, but then immediately censures Lorenz for not doing so. Secondly, he offers his own definition of the term—an unstable section separated from surrounding stable "mo-

Transitional sections may be dictated by the stage action and function as musical analogies for dramatic hinges such as introductions, interruptions, and asides. For example, a transition is found between *Wk*.III.P.3 and P.4 which marks the departure of Sieglinde and prepares for Wotan's arrival in the following period. Similarly, Siegfried's lines in mm. 261–79 of *Gd*.III form a transition between the first two periods of the act which is articulated dramatically by the diving and surfacing of the Rhinemaidens. Siegmund's tales of his past in the first act of *Die Walküre* (P.6–P.8) are also separated by transitional sections in which Hunding and Sieglinde encourage him to continue. Significant stage action may occur in these sections (such as Siegfried's disguised arrival on Brünnhilde's rock in the transition between *Gd*.I.P.15 & P.16) but this does not alter their dramatically transitional nature.

Nearly all of the orchestral transitions in the *Ring* are labeled by Lorenz as transitional in the present sense: that between the first two scenes of *Rheingold*, the ascent and descent to and from Nibelheim, the music accompanying Siegfried through the fire in *Siegfried* III, and that between the scenes in *Götterdämmerung* I.[39] Transitional sections are also typically found as introductions (in the manner of a preceding recitative) to those more self-contained sections of the *Ring* such as Waltraute's narrative, or Siegfried's tales in the last act of the same opera.

Understanding that transitional sections arise out of dramatic necessity is the only way to explain a curious aspect of their use. Frequently, different transitional sections, such as a "postlude and transition," follow one another directly. Thus the music between the scenes in *Gd*.I is divided into a "postlude to P.11" (mm. 924–66), a "transition (mm. 967–76), and a "prelude to P.12" (mm. 977–1019). While this division is apparent musically through the change in motives (with Brünnhilde's motive signaling the beginning of the next scene) in other cases the musical aspect is less convincing than the rhetorical or dramatic sense. Such is the case with the transition between *Gd*.I.P.13 and P.14 which Lorenz analyzes as a (formed) transition (mm. 1171–99) and an "introduction to the narrative" (mm. 2000–2020) without any compelling musical reason to do so.

---

dalities"—and then evaluates Lorenz's use of the term according to his own just-given definition (obviously finding it wanting). Finally, he makes no attempt to discern what *Lorenz* meant by the term, and obscures entirely the distinction between these unnumbered transitional sections and transitional sections such as introductions and codas within the periods themselves.

39. Two notable exceptions are Siegfried's Rhine Journey (*Gd*.Vor.P.3) and the Funeral March (*Gd*.III.P.7). Lorenz does refer to the former as a postlude to the entire Vorspiel. The ascent and descent to and from Nibelheim in *Rh*. are only half transitional, as Lorenz begins the next period when the mood of that period is reached; i.e., m. 1831 and m. 2795. Thus, the anvils occur not in the transition but in the period portion of the descent, but fall in the transition section of the ascent.

Although Lorenz is not consistent in his use of either the concept or his terminology, these unnumbered transitional sections are an important aspect of his analyses for they point to an excess, a flowing over of the period boundaries with a more fluid type of music. They imply a different kind of music from that of the periods themselves: perhaps even a less structured type of music (though Lorenz argues that many of them are structured according to his formal types). This fundamental qualitative difference has seldom, if ever, been noted by his critics. Abbate and Parker's assertion that Lorenz "ignored self-evident distinctions between more ordered and less ordered music, between loosely rhythmic prose and periodic phrasing, between clear diatonicism and deliberate harmonic obfuscation" is simply not true.[40] To study each analysis is to see quickly that Lorenz did not regard all periods as equal: some are described as introductory, others as transitional; some are said to be very free in character, while others are clearly formed. On cursory examination, however, Lorenz's work does give this impression. But this distinction has even further resonance: if Wagner's music is characterized by discrete periods—unified both tonally and formally—linked by more fluid transitional sections, as Lorenz suggests, then how is this different from traditional opera? Has Lorenz in spite of himself found Wagner's "numbers" under the guise of the poetic-musical periods?

When presenting the individual formal types of the periods in the largest section of the volume, Lorenz gives less emphasis to their tonal structure than might seem called for by his own introduction to the topic. There Lorenz used Wagner's own voice to establish tonality as the primary determinant of the poetic-musical period (by citing the *Oper und Drama* passage). His table of the periods of the *Ring* does list a tonic key for every period. Yet in practice, these "tonics" are often nebulous creations which seem to hold little authority over the music they are said to dominate.

As a rule, the shorter the period, the more convincing Lorenz's tonics are. For example, there is no doubt that Brünnhilde's Awakening (*Sf*.III.P.8) is based around a tonal center of C. Even the longest periods typically return to their "tonics" at the conclusion. The problem arises, especially with these longer periods, with the question of what it means in opera to be "in" a tonic in the first place. To call D major the "tonic" of *Le nozze di Figaro* because the overture and fourth-act finale are in that key may be questionable, yet there seems to be no doubt that the return to D major for the finale does function as a key of resolution, or at least as a type of musical signifier for that dramatic resolution. If a significant stretch of music begins and ends in the same key, even if various other tonalities are passed through between these tonic pillars, the return of the initial tonality acts in a similar manner: as a sonic signifier for a return, a resolution. But what of all the music in between? In most cases, tonality in opera does not (and often

---

40. Abbate and Parker, "Introduction: On Analyzing Opera," 14.

cannot) have the controlling function it might in symphonic music. There are passages, acts, and even operas for which a compelling case can be made for tonal organization. Yet for every unambiguous example of such tonal organization, other instances—perhaps even in the same work—can be cited where this rule does not obtain. Lorenz can hardly be blamed for not solving an issue which remains contentious even today, almost sixty years after his death.

Lorenz is clear that he is most interested in the big picture. It is not his intent to provide a detailed analysis of every chord of the work. For Lorenz, just being able to analyze Wagnerian tonality was enough. By proving that conventional tonality was still operative in Wagnerian opera, and that Wagner was by no means responsible for the *dissolution* of tonality, but instead had "*intensified* [it] to almost demonic proportions,"[41] Lorenz was making an ideological point.

His use of Riemann's harmonic function symbols is intended to show this large-scale harmonic movement. While his overview may at times be crude and over simplistic, it does have the advantage of indicating clearly and immediately the tonal symbolization of the drama. He is seldom totally unjustified in his choice of tonic for a period. He allows periods to begin in keys other than the tonic (by way of introduction, generally), and even occasionally to end in other keys as well (for dramatic reasons).

Lorenz's discussion of unending melody presented the various types of Wagnerian cadence used at the ends of periods; in addition to the ubiquitous linking cadence (which may go just about anywhere), periods may conclude with a half-cadence (either "in" or "on" the dominant). Harmonically, several of these cadences can be understood as tonic; for example a shift from a dominant seventh on G to a minor chord on E would still be a tonic cadence, albeit linking: a move to the *Leittonwechselklang* of the expected tonic, C major.

One glaring contradiction does stand out amongst Lorenz's analyses when it comes to the tonal determination of the periods. Although this is supposed to be the foremost consideration, preceding and resulting in the formal structure of the periods, twice in his analyses Lorenz allows adjacent poetic-musical periods (in different keys) to create together the overall form of the section. In both of these cases—the Mime/Wanderer scene (*Sf*.I.P.6 & P.7) and the Brünnhilde/Sieglinde arrival on the Valkyrie rock (*Wk*.III.P.2 & P.3)—dramatic considerations demand their treatment as wholes, despite their obvious contravening of the period principle. (Interestingly, these scenes have a similar overall form: the first a rondo form, and the second a refrain form.)

Close examination of the analyses reveals a similar compromising tendency in period after period. This ought not to be seen as a catastrophic

---

41. Lorenz, "Tonalität in Tristan," 186.

fault of Lorenz's methodology, but rather as a testament to his belief in Wagner's genius. The overall pattern in Lorenz's work is the presentation of general principles which are then adapted by Wagner under the pressure of the moment. These general principles were held to be the equivalent of universal law by Lorenz, or at least to hold the status of Idea which must be made concrete in specific instances. To his mind, the many variations, substitutions, and even contradictions which he is obliged to invoke in his analyses do result in fundamentally different forms, despite their surface resemblance.[42] Again and again he admires the multiplicity of forms found in Wagner's works:

> From the whole contemplation, one can see what an unprecedented diversity prevails in Wagnerian forms, despite the fact that everything can be attributed to a few formal types.[43]

Lorenz employed various sorts of analytical sleights of hand to explain the diversity of Wagnerian form. While to us it is clear that he is led by his methodological zeal to conjure up all sorts of tidy (and often fictive) symmetries and parallels, to him they simply seemed logical extensions of his beliefs; we may be able to see the ideological lens through which Lorenz viewed the works, but to him it was invisible.

Lorenz relies on free or opposite symmetry to explain the structure in not quite half of the periods and transitional sections of the *Ring*.[44] He employs the concept just about equally in all four works. Typical examples of the kind of motivic substitution allowed by Lorenz in order to create such "symmetry" is the replacement of the Fluchtmotiv with the Liebesmotiv in *Wk*.I.P.6 and *Wk*.II.P.13, and the substitution of the Verfolgung motive for the Fluchtmotiv in *Wk*.II.P.9. Similarly, in the first act of *Siegfried* Lorenz equates the Nothungphrase and the Schwertmotiv in several instances (e.g., P.10). These examples point to one consequence of Lorenz's understanding of leitmotives: they are regarded as absolutes, with a clear Ur-form of the motive to which later occurrences are held up in comparison. There is no attempt to sort out the various motivic "families" found in the *Ring* (to use Deryck Cooke's expression). Thus the Fluchtmotiv and the Liebesmotiv can be "substituted" for one another as separate, distinct motivic entities, even though—on another level—they are closely related. His use of opposite symmetry is also free; for example, *Gd*.II.P.13 is a Bogen form in which the outer sections are related by opposite symmetry: in the HS, Siegfried lashes out at Brünnhilde, while in the Rp he praises Gutrune. In *Sf*.II.P.14, two strophes are in opposite symmetry where the first concerns the disposal of

---

42. Recall his comparison of his formal types to species in nature, as presented in chapter 3.
43. Lorenz, "Orchestereinleitungen," 176.
44. They are used in approximately 96 of 209 of these.

Mime's body and the second, the disposal of Fafner's (each strophe contains the expected motives pertaining to these characters). This symmetry is obviously of a dramatic nature, and Lorenz's use of it is further proof of his essentially dramatic orientation despite his claims to the contrary.

The most striking thing about the various symmetries alleged in Lorenz's analyses (straightforward symmetry as well as free and opposite) is that their credibility is based almost entirely on *how* Lorenz describes them; their essence is rhetorical, rather than necessarily analytical. Thus, formal sections are equated on the basis of "strong motives," or "preparatory motives" (e.g. *Wk*.II.P.7.A), through "contrasting motives," or even according to the "underlying sense of the motives" (as in *Sf*.III.P.2, where the underlying sense is dramatic). There are many other instances of such equation; for example, a formal equivalence may be made for sections on the basis of their containing "motives pertaining to x," where x may be a different character each time. Sometimes the equivalence rests entirely on Lorenz's choice of words: in *Gd*.II.P.8 the HS and Rp of a Bogen form are balanced by noting that "Hagen has the floor" (i.e., holds the attention of all) in the HS and that the Rp contains a motive from the Hagenwacht ("Die eigne Braut"). He may equate textual sense with musical motives, as in *Gd*.I.P.13. where Brünnhilde's words in St.1 ("Walvaters Bann zu brechen") are balanced musically by the Bannphrase in St.2.[45] Once he invokes the concept of an "ideal Bogen" on the basis of the dramatic action, since the HS has to do with a sword (*Sf*.I.P.3). It also depends on which motives Lorenz chooses to discuss, as he occasionally does not mention them all; thus he ignores the Rittmotiv in the third act prelude of *Siegfried* even though it pervades the entire period. Again, it is important to emphasize that Lorenz regarded these departures from exact symmetry as virtues, and as evidence of Wagner's compositional prowess; he writes over and over how wonderfully free the symmetry of this or that period is. All of these analytical dodges stem from Lorenz's reluctance to admit the primacy of the drama in his analytical considerations.

Lorenz has several other techniques for demonstrating formal equivalence. Themes may be rearranged in formal sections and subsections upon their repetition (as in *Gd*.I.P.14). Further, various types of repetition, not just motivic, are invoked to create form. Thus, a Bogen may be discerned on the basis of dynamic contrast (loud-soft-loud, as in *Gd*.II.P.7), tonality (both HS in E minor, *Rh*.P.12), or character presence, whether singing or not (e.g. the Valkyrie choruses making up the HS of the large "dynamic" rondo of *Wk*.III.P.4). Lorenz even uses form to create form: the outermost sections of the composite, perfect Bogen of *Sf*.II.P.5 are both Bars with opposite symmetry and some motivic similarity. Once, Lorenz explains the

---

45. Lorenz discusses this case in one of his aesthetic asides in the chapter dealing with the higher forms. *Geheimnis* I: 276.

presence of an important motive (the Siegfried motive) in St.2 but lacking in St.1 with the comment that the first Stollen contains an "ideal storage place" for the motive.[46]

Lorenz frequently attempts to equalize the proportions of the sections in his forms through various techniques. Sometimes he does not count measures of silence (or of little activity) as part of the form, as for instance, in Gutrune's monologue. His treatment of such "unsymphonic places" varies: sometimes he discounts them from the formal count (as in *Rh*.P.5 & P.7); at other times, he does not (as in *Wk*.III.P.11). *Rh*.P.9 has an insertion into the form, and some measures unaccounted for, which Lorenz refers to as "Luftpause" within the symphonic structure.[47] Along the same lines, the "interruption" or "development" sections that Lorenz allows in his forms are not included when considering the overall proportion of the form.[48] He also will convert one meter into another if it will equalize the proportions for his table. For instance: in *Gd*.II.P.5, five measures of duple time (mm. 691–95) are inserted into the prevailing triple meter of the section. These Lorenz converts to three and one-half measures of triple time, thus making the first Stollen 23½ measures long, and almost identical in size to the 23–measure second Stollen.

Put simply: Lorenz's forms are not all created equal. There are so many things which are deemed to create formal equivalence that it is difficult to extract common principles from his analyses. To examine all of Lorenz's Abgesänge, for example, would be to discover as many variations as there are examples. The Abgesang may contain entirely new motives, a combination of new and old motives, or simply extend and develop motives from the Stollen.[49] There are varying degrees of formal articulation found in Lorenz's periods. Some are subject to almost microscopic analysis, with every motive and harmonic turn listed, while others are scarcely divided at all. Siegfried's Funeral March is a good example of the latter (*Gd*.III.P.7): Lorenz notes only that the rhythm of Trauerklage recurs eleven times in the period, and acts as a refrain. The second and third periods of *Wk*. I are similarly under articulated, as is *Rh*.P.19.[50]

---

46. Ibid., 198.

47. Ibid., 95.

48. Examples of this may be found in *Wk*.III.P.1 and *Gd*.III.P.6.

49. Willi Schuh, *Formprobleme bei Heinrich Schütz* (Leipzig: Breitkopf & Härtel, 1928; reprint Niedeln, Liechtenstein: Kraus Reprint, 1976) finds Bar forms most commonly in a-a-a and a-b-c patterns in Schütz's works, and less often in the expected a-a-b or a-b-b (Gegenbar) patterns. In his opinion, identical Stollens followed by a contrasting Abgesang is not a requirement of the Bar form, but rather a special case. The essence of Schuh's Bar is two *Ansätze* followed by an *Auslösung*.

50. Another under-articulated period (*Wk*.I.Vorspiel) is considered in much more detail by Lorenz in "Die Orchestereinleitungen der Festspiel-Werke 1934," 173. Interestingly, it is analyzed here as a Gegenbar rather than as a double Bogen form as in *Geheimnis* I (98–99). Lorenz did not recognize the reversed Bar form until the publication of *Geheimnis* II in 1926.

The task of evaluation is made even more difficult because of obvious errors and omissions made by Lorenz. Not infrequently, the period boundaries given by Lorenz in his table of the *Ring*'s poetic-musical periods do not agree with those given in the later, detailed analysis of the periods. Boundaries overlap or do not meet, leaving some measures unaccounted for. In one instance, five measures are included in one period (*Sf*.II.P.7), but analyzed within the next (P.8). Lorenz appears not to notice these discrepancies.[51]

Regardless of these technical problems, it should be apparent that Lorenz's work is far less monolithic than is often maintained. His period boundaries are by no means cast in stone: some changed in the interval between their first appearance in his dissertation and their publication as the first volume of *Das Geheimnis der Form*, others vary within *Geheimnis* I itself (whether deliberately, or erroneously it is difficult to know).[52] As already mentioned, Lorenz himself regarded these boundaries as only provisional, open to refinement by later analysts.[53] The periods themselves show varying degrees of articulation and formal organization. Some, Lorenz notes, reveal a lack of clarity and are "somewhat irregular" or transitional in nature. In addition, Lorenz occasionally offers the reader a choice: for example he notes that the transitional horn canon between the first two scenes of *Götterdämmerung* II could belong to either P.1 or P.2.[54]

It is a curious—even paradoxical—result of Lorenz's analytical technique that while most often the broad outlines of the periods and their governing forms make sense, so too do many of the smallest sections and individual details. Small Bogens and Bars may be found again and again in Wagner's works. It is the analyses of what might be termed the "middle" level—found primarily in the internal forms of the complex periods—which cause the most difficulty.[55] These internal forms are often under-articulated and frequently seem rather cobbled together (as, for example, in an Abgesang

---

51. They are all indicated in the table for the *Ring* given in appendix 2. I have corrected these errors, where possible, on the basis of what I believe Lorenz meant. Some small discrepancies are most likely typographical errors.

52. There are approximately 12 such changes which may be discerned by comparing the respective tables in the dissertation (pp. 17–32) and *Geheimnis* I (pp. 23–46).

53. Indeed eight periods change their governing form between the dissertation and *Geheimnis* I:
    1) *Gd*.II.P.12: from strophic to complex strophic
    2) *Wk*.II.P.7.A: from Bogen to Bar
    3) *Wk*.I.P.12.B.a: from potentiated Bogen to complex strophic
    4) *Gd*.III.P.3: from potentiated Bogen to potentiated Bar
    5) *Gd*.III.Üb. btw. P.1/P.2: from potentiated Bar to complex Bar.
    6) *Gd*.III.P.4: from complex, perfect Bogen to complex strophic
    7) *Rh*.P.17: from complex, perfect Bogen to potentiated Reprisenbar
    8) *Sf*.III.P.14: from un-unified successive form to complex Bar

54. See *Geheimnis* I: 198 and 229–31.

55. Some simple forms, too, are not fully convincing.

consisting of several smaller forms in a row). Sometimes internal sections which are not part of a smaller form (i.e., which conclude the large St. of a Bar, but are not part of the Bogen which makes up most of this St., for example) seem like motivic listing rather than a convincing formal entity.

It is this odd result that leads Adorno to regard Wagnerian form as an empty shell.[56] Lorenz's forms are "superimposed from outside and end up as the nameless schematic patterns that they are when they articulate the abstract beat at the outset."[57] His final conclusion is that

> Wagner's forms, even the paradoxical "Bar"-form which negates the flow of time within which it moves, all fail to do justice to time. Mephistopheles's saying, "It might just as well never have been," has the final word. . . . [Wagner's] music acts as if time had no end, but its effect is merely to negate the hours it fills by leading them back to their starting-point.[58]

I believe that Adorno was lead to this conclusion by the tendency of Lorenz's forms to be quite convincing in their external contours while often problematic in content. They almost seem to make the actual music between the formal division points irrelevant: it is enough that they fill the requisite number of measures. In Adorno's time, Lorenz's view of Wagnerian form was so universally accepted that the former presents it as received truth by presupposing Lorenz's method and conclusions when broaching the subject in the first place. We ought to read the following as a critique of *Lorenz's* view of Wagnerian form rather than of Wagnerian form *per se*:

> The giant packages of [Wagner's] operas are divided up by the notion of striking, of beating time. The whole of the music seems to have been worked out first in terms of beat, and then filled in . . . as if the evenness of beat allowed entire scenes to be grasped at a glance, rather like simplifying fraction-sums by "canceling." . . . Wagner's use of the beat to control time is abstract; it is no more than the idea of time as something articulated by the beat and then projected onto the larger periods. The composer pays no heed to what takes place within time. . . . [his] use of the beat is a fallacious method of mastering the empty time with which he begins, since the measure to which he subjects time does not derive from the musical content, but from the reified order of time itself.[59]

Even if Adorno did not have Lorenz in mind when he wrote this passage, he manages to hit on both the great strength and great weakness of Lorenz's analyses, understood in an abstract sense: while clear and almost immediately

---

56. Theodor Adorno, *In Search of Wagner*, trans. Rodney Livingstone (London: Verso, 1991 [first pub. 1952]), 42.
57. Ibid.
58. Ibid.
59. Ibid., 33.

graspable by readers/listeners, they are nonetheless strangely empty, "a graphic game, without power over the actual music."[60]

The central question for any evaluation of Lorenz is to what extent his aesthetic presuppositions ultimately informed his analyses. In short: is Lorenz a formalist, despite himself? Certainly, in practice—at least at the level of detail—unlike Kurth or Halm, Lorenz does give priority to score over sound—a position which Ian Bent has linked with modernism, and hence formalism.[61] Several of Lorenz's contemporaries seem to have sensed this. Rudolf von Tobel was perhaps the first to point to a certain static quality of his analyses (Lorenz's claims to the contrary notwithstanding)—ironically, however, since Tobel's own form-dynamic analysis is heavily indebted to Lorenz. Tobel's "principal type of dynamic process" is the Bar form, which he takes from Lorenz, but notes that

> Lorenz did not conceive of his notion of Bar form dynamically enough: he follows the alternation of the themes (just as in the now superseded manner of looking at form), illustrates it with letters, and everywhere detects Bar forms independent of dynamic processes wherever the schema M-M-N emerges in the order of the themes. . . . For architectonic forms, doubtless this suffices, but dynamic waves constitute a *fundamentally different formal principle* . . . Lorenz's discoveries are nevertheless not wrong, but they do not grasp the formal process in its innermost and most essential [details] which are based in dynamic events, since Lorenz pursues the alternation of themes only and not their *dynamic function* as well.[62]

Tobel's quarrel with Lorenz seems to stem principally from the way the latter presents his analyses; it is largely a dispute over rhetoric, for Tobel's own analyses are virtually indistinguishable from Lorenz's. His criticisms come from within the expressive aesthetic and do not question its basic premises, and so we have not really answered the question. Is Lorenz a formalist? We will return to this question after briefly surveying the reception history of *Das Geheimnis der Form*.

But first, a few summary remarks about the work as a whole. In many respects, Lorenz's *Das Geheimnis der Form* is more of a demonstration of an aesthetic than a proper analytical system. It is entirely deductive in character, not empirical at all; Lorenz's flexible analytical paradigm mirrors the subjectivity of his aesthetic presuppositions. Lorenz takes his cue in all things

---

61. Ian Bent, ed., *Music Analysis in the Nineteenth Century*, vol. 2: *Hermeneutic Approaches* (Cambridge: Cambridge University Press, 1994), 37.

62. Rudolf von Tobel, *Die Formwelt der klassischen Instrumentalmusik* (Bern and Leipzig: Paul Haupt, 1935), 234. Hellmut Federhofer makes the same point in *Beiträge zur musikalischen Gestaltsanalyse* (Graz: Akademische Druck- und Verlagsanhalt, 1950), 29. [= "Musikalische Form als Ganzheit," Habilitationsschrift, Graz University, 1944].

from Wagner and his works, both literary and musical. The abiding value of Lorenz's work is perhaps three-fold: first, it represents an exhaustive, and still unsurpassed synthesis of Wagner's compositional and dramatic technique; second, it provides a superb document of the expressive aesthetic in practice; and third, it unquestionably forms the basis of modern Wagnerian analytical research (not to mention operatic analysis in general). That Lorenzian questions of large-scale tonal and motivic structures in operatic acts (and entire operas) continue to arise in writings about operatic analysis is only confirmation of their continuing relevance.

Chapter Six

The Reception of
Lorenz's Analytical Method

The following survey of the critical response to Lorenz's work is divided into three sections. The first two chronicle its reception in German-speaking countries before and after the Second World War, and the third is devoted to its reception abroad (primarily in English-speaking countries). It makes no claim to being exhaustive. As is well known, writings about Wagner and his works are legion, and a large number of these works mention Lorenz as well. I have tried to account for the primary critical responses to Lorenz through a representative sampling of this literature. It is by no means a complete account of Wagner research, even in the circumscribed field of Wagnerian form. Most of these accounts could be engaged on their own terms, but (for the most part) I have resisted the temptation to do so, preferring instead simply to present them and comment upon their ideological positioning. With the English-language reception in particular, it should be readily apparent how frequently Lorenz has been misrepresented and misunderstood.

Contemporary Reception in Germany

Initial response to Lorenz's work falls into several related categories which represent differing stages in the reception of *Das Geheimnis der Form*. First and foremost there are reviews in the scholarly press and citations of the books in other works of musical scholarship. There are also several whole articles devoted to Lorenz and his analytical technique. All three types of initial response are remarkable for their uniformly positive tone and glowing recommendations. The next level of reception encompasses those new studies written in direct response to Lorenz's work which employ his analytical technique on the works of other composers. While it is difficult to assess Lorenz's actual influence on a number of these studies, in many cases it is unambiguous, as the authors themselves acknowledge their debt to their predecessor. In several instances, these satellite works are by students of Lorenz from Munich University.

Without exception, the reviews of Lorenz's work in the scholarly litera-
ture are entirely rhapsodic.[1] Over and over the same refrain is sounded:
Wagner has at last been freed from the reproach of formlessness, thanks to
Alfred Lorenz's pathbreaking work.

> Lorenz has not only forever brought to an end the silly fable of Wagner's lack of
> form, he has also provided meticulous, scientific proof that Wagner must be
> regarded as one of the most colossal and innovative creators [*Neuschöpfer*] in
> the realm of form that ever lived.[2]

The reviews typically offer a précis of Lorenz's approach—the tonally determined poetic-musical period internally organized into a single formal
type—which emphasizes its systematic and rigorous nature; one reviewer
compares Lorenz's careful presentation of the forms in the *Ring* to the layout of a botany textbook.[3]

It is clear from these reviews that Lorenz's work was received and understood according to the dictates of the then prevailing expressive aesthetic
position. No reviewer questions such Lorenzian conceptions as free or opposite symmetry, or motivic substitution. Likewise, Lorenz's claim to have
bracketed off the drama from the music is not taken at face value—for such
a division between form and content is impossible according to this aesthetic viewpoint—but rather as a heuristic, rhetorical gesture intended to
distance the author from the customary leitmotivic interpretations of
Wagner's music which then passed for analysis. Certainly, when compared
with these earlier "analyses," Lorenz *does* deal with purely musical matters, it is just that his definition of the purely musical is colored by his belief
in music as expression. In other words, reviewers felt satisfied that Lorenz
engaged the drama through the music itself, as the two are inseparable.
Siegfried Günther expresses this nicely with the term "psychological form":

---

1. A selection of these is included in the bibliography of the present work. It will be immediately apparent that a large number of these are by Karl Grunsky, and his son, Hans Alfred.
In the following discussion of these reviews, I have been careful not to rely entirely on the
opinions of the Grunskys, but to compare these to those of several other reviewers. Nevertheless, the reviews are not markedly different in tone.

To the aforementioned reviews should be added two longer pieces which describe Lorenz's
methodology; these are in fact review-articles of the private printing of Lorenz's dissertation:
Karl Grunsky, "Die Formfrage bei Richard Wagner"; Arthur Seidl, "Ist Richard Wagner
'Romantik' oder bedeutet er vielmehr 'Klassik'—'Form-Auflösung' oder 'Gesetzes-Erfüllung'?"
in *Deutsches Musikjahrbuch* 2/3, ed. Rolf Cunz (Essen: Th. Reismann-Grone, 1925), 126–30.
The Grunsky article provides the first mention of Lorenz's work I have found.

2. Hans Alfred Grunsky, "Über Alfred Lorenz's 'Der musikalische Aufbau von Wagners
Tristan und Isolde'," [Review *of Das Geheimnis der Form bei Richard Wagner*, vol. 2: *Der
musikalische Aufbau von Richard Wagners 'Tristan und Isolde'*, by Alfred Lorenz.] *Zeitschrift
für Musik* 94 (1927): 559.

3. Karl Grunsky, "Die Formfrage bei Richard Wagner," 439.

It is by no means an absolute, abstract, purely intellectual, formal type of analysis . . . but more of an articulative type—a will to find form, always beginning with formalistic means, but developing far beyond this and anchored, before all consciousness, in living feeling. In this analysis, which aims at deep-seated correspondences and often calls for draconian substitutions, the author is obliged to accept so many restrictions that the identities (i.e., the external form) can barely be recognized as decisive. Fundamentally, this gives rise to a new concept of form: that of *"psychological"* form.[4]

Günther was not alone in praising this aspect of Lorenz's work; his point is reiterated in several places by Hans Alfred Grunsky:

Lorenz is the first to shed light on the true and deepest nature of the *Gesamtkunstwerk*. It is a magnificent sight [to see] how, in the end, all the poetic-musical periods combine to form an immense poetic-dramatic total structure [*Gesamtbogen*]. . . . But soon the reader will realize that the individual period is identical in its musical form with the form of the inner psychological development of the drama. For Wagner today appears to us mightier than ever.[5]

Reviewers also typically praise the elegance and simplicity of Lorenz's method, and in particular its accessibility to amateurs.[6] The wider implication of *Das Geheimnis der Form* is frequently noted: that Lorenz's approach can shed light on both pre- and post-Wagnerian works.[7] One article by Hans Alfred Grunsky, entitled "Neues zur Formenlehre," is particularly noteworthy for its enthusiastic advocacy of Lorenz's "new" teachings on musical form.[8]

---

4. Siegfried Günther, Review of *Das Geheimnis der Form bei Richard Wagner*, vol. 1: *Der musikalische Aufbau des Bühnenfestspieles 'Der Ring des Nibelungen'*, by Alfred Lorenz. *Zeitschrift für Musikwissenschaft* 8 (1925): 50.

5. Hans Alfred Grunsky, "Über Alfred Lorenz's 'Der musikalische Aufbau von Wagners Tristan und Isolde'," 560.

6. "The ingenious simplicity of Lorenz's new method is self-explanatory." Hans Alfred Grunsky, "Über Alfred Lorenz's 'Der musikalische Aufbau von Wagners Tristan und Isolde'," 561.

7. "From his Wagnerian analyses, entirely new light falls on the formal art of other composers, both before and after Wagner, and permits this to be grasped in a much more fundamental way than was possible earlier." Otto Baensch, Review of *Das Geheimnis der Form bei Richard Wagner*, vol. 2: *Der musikalische Aufbau von Richard Wagners 'Tristan und Isolde'*, by Alfred Lorenz. *Zeitschrift für Musikwissenschaft* 9 (1927): 600.

8. Hans Alfred Grunsky, "Neues zur Formenlehre," *Zeitschrift für Musikwissenschaft* 16 (1934): 84–91. This article by Grunsky attempts to extend Lorenz's new formal theory by proposing several "Mischformen" which are comprised of various combinations of the three "Grundformen" discovered by Lorenz: the Bogen, the Bar, and the Gegenbar (this latter form named by Grunsky himself). Only one of these hybrid forms—the Reprisenbar—was found by Lorenz: Grunsky suggests that the basis of the Reprisenbar is a marriage between the Bar and the Bogen (m-m-n-m). Grunsky's other hybrid forms are the echo Bogen (Bogen + Gegenbar: m-n-m-m), the echo Bar (Bar + Gegenbar: m-m-n-n), the double Bar (Gegenbar + Bar: m-n-n-m, or m-n-n-o), and the four-part Bogen progression (Bogen + Bogen: m-n-m-n). These suggestions appear to be an attempt on the part of Grunsky to account for the various permutations of binary form—to bring binary structures into the fold, as it were. I have not found Grunsky's terminology adopted by any other scholar.

During the late 1920s and 1930s, Lorenz went out of his way to publicize and popularize his research, primarily through the publication of introductory articles in such widely read (at least by Wagnerians) journals as the *Bayreuther Blätter* and the *Bayreuther Festspielführer*. The appearance of these articles can therefore be seen as an implicit (occasionally explicit) endorsement of Lorenz's work on the part of the Bayreuth establishment. As we have seen, he also offered courses in his research in Munich at the University. These efforts proved worthwhile, as Lorenz's findings were soon being disseminated as received truth not only within the specialized field of Wagner studies, but also in general textbooks of music history and musical form.[9] For example, Hans Joachim Moser's *Geschichte der deutschen Musik* (1924, 2/1928) gives an extensive overview of Lorenz's method, complete with examples.[10] Richard Eichenauer's very basic introduction to musical form contains a brief discussion of Lorenz's work, although Lorenz is not mentioned by name. Eichenauer writes that

> Wagner's music drama is not musically "formless" and does not stretch along the thread of the action, like some endless tapeworm, without revealing large musical forms; rather, recent research has proven that it shows clearly recognizable musical divisions in well-known shapes.[11]

Other examples could easily be added to these two.[12]

What is noteworthy about all of these early notices is their uniformly positive viewpoint. To be sure, several reviewers express the occasional cavil about this or that small point, but none ever questions the soundness or appropriateness of the approach in toto.[13] Rudolf von Tobel's criticisms of Lorenz, discussed in the previous chapter, have less to do with the details of Lorenz's analyses than with the language in which they are expressed, and his own analyses are almost indistinguishable from Lorenz's own.[14] In fact,

---

9. With regard to the former category, praise for Lorenz's work occupies a major place in Otto Strobel's 1943 survey of Wagnerian scholarship: "Ziele und Wege der Wagnerforschung."

10. Hans Joachim Moser, *Geschichte der deutschen Musik*, vol. 3, *Vom Auftreten Beethovens bis zur Gegenwart*, 2nd ed. (Stuttgart: Lokay, 1928; reprint, Hildesheim: Georg Olms, 1968), 255–60. This section is largely unchanged from the first edition of Moser's work (1924), where the references are to Lorenz's dissertation rather than its printed form as *Geheimnis* I.

11. Richard Eichenauer, *Von den Formen der Musik* (Wolfenbüttel und Berlin: Georg Kallmeyer, 1943), 93. Like Lorenz, Eichenauer was an early supporter of the Nazi movement, and is most (in)famous for his 1932 study *Musik und Rasse*, 2nd ed. (Munich: Lehmann, 1937). He was not a trained musicologist. On Eichenauer, see Pamela M. Potter, "Trends in German Musicology, 1918–1943: the Effects of Methodological, Ideological, and Institutional Change on the Writing of Music History," (Ph.D. dissertation, Yale University, 1991), 64–68.

12. Lorenz himself provides several in *Geheimnis* IV: 193.

13. Thus, for example, Siegfried Günther quarrels with aspects of Lorenz's tonal line (*Geheimnis* I: 58) in the review cited above in note 4, and Karl Grunsky wishes that Lorenz had given names to some of the self-standing "numbers" in the *Ring* ("Formfrage bei Richard Wagner," 439), but acknowledges that Lorenz wanted to avoid the old saw about "number opera."

14. See above, p. 170.

I have encountered just one extensive disagreement with Lorenz's analyses during this period, and this is simply one of degree rather than of kind. In 1942 Theodor Veidl published an "Entgegnung" to Lorenz's analysis of the *Tristan* prelude in which he argues that Lorenz distorts the thematic content of the prelude, which is really a type of rondo form, rather than a perfect Bogen, as Lorenz believed.[15] The alacrity with which even this small criticism is refuted in an article of the same year by Herbert von Stein is further testament to the influence and esteem given to Alfred Lorenz's work.[16]

The further fruitfulness of Lorenz's approach to questions of musical form may be judged by the veritable cottage industry of Lorenzian treatments of the music of other composers. Works by Bach,[17] Beethoven,[18] Bruckner,[19] Liszt,[20] Humperdinck,[21] Richard Strauss,[22] and even Giacomo

15. Theodor Veidl, "Die formale Gestaltung des Tristan-Vorspiels: Eine Entgegnung," *Die Musik* 34 (1942): 127–30. Lorenz's analysis of the *Tristan* prelude was first published in the *Zeitschrift für Musikwissenschaft* in 1923, and is reprinted verbatim in *Geheimnis* II. It appears in translation by Robert Bailey in Richard Wagner, *Prelude and Transfiguration from* Tristan und Isolde, Norton Critical Score, ed. Robert Bailey (New York: Norton, 1985), 204–20.

16. Herbert von Stein, "Die formale Gestaltung des Tristanvorspiels," *Die Musik* 35 (1942): 78–79.

17. Wilhelm Luetger, "Bachs Motette Jesu meine Freude," *Musik und Kirche* 4 (1932): 97–113.

18. Otto Baensch, "Der Aufbau des 2. Satzes in Beethovens IX. Symphonie," *Bayreuther Festspielführer* (1925): 238–46; Baensch, *Aufbau und Sinn des Chorfinales in Beethovens neunter Symphonie* (Berlin and Leipzig: Gruyter, 1930); Josef Braunstein, *Beethovens Leonore-Ouvertüren: eine historisch-stilkritische Untersuchung* (Leipzig: Breitkopf & Härtel, 1927).

19. Hans Alfred Grunsky, "Der erste Satz von Bruckners Neunter: ein Bild höchster Formvollendung." Lorenz also refers to a book-length study by Grunsky, entitled *Formenwelt und Sinngefüge der Bruckner-Symphonien*. This work seems never to have been published. Although it does appear in Leopold Nowak's bibliography for Bruckner in the *New Grove*, it is not listed in any national bibliography available to me. An unpublished letter of 5 May 1933 from Hans Alfred Grunsky to the Kultusministerium (BDC Hans Alfred Grunsky file) explicitly states that it was not published owing to the collapse of its publisher. On Lorenzian treatments of Bruckner, see Stephen McClatchie, "Bruckner and the Bayreuthians; or, *Das Geheimnis der Form bei Anton Bruckner*," in *Bruckner Studies*, ed. Timothy L. Jackson and Paul Hawkshaw (Cambridge: Cambridge University Press, 1997), 110–21.

20. Joachim Bergfeld, *Die formale Struktur der symphonischen Dichtungen Franz Liszts* (Inaugural Dissertation, Berlin, 1931; Eisenach: Philipp Kühner, 1931).

21. H. Kuhlmann, "Stil und Form in der Musik von Humperdincks Oper 'Hänsel und Gretel'," (Ph.D. dissertation, Marburg, 1930); cited by Lorenz, *Geheimnis* IV: 193.

22. Edmund Wachten, *Das Formproblem in den sinfonischen Dichtungen von Richard Strauß (mit besonderer Berücksichtigung seiner Bühnenwerke)* (Straßburg: P. Heitz, 1933); Wachten, "Der einheitliche Grundzug der Straußschen Formgestaltung," *Zeitschrift für Musikwissenschaft* 16 (1934): 257–74; Heinz Röttger, "Das Formproblem bei Richard Strauss, gezeigt an der Oper 'Die Frau ohne Schatten' mit Einschluß von 'Guntram' und 'Intermezzo'," (Ph.D. dissertation, Munich, 1937; Berlin: Junker and Dünnhaupt, 1937).
Röttger's book duplicates Lorenz's analytical technique almost exactly for the three Strauss works under consideration: all are divided into poetic-musical periods, determined by key, which then themselves are shaped according to certain recurring formal types. Röttger employs all of Lorenz's analytical apparatus, including the notion of motivic substitution and free

Puccini[23] were examined along Lorenzian lines, and their formal structures (complete with Bogens and Bars) illustrated in tabular form in imitation of Lorenz's Wagner analyses.[24] It is noteworthy that, with the exceptions of Bach and Beethoven, each of these composers has been accused of "formlessness" in their own right; Lorenz's defense of Wagnerian form is thus mustered in support of other "progressive" composers. Many of the above-mentioned studies contribute to the burgeoning literature of the expressive aesthetic movement, either through discussion of Schopenhauerian aesthetics or of psychological form (form-as-rhythm). Each explicitly credits Lorenz with the discovery of the analytical technique employed, and most use Lorenzian analytical charts to diagram the works under consideration.[25]

The remarkable uniformity of critical opinion about Lorenz's work during his lifetime may be attributed to the then prevailing philosophical and aesthetic climate. *Das Geheimnis der Form* was the right book at the right time. It is at once a reflection of the *Zeitgeist* of interwar Germany—not only philosophically, aesthetically, and psychologically, but also politically— and a contributing factor to that sociological situation. Further elaboration of the cultural and ideological context of *Das Geheimnis der Form*, although certainly an integral part of its reception, must nevertheless be deferred to the next chapter. The complicity of Lorenz's method with the goals and methods of National Socialism—not to mention their shared cultural

---

and opposite symmetry. Interestingly, unlike Lorenz, Röttger is explicit that the dramatic content of the periods is a major criterion for their determination. His preface acknowledges his debt to Lorenz, and notes that Strauss himself had seen and approved his work. (The book is dedicated to Strauss.)

23. Walter Maisch, *Puccinis musikalische Formgebung untersucht an der Oper 'La Bohème* (Neustadt a.d. Aisch: P.C.W. Schmidt, 1934).

24. One book even employs a Lorenz-like analytical technique on the music of Heinrich Schütz: Willi Schuh, *Formprobleme bei Heinrich Schütz*. Schuh's work is also heavily influenced by Ernst Kurth. Schuh posits an alternation between static forms (A-B-A) and dynamic forms (A-A-B)—that is, between Bogen and Bar—which underlies every historical era. Schütz's, like Wagner's, was a dynamic era.

25. Among a list of studies which employ his methodology (*Geheimnis* IV: 193), Lorenz includes several works which have not been available to me: Paul Egert, "Beiträge zur Geschichte der Klaviersonate nach Beethoven," (Ph.D. diss., Munich University, 1928) [likely a student of Lorenz]; Carl Heinzen, *Bachs Inventionen und Symphonien*; Willy Salomon, *Carmen*. Lorenz notes that these last two works are not yet published; I have been unable to find any trace of them.

In this context, it is appropriate to mention Ilmari Krohn's studies of Bruckner's and Sibelius's symphonies: *Der Formbau in den Symphonien von Jean Sibelius* (Helsinki: Finnische Literaturgesellschaft, 1942); *Anton Bruckners Symphonien: Untersuchung über Formenbau und Stimmungsgehalt* (Helsinki: Finnische Literaturgesellschaft, 1955–57). In these works, Krohn analyzes the formal structure of each symphony according to a synthetic hierarchy of structural levels (Taktfuß, Zeile, Period, Strophe [or Stollen], Reihe, Gefüge, etc.) which bears a close resemblance to Lorenz's hierarchic structures. Krohn also speaks of formal rhythm and of Bogen and Bar forms in these works. Nevertheless, his method appears to have been developed independently of Lorenz's.

roots, as well as Lorenz's close personal ties to the movement—accounts for the radically different reception afforded Lorenz's work in the aftermath of the Second World War.

Post-War Reception in Germany

The issue of collective guilt and individual involvement during the Nazi regime is far from straightforward, not simply within the relatively small musicological community, but within German society as a whole. Even today many Germans appear to suffer from collective amnesia about the war years.[26] The de-Nazification trials which a large portion of German society was forced to undergo in the late 1940s served, in many respects, to band Germans together in general agreement to forget the entire Hitler period. In recent years, however, many younger Germans have made tentative attempts to come to terms with the Nazi years, and with the activity of currently prominent Germans during those years. As more and more of those directly involved pass away, it is easier to discuss such matters in objective terms.[27]

For many, to posit any continuity between National Socialist and post-War Germany is seen as impossible. Yet, to take only one relevant example, the victorious Allies did not remove a single professor from a chair in any German university. Many scholars closely identified with the Nazi movement continued to thrive—teaching and publishing—until their deaths. This is indeed the case in Wagner studies. Essays by Hans Alfred Grunsky, for example, the author of a monograph entitled *Seele und Staat: Die psychologischen Grundlagen des nationalsozialistischen Siegs über den bürgerlichen und bolschewistischen Menschen,*[28] are to be found in the official program book of the Bayreuth Festival in the 1950s. Grunsky continued his advocacy of Lorenz's analytical technique throughout this time, most notably in a piece about the "symphonic structure" of the third act of *Tristan.*[29] Likewise, a 1962 monograph by Herbert von Stein—Lorenz's defender in the 1942 *Die Musik* exchange discussed above—uses Lorenzian analysis to support his contention that the forms of absolute music are used

---

26. For example, consider the recent fractious debate amongst many German historians and other intellectuals about the singularity of the Holocaust (the so-called *Historikerstreit*). For a collection of many of the relevant documents, see *Forever in the Shadow of Hitler?*, trans. James Knowlton and Truett Cates (Atlantic Highlands, N.J.: Humanities Press, 1993).

27. For German musicology, there is the invaluable work of Pamela Potter, "Trends in German Musicology," and to a lesser extent, Michael H. Kater, *The Twisted Muse: Musicians and Their Music in the Third Reich* (New York: Oxford, 1997).

28. Berlin: Junker & Dünnhaupt, 1935.

29. Grunsky stopped using his middle name after the war. Hans [Alfred] Grunsky, "'Tristan und Isolde': Der symphonische Aufbau des dritten Aufzugs," *Zeitschrift für Musik* 113 (1952): 390–94. I discuss Grunsky and his activities in "Bruckner and the Bayreuthians," 117–20.

to convey the drama in Wagnerian opera.[30] In fact, recent research has high-lighted an essential continuity in some Wagnerian circles between Weimar, the Third Reich, and even post-war Germany, so it is not entirely surprising that Lorenz was still influential after the war.[31]

But by far the most influential espousal of Lorenz's methodology amongst post-war Wagnerians was that of Curt von Westernhagen. Westernhagen offers a prime example of a scholar sympathetic to the Nazi cause who was nevertheless able to further his career in post-war Germany (indeed, Westernhagen's influence as a Wagner scholar has been comparatively recent).[32] His 1956 book on Wagner, *Richard Wagner: Sein Werk, sein Wesen, seine Welt* (Zurich: Atlantis) discusses *Das Geheimnis der Form* in some detail, as one of two "fundamental and conclusive" works on Wagner.[33] Westernhagen presents Lorenz's method clearly and concisely, but in a context and terms which reveal the author's deep sympathy with the expressive aesthetic.[34] Lorenz's analytical technique is not treated as something objec-

---

30. Herbert von Stein, *Dichtung und Musik im Werk Richard Wagners* (Berlin: Gruyler, 1962), especially chapter 3: "Die Form der Musik Wagners."

A 1952 article by Willy Hess on *Die Meistersinger* also employs uncritically Lorenz's analyses of that work: Willy Hess, "'Die Meistersinger von Nürnberg': Ihre dichterisch-musikalische Gesamtform," *Zeitschrift für Musik* 113 (1952): 394–97.

31. See, for example, Fredric Spotts, *Bayreuth: A History of the Wagner Festival* (New Haven and London: Yale University Press, 1994).

32. Westernhagen's work during the period of Nazi Germany includes: *Richard Wagners Kampf gegen seelische Fremdherrschaft* (Munich: Lehmann, 1935); "Gobineau," *Bayreuther Festspielführer* (1937): 161–66; "Magie der Tat," *Bayreuther Festspielführer* (1939): 142–47; and "Wagner und das Reich," in *Neue Wagner-Forschungen: Erste Folge*, ed. Otto Strobel (Karlsruhe: G. Braun, 1943), 43–73. Zelinsky, in *Richard Wagner: Ein deutsches Thema*, 282, notes that Westernhagen never renounced these writings. His post-war books on Wagner have been accused of betraying too great a "love" of Wagner: John Deathridge has dismissed as hagiography his 1968 (Eng. trans., 1978) biography of Wagner (*19th-Century Music* 5 [1981]: 84–88). Westernhagen joined the NSDAP on 1 February 1930, and was Pg. 203950 (BDC Westernhagen file).

Westernhagen's post-war position is similar to that of Otto Strobel, director of the Bayreuth archives until his death in 1953 (and formerly director of the Richard-Wagner-Forschungsstätte founded by Hitler in 1938). On Strobel, see Stephen McClatchie, Review of Fredric Spotts, *Bayreuth: A History of the Wagner Festival*, *Cambridge Opera Journal* 7 (1995): 283 n. 13.

33. The other theory, which Westernhagen refers to as the "principle of thematic development," is that of Walter Engelsmann: *Wagners Klingendes Universum* (Potsdam: Müller & Kiepenheuer, 1933); Engelsmann, "Die 'Konstruktion' der Melodie in Wagners 'Tristan und Isolde'," *Bayreuther Festspielführer* (1938): 145–56. Engelsmann attempts to discover a work's motivic seed or seeds—its *Werkthema*—and account for its manipulation on the part of the composer to construct the work. Very often these archetypal motivic gestures are then interpreted on a psychological basis; for example, in the *Ring* the descending major second associated with the Rhinemaidens' cry is said to represent *Freude* or *Glück*, while its minor analogue, associated with "Wehe!," signifies *Angst* or *Schmerz*.

34. All of Lorenz's key concepts, such as motivic substitution, free and opposite symmetry, formal potentiation, etc. are mentioned by Westernhagen, who also accepts the applicability of Lorenz's method to the works of other composers.

tive and disassociated from aesthetic questions; rather, Westernhagen encloses it in a chapter ("Das Bewußte und das Unbewußte") devoted to the question of artistic inspiration versus reflection. (Westernhagen, like Lorenz, believes in the primacy of inspiration, which is then subjected to conscious "working out" on the part of the composer.) Several of his comments read like Lorenz's own:

> And now, if one would not pursue formal analysis, one should forget all names and technical terminology; one needs only to hold before one's eyes the image, in detail and in aggregate, in atom and in universe, of how the same powers work to build a shape and create a cosmos. As well, whoever would penetrate more deeply into the secret of form need not, because of that, study all of Lorenz's analyses; even less need he agree with every single case, since the element of subjectivity is never completely eliminated. He must also acknowledge that a remnant will always remain that cannot be accounted for theoretically. . . . Despite these reservations that I would like to make, the study of Lorenz's work yields lasting, practical benefits.[35]

Westernhagen, like Lorenz, here appears to regard analysis as only a technique designed to attune the listener to the true essence of the work: the most desirable goal of an analysis is to make itself superfluous to the reader. His work may be seen as perhaps the final manifestation of the Old Bayreuthian aesthetic of music as expression which had unquestionably fallen into disrepute after the war.[36]

More symptomatic of postwar concerns was the strong rearguard action embodied in Theodor Adorno's socio-political interpretation of Wagner, with its underlying claims for work immanence and aesthetic autonomy (*Versuch über Wagner*, 1952). Significantly, Adorno's work represents the first large-scale attack on Lorenz's method in any language.[37] His "demystification" of Wagnerian form—despite being couched as an absolute—is properly read as a demystification of *Lorenz's* view of Wagnerian form; by

---

35. Westernhagen, *Wagner: Sein Werk, sein Wesen, seine Welt*, 85.

36. Westernhagen's later Wagner biography, as well as his study of Wagner's composition sketches for the *Ring*, continues to speak highly of Lorenz.

37. The very first negative assessment of Lorenz that I have found is from 1948, and occurs—almost as an aside—in Jacques Handschin's brief discussion of Wagner in his music history textbook:

> If Alfred Lorenz's well-known books undertake the task of presenting Wagner's works as model examples of form and structure on the basis of mere harmonic and tonal correspondences, then I can only say once again: not everything that is form to you is form to me. To me, Wagner's music—like Bruckner's and Reger's—is more flow and urgency [*mehr Fluß und Drang*] than form.

Musikgeschichte im Überblick, 2nd ed. (Lucerne & Stuttgart: Räber, 1964), 367. (This sentence is unchanged from the first edition).

that time the two had become inextricably intertwined. Adorno's approach is a deliberate attempt to rescue Wagner from himself, and from those forces in history that had co-opted him to their own ends. It is a deliberately antimonumental approach, which resists as ideologically suspect any attempt at totalization—the very core of Lorenz's treatment of Wagner.[38]

Apart from Adorno, however, Wagnerian scholarship remained generally silent—indeed almost moribund—in the immediate post-war years.[39] One article, from 1962, suggests the turning of the tide against Lorenz. In "Richard Wagners musikalische Gestaltungsprinzipien," Georg Knepler acknowledges Lorenz's central role in combating the charge of Wagner's "formlessness," but concludes that

> Lorenz's Gestaltist [*erkenntnistheoretische*] orientation is old-fashioned and the one-sided position does not permit fundamental judgements. Lorenz's results must certainly be considered, but they can not be taken as the last word on the subject.[40]

Knepler's considered assessment of Lorenz is particularly striking when compared to the one-sided polemics soon to emerge from the pen of Carl Dahlhaus. While the ultimate result of both critical stances is the complete dismissal of Lorenz's work, Knepler's is remarkable for its recognition of Lorenz's differently oriented ideological stance.

Dahlhaus's antipathy towards Lorenz's Wagner analyses is well known to those possessing even passing acquaintance with his groundbreaking Wagner studies.[41] During the discussion following a paper on the poetic-musical period, Dahlhaus makes this abundantly clear:

---

38. Adorno's view of Lorenz is discussed in greater detail above, pp. 169–70.

39. A glance at the extensive bibliography (arranged chronologically) which accompanies Barry Millington's article on Wagner in *The New Grove Dictionary of Opera* (1992) will corroborate this point. There is a marked decrease of publications about Wagner from the late 1940s to the end of the 1950s, particularly when compared to the decades immediately preceding and following this time.

40. Georg Knepler, "Richard Wagners musikalische Gestaltungsprinzipien," *Beiträge zur Musikwissenschaft* 5 (1963): 33.

41. The most important of these are as follows, arranged in order of first publication: "Wagners Begriff der 'dichterisch-musikalischen Period'," in *Beiträge zur Geschichte der Musikanschauung im 19. Jahrhunderts*, ed. Walter Salmen, vol. 1 of *Studien zur Musikgeschichte des 19. Jahrhunderts* (Regensburg: Gustav Bosse, 1965), 179–94; "Formprinzipien in Wagner's 'Ring des Nibelungen'," in *Beiträge zur Geschichte der Oper*, ed. Heinz Becker (Regensburg: Gustav Bosse, 1969), 95–129; *Richard Wagner's Music Dramas* (1971), trans. Mary Whittall (Cambridge: Cambridge University Press, 1979); "Issues in Composition," In *Between Romanticism and Modernism: Four Studies in the Music of the Later Nineteenth Century*, trans. Mary Whittall (Berkeley: University of California Press, 1980 [German ed., 1974]), 42–78; "Wagners dramatisch-musikalischer Formbegriff," in *Colloquium 'Verdi-Wagner' Rom 1969*, ed. Friedrich Lippmann, vol. 11 of *Analecta Musicologica* (Cologne: Böhlau, 1972), 290–303; "Tonalität und Form in Wagners 'Ring des Nibelungen'," *Archiv für Musikwissenschaft* 40 (1983): 165–73; (with John

For my paper I have worked through the analyses of *Walküre* and *Rheingold*, and unfortunately must say that I did not find a *single* analysis without error. It seems to me that Lorenz's analyses presuppose an idea of form which, in its combination of little stones into arches, symmetries, and reprises, is contrary to Wagner's idea of form.[42]

The main points of his Lorenz critique are easily summarized.

First, and most essentially, Dahlhaus's understanding of Wagnerian form is not the same as Lorenz's. This leads him to claim that Lorenz's methodology is entirely inappropriate for Wagner's music. To Dahlhaus, Wagner's mature music dramas are constructed of a "web" of themes (the leitmotives) which create their musical form. This form is not architectonic, and does not involve the extended elaboration of a few thematic ideas; rather it is "web-like," a polythematic network. He expresses this idea most concisely in the *New Grove Wagner*:

Form as "architecture" was replaced by form as "web" (Lorenz did not appreciate this when he defended Wagner's music against charges of "formlessness" by trying to reduce it to *Bogen* and *Bar* forms; rather, he should have demonstrated the inapplicability to Wagner's music of the formal concept on which the criticism was based).[43]

Dahlhaus's belief in the essential flexibility and unschematic nature of Wagnerian form, embodied in the rejection of architectural form, is also discernible in his idea of "logical" form. This concept, which stresses what Dahlhaus sees as the ad hoc nature of Wagnerian forms (form as development), is freely interchanged with that of form-as-web in his writings.[44]

Dahlhaus argues for the essentially prose-like character of Wagner's music. In his opinion, Wagner abandons quadratic (i.e. periodic) phrase construction—the hallmark of the classic-romantic style—after *Lohengrin*. Thus an analytical technique such as Lorenz's, premised upon music organized in balanced and recurring phrases is entirely inappropriate for Wagner's mature works where this architectonic principle does not obtain in the least.

These principal beliefs provide the framework of Dahlhaus's attack upon Lorenz.[45] At its core is the assertion that Lorenz falsified Wagner's intent in his adoption of the poetic-musical period principle from *Oper und Drama* as the basis for his analytical technique. According to Dahlhaus, under this

---

Deathridge) *The New Grove Wagner* (New York: Norton, 1984); "The Music," in *Wagner Handbook*, ed. Ulrich Müller and Peter Wapnewski, trans. and ed. John Deathridge (Cambridge, MA: Harvard University Press, 1992 [first pub. 1986]), 297–314.

42. Dahlhaus, "Wagner's Begriff der dichterisch-musikalischen Periode," 189.

43. Dahlhaus, *The New Grove Wagner*, 126.

44. See, for example, Dahlhaus, *Richard Wagner's Music Dramas*, 128.

45. This may be found in its most concentrated form in Dahlhaus, "Formprinzipien in Wagners Ring des Nibelungen."

rubric Wagner meant a section of approximately eight to thirty measures (certainly not the hundreds of measures proposed by Lorenz). He also suggests that although Wagner is unequivocal that a poetic-musical period is based upon a single tonic, to assert that every section based upon a single tonic is a poetic-musical period is "logically tenuous."[46]

After attacking the basis of Lorenz's analytical technique, Dahlhaus turns to the details. One by one he quarrels with Lorenz's period divisions, his notions of symmetry, his conception of the symphonic melos and unending melody, the apparent static nature of Lorenz's formal types, and the widely differing sizes and proportions of his periods and forms. Each of Lorenz's principles, he suggests, is a figment of his "own imagination, conjured up in apologetic zeal."[47] But Dahlhaus makes no attempt to comprehend why Lorenz came up with these ideas in the first place; for one so interested in aesthetics, Dahlhaus seems to have shown little concern for the aesthetic foundations of Lorenz's work.

Dahlhaus's apparent blindness to Lorenz's analytical presuppositions in the field of aesthetics and philosophy is perhaps not surprising once we consider his own historical position. Like Adorno's work, that of Dahlhaus is a reaction to the totalizing and hierarchizing tendencies of pre-war scholarship. With his radically different approach to Wagner, Dahlhaus makes a clear attempt to distance himself from the excesses of the Bayreuth Circle and other pre-war Wagnerians. By proposing a new paradigm through which to understand Wagner, he aims to disassociate the latter from the now ideologically suspect older paradigms. Yet in so doing, Dahlhaus frequently oversteps the mark. If Lorenz may be criticized for inflexibly insisting that all of Wagner's music is perfectly structured tonally and formally, Dahlhaus too may be censured for his own inflexible insistence on the opposite.[48] To borrow Joseph Kerman's criticism of Lorenz, Dahlhaus's Lorenz critique is a "*reductio ad absurdum* of certain valid insights."[49]

Following Dahlhaus's death in 1989, a number of studies of his work and influence have appeared. One in particular, by James Hepokoski, is

46. Dahlhaus, "Wagners Begriff der 'dichterisch-musikalischen Period'," 180.

47. Dahlhaus, "Issues in Composition," 60.

48. Anthony Newcomb, among others, has pointed out this reactionary character of Dahlhaus's Wagner scholarship; see "The Birth of Music out of the Spirit of Drama," 39–40. Both Newcomb and William Kinderman (in a personal letter) argue that Dahlhaus obscures or minimizes the large-scale structural techniques and symmetries in Wagner's music in his insistence on concentrating on only short sections of the works at a time, and in resisting any attempt to totalize his findings. Christopher Wintle has shown through a comparison of analyses of the same section of *Tristan* by Lorenz, Schoenberg, and Dahlhaus, how Dahlhaus regularly ignores and distorts large-scale tonal movements: "Issues in Dahlhaus," *Music Analysis* 1 (1982): 341–55, esp. 345–51.

49. Joseph Kerman, *Opera as Drama*, rev. ed. (Berkeley & Los Angeles: University of California Press, 1988), 170. The comment is unchanged from the original (1956) edition.

helpful in its attempt to position Dahlhaus and his writings within the post-war intellectual climate of divided Germany.[50] Hepokoski's primary concern is Dahlhaus's response to the central German epistemological crisis of the 1960s and 1970s: the collapse of positivism and the rise of the Marxist left. He argues persuasively that Dahlhaus be numbered amongst the culturally conservative right who were anxious to "shelter the German romantic canon from [the] ideology critique" of the left.[51] This is particularly noticeable in Dahlhaus's discussion of the musical work, about which Hepokoski writes:

> [Dahlhaus's] principal strategy was, first, to insist that as concrete art works [the Austro-Germanic canon] were conceived primarily under the category of aesthetic autonomy . . . and second, to argue that historians should generally stress primary, not secondary categories. This permitted "great music" to continue to be considered principally within the realm of aesthetics, as a type of socially functionless, nonauthoritarian discourse.[52]

In the case of Wagner, then, this belief allows Dahlhaus to bracket off what he calls the "intellectual and political significance" of Wagner's work as a "part of history [which can now] be regarded with the historian's detachment."[53] (In other words, Dahlhaus dismisses as unimportant the common roots of Wagner's style and National Socialism, as well as the protofascist elements of the works themselves, not to mention the association of Bayreuth with the Nazis.) Hepokoski calls these words "highly charged," and suggests that they "cannot be understood apart from the resistance against which they were written."[54]

On the surface, it is apparent that Dahlhaus's own historical position and the intellectual climate during which his Lorenz critiques were written contributed not only to the polemical nature of these writings, but also to their fundamental negative orientation. Certainly the ideological complicity of Lorenz's work was anathema to Dahlhaus. But Dahlhaus's conservative stance in the face of the intellectual debates of his day suggests a strange affinity between him and Lorenz in their similar insistence on the immanence of art and its remove from mundane concerns. Both may be located within the traditions of German idealism.

One of Dahlhaus's contemporaries, Rudolf Stephan, attempted to obliterate Lorenz's influence by returning to Guido Adler's 1904 suggestion that Wagner's operas were organized according to the (albeit hidden) principle

---

50. James Hepokoski, "The Dahlhaus Project and Its Extra-Musicological Sources," *19th-Century Music* 14 (1991): 221–46.

51. Ibid., 225.

52. Ibid., 222.

53. Dahlhaus, *Richard Wagner's Music Dramas*, 1.

54. Hepokoski, "Dahlhaus Project," 226.

of recitative and aria.[55] Stephan expands this thought into a theory of contrast between tightly organized and more diffuse music, which he terms *Attraktionszentren* and *Durchführung*.[56] Common to both Stephan and Dahlhaus is an attack on Lorenz's period boundaries and other details of the analyses without any consideration of their founding principles. Stephan's desire to reject Lorenz and all that he stood for leads him to such statements as the following, written as if to erase the very fact of Lorenz's existence from the field of Wagner scholarship:

> The foundation of Wagner's musical form—which certainly appears less secretive—is the development technique of the classical sonata.[57]

Egon Voss makes the same point in even stronger terms:

> Lorenz did not prove by means of his analyses that Wagner's music is well structured, nor in what way it is structured; what he did was to confirm the reproach that his music is formless. The secret of form, which Lorenz thought he had discovered, revealed itself as the principle of formlessness. Wagner's music dramas are indifferent towards specifically musical form, and in this sense they are in fact lacking in form.[58]

To be sure, Stephan, Dahlhaus, and Voss make valid observations concerning certain problems and inconsistencies in Lorenz's work (many of which have already been pointed out at the conclusion of the previous chapter); I do not wish to minimize their important role in this respect, but only to make the obvious point that their work too is a product of a given time and historical situation. Antipathy towards the Nazi regime of their youth, as well as their own places within the very different postwar musical climate, may have lead them to overstate their case somewhat with regard to Lorenz. Some scholars, such as Egon Voss and Reinhold Brinkmann, make explicit Lorenz's ties—both intellectual and personal—to the National Socialist state, but all avoid any systematic account of these connections.[59]

---

55. Guido Adler, *Richard Wagner: Vorlesungen gehalten an der Universität zu Wien* (Leipzig: Breitkopf & Härtel, 1904).

56. Rudolf Stephan, "Gibt es ein Geheimnis der Form bei Richard Wagner?" in *Das Drama Richard Wagner als musikalisches Kunstwerk*, ed. Carl Dahlhaus, vol. 23 of *Studien zur Musikgeschichte des 19. Jahrhunderts* (Regensburg: Gustav Bosse, 1970), 9–16.

57. Ibid., 14.

58. Egon Voss, "Once again: The Secret of Form in Wagner's Works," *Wagner* 4 (June 1983): 78 [German pub. in *Theaterarbeit an Wagners 'Ring'*, ed. Dietrich Mach (Munich: R. Piper, 1978)].

59. Reinhold Brinkmann, "'Drei der Fragen stell' ich mir frei': Zur Wanderer-Szene im 1. Akt von Wagners 'Siegfried'." To my knowledge, Brinkmann is the first scholar to highlight the ideological component of Lorenz's thought:

> Without a doubt, Lorenz's method of forcing each separate individual into the totality of a higher, self-replicating, abstract unity is not only inherently ideological in terms of form, it

Instead of attempting to reconstruct (and thereby exorcize?) Lorenz's aesthetic and philosophical context with their criticisms of his work, post-war German scholars have preferred to reject Lorenz out of hand; paradoxically, this results in *Das Geheimnis der Form* becoming a palimpsest upon which new formal paradigms are written in response and reaction to its erased, but unconsidered, preoccupations.

English-Language Reception: Lorenz as Artifact

Das Geheimnis der Form was slow to attract the attention of non-German readers. It was not reviewed in any of the major musicological journals. The first significant mention of Lorenz which I have located is found in Gerald Abraham's *A Hundred Years of Music*, from 1938.[60]

Abraham presents the basic principles of the method, and then reproduces Lorenz's analyses for the first act of *Die Walküre*, during the course of which he writes of Lorenz's ability "to demonstrate . . . how completely the basic principles of musical form underlie the vast musical-dramatic structures of Wagner's mature works."[61] Although he expresses some reservations about the odd analytical detail (suggesting that Lorenz occasionally strains an analytical point to fit into his theory), Abraham's overall tone is admiring, even to the point of writing approvingly of several of Lorenz's higher forms. He concludes with the observation that

> [t]he result of Lorenz's great analytical work is to demonstrate conclusively that as long as Wagner was true to his own axiom that the poetic-dramatic stuff of opera music be essentially "musical" (i.e., emotional) and not intellectual (argument or narrative), his work was cast in coherent and more or less clear musical forms; and that when argument and narrative do intrude . . ., though they injure the form, they do not destroy all vestiges of it.[62]

Abraham's recognition of a distinction between more and less organized music is particularly striking in light of subsequent claims to the contrary amongst some of Lorenz's later critics.

---

clearly represents the aesthetic counterpart of that ideology of community and people [*Gemeinschafts- und Volksideologie*] which increasingly dominated Germany in the second decade of this century, and to which Lorenz himself submitted with particular zeal. (120)

He thereby suggests treating Lorenz as an historical figure, and indeed considers him infrequently in the remainder of the article, unlike the Dahlhaus's apparent obsession with him.

60. Ernest Newman's monumental biography of Wagner, which appeared between 1933 and 1946, mentions Lorenz twice in passing, merely noting the appearance of his "remarkable books" on Wagner's musical form: *The Life of Richard Wagner*, vol. 1 (New York: Knopf, 1933; reprint Cambridge: Cambridge University Press, 1976), 66 n.1.

61. Abraham, *A Hundred Years of Music*, 121. Abraham presents Lorenz's *Walküre* analyses in simplified form; he does not, for instance, bring up the notions of motivic substitution, or free or opposite symmetry.

62. Ibid., 128.

As was the case with the German scholars, little work was done on Wagner during the decades immediately following the war. During this time, however, we do find the first English criticism of Lorenz's method. In an article on "The Structural Methods of the Ring," A.E.F. Dickinson argues against Lorenz's view of Wagnerian form. To Dickinson, the formal basis of the *Ring* (and by extension, the rest of the mature works) is a text-oriented loose structure which eschews set patterns. His main quarrel with Lorenz concerns the seemingly endless number of variations possible for a single formal type:

> A hypothesis that every scene in 'The Ring' be considered as a series of *set* patterns is most improbable, and cannot be justified except by interpreting a given pattern so loosely as to convey nothing significant. . . . [A]ny attempt to tie every 'period' to a melodic formula [like Bogen and Bar] soon loses contact with structural realities, as may be expected. It is like forcing sonata-form on a classical concerto first movement.[63]

Notice, however, that Dickinson makes no reference to the aesthetic and philosophical reasons for Lorenz's belief in this process of continual variation amongst formal types.

During this relatively fallow period of Wagnerian scholarship, the existence of Lorenz's work began to become more general knowledge as the initial, uncritical assessment of scholars such as Abraham and Newman were disseminated in general works of musical scholarship. Thus, in Donald J. Grout's *A History of Western Music* we read:

> Wagner wrote his acts in sections or "periods," each of which is organized in some recognizable musical pattern, most often AAB (*Bar* form) or ABA (3 part, or *Bogen* [arch] form). . . . Periods are grouped and related so as to form a coherent pattern within each act, and each act in turn is a structural unit in the shape of the work as a whole.[64]

That this passage has remained, unchanged, in all subsequent editions up to and including the fourth (1988) demonstrates the continuing influence of Lorenz's ideas on nonspecialists.[65] It frequently finds its way into program notes as well, as the following sentence from the notes for a 1989 Toronto Symphony concert performance of the first act of *Die Walküre* attests: "[B]alanced forms are present even in the smallest details, as Alfred Lorenz has shown in a bar-by-bar analysis of this act."

The popularization of Lorenz was helped by the appearance of a new analytical work in English based upon Lorenz's analytical technique.

---

63. A[lan] E[dgar] F[rederic] Dickinson, "The Structural Methods of the 'Ring': I. The Word and the Orchestra," *Monthly Musical Record* 84 (May 1954): 89.

64. Donald J. Grout, *A History of Western Music* (New York: Norton, 1960), 565.

65. It does not appear in the fifth edition, 1996.

Siegmund Levarie's *Mozart's "Le Nozze di Figaro": A Critical Analysis* follows *Das Geheimnis der Form* in being a book-length study of a single operatic work.[66] It proceeds, number by number, to detail the formal organization of Mozart's masterpiece, and even includes such quintessential Lorenzian techniques as detailed charts illustrating text-derived formal symmetries. (Like Lorenz, Levarie employs Riemann's function symbols.) Levarie's respect for *Das Geheimnis der Form* is nowhere more clear than in those places in *Figaro* where Lorenz himself had offered a solution; Levarie writes, regarding the fourth-act finale:

> The spadework done by Alfred Lorenz in exposing the unified form of finales in Mozart's operas has brought to light many beauties of the finale now under discussion. Imitation is the most honest form of flattery, it is said. The greatest tribute one can pay to Lorenz at this moment is to follow literally the solution suggested by him.[67]

Given the close ties between Lorenz and Levarie, it is not surprising that the reaction against the former has made a casualty of the latter as well, despite the undeniable insight Levarie is able to bring to Mozart's opera.

Apart from Dickinson's reservations, Lorenz is not really engaged critically during this time. Certainly, some criticisms were beginning to be voiced—Kerman's *Opera as Drama* is typically prescient in this regard—but these are by far minority views.[68] This situation begins to change in the late 1960s with the explosion of Anglo-American Wagnerian scholarship in response to the stimulus of its slightly earlier reawakening in Germany under Dahlhaus and his colleagues. While many (if not all) studies of Wagner's music mention Lorenz's work, the influence of this new German school is seen in the almost unanimously negative assessment his work is given. It is important to emphasize here that while the Germans may have ideological reasons for not according Lorenz that unbiased critical evaluation which is his due, Anglo-American scholars have no such impediment. They simply have not done so.

English-language studies of Wagner differ in one important respect from their German counterparts, however. While criticism of Lorenz often seems to be the raison d'être of much German work, Lorenz and his findings

---

66. Chicago: University of Chicago Press, 1952.

67. Ibid., 219. Likewise, for the second-act finale, Levarie simply translates a large section of Lorenz's 1927 essay "Das Finale in Mozarts Meisteropern," and notes that "as a proper tribute to him, my words now yield to his" (108).

68. Kerman, in *Opera as Drama*, calls Lorenz's work "fantastic special pleading" (170), and writes that the assumptions and procedures are questionable enough, but the main point is this: the system is in fact a pre-existing, purely musical one, for which dramatic details are regularly invoked to "explain" musical details which do not fit. The "explanation" is made with a logical naivete that matches the dramatic insensitivity (12).

often form the starting point for new work, which generally departs markedly from Lorenz's view. Within these new studies, criticisms of Lorenz's analytical enterprise are raised which are often convincing. Thus, Daniel Coren points to Lorenz's inconsistency in applying his own formal principles.[69] Likewise, David Murray highlights the tension between the relative importance of formal and tonal considerations between Lorenz's methodology and his analyses.[70] Lorenz's omissions and distortions have also received scrutiny. Patrick McCreless has noted Lorenz's disregard for the marked stylistic shift between the second and third acts of *Siegfried*,[71] and William Kinderman has shown how Lorenz obscures Wagner's use of large-scale recapitulation for dramatic means.[72] These points are all worth suggesting (I have mentioned all of them myself in the previous chapter), yet are only offered incidently, as it were, on the way to a larger analytical insight. Within such studies, Lorenz becomes part of current debate. The way in which his views are presented becomes something of a gauge for the author's own views on Wagnerian form.

Of recent Wagner scholarship, Thomas Grey's *Wagner's Musical Prose* is perhaps the most sympathetic to Lorenz. Grey's main point is that Wagnerian form supersedes the constraints of thematic contrast and reprise in absolute music by presenting a dynamic and evolutional model for form analogous to drama; he argues that Lorenz's primary fault lies in his insistence on alternation and return in his forms—that is, for emphasizing architectonic rather than logical form.[73] Nevertheless, Grey tends to accept Lorenz's basic premise by discussing the formal sections—"periods"—found in Wagner's works. He even allows that many of Lorenz's large forms work:

> [*Rh*.P.15] is one of many cases in which a larger unit identified by Lorenz . . . is indeed audible as a formal entity, while his scanning of its putative interior form obscures the subtlety of an "evolving" design in favor of artificial symmetries.[74]

69. Daniel Coren, "Inspiration and Calculation in the Genesis of Wagner's *Siegfried*," in *Studies in Musicology in Honor of Otto E. Albrecht*, ed. John W. Hill (Kassel: Bärenreiter, 1980), 286.

70. Murray, "Major Analytical Approaches to Wagner's Musical Style," 216.

71. McCreless, *Wagner's "Siegfried"*, 88, 105–107, 189. He claims that Wagner abandoned the poetic-musical period principle after the first act of *Tristan*. McCreless writes admiringly, however, of Lorenz's *Rheingold* analyses, and indeed of many of the details of his analyses of *Siegfried*.

72. Kinderman, "Dramatic Recapitulation in Wagner's *Götterdämmerung*," 101–12.

73. Grey, *Wagner's Musical Prose*, 59, 278. Elsewhere he writes that it was impossible to extrapolate "generalized formal models from musical procedures supposedly predicated on the individual dramatic material at hand," and that this is the "root of Lorenz's failure"; Thomas Grey, ". . . *wie ein rother Faden*: On the Origins of 'Leitmotif' as a Critical Construct and Musical Practice," in *Music Theory in the Age of Romanticism*, ed. Ian Bent (Cambridge: Cambridge University Press, 1996), 187.

74. Grey, *Wagner's Musical Prose*, 232 n. 43.

Somewhat contradictorily, he later writes that Lorenz's used "questionable" criteria to determine the shape of his individual poetic-musical period—if "many" larger units (i.e., poetic-musical periods) work, how then can their premise be questionable? [75] A similar contradiction undermines his insight that Lorenz did not ignore the text or stage action; in one place he writes that "Lorenz by no means ignored the text or stage action," while in another he writes that his "indefatigable cataloguing of strophic, 'Bar,' and 'arch' forms . . . often (though by no means always) short-chang[es] the formative role of text and stage action."[76] Still, Grey does understand that Lorenz's "larger or 'composite' periods do nonetheless reflect an important aspect of Wagner's procedures that Dahlhaus, in turn, tends to overlook: the emphasis in *Opera and Drama* on the 'evolutionary' cohesion of smaller units (periods) into musical-dramatic scenes or even acts."[77] Grey's text does not mention Lorenz's aesthetic and philosophical underpinnings, and his claim that the idea of the poetic-musical period only provided Lorenz with his criterion of tonal closure is simply incorrect, as I hope to have demonstrated in previous chapters.[78]

Grey's thoughtful and nuanced treatment of Lorenz contrasts markedly with Warren Darcy's neo-Lorenzian study of *Das Rheingold*. Indeed, the two could hardly be more different. Darcy explicitly sets out to counter what he terms the "Dahlhaus myth" of form-as-web; instead he argues that, in *Rheingold* at least, Wagner still subscribed to the form-as-architecture idea. He admits that he is open to the charge of trying to resuscitate Lorenz, and does not really refute this; he replaces Lorenz's "periods" with "episodes," but continues to find Bars and Bogens and often agrees with his predecessor's analyses.[79] His central quarrel with Lorenz seems to be one of terminology; he backs off from the latter's insistence on "ground[ing] his own analyses in Wagner's prose writings."[80] Ironically, what might seem to be his most crucial difference from Lorenz—his use of Schenkerian analysis—most strongly recalls the very premise of Lorenz's own approach: the demonstration that Wagner's works were not formless. Darcy aims to prove the unity of his episodes and the work as a whole by demonstrating that they make Schenkerian sense; he speaks of the "symmetrical macro-structure of *Das Rheingold*" and provides Schenkerian background graphs for the entire opera.[81]

---

75. Ibid., 279.

76. Ibid., 13 n. 21, 206.

77. Ibid., 206–207.

78. Ibid., 182.

79. Warren Darcy, *Wagner's* Das Rheingold (Oxford: Clarendon Press, 1993), 57–61; see especially p. 61 n. 2. As with Lorenz, Darcy's "episodes" are often separated by (non-episodic) transitions.

80. Ibid., 60.

81. Ibid., 216–17.

Within more recent literature, there is an increasing propensity to see Lorenz historically; John Deathridge, for instance, writes that "Lorenz's position in the history of Wagner research is seldom noted in judgments of his methods."[82] Numerous surveys of analysis (operatic or otherwise) or of Wagnerian scholarship have attempted to assess Lorenz's historical position in varying degrees of detail.[83] Although none of these works is able to do justice to the full intellectual context of Lorenz and the expressive aesthetic, they nevertheless make some very important points. For example, they all credit Lorenz with being the first to deal with Wagnerian formal questions in a detailed, systematic manner, and many correctly point out that Lorenz explicitly aimed to counter the charge that Wagner's music was formless. His was the first sustained attempt to elevate Wagnerian analysis to more than just catalogues of leitmotives and their appearances. As well, Lorenz was among the first to recognize the structural importance of tonality in operatic works. Carolyn Abbate and Roger Parker have written aptly that "it is possible to see much of later-twentieth-century analysis of Wagner as Lorenzian fallout, whether through judicious adaptation of his thought, or through critical reaction to it."[84] This is particularly the case for those operatic analyses based on the premise of a structural use of tonality, generally in tonally unified sections. In their survey of operatic analysis, then, they refer to the work of Robert Bailey, Patrick McCreless, and Anthony Newcomb (we might add William Kinderman and Warren Darcy) as "Neo-Lorenzian."[85] Many of these historical treatments (Deathridge's in particular) mention Lorenz's metaphysical inclinations and position within the Schopenhauerian-Wagnerian aesthetic position. Some even acknowledge his debt to Gestalt psychology.[86] Most are silent, however, about Lorenz's National Socialist ties.[87]

The real problem with most of these writings, from the present point of view, is that none was intended as a detailed account of Lorenz and his methodology. Writers have had to be content with pointing out the influences on Lorenz, without examining them in any detail. Despite this glar-

---

82. John Deathridge, "A Brief History of Wagner Research," in *Wagner Handbook*, trans. and ed. John Deathridge (Cambridge, MA: Harvard University Press, 1992 [first pub. 1986]), 214.

83. Many of these studies have already been referred to: David Murray, "Major Analytical Approaches to Wagner's Musical Style"; Anthony Newcomb, "The Birth of Music Out of the Spirit of Drama"; Deathridge, "A Brief History of Wagner Research"; Ian Bent, *Analysis*; Susanna Gozzi, "Nuovi orientamenti della critica wagneriana," *Rivista italiana di musicologia* 19 (1984): 147–77; Carolyn Abbate and Roger Parker, "Introduction: On Analyzing Opera"; *The New Grove Dictionary of Opera*, s.v. "Analysis," by Carolyn Abbate.

84. Abbate and Parker, "Introduction: On Analyzing Opera," 15.

85. Ibid., 16.

86. Bent, *Analysis*, 47.

87. They are discussed in general terms in Barry Millington, *Wagner*, rev. ed. (London: Dent, 1992), 135–36.

ing lack, many—too eagerly—have rushed to claim that "the seemingly indigestible lump of Lorenz has finally been broken down, its nutritious portions digested, its harmful ones expelled."[88] Too often the historicization of Lorenz seems to be a vain attempt to simply be rid of him. It may not be out of place to suggest that such eagerness might indicate a continuing obsession with its subject. Seen in this light, Abbate and Parker's concluding comment is ambiguous, at once a considered assessment and a wistful hope:

> Lorenz should be read not because he discovered a last secret but within the context of his training and time. If we can thus make *Das Geheimnis der Form* an artifact, we can free ourselves from anxiety about its influence.[89]

For Lorenz to be truly useful—and to avoid misreading his work—this anxiety must be faced.

While the Germans are at least aware—all too aware—of the intellectual context of Lorenz's work, virtually all English-language commentators ignore or misrepresent the aesthetic and philosophical foundations of Lorenz's thought. From Abraham and Dickinson on, critics betray their ignorance of (or, more likely, their skepticism about) this crucial component of Lorenz's work. Curiously, only Robert Gutman comes near to pinpointing the character of the expressive aesthetic in his overwhelmingly critical biography of Wagner; Gutman writes that the arguments of Lorenz and his disciples are "seemingly theological in spirit, in that they depend upon the very special insights of faith."[90] While Gutman clearly means this to be a negative comment, it may also be read as an accurate assessment of the very nature of the aesthetic position.

A wider historical picture may also account for some of the more recent considerations of Lorenz and his position within current debate about operatic analysis and its relationship to postmodern thought. Some recent analytical work on Wagner has been characterized by the influence of paradigms derived from literary theory.[91] This influence is nowhere more clear than in the burgeoning field of operatic analysis. Opera attracts particular attention within this critical climate because of its very nature: a hybrid form which often resists attempts to tame its unruly marriage of music, poetry, and drama through systematization or reduction. For several years,

---

88. Newcomb, "Birth of Music," 39.

89. Abbate and Parker, "Introduction: On Analyzing Opera," 14–15.

90. Robert W. Gutman, *Richard Wagner: The Man, His Mind, and His Music* (New York: Harcourt, Brace, & World, 1968), 387.

91. Carolyn Abbate's Wagner analyses in particular: "Opera as Symphony: A Wagnerian Myth"; "Wagner, 'On Modulation,' and *Tristan*"; and the final two chapters of *Unsung Voices*: "Wotan's Monologue and the Morality of Musical Narration," and "Brünnhilde Walks by Night."

clarion calls have been sounded by a number of American scholars for a multivalent type of operatic analysis—one that considers the integration (or lack thereof) of all of the components of opera, without privileging one (such as music) above another.[92] Such analysis typically adopts the technique of deconstruction, and picks at the gaps, absences, and disjunctions in the text in order to unravel or problematize traditional interpretations and meanings.[93]

Within this literature, Lorenz is seen as the founder of a particular type of operatic analysis that is itself based on Wagnerian criteria: one reductively preoccupied with finding unity and order. This interpretation suggests that critics still evaluate opera according to the Wagnerian model embodied in Lorenz's books. A fairly lengthy quotation from one such assessment will serve to make the point.

> Much has been written about Lorenz's Wagner analyses, but for the moment it is sufficient to stress its aesthetic dimension: that *beauty* can reside only in absolute and definable formal symmetries, and that Wagner's music thus had to be defined as possessing no extraneous or unaccountable moments, no noise. Not for Lorenz the idea that Wagner's works evoke an illusion of coherence only to subvert it, or that they try both to confirm or establish something—a value, a pattern of coherence, a system, a genre—and call it into question. Reductive interpretations like Lorenz's make the work all too familiar, and merely emphasize features—like formal symmetry—that it holds in common with the derivative and the banal.[94]

This critical shift marks a movement from a New Critical approach to Lorenz in which his work (and his work alone) forms the subject for discussion, to a poststructural approach to Lorenz, whereby he himself is under scrutiny. Within the self-referential play of poststructuralism, scholarship itself emerges as a subject for scholarship. This is not necessarily a bad thing, but the shift of critical attention from Lorenz's work to Lorenz himself has resulted in a gross distortion and oversimplification of the issues raised by his analyses. This fetishization of Lorenz has led to his emergence in much recent literature as a symbol—a bogeyman—for all that is bad about unifying analyses.

The English-language reception of Lorenz enfolds a paradox. Since most writers have ignored Lorenz's aesthetic and philosophical background and

---

92. Carolyn Abbate, Roger Parker, James Webster, and Harold Powers are principal among these scholars. The *Cambridge Opera Journal*, edited by Parker and a colleague from the literary side of the equation, is proving to be the primary sounding board for such views.

93. Indeed, such disjunctive moments form the basis for Carolyn Abbate's theory of narrative in operatic music, formulated in *Unsung Voices*. For a more detailed consideration of postmodern thought on current analysis, and Abbate's book in particular, see my review-essay "Towards a Post-Modern Wagner," *Wagner* 13 (1992): 108–21.

94. Abbate and Parker, "Dismembering Mozart," 193.

political beliefs, *Das Geheimnis der Form* is has largely been understood as an objective study of musical structure, whether useful or misguided. Just as Lorenz's work originated in an attempt to rescue Wagner from the reproach of "formlessness," so too does it now seem to rescue Wagner from the taint of metaphysical speculation and Nazi ideology and propaganda—a taint which the present work argues lies at the heart of *Das Geheimnis der Form*.

Chapter Seven

Alfred Lorenz and German Nationalist Ideology

Is Alfred Lorenz a formalist? Certainly recent scholars have thought so. Thomas Grey, for example, writes of the "grand failure of Alfred Lorenz's analytical project to exonerate the music dramas before the tribunal of a modern, formalist aesthetic."[1] Likewise, Carolyn Abbate allies Lorenz with a purely musical school of operatic analysis that she calls "formalist" and "anti-representational," and places it in opposition to one more interested in how the music traces or represents the drama, which she terms "symbolist."[2] But Lorenz's aesthetic and philosophical background is that of the *Geisteswissenschaften*—what I have called the expressive aesthetic position. Perhaps Lorenz effects a reconciliation of the two? If it would be true, as I have argued, that a strictly formalist and a strictly expressive aesthetic position are incompatible, it is illogical to claim that Lorenz somehow synthesizes the two, despite a certain heuristic temptation to do so. The formalist and expressive aesthetic positions proceed from quite different understandings about the nature and essence of works of art. The formalist position takes as its basis the phenomenal world, with works of art being absolute and autonomous things unto themselves. The expressive position, on the other hand, exists at one remove from the here and now; individual works of art are only communicative channels between the creator and the recipient, both of whom are focused upon the essential content of the work, rather than upon the form of its external manifestation. In other words, the external form of a work is a reflection of its internal essence, rather than some separate and distinct conceptual category. Even the term "absolute music," which seems central to formalism, can be used in various ways. A strictly formalist viewpoint disentangles it from the metaphysics of absolute music of the early Romantics, whereas for a purely expressive aesthetic, metaphysics is central.

---

1. Thomas S. Grey, ". . . *wie ein rother Faden*: On the Origins of 'Leitmotif' as a Critical Construct and Musical Practice," in *Music Theory in the Age of Romanticism*, ed. Ian Bent (Cambridge: Cambridge University Press, 1996), 187.
2. *The New Grove Dictionary of Opera* (1992), s.v. "Analysis," by Carolyn Abbate.

The relationship between the formalist and expressive aesthetic positions in Lorenz is more complex than a mere synthesis or reconciliation. While Lorenz's approach has elements of a traditional *Gefühlsästhetik*—for example, his recourse to the metaphysics of absolute music in order to privilege content—his emphasis on the autonomous and quantifiable structures of Wagner's music dramas certainly aligns it more readily with formalism. There is no question that Lorenz is obsessed with formal perfection and tidy symmetries; indeed, he is quite clear that value can reside only in formal unity: "form is nothing superficial; rather it is the sensation of large-scale rhythm in the flow and structure of the music."[3] Yet, at the same time, his discussion of form assumes its dynamic and evolutionary nature, and—as we have seen—seems to have been derived from such contemporaries as August Halm, Ernst Kurth, and the Gestaltists. Lorenz himself writes (comparing himself with Kurth) that "I too refuse to see form as 'static' in any way; it is a *dynamic* process."[4] Form for Lorenz, as for Halm and Kurth, seems to be a perceptual category; his understanding of form is experiential, based on the listener, and hence idealistic.

Lorenz's aesthetic principles allow for an evolutionary, dynamic view of form. For instance, his notions of motivic substitution and free and opposite symmetry (derived from Max Dessoir) reflect his Schopenhauerian belief in the *psychological necessity* of inexact repetition. Just as no human emotion is ever the same, but is always varied by subtle admixtures and shadings, so too must be the concrete artistic manifestations of these emotions: music itself. This principle Lorenz extends to his forms in general. Rather than compromising the soundness of the methodology, the many, often substantial differences encountered, for instance, among Lorenz's Bar forms are a testament to the power and fecundity of Wagner's genius in varying these few, ideal types. That Lorenz's aesthetic beliefs result in the logical impossibility of any separation of form from content in his analyses goes without saying—despite his own claims to the contrary.

As we have seen, in practice Lorenz does acknowledge the rhetorical basis of his periods and he does evince an interest in form as a bearer of dramatic and expressive meanings. It seems clear, then, that the double-function hypothesis for the leitmotive is only a feint. Here, for heuristic reasons, Lorenz becomes a ventriloquist for a formalist approach, but—at a more fundamental level—he follows Schopenhauer and Wagner in understanding "music" as a direct copy of the will itself, unmediated by any representation. It is thereby vested with all the power and authority enjoyed by the *Ding an sich*, or essence, within an idealistic philosophical system. (Like Wagner, Lorenz also employs the idea of "drama" as a syn-

---

3. Alfred Lorenz, "Richard Wagner, ein Meister des musikalischen Aufbaues," *Die Sonne* 10 (1933): 69.

4. Alfred Lorenz, "Ernst Kurths *Musikpsychologie*," *Die Musik* 23 (1930): 186.

onym for this absolute essence or will.[5]) But there is a subtle distinction in Schopenhauer when he discusses music. On the one hand, he equates music with the will (thus making it equivalent to the *Ding an sich*), but on the other, he speaks of it as a "copy" of the will, thus asserting the existence of some essential will that is not a copy of anything else. The will is thus paradoxically the origin and content of all music.

When Lorenz speaks of "music," he is really speaking of the will itself. Thus, when he argues that all the component arts of the *Gesamtkunstwerk* are, in a sense, musical, he means this in a two-fold sense. First, they all have the same essential origin in the will, but whereas music is a direct manifestation of the will itself, the other arts exist at one remove, as representations.[6] Second, Lorenz suggests that the principles of musical form are operative in bringing the initial impulse of these arts to fruition. Artistic products are rhythmically divided and rationally shaped concrete manifestations of the will. It is in this sense that Lorenz's claim that "musical form seizes hold of the entire poetic course and becomes the sculptor of the drama" must be understood.[7]

Thus, when Lorenz claims to consider purely musical matters only, whether these be the "musical" function of the leitmotives, or the allegedly musical free and opposite symmetries, he is in fact doing so, but only according to his own implied definition of the term. Recognition of this requires a different interpretation of aspects of Lorenz's analytical methodology, the poetic-musical period in particular. As we have seen, this latter has strong dramatic and rhetorical components to its constitution. Since the drama itself is a manifestation of will—that is, of music—Lorenz's claim is justified according to the dictates of his own aesthetic suppositions.

As perceptual entities—*Gestalten*—many of Lorenz's forms work perfectly well in practice, largely owning to their rhetorical basis. That they range in size from a dozen to hundreds of measures is not a flaw according to his aesthetic presuppositions; for example, Lorenz writes:

> For me, musical forms are "Gestalt-qualities" in the sense of the philosopher Christian von Ehrenfels; i.e., forms independent of their absolute size, to be perceived only in the relative proportional relationship of their parts. . . . Absolute size, like that presented by Riemann's eight-measure period, obscures the more important awareness of architectonic symmetries.[8]

---

5. In his earlier, pre-*Beethoven*, theoretical writings, Wagner uses the idea of "drama" rather than "music" to convey this essential, original sense.

6. There is obviously a value judgment at work in this Schopenhauerian hierarchy of the arts in which all other arts are seen as "lesser music."

7. *Geheimnis* IV: 4.

8. Alfred Lorenz, "Worauf beruht die bekannte Wirkung der Durchführung im 1. Eroicasatze," *Neues Beethoven-Jahrbuch* 1 (1924): 166.

If further proof is needed that Lorenz is not an unregenerate formalist, consider his frequent appeals to his readers to "adopt a higher viewpoint" when considering certain issues, and his insistence on the occasional necessity for conjecture.[9] Here Lorenz employs the idealistic privileging of insight and creativity over "pedantic correctness"—which he acknowledges is not to be found in all of his analyses.[10] It *is* difficult to accept all of the details of his analyses. Lorenz is inconsistent in articulating the inner forms of his larger structures, and sometimes seems only to list motives. His choice of motives on which to focus is not rigorous; the analyses seem to include and exclude motives depending on how well they "work." At times, the analyses seem strangely empty, as Adorno seems to have sensed.

Consideration of Lorenz's aesthetic and philosophical background is crucial for properly understanding his analytical methodology. Contrary to Schenker's analytical technique, one cannot divest Lorenz's method of its aesthetic and philosophical underpinnings and hope to distill a useful remainder.[11] There isn't one. And yet, despite the significance of this aesthetic and philosophical background, it is the formal structures revealed by his analysis that seem most important to Lorenz. Ultimately, there is an unresolved tension in *Das Geheimnis der Form* between aesthetic issues and his formalist way of expressing them. Lorenz does celebrate the autonomous and self-referential power of music, and certainly does go beyond the exegetical (hermeneutic) aims of the *Leitfaden* literature, which simply traces the motives and the drama. He does so, that is, for *aesthetic* reasons: a committed belief in the Wagnerian-Schopenhauerian aesthetic position and in the resulting dynamic understanding of musical form. For the most part, however, he does not use experiential language to express these insights, and the pages and pages of tables, graphs, and numbers in *Das Geheimnis der Form* certainly appear static, objective, and scientific.

Ian Bent has recently pointed out that modern readers are often "word-blind" to nineteenth-century writing about music; in fact, according to Bent, much of twentieth-century understanding of "proper analytical writing" developed as a conscious negation of nineteenth-century ideals. His discussion includes a quotation from George Steiner that links this phenomenon to the advent of modernism:

> Our contemporary sense of the poetic, our often unexamined presumptions about valid or spurious uses of figurative speech have developed from a conscious negation of *fin de siècle* ideals. It was precisely with the rejection, by the Mod-

---

9. For example, *Geheimnis* I: 296, 157–58.
10. *Geheimnis* III: 187.
11. For an account of this process as it relates to Schenker, see William Rothstein, "The Americanization of Heinrich Schenker," in *Schenker Studies*, ed. Hedi Siegel (Cambridge: Cambridge University Press, 1990), 193–203.

ernist movement, of Victorian and post-Victorian aesthetics, that the new astringency and insistence on verifiable structure came into force.[12]

Alfred Lorenz is part of this modernist move in analysis—giving priority to score over sound, unlike Kurth—yet all the while he is tinged by anti-modernist nostalgia.[13] Indeed Lorenz's text is irreparably rent with these conflicts. For aesthetic and ideological reasons, he could not embrace a modernist preoccupation with form and structure unreservedly.[14] Not only would it contravene the aesthetic of the *Gesamtkunstwerk* and the indissolubility of form and content that that entailed, it would also be understood according to the cultural politics of the day as an anti-Wagnerian (and hence un-German) gesture. This essentially reactionary position is typical of Lorenz's politics.

Ultimately, it is to culture and politics that we must turn in order to understand Alfred Lorenz. Despite sharing many of the aesthetic and philosophical foundations of the dynamic and experiential *Geisteswissenschaften*, Lorenz's aim, finally, is ideological rather than modernist or hermeneutic: the demonstration that Wagner's music was *not* formless; that it was, basically, tonal (and certainly was not "atonal"). Even if we want to insist that Lorenz is a formalist, his "formalism" is neither positivistic nor objective, for it is closely bound up with ideological and nationalistic issues: by revealing the form and logic behind Wagner's works, Lorenz in a sense validates them as *echte deutsche Kunst*.[15]

By arguing that Lorenz is part of a new, modernist discipline of "analysis" but also resistant of this move, we can tap into a stream of "reactionary modernism" in Germany. Jeffrey Herf has traced this process whereby "alien" technology (a product of Western *Zivilisation*) is transformed and mapped onto *Kultur*.[16] He examines the writings of men such as Oswald

---

12. George Steiner, *After Babel: Aspects of Language and Translation* (London: Oxford University Press, 1977), 14–15, cited in *Music Analysis in the Nineteenth Century*, ed. Ian Bent, vol. 2: *Hermeneutic Approaches* (Cambridge: Cambridge University Press, 1994), 36.

13. For the idea of privileging "score over sound," i.e. visual symmetries, connections, etc., that "work" on paper but may not be obvious aurally, see ibid., 37.

14. Lorenz was not alone in this; see, for example, Karl Grunsky's attack on Eduard Hanslick in his *Musikästhetik* (Leipzig: G.F. Göschen, 1907), 22. As Lee Rothfarb notes in his discussion of this passage ("Hermeneutics and Energetics: Analytical Alternatives in the Early 1900s," *Journal of Music Theory* 36.1 [1992]: 45) their positions were not very far apart.

15. Confirmation of this ideological project may be found in Karl Grunsky's argument that Anton Bruckner (promoted as Wagner's heir by many cultural conservatives, Wagnerians, and, later, National Socialists) also heard Wagner's works as absolute music and was concerned only with their pure form: "even at that time [Bruckner] heard almost in a Lorenzian manner [*lorenzisch*], and . . . had an equal understanding of the secret of Wagner's musical form." Grunsky, *Fragen der Bruckner-Auffassung* (Stuttgart: Heyder, 1936), 13.

16. Jeffrey Herf, *Reactionary Modernism: Technology, Culture, and Politics in Weimar and the Third Reich* (Cambridge: Cambridge University Press, 1984). See pp. 11–17 for a definition of reactionary modernism.

Spengler, Ernst Jünger, Martin Heidegger, and others, and notes that reactionary modernism entailed a preoccupation with form and structure: "The reactionary modernists were nationalists who . . . point[ed] instead to the outlines of a beautiful new order replacing the formless chaos due to capitalism in a united, technically advanced nation."[17] Herf clearly links such thought with fascism and National Socialism, which "promised creativity, beauty, aesthetic form, and the spiritual unity of the nation in place of materialism, positivism, and formless, soulless and chaotic liberalism."[18]

The connection between Lorenz and National Socialism is not simply biographical. Understanding Lorenz as a reactionary modernist may help to uncover latent ideological aspects of his analyses that mark him clearly as caught up in the cultural politics of his day. As many scholars have shown, there is a demonstrable connection between the late-Romantic idealistic-transcendentalist tendencies of cultural conservatives and subsequent Nazi appeals to the "great German tradition."[19] Wagner, unsurprisingly, plays a central role.

Recent work in cultural theory has highlighted the Western tendency to create Others against which we define ourselves. For late nineteenth-century Germany, this tendency was expressed in a distinction between *Kultur* and *Zivilisation*. By the latter was meant Anglo-French civilization based on the Enlightenment ideals of rationalism, empiricism, and utility. German cultural conservatives—among whom may be numbered Richard Wagner—understood this as a world of external form, devoid of spiritual values and distracted by manners, superficiality, and dissimulation, in which true freedom was impossible. This bourgeois-liberal world was contrasted with an ideal of German *Kultur*: one concerned with "inner freedom" and authenticity; with essence rather than appearance; and with truth rather than sham. *Kultur* was a matter of spiritual cultivation rather than external form, and necessitated the "overcoming" through transcendence of material concerns and limitations. For many conservatives, the Wagnerian *Gesamtkunstwerk* was an unsurpassable synthesis and expression of *Kultur*, and Bayreuth was seen as a shrine to the transcendence of life and reality by art and imagination.[20] By the end of the nineteenth century, a connection

---

17. Ibid., 2.

18. Ibid., 31.

19. See, for example, Modris Eksteins, *Rites of Spring: The Great War and the Birth of the Modern Age* (Toronto: Lester & Orpen Dennys, 1989); Fritz Stern, *The Politics of Cultural Despair: A Study in the Rise of the Germanic Ideology* (New York: Anchor, 1965); William McGrath, *Dionysian Art and Populist Politics in Austria* (New Haven: Yale University Press, 1974). Fritz K. Ringer discusses this cultural crisis as it was reflected by the academic community in his *The Decline of the German Mandarins: The German Academic Community, 1890–1933* (Cambridge, MA: Harvard University Press, 1969).

20. The above account has largely been derived from Eksteins, *Rites of Spring*, 76–80. Thomas Mann's *Betrachtungen eines Unpolitischen* (Berlin: S. Fischer, 1918) was an influential expression of this attitude, from which Mann was later to distance himself.

between cultural conservativism and Bayreuth had been firmly made—indeed, very often in the pages of the *Bayreuther Blätter* itself.[21]

Cultural conservatives aimed for the aesthetic rejuvenation of society and the overcoming of cultural decadence also advocated by Wagner in his late writings (mostly published in the *Bayreuther Blätter*).[22] This hoped-for cultural and political revolution was essentially reactionary, however, and so it is not surprising that the cultural conservatives were among those most disaffected with the liberal Weimar republic after Germany's defeat in World War I. Nor is it surprising that many of these men were attracted by the conservative and nationalistic National Socialists. In *The Dialectic of Enlightenment*, Theodor Adorno and Max Horkheimer have argued that the myth and modernism characteristic of German rejection of Enlightenment values in favor of *Kultur* are inextricably linked with right-wing ideologues.[23] Such anti-Western tendencies were vindicated and even intensified by the German loss in 1918.

In his account of the intellectual foundations of Nazism, Fritz Stern points out the works of Paul de Lagarde, Julius Langbehn, and Arthur Moeller van den Bruck as examples of what he calls the "politics of cultural despair" that provided fertile soil for the National Socialist movement.[24] All three were anti-Semitic critics of existing Germany, and all looked for a *Führer* figure to embody the body politic, unifying and purging it of internal conflict. With a mixture of cultural despair and mystical nationalism, they promulgated an ideology of mythical *Deutschtum* and demanded the creation of political institutions to effect and preserve this. All were explicitly antirational: they depreciated reason and exalted prophetic intuition. In an elegant formulation, Stern writes that the aim of the conservative revolution was to "destroy the despised present in order to recapture an idealized past in an imaginary future."[25]

The idealistic devaluation of appearance and the antirational valorization of subjective feeling and experience over intellectual activity is characteristic of a preoccupation with *Kultur*. For example, Langbehn's highly influential *Rembrandt als Erzieher* of 1890 proclaims the virtue of irrationality and denounces the intellectualistic and scientific bent of German culture and the increasing conformity of German life at the expense of (artistic)

---

21. Frederic Spotts, *Bayreuth: A History of the Wagner Festival* (New Haven and London: Yale University Press, 1994) admirably demonstrates the link between Wagner and the cultural conservatives.

22. I leave to others the untangling of the threads of influence between Wagner and other conservative writers. Certainly Wagner was not writing in a vacuum and must have been aware of other, similar thinkers.

23. Max Horkheimer and Theodor W. Adorno, *Dialectic of Enlightenment*, trans. John Cumming (New York: Continuum, 1986).

24. Stern, *The Politics of Cultural Despair*.

25. Ibid., 6–7, from which the above account was derived.

individuality. Likewise, Lagarde's success lay in his uncanny ability to analyze the national psyche—which he did largely by intuition (which he valued more highly than facts): "[s]uch a matter I do not learn piece by piece, but I see it at once or not at all."[26] Others have noted how *völkisch* ideology accentuates individual subjectivity.[27] As we have seen, each of these things has its parallel in Lorenz's work.

The antimodernist, conservative distinction between *Kultur* and *Zivilisation* also lies at the heart of Heidegger's *Being and Time*, with its paeans to destiny and authenticity.[28] Heidegger's concern with the ontology of Being—which, as phenomenological presence he valorizes over reason, historical consideration, and even individual subjectivity—and "spontaneous 'pre-understanding'" gives his work a lofty viewpoint that very much minimizes the importance of the individual. The individual is not authentic. Instead, art is held up as the repository of authenticity: in art alone—as in van Gogh's representation of peasant shoes—do we find phenomenological truth manifested ("the presence of the god").[29] But for Heidegger, art is not the expression of an individual subject; instead, the subject is simply the medium through which the truth of the world speaks itself. We need to open ourselves passively to the work. While Heidegger equates art with people and politics, he is also clear that it preexists them: the origin of art is art. Indeed, the artist is inconsequential compared to the work. Heidegger's devalorization of the human figure goes so far as to say that it is the *work* which makes creators even possible:

> The more solitarily the work, fixed in the figure, stands on its own and the more clearly it seems to cut all ties to human beings, the more simply does the thrust come into the Open that such a work *is*, and the more essentially is the extraordinary thrust to the surface and the long familiar thrust down.[30]

Significantly, Heidegger links form with Being itself: "the beautiful does lie in form, but only because the *forma* once took its light from Being as the isness of what is."[31]

---

26. Cited by Ludwig Schemann, *Paul de Lagarde: Ein Lebens- und Erinnerungsbild*, 3rd ed. (Leipzig: Matthes, 1943), 132; also "Anyone who does not want to see the totality in the individual instance, the whole in one, should at least not pester me with his opinion." (Lagarde, *Aus dem deutschen Gelehrtenleben: Aktenstücke und Glossen* [Göttingen: Dieterich, 1880], 6). Both cited by Stern, *Politics of Cultural Despair*, 36.

27. Herf, *Reactionary Modernism*, 15.

28. Martin Heidegger, *Being and Time*, trans. John Macquarrie and Edward Robinson (New York: Harper & Row, 1962).

29. Heidegger's thoughts about art are found in "The Origin of the Work of Art," in *Poetry, Language, Thought*, trans. Albert Hofstadter (New York: Harper Colophon Books, 1971). See also Joseph J. Kockelmans, *Heidegger on Art and Art Works* (Dordrecht: Martinus Nijhoff, 1985).

30. Heidegger, "The Origin of the Work of Art," 66.

31. Ibid., 81.

Heidegger offers an interesting comparison with Alfred Lorenz. Both men had personal and professional ties with National Socialism, and the writings of both have been linked with Nazi ideology. Indeed Adorno once wrote that Heidegger's "philosophy is fascist right down to its most intimate components."[32] The idealistic origins of Heidegger's views should be apparent, and others have discussed their essential complicity with National Socialist thought.[33] Like Lorenz, the extent of Heidegger's ties with Nazism were not apparent at first, but quickly became evident when in 1953, without a word of explanation, he published his 1935 lectures *Einführung in die Metaphysik* (in which the question of Being is tied to the success of the National Socialist revolution.[34] Lorenz's Nazism has had to wait longer to be uncovered. In *The Jargon of Authenticity*, Adorno links Heidegger with reactionary politics, and it is striking just how much of his critique may be applied to Lorenz. When Adorno notes that jargon "sees to it that what it wants is on the whole felt and accepted through mere delivery, without regard to the content of the words used," he could be describing the language of much of Lorenz's *Das Geheimnis der Form*: perfect Bars and Bogens, spiritual symmetry, expression of the will and so on.[35] The jargon of authenticity places certain absolutes—blood, race, soil, form— beyond rational justification, and serves as a mode of magical expression, much like Benjamin's "aura."[36] A number of writers have discussed the early twentieth-century transference of the reactionary (indeed Wagnerian) aesthetic criteria under discussion into the political sphere.[37] Benjamin sees this "aestheticization of politics" as a logical result of fascism.[38]

It is clear that the political stakes were high, even within apparently unrelated fields like music. In critical polemics against atonality or modernism, there tends to be more under discussion than just musical style: in

---

32. Theodor Adorno, letter in *Discus*, January 1963; reprinted in the editorial postface to volumes 5 and 6 of his *Musikalische Schriften*. Cited by Philippe Lacoue-Labarthe, *Heidegger, Art and Politics*, trans. Chris Turner (Oxford: Blackwell, 1990), 105.

33. See, for example, Richard Wolin, *The Politics of Being: The Political Thought of Martin Heidegger* (New York: Columbia University Press, 1990).

34. It was a review by Jürgen Habermas that first brought this issue to light; see Richard Wolin, ed., *The Heidegger Controversy: A Critical Reader* (Cambridge, MA: MIT Press, 1993), 186–89.

35. Theodor W. Adorno, *The Jargon of Authenticity*, trans. Knut Tarnowski and Frederic Will (Evanston: Northwestern University Press, 1973), 8.

36. Ibid., 9.

37. See, for example, Peter Viereck, *Metapolitics: The Roots of the Nazi Mind* (New York: Capricorn Books, 1961); Rainer Stollmann, "Fascist Politics as a Total Work of Art: Tendencies of the Aestheticization of Political Life in National Socialism," trans. Ronald L. Smith, *New German Critique* 14 (1978): 41–60.

38. Walter Benjamin, "The Work of Art in the Age of Mechanical Reproduction," chapter in *Illuminations*, ed. and with an introduction by Hannah Arendt, trans. Harry Zohn (New York: Harcourt, Brace & World, 1968), 243. This 1936 essay seems to have coined the term "aestheticization of politics."

fact, there is a tendency to see such musical developments as symptomatic of larger decadence in society. As Pamela Potter has recently demonstrated, German musicology did not stand innocently aloof from society; from the outset it was pressed into service to aid in constructing the cultural nation, and this process certainly continued under the Nazis.[39] In fact, Potter argues persuasively that musicology as a discipline has been largely Germanocentric from its beginnings.[40] She cites a typical formulation by Friedrich Blume to this effect:

> German musicology has to preserve one of the noblest commodities of German culture. Music has always been one of the liveliest and most characteristic expressions of the German spirit. The German *Volk* has for centuries erected for itself and for its destiny a "victory boulevard" [*Siegesallee*] of great monuments. Given this fact, the direction of any music research that takes its obligations to the *Volk* and state seriously has become clear. The heritage of German music dictates its duties. Even if earlier research often went off in several futile directions and sacrificed a living bond with the ordinary for the pursuit of the extraordinary, a National Socialist musicology can only proceed from the living core of German music, laying the periphery around it, orienting remote problems around this center.[41]

Apart from the explicit mention of "National Socialist musicology," this passage might have been written during much of the twentieth century. Potter's work reveals that, despite their reputed anti-intellectualism, the Nazis gave musicology extensive state support—in fact, for cultural-political reasons, it seems that they gave it *more* attention than previous re-

39. Pamela Potter, "Trends in German Musicology, 1918–1945: The Effects of Methodological, Ideological, and Institutional Change in the Writing of Music History" (Ph.D. dissertation, Yale University, 1991); Potter, "Musicology under Hitler: New Sources in Context," *Journal of the American Musicological Society* 49 (1996): 70–113.

There are only a few studies that trace the cultural and ideological role of music in building the German cultural nation: Jörg Theilacker, *Der erzählende Musiker: Untersuchung von Musikerzählungen des 19. Jahrhunderts und ihrer Bezüge zur Entstehung der deutschen Nationalmusik*. Münchener Studien zur literarischen Kultur in Deutschland (Frankfurt am Main: Peter Lang, 1988); Celia Applegate, "What is German Music? Reflections on the Role of Art in the Creation of the Nation," *German Studies Review: Special Issue—German Identity* (Winter 1992): 21–32.

Sanna Pederson points out how the symphony became a problem in the nineteenth century: bound to German identity, it became tied to the question "what is German?"; "On the Task of the Music Historian: The Myth of the Symphony after Beethoven," *repercussions* 2 (Fall 1993): 5–30.

40. Potter, "Musicology under Hitler," 107–108. She also adds that this orientation survived both denazification and emigration.

41. Friedrich Blume, "Deutsche Musikwissenschaft," in *Deutsche Wissenschaften. Arbeit und Aufgabe. Dem Führer und Reichskanzler zum 50. Geburtstag* (Leipzig, 1939), 16; cited and trans. Pamela Potter, "Musicology under Hitler," 79.

gimes.[42] For Lorenz, this intellectual climate was certainly conducive to scholarship, as a glance at his many articles of the 1930s reveals.

In the field of literary criticism, Peter Hohendahl has drawn on Jürgen Habermas's notion of the "public sphere" and its institutions to chronicle the process of establishing a German national literature.[43] He is particularly concerned with the institution of art, which Peter Bürger defines as "the notions about art (definitions of function) generally held by a given society (or by particular classes or strata) viewed from the perspective of their social determinacy."[44] The work of George Mosse, who examines the role of form and myth in the creation of a national synthesis, has also helped to illuminate the construction of a German national identity.[45] A similar project for the field of music(ology) is long overdue, although David Dennis's recent book about Beethoven is a start.[46] It is within this (yet unwritten) context that we must situate Lorenz.

The work of Alfred Lorenz plays an important role in remaking Wagner into a monument to the great German tradition rhapsodized by the Nazis. By proving the unity and formal perfection of the music dramas by analysis, Lorenz helps remove the taint of "decadence" that still clung to Wagner owing to his earlier association with Jews, liberals, modernists, symbolists, and hysterics.[47] Lorenz focuses particularly on two "German" elements:

---

42. While there is no question that the Nazis mistrusted intellectuals (the classic demonstration remains Edward Yarnell Hartshorne Jr., *The German Universities and National Socialism* [Cambridge, MA: Harvard University Press, 1937]), after 1937, Goebbels attempted to downplay the anti-intellectual character of the movement. During the war, he gave high priority to book production and promoted scholarly works for their propagandistic value. See Potter, "Musicology Under Hitler," 108–09, and Potter, "Did Himmler *Really* Like Gregorian Chant? The SS and Musicology," *Modernism/Modernity* 2.3 (1995): 45–47.

43. Peter Uwe Hohendahl, *Building a National Literature: The Case of Germany 1830–1870*, trans. Renate Baron Franciscono (Ithaca and London: Cornell University Press, 1989); Hohendahl, ed. *A History of German Literary Criticism, 1730–1980* (Lincoln: University of Nebraska Press, 1988). (The reference is to Jürgen Habermas, *Strukturwandel der Öffentlichkeit* [1962], translated by Thomas Burger with the assistance of Frederick Lawrence as *The Structural Transformation of the Public Sphere: An Inquiry into a Category of Bourgeois Society* [Cambridge, MA: MIT Press, 1989])

44. Peter Bürger, *Vermittlung-Rezeption-Funktion: Ästhetische Theorie und Methodologie der Literaturwissenschaft* (Frankfurt a. M.: Suhrkamp, 1979), 176, cited by Hohendahl, *Building*, 30.

45. George Mosse, *The Nationalization of the Masses: Political Symbolism and Mass Movements in Germany from the Napoleonic Wars through the Third Reich* (New York: Howard Fertig, 1975); Mosse, *Mass and Man: Nationalist and Fascist Perceptions of Reality.* (New York: Howard Fertig, 1980).

46. David Dennis, *Beethoven in German Politics, 1870–1989* (New Haven: Yale University Press, 1996).

47. For the cultural link between Wagnerian and the "irrational," hysterical woman, see Thomas S. Grey, *Wagner's Musical Prose: Texts and Contexts* (Cambridge: Cambridge University Press, 1995), 246. For Wagner reception in general, see David L. Large, William Weber, and Anne Dzamba Sessa, eds., *Wagnerism in European Culture and Politics* (Ithaca and London: Cornell University Press, 1984).

Beethoven and the Bar form. In the first, Lorenz takes his cue from Wagner himself, who explicitly aligned his ideas of musical form with Beethoven's symphonies and presented himself as the composer's true heir.

> The cumulative mass of forms I have found in Wagnerian music drama are not rooted in Wagner's operatic predecessors but in *Beethoven's symphonies*, proving the truth of Wagner's claim that the symphony had flowed into his own dramatic works.[48]

This appeal to Beethoven not only linked Wagner with his great predecessor but also served to rescue Wagner's works from the taint of the theater.[49]

In his writings, Lorenz emphasizes the inherent Germanness of Bar form, which he suggests is "especially familiar to German feeling." Bar form, not surprisingly, is the most predominant form in the overtly nationalistic *Die Meistersinger von Nürnberg*.[50] It is at the root of both the songs of the medieval *Meistersinger* and the later German lied, and Lorenz shows how it structures both symphonies and music dramas, all of which are the same when seen from the perspective of the "smallest crystals of latent musical form" (*Formtriebs*).[51] Karl Grunsky makes explicit the connection between musical form, Lorenz's method, and *völkisch* ideology:

> In his Wagner books, Alfred Lorenz develops a *Formenlehre* of rigorous, logical consistency for the music drama. And in just this the unity of German music shows itself, in which the simple and the complex are clearly linked. . . . Let there be no division between lied and symphony, as if one were for the uneducated masses, while the symphony is for those who are cultured [*Gebildete*]. On the contrary, the spirit of the German people [*deutscher Volksgeist*] moves in both. In the artistic relationship and arrangement we recognize the *Volk* at work, as though in a simple song that makes such an impression that it is widely distributed.[52]

As was discussed in chapter one, Lorenz's work often includes an indication of his political views. For example, many nationalistic comments in

---

48. Lorenz, "Worauf beruht die bekannte Wirkung der Durchführung im 1. Eroicasatze," 183.

49. David Dennis discusses the Wagnerian association of Beethoven and German nationalist ideology around the turn of the century in *Beethoven in German Politics*, 52. See also pp. 115–74 for an account of right-wing and Nazi appropriations of Beethoven, including the National Socialist assocation of Hitler with Beethoven (150–52).

50. Lorenz, *Geheimnis* I: 103; *Geheimnis* III: 8–10. Lorenz's follower Hans Alfred Grunsky goes farther and argues that Bar form is rooted in the (German) philosophical constructs of Jakob Böhme and Georg Wilhelm Friedrich Hegel; see Stephen McClatchie, "Bruckner and the Bayreuthians; or, *Das Geheimnis der Form bei Anton Bruckner*" in *Bruckner Studies*, ed. Timothy L. Jackson and Paul Hawkshaw (Cambridge: Cambridge University Press, 1997), 110–21.

51. Karl Grunsky, *Volkstum und Musik* (Eßlingen a.N: Wilh. Langguith, 1934), 23.

52. Ibid.

the *Meistersinger* volume of *Das Geheimnis der Form* may be read in light of the contemporary situation in Germany; certainly Hans Sachs's final speech ("Habt acht!"), to which Lorenz refers as a "magnificent warning," is given an explicitly contemporary interpretation:

> "Habt acht . . ." which in the present time, two generations after its writing, ought to have continued to resound in our ears, despite that fact that now it is not princes who plant their foreign trinkets in our land.[53]

The *Parsifal* volume goes even further. In the preface dated May 1933, Lorenz implicitly equates Parsifal with Hitler when he argues that the character had heretofore been interpreted as too weak or soft: "in this work, Wagner spoke his prophetic thoughts about leadership and resurgence (*Führertum und Wiederaufstieg*) and entrusted to [that leader] a lofty mission."[54] His nationalistic interpretation extends even to arguing that the work provides the "foundation of a new *Parsifal* religion" which draws on the thought of medieval German mystic, Meister Eckhardt.[55]

In an article in the Hitler Youth periodical *Wille und Macht*, Lorenz implies a connection between National Socialist ideology and his own analytical method. He presents Wagner's art as a symbol for German youth and as a bulwark against both reaction and cultural bolshevism.[56] Indeed, Wagner himself is to be understood as a revolutionary precursor of the National Socialist fight against Jewish art. To be a Wagnerian, avers Lorenz, is not to be reactionary or old fashioned; this misunderstanding he attributes to Jewish influence. The "destructive liberal mess" (*zerstörendes liberalistisches Durcheinander*) of modern music is the exact opposite of the "organic, community-building, National-Socialist world view" (*organische, gemeinschaftbildende nationalsozialistische Weltanschauung*) seen in Wagner's works:

> In Richard Wagner's music the essences of our world view are made real. In his *Gesamtkunstwerk* he even managed to bring about the unification of *all* the arts into a marvelous whole, just as Hitler did with the German people.[57]

A suggestive parallel exists between this "marvelous whole" of German society under Hitler and that of Wagner's music dramas as analyzed by

---

53. *Geheimnis* III: 169.
54. *Geheimnis* IV: preface. See chapter 1, pp. 19–20, for more about Lorenz's interpretation of *Parsifal*.
55. Ibid., 62–66, especially 63–64. He also argues that *Parsifal* corresponds with Wagner's later prose works, the so-called *Regenerationslehre*.
56. Alfred Lorenz, "Richard Wagner als Musiker." *Wille und Macht* 1 (1 November 1933): 24–28.
57. "Richard Wagner als Musiker," 27.

Lorenz. In both, the individual (person/form) is submerged into the collective whole, with parts only achieving validity in relation to the larger structure. Regionally, the NSDAP (and hence Germany as a whole after 1933) was organized into interlocking units or administrative districts, each with their respective leaders: a region (*Gau*) contained several districts (*Kreise*) that were made up of local groups (*Ortsgruppen*) comprised of cells (*Zellen*) formed by blocks (*Blöcke*). Analytically, Lorenz argues for the organic growth of Wagner's works from the seeds of Lorenz's formal types. He finds these formal patternings interpenetrated across all levels of Wagner's work: a small Bar form may also be the first Stollen of a larger Bar, which is also part of a still larger structure, and so on, up to the level of the act, and finally of the opera as a whole.

During the Third Reich, Lorenz's work was understood in a cultural-political sense. Indeed, Lorenz was allowed to remain on the faculty of Munich University past the normal age of retirement precisely because his work was deemed important for "cultural-political reasons."[58] Karl Grunsky's *Kampf um deutsche Musik!* (the cover of which shows a lyre ["music"] being pulled from the muck by a German flag) traces an alleged "reaction" against Wagner and the nineteenth century. Employing National-Socialist "racial science," Grunsky links "modern" with "Jewish" and argues that the true salvation of German music will come by and through Wagner alone. To bolster his point, Grunsky offers an almost hysterical list of "Jewish" epithets thrown at Wagner, and states clearly that Hitler alone can save Wagner from such trash.[59] It is clear that Lorenz can stand in metonymically for Hitler in terms of form, for he is mentioned immediately afterwards: he saves Wagner from these things too—especially from the "Jewish" reproach of "formlessness."[60] Karl Grunsky thus explicitly equates anti-Semitism and Nazism with Lorenz's approach. His son, Hans Alfred, goes a step further and explicitly links them:

> The most wonderful [thing] about this new science of form, however, is that it corresponds completely to the ideal that the most recent generation of academic

---

58. See chapter 1, pp. 8–9.

59. Many are untranslatable: "Wagner selber galt als Unhold; man schalt ihn Dilettanten, Blechschmied, Sophisten, Homunculus, Dalai Lama [!], Marat. . . . Er hieß Narr, Spektakelmacher, Nervenzerrütter, Volksverführer, Grobian, Straßenjunge, Landplage und Gottesgeißel, Speichellecker, Winkelpedant, Münchhausen, Moloch, Oelgötze, moralische Wasserpest, ein Gründer, Spekulant und Hochstapler, ein Henker, Vandale und Antichrist der Kunst, ein Schaute, Bandit und Beelzebub, ein Thersites und Megatherion, ein Satyr und Marsyas, ein Cagliostro und Heliogabal." Karl Grunsky, *Kampf um deutsche Musik!* (Stuttgart: Erhard Walther, 1933), 67.

60. Ibid., 68. Although Grunsky does not directly link this reproach with Jewishness, the context makes it clear. Not only does it follow the harangue of "Jewish" epithets for Wagner, Grunsky cites a statement by the Jewish writer Franz Werfel to the effect that Germans are not bound by form.

works correctly demands: it is not lifeless, but is intimately connected with art, with life, and with the *Volk*. [Lorenz's] works . . . find their true niche in the *Volk*, i.e., in this case in all serious music listeners, as well as in all interpretative artists, from conductors and directors to singers and instrumentalists, for they lead *from the recognition of form* [Formerkennen] *to the experience of form* [Formerleben].[61]

Here the younger Grunsky invokes the experiential emphasis of Lorenz's work, which—as we have seen—is part of an idealistic devaluation of appearance and an antirational valorization of subjective feeling and experience over intellectual activity. Such an approach is not dissimilar to the servile position before Art advocated by Heidegger.

Not only did Lorenz's work appear in the *Bayreuther Blätter* and the *Bayreuther Festspielführer* with the implicit endorsement of the Bayreuth establishment, it was also published and discussed such general periodicals as *Die Sonne, Wille und Macht, Deutsches Wesen*, and *Völkische Kultur*. Lorenz's seventieth birthday was marked by an article in the Munich-based *Völkischer Beobachter* that included a photograph of him wearing his party membership pin.[62] Lorenz's National Socialist credentials were so impeccable and his work connected with the prevailing ideological climate on so many levels that it may have been risky to attack him.[63] This may account for the curious note in Tobel's *Die Formwelt der klassischen Instrumentalmusik* to the effect that his treatment of and disagreement with Lorenz was already to be found in the original version of the work (his 1928 dissertation).[64] No substantive criticism of Lorenz's work was published before the end of World War II. On a number of fronts, Lorenz was impregnable.

Such an ideologically oriented evaluation of Lorenz as the present one is part of a recent tendency which has loosely been termed the "new historicism." It has been aptly described as being concerned with the "historicity of texts and the textuality of history."[65] I have attempted to engage equally

---

61. Hans Alfred Grunsky, "Form und Erlebnis," *Bayreuther Festspielführer* (1934): 170.

62. "Der Entdecker der Wagnerschen Formprinzipien: Zum 70. Geburtstag von Universitätsprofessor Alfred Lorenz," *Völkischer Beobachter*, 11 July 1938.

63. See chapter 1, pp. 15–17. I offer this only as a possible suggestion for the notable lack of criticism of Lorenz's work. Certainly, as Pamela Potter has pointed out to me, the Party controls were not as rigid as one might imagine, and some scholars—Wilibald Gurlitt, for example—did not hesitate to attack influential figures.

64. Rudolf von Tobel, *Die Formwelt der klassischen Instrumentalmusik* (Bern and Leipzig: Paul Haupt, 1935), 236 n.11.

65. Louis Montrose, "Renaissance Literary Studies and the Subject of History," *English Literary Renaissance* 16 (1986): 8. Within musicology, elements of new historicism may be seen in the writings of Leo Treitler, *Music and the Historical Imagination* (Cambridge, MA: Harvard University Press, 1989); Treitler, "The Politics of Reception: Tailoring the Present as Fulfilment of a Desired Past," *Journal of the Royal Musical Association* 116 (1991): 280–98; Gary Tomlinson, "The Web of Culture: A Context for Musicology," *19th-Century Music* 7

both sides of the equation in exploring the historical, aesthetic, and philosophical context of Lorenz's work, as well as its role in promulgating a particular view of Wagner's works. A new historical approach requires explicating works of art not only as products of their social situation ("historicity of texts") but also as cultural agencies actively helping to construct that very social situation. Thus the shared origins of Nazism and the expressive aesthetic has been shown to have an impact upon Lorenz's analytical methodology in a significant fashion, and his own Nazi background is seen to shape both the form and content of his work. The changing reception of *Das Geheimnis der Form* is also relevant to such an approach, since according to new historicism, not only historical documents (like Wagner's works) but also the documents of history as a discipline—its books, articles, and reviews, as well as its scholarly controversies, reevaluations, and revisions—are fair game for assessment, and indeed play a significant role in creating our understanding of a work ("textuality of history"). This latter component suggests that no text is ever complete in itself, but instead is constituted by each reader according to his own beliefs and background.[66] Texts therefore change in meaning throughout history (as our reception history of *Das Geheimnis der Form* has shown) as historical knowledge deepens our perspective of the past, and current circumstances color our preoccupations in the present.

Lorenz and his reception can serve therefore as a cautionary tale: not only of the danger of misrepresentation when a subject is divorced from its own historical, aesthetic, and philosophical context, but also in a wider sense relevant to our own discourse. *Das Geheimnis der Form* suggests a need to be conscious of our own ideological suppositions and how they inform our scholarship (even in the very choice of subjects to be brought under scrutiny), and also to be aware of the futility of elevating our judgments to the status of received truth, of some insoluble *Geheimnis* finally solved.

(1984): 350–62; Lawrence Kramer, *Music as Cultural Practice 1800–1900* (Berkeley and Los Angeles: University of California Press, 1990). In the present context, it is significant that Carolyn Abbate's article on analysis in the *New Grove Dictionary of Opera* devotes half of the space to a category entitled "ideologies."

66. This notion is, of course, that which Julia Kristeva has termed "intertextuality"; see her "Word, Dialogue and Novel," in *The Kristeva Reader*, ed. Toril Moi (New York: Columbia University Press, 1986), 34–61, esp. 35–39.

Appendix One

Lorenz's Formal Types

A. Simple Forms

1. Strophic   a–a
           a. Variation form: $a–a^1–a^2$

2. Simple Bogen form   a–b–a
           sections known as Hauptsatz (HS)–Mittelsatz (MS)–Reprise (Rp). If "b" is of the greater importance, "a" becomes a Rahmensatz (VRS = Vorderer Rahmensatz; SRS = Schließender Rahmensatz)

3. Expanded Bogen form   a–b–c–MS–a–b–c
           outer sections are multithematic

4. Perfect Bogen   a–b–c–MS–c–b–a
           HS is mirrored in the Rp

5. Rondo form $a–x–a–y–a–z\ (x^1)–a$

6. Refrain form   if a in 5. is of less importance than the linking sections, this is refrain form

7. Bar form   a–a–b
           Stollen (St.), Stollen, Abgesang; St.II often in different key

8. Reprisenbar   a–a–b–a (o)
           music from St. recurrs in Abgesang, (o) may be a coda; if the St. are of greater importance than the Abg., this form resembles sonata form

9. Gegenbar   a–b–b
           Aufgesang (Aufg.), Nach-Stollen (NSt.), Nach-Stollen

B. Potentiated Forms

1. Potentiated Bogen	each section of Bogen form is itself in Bogen form i.e. A (cdc)–B (efe)–A (cdc)
2. Potentiated Bar	each section of Bar is itself in Bar form i.e. A (ccd)–A (ccd)–B (eef)

Likewise one can have potentiated Gegenbar form, Rondo, and Refrain forms

C. Composite Forms

A large variety is possible; for example, the HS of a large Bogen form can be in Bar form while the MS can be strophic

D. Successive Forms

On rare occasions, a period is constructed of small forms one after the other which do not together form a type B. or C. form

Lorenz's Analysis of the Poetic Musical Periods of *Der Ring des Nibelungen*

This appendix is included only for ease of reference, and should be read in conjunction with the body of the text. An attempt has been made to indicate the higher forms through spacing; formal types for the higher forms may be found in figure 4.14. For the reader's convenience, the figures in parenthesis refer to the page, system, and measure number of the widely available Schirmer vocal scores. The figures in square brackets are measure numbers. Following Lorenz, references to tonality employ Riemann's function symbols.

Das Rheingold

Vorspiel: E-flat major (1/1/1–5/3/4) [1–136]
           Form: Simple strophic
Period 1: E-flat major (5/4/1–27/2/4) [137–447]
           Dramatic Content: Innocent play of the Rhine maidens in the depths of the Rhine
           F: Potentiated perfect Bogen
Übergang: (28/1/1–31/1/2) [448–513]
           D.C: Alberich's play with the maidens
           F: Simple expanded Bogen
Period 2: C major (beginning in D) (31/1/3–47/3/2) [514–662]
           D.C: Celebration of the gleaming Rheingold
           F: Composite double Bogen
Period 3: C minor (47/3/3–53/6/2) [663–748]
           D.C: The cursing of love
           F: Simple Bar
Übergang: (53/6/3–54/5/8) [749–768]
           F: Simple strophic + transition

[*Das Rheingold*]

Period 4: D-flat major (55/1/1–58/1/4) [769–826]
          D.C: Greeting of Walhalla
          F: Simple Bogen

Period 5: D minor (58/2/1–63/2/3) [827–913]
          D.C: Godly worries
          F: Simple perfect Bogen

Period 6: E minor (63/3/1–67/4/4) [914–983]
          D.C: Freia's flight
          F: Potentiated perfect Bogen

Period 7: F major (also minor) (68/1/1–73/2/5) [984–1093][1]
          D.C: Appearance of the giants
          F: Simple perfect Bogen

Period 8: D major (half cadence) (73/3/1–77/4/1) [1094–1183]
          D.C: Climax of the conflict between the gods and the giants
          F: Simple perfect Bogen

Period 9: F-sharp minor (ending in *(D)Tp*) (77/4/2–84/2/5) [1184–1312]
          D.C: Loge's appearance
          F: Simple Bogen

Übergang: 3 measures

Period 10: D major (beginning in *D*) (84/3/2–97/5/5) [1316–1584]
          D.C: Loge awakens the greed for gold
          F: Composite refrain

[Lorenz omits mm. 1585–86]

Period 11: F major (ending in minor, half cadence) (98/1/1–102/4/5) [1587–1668]
          D.C: Freia taken away by the giants
          F: Simple Bogen

Period 12: E minor (103/1/1–110/2/3) [1669–1803]
          D.C: The gods' aging
          F: Composite Bogen

Nachspiel: (110/3/1–111/5/4) [1804–1830][2]
          F: Coda to P.12 (Bar) + transition (strophic)

Period 13: B minor (111/5/5–134/4/6) [1831–2319]
          D.C: Alberich's might
          F: Potentiated Bogen

Period 14: A minor (134/5/1–137/1/3) [2320–2353]
          D.C: The gods parley with Alberich
          F: Composite refrain

---

1. In the table of poetic-musical periods, Lorenz places the division between m. 1092 and m. 1093, but in his detailed analyses makes it one measure later; the latter makes more sense. Likewise, in the table, P.8 concludes with m. 1182.

2. Erroneously begins with m. 1803 in the table.

[**Das Rheingold**]
Period 15: A major (half cadence) (137/2/1–155/6/4) [2354–2774]
        D.C: Alberich's defeat
        F: Composite expanded Bogen
Nachspiel: (156/1/1–156/3/8) [2775–2794]
Period 16: C major (156/4/1–181/2/3) [2795–3255]
        D.C: Completion of the deeds necessary for the release of
        Freia
        F: Rondo with composite strophic prelude
[Lorenz omits mm. 3256–3260]
Period 17: E-flat major (181/3/5–203/2/1) [3261–3665]
        D.C: Redemption of Freia
        F: Potentiated Reprisenbar
Period 18: B-flat major (203/2/2–208/2/2) [3666–3712]
        D.C: Dispelling of the mists
        F: Simple refrain
Period 19: D-flat major (208/3/1–221/6/4) [3713–3897]
        D.C: Entry of the gods into Walhalla
        F: Composite Bogen

Die Walküre

Act I

Vorspiel: D minor (1/1/1–5/4/4) [1–121]
        F: Simple Bogen

Period 1: D minor (5/3/1–6/5/7) [114–156][3]
        D.C: Siegmund's exhaustion
        F: Simple Bogen
Übergang: (7/1/1–7/3/2) [157–169]
        D.C: Sieglinde sees the stranger
        F: Simple supporting Bogen to P.1
Period 2: D minor (7/3/3–10/3/1) [170–242]
        D.C: Sieglinde attends to the guest
        F: Simple Bar
Period 3: D minor (10/3/2–13/3/5) [243–315]
        D.C: Siegmund recognises his love, and would depart
        F: Simple Bar

---

3. This overlap is correct, and is mentioned by Lorenz on p. 89. The first period proper
begins with m. 122.

[*Die Walküre I*]

Period 4: D minor (ends in major, then transitional) (13/3/5–15/5/6)
           [316–380]
           D.C: Siegmund decides to remain
           F: Successive forms (coda-like)

Period 5: C minor (begins in °S, half cadence) (16/1/1–18/2/1)
           [381–423]
           D.C: Hunding's entry
           F: Simple perfect Bogen

Period 6: B-flat major (begins: *(D)Sp*; ends: D^7) (18/2/1–20/4/6)
           [423–470]
           D.C: Hunding as host
           F: Composite perfect Bogen

Übergang: 5 measures

Period 7: G minor (21/2/2–24/3/1) [476–530]
           D.C: First section of Siegmund's narrative
           F: Simple strophic

Übergang: (24/3/2–25/1/3) [531–540]

Period 8: A minor (25/1/4–28/1/1) [541–586][4]
           D.C: Second section of Siegmund's narrative
           F: Simple Bar

Nachspiel: 7 measures

Period 9: C minor (half cadence) (28/2/4–32/3/6) [594–674]
           D.C: Third section of Siegmund's narrative
           F: Simple expanded Bogen

Period 10: C minor (begins in °D) (32/4/1–36/4/6) [675–789]
           D.C: Hunding's discovery
           F: Composite Bogen (shortened Rp)

Period 11: C major (arising from dissonant chords; ends in minor)
           (37/1/1–42/4/6) [790–925]
           D.C: Sword monologue
           F: Simple refrain (strophic)

Period 12: G major (begins in *Tp*) (42/4/7–77/5/6) [926–1523]
           D.C: Love Scene
           F: Expanded Bogen

           A.a E major (begins in minor, ends with trans. to *(D^7)G*)
                (42/4/7–47/2/4) [926–1021]
                     D.C: Sieglinde's narrative about Wälse
                     F: Simple expanded Bogen

---

4. Lorenz says that the period ends with m. 587. This must be an error made in consequence of adding (incorrectly) an extra measure to the second Stollen of his analysis.

[*Die Walküre I*]

      A.b G major (middle in minor) (47/2/5–51/4/3) [1022–1086]
            D.C: Wälsung rejoicing
            F: Simple strophic
      B.a B-flat major (52/1/1–58/1/1) [1087–1169]
            D.C: Picture of love and spring
            F: Composite strophic
      B.b [modulatory] (58/1/2–61/2/3) [1170–1218]
            D.C: True life spring and love
            F: Potentiated Bogen
      B.c [modulatory, then returning to G major] (61/2/4–63/3/6)
            [1219–1258]
            D.C: Joy in gazing
            F: Simple strophic
      C.a E major (then trans. to *D*) (63/4/1–70/1/1) [1259–1377]
            D.C: Sieglinde recognises the Wälsung
            F: Potentiated Bogen
      C.b G major (middle in *Tp*) (70/1/2–77/5/6) [1378–1523]
            D.C: Siegmund wins the sword
            F: Simple strophic

Act II

Vorspiel: A minor (end in *D*⁺) (78/1/1–81/1/4) [1–73]
            F: Simple Bar
Period 1: D minor (81/2/1–85/4/5) [74–154][5]
            D.C: Wotan sends Brünnhilde to battle
            F: Simple Bar
Period 2: C minor (end in *Tp*) (86/1/1–90/3/6) [155–252]
            D.C: Confrontation between Wotan and Fricka
            F: Simple Bar
Period 3: A-flat minor[6] (90/4/1–95/4/3) [253–344]
            D.C: Fricka's lament
            F: Simple Bar
Period 4: C major (95/4/4–99/1/5) [345–414]
            D.C: Wotan's calmness
            F: Simple Bar
[Lorenz omits mm. 415–416]

---

5. Although Lorenz makes the division between m. 153 and m. 154 in both the table and the heading of the analysis, it is clear from the analysis itself—as well as the score—that the division is off by one measure.

6. I.e., not G-sharp minor; see Lorenz's note on p. 30.

[*Die Walküre II*]

Period 5:   C minor (begins in *(D)* ⁺*Tp*; ends in *Tp*) (99/2/3–108/1/8)
            [417–588]
            D.C: Fricka's victory
            F: Composite strophic

Period 6:   G minor (MS in F minor; end in *Tp*) (108/2/1–110/4/5)
            [589–647]
            D.C: Brünnhilde's question
            F: Successive forms (without unity)

Übergang: (110/4/6–111/2/2) [646–663][7]

Period 7:   A minor (half cadence) (111/2/3–136/6/5) [664–1107]
            D.C: Wotan's answer and decision
            F: Bar

            A.   A minor (begins in *Leittonwechselklang* of *D*; ends in major)
                 (111/2/3–117/4/1) [664–776]
                        D.C: Intro. and preliminary history up to
                        construction of Valhalla
                        F: Simple Bar
            B.   A minor (ends in °*D*) (117/4/1–120/2/3) [777–814]
                        D.C: The threat
                        F: Simple Bar
            C.   A minor (120/2/4–123/4/3) [815–872]
                        D.C: The longed-for but impossible free hero
                        F: Simple Bar
            D.   C minor (123/4/4–130/2/4) [873–988]
                        D.C: Wotan's despair
                        F: Successive forms (coda-like)
            E.   [return to A minor] (130/3/1–133/1/4) [989–1036]
                        D.C: Argument between Brünnhilde and Wotan
                        F: Simple strophic
            F.   A minor (133/2/1–136/6/5) [1037–1107]
                        D.C: Wotan's rage
                        F: Simple Bar

Period 8:   A minor (136/6/6–138/3/9) [1107–1158]
            D.C: Brünnhilde's sadness at this decision
            F: Successive forms (coda-like)

Period 9:   F minor (138/4/1–152/1/5) [1159–1439]
            D.C: The flight of the Wälsungs
            F: Potentiated Bogen

---

7. The overlap with the preceding period is correct.

[*Die Walküre II*]
Übergang: (152/1/6–152/3/9) [1440–1461][8]

Period 10: F-sharp minor (half cadence in *D*) (152/4/1–159/1/1)
[1462–1617]
D.C: The Valkyrie appears to Siegmund
F: Potentiated Bar
Period 11: F-sharp minor (half cadence) (159/1/2–164/4/1) [1618–1715]
D.C: Siegmund refuses to follow her
F: Potentiated Bar
Period 12: F-sharp minor (half cadence in *Tp*) (164/4/2–172/4/2)
[1716–1847]
D.C: Transformation in Brünnhilde's soul
F: Potentiated Bar
[m. 1848 called the "Nullpunkt" of the scene by Lorenz]

Period 13: D minor (172/4/4–183/5/4) [1849–2065]
D.C: Siegmund's last battle
F: Composite Bar

Act III

Period I: B minor (end in °*D*) (184/1/1–207/2/1) [1–266]
D.C: Assembly of the Valkyries
F: Composite Bar
Period 2: D minor (207/2/1–219/4/4) [267–408]
D.C: Brünnhilde's flight
F: Simple Bogen (together with P.3)
Übergang: 7 measures
Period 3: G major (begins in *Tp*) (220/3/1–229/2/4) [416–561]
D.C: Prophecy about Siegfried
F: Simple Bogen (together with P.2)
Nachspiel: 10 measures
Übergang: (230/1/2–223/1/1) [572–589]
D.C: Brünnhilde hidden
F: Simple Bogen
Period 4: D minor (end in *Tp*) (233/1/2–242/1/5) [590–653]
D.C: Wotan before the Valkyries
F: Simple rondo
Period 5: G minor (243/1/1–246/1/3) [654–716]
D.C: Wotan confronts Brünnhilde
F: Composite Bogen

8. Although Lorenz gives m. 1439 as the first measure of the transition, m. 1440 is more likely.

[*Die Walküre III*]
Übergang: (246/1/4–246/4/1) [717–731]
          D.C:Brünnhilde bows to punishment
          F: Simple Bar
Period 6: F minor (246/4/2–249/2/5) [732–784]
          D.C: Wotan casts her out of the Valkyries
          F: Simple Bar
Period 7: F minor (249/3/1–251/2/6) [785–831]
          D.C: Wotan banishes her
          F: Simple Bar
Period 8: B-flat minor (251/3/1–261/1/3) [832–908]
          D.C: Shame of punishment
          F: Simple expanded Bogen

Abrundung: (261/1/4–262/2/3) [909–936]
          F: Simple Bogen
Rückkehr to B minor: (262/2/4–264/5/2) [937–979]
          F: [coda to P.1]
Period 9: E minor (end in major) (265/1/1–274/3/3) [980–1201]
          D.C: Brünnhilde justifies her deed
          F: Composite rondo
Period 10: A-flat major (274/3/4–278/3/2) [1202–1288]
          D.C: Wotan justifies his anger
          F: Composite perfect Bogen
Übergang: (278/3/3–280/3/2) [1289–1332]
          F: Simple Bar
Period 11: B minor (280/3/2–284/4/2) [1333–1410]
          D.C: Brünnhilde's news about Siegfried; Wotan is unmoved
          F: Simple Bar
Period 12: D major (MS in C minor) (284/4/3–289/3/2) [1411–1487]
          D.C: Brünnhilde's despairing plea to alleviate her shame
          F: Composite expanded Bar
Period 13: E major (289/3/3–304/5/4) [1488–1732]
          D.C: Wotan grants her request
          F: Composite Bogen (concentrated Rp.)

Siegfried
Act I

Vorspiel: B-flat minor (1/1/1–4/5/4) [1–132]
          F: Composite perfect Bogen

Period 1: B-flat minor (4/6/1–10/3/4) [133–249]
          D.C: Mime's worries
          F: Simple double Bogen

[*Siegfried I*]

Period 2:   G major (half cadence) (11/1/1–16/1/4) [250–341]
            D.C: Siegfried's cheerfulness
            F: Potentiated Reprisenbar

Period 3:   G minor (16/1/5–46/1/1) [342–1181]—divided into the
            following sections:[9]

  A.   G minor / D minor (16/1/5–20/4/6) [342–499]
        D.C: Siegfried smashes the sword and gets angry
        with Mime
        F: Simple rondo

  B.   F minor (20/4/7–23/4/8) [500–589]
        D.C: Mime praises his own care of Siegfried (false
        father)
        F: Simple Bogen

  C.   D minor / G minor (24/1/1–29/2/7) [590–772]
        D.C: Siegfried's abhorrence of Mime
        F: Successive forms

  D.   D major (29/3/1–31/4/1) [773–?829]
        D.C: Siegfried's love of nature
        F: Simple strophic

  E.   G minor (31/4/2–36/2/7) [?830–943]
        D.C: Siegfried's impetuous questions about his
        parents
        F: Successive forms

  F.   D minor / F minor (36/3/1–42/1/4) [944–?1079]
        D.C: Mime's narrative of Siegfried's birth (true
        parents)
        F: Successive forms

  G.   (C) G minor (ends in major) (42/1/5–46/1/1) [?1180–1181]
        D.C: Siegfried's impetuous demand for the sword
        F: Successive forms

Period 4:   B-flat major (46/1/2–48/4/2) [1182–1254]
            D.C: Siegfried's wanderlust
            F: Simple Bogen

Period 5:   B-flat minor (48/4/3–50/2/6) [1255–1288]
            D.C: Mime's need
            F: Simple double Bogen

Period 6:   C major (50/3/1–66/1/4) [1289–1634]
            D.C: Wotan wins the riddle contest
            F: Potentiated rondo (together with P.7)

---

9. Lorenz does not give the boundaries for each of the internal divisions. I have derived these from Lorenz's analyses of the period, although several remain conjectural.

[*Siegfried I*]
Period 7:   F minor (ending in °*S*) (66/1/5–75/3/9) [1635–1854]
                 D.C: Wotan's three questions to Mime
                 F: Potentiated rondo (together with P.6)
Abrundung: reprise of beginning and return to C major (75/4/1–77/1/2)
                 [1855–1884]
                 [F: Outer HS of rondo]
Übergang: (77/1/3–77/5/5) [1885–1903]

Period 8:   C minor (end in *Ltwk.* of *T*) (78/1/1–81/1/2) [1904–1947]
                 D.C: Mime's paroxysm of fear
                 F: Simple Bar
Period 9:   G minor (beg. in *Ltwk.* of *D*) (81/1/3–98/1/7) [1948–2263]
                 D.C: Mime's and Siegfried's discussion about fear
                 F: Composite refrain
Period 10: G major (end in *D*) (98/2/1–106/1/2) [2264–2429]
                 D.C: Siegfried files the sword
                 F: Simple strophic

Period 11: D minor (end in major) (106/1/3–116/4/4) [2430–2626]
                 D.C: Siegfried heats the sword until it is red-hot
                 F: Potentiated refrain
Period 12: D major (end in *D*) (117/1/1–119/4/2) [2627–2691]
                 D.C: Mime prepares the drink
                 F: Composite Bogen
Period 13: F major (119/4/3–126/2/3) [2692–2781]
                 D.C: Siegfried hammers the metal
                 F: Composite Bogen
Period 14: D major (beg. in Ltwk. of *T*) (126/2/4–135/5/8) [2782–2983]
                 D.C: Sword and drink finished
                 F: Successive forms (coda-like)

Act II

Vorspiel: F minor (136/1/1–138/5/5) [1–95]
                 F: Potentiated Bar
Period 1:   B minor (138/6/1–142/1/2) [96–165]
                 D.C: Alberich worried
                 F: Simple expanded Bogen

Period 2:   F minor (beg. in °*D*) (142/1/3–146/3/1) [166–239]
                 D.C: Alberich's rage
                 F: Gegenbar (together with P.3)
Period 3:   F minor (146/3/2–149/3/4) [240–302]
                 D.C: Antithesis Wotan/Alberich
                 F: Gegenbar (together with P.2)

[*Siegfried II*]
Übergang: (149/3/5–151/3/4) [303–347]
    F: Simple expanded Bogen
Period 4: F major (151/3/5–158/1/2) [348–474]
    D.C: Wotan's superiority
    F: Composite perfect Bogen
Rückkehr: to F minor (158/1/3–160/5/2) [475–529][10]
    F: Simple supporting Bogen

Period 5: D minor (160/5/3–167/3/1) [530–644]
    D.C: Description of Fafner
    F: Composite perfect Bogen
Period 6: D minor (167/3/1–171/1/4) [644–713]
    D.C: Siegfried drives Mime away
    F: Simple perfect Bogen

Period 7:[11] E major (beg. in $(°S)°S$) (171/1/5–183/1/3) [714–929][12]
    D.C: Siegfried in the peacefulness of the woods
    F: Composite rondo
Period 8: F major (end in *Tp*) (183/2/1–190/3/7) [930–1098]
    D.C: Siegfried calls and conquers the dragon
    F: Composite Bogen (shortened Rp)
Period 9: F minor (beg. in *Ltwk.* of *T*; end. D^+) (190/4/1–194/3/6)
    [1099–1170]
    D.C: Fafner's death
    F: Simple perfect Bogen
Übergang: 10 measures
Period 10: E major (195/1/4–197/4/2) [1179–1212]
    D.C: Siegfried understands the woodbird
    F: Simple strophic
Period 11: B-flat minor (end in major) (197/4/3–207/4/4) [1213–1379]
    D.C: Siegfried wins the hoard
    F: Successive forms (half-unified)
        1. Siegfried in the cave (squabble of the dwarves)
        2. Siegfried contemplates Ring and Tarnhelm
Period 12: E major (208/1/1–210/2/2) [1380–1411]
    D.C: Woodbird warns Siegfried of Mime
    F: Simple strophic

---

10. Lorenz's analysis of this Rückkehr, however, begins with m. 480.

11. In the table, Lorenz erroneously says that P.6–15 form the larger period.

12. In the table and in the heading of the analysis, Lorenz counts mm. 930–34 within P.7, but his analysis only goes as far as m. 929. He discusses these measures within P.8. I have therefore revised the period boundaries to reflect the analytical discussion.

[*Siegfried II*]
Period 13: D major (210/2/3–222/3/1) [1412–1645]
      D.C: Mime's attempt to poison Siegfried and death
      F: Composite Bogen (shortened Rp)
[2 measures unaccounted for by Lorenz]
Period 14: B minor (222/3/4–225/2/5) [1648–1701]
      D.C: Siegfried buries his enemies
      F: Simple strophic
Übergang: (225/3/1–226/3/3) [1702–1723]
      F: Potentiated Bar
Period 15: E minor (beg. in *Ltwk.* of *T*) (226/3/4–230/1/3) [1724–1792]
      D.C: Siegfried feels his isolation
      F: Simple Bogen
Period 16: E major (230/4/1–238/6/4) [1793–1910]
      D.C: Woodbird tells of Brünnhilde
      F: Simple Bar

Act III

Vorspiel: G minor (239/1/1–242/2/2) [1–73]
          F: Composite expanded Bar

Period 1:   G minor (242/2/3–247/4/4) [74–189]
          D.C: The Wanderer invokes Erda
          F: Composite expanded Bar
Period 2:   begins in A-flat major; half cadence A-flat minor (247/4/5–
          250/3/6) [190–245]
          D.C: Erda will not be questioned
          F: Simple perfect Bogen
Period 3:   E-flat major (half cadence in minor) (250/3/7–254/2/1) [246–
          311]
          D.C: Brünnhilde's guilt
          F: Simple perfect Bogen
Period 4:   G minor (end in major) (254/2/2–261/1/4) [312–439]
          D.C: Wotan's superiority and joy in resignation
          F: [HS to perfect Bogen of entire Erda scene]

Period 5:   E-flat major (beg. in *S*⁺; end. in *(D)D*) (261/2/1–272/1/3)
          [440–628]
          D.C: Wotan's paternal feelings for Siegfried
          F: Potentiated refrain
Period 6:   F minor (end major) (272/2/1–281/2/4) [629–769]
          D.C: Wotan as Siegfried's enemy
          F: Potentiated Bar

[*Siegfried III*]
Verwandlungsmusik: (281/3/1–285/2/4) [770–833][13]
        F: Composite perfect Bogen
Period 7: E minor (major) (285/2/3–296/3/5) [832–1066]
        D.C: Siegfried finds Brünnhilde
        F: Potentiated Bogen
Period 8: C major (296/4/1–301/2/5) [1067–1146]
        D.C: Brünnhilde's awakening
        F: Potentiated Bar
Period 9: C major (301/3/1–306/2/5) [1147–1239]
        D.C: Brünnhilde's blessed fortune
        F: Simple expanded Bogen
[3 measures not counted by Lorenz]
Period 10: E-flat major (beg. in *S*; half cadence) (306/3/4–308/3/4)
        [1243–1278]
        D.C: Siegfried's tender wooing
        F: Composite strophic
Period 11: E-flat major (end in *Tp*) (308/3/5–314/4/2) [1279–1389]
        D.C: The battle for love
        F: Composite Bar
Period 12: C minor (ending in Übergang to E) (314/4/3–318/3/8) [1390–
        1477]
        D.C: Brünnhilde feels her wisdom depart
        F: Composite refrain
Period 13: E major (318/4/1–322/1/7) [1478–1559]
        D.C: Brünnhilde defends the clarity of her spirit
        F: Simple Bogen
Period 14: A-flat major (322/2/1–325/4/2) [1560–1617]
        D.C: Siegfried's fervent wooing
        F: Composite Bar
Period 15: C major (beg. in °*Sp*) (325/4/3–337/4/5) [1618–1789]
        D.C: The triumph of love—falls into 3 sections
        F: [Composite Bar][14]
            A. Siegfried's rejoicing (to 1648) [half cadence on C]
            (Composite Bar)
            B. Brünnhilde's rejoicing (to 1712) [full cadence in B
            major (parallel major of *Ltwk.* of *D*] (Composite Bar)
            C. Love's decisiveness (Potentiated Bar)

---

13. This overlap is correct.
    14. Although Lorenz nowhere states this explicitly, and discusses the three sections quite separately.

Götterdämmerung

Vorspiel[15]

Period 1:   E-flat minor (ending in key of *(°S)Tp* without resolution) (1/1/
            1–19/2/1) [1–304]
            D.C: Norn scene
            F: Composite refrain
Period 2:   E-flat major (19/2/2–37/3/5) [305–639]
            D.C: Siegfried's departure from Brünnhilde
            F: Composite Bogen (concentrated Rp)
Period 3:   E-flat major (37/3/6–44/5/8) [640–892]
            D.C: Siegfried's Rhine Journey
            F: Successive forms (coda-like)

Act I

Period 1:   B minor (end in major) (45/1/1–46/4/2) [1–39]
            D.C: Splendour of the Gibichungen
            F: Simple Bogen
Period 2:   B minor (end in *D*⁺) (46/4/3–47/4/5) [40–71]
            D.C: What the Gibichungen lack
            F: Simple perfect Bogen
Period 3:   B major (half cadence) (47/4/6–48/3/4) [72–85]
            D.C: Advice about Brünnhilde
            F: Simple Bar
Period 4:   B minor (48/3/5–51/4/1) [86–149]
            D.C: Advice about Siegfried
            F: Successive forms (half-unified)
Period 5:   G minor (end in major) (51/4/2–56/2/1) [150–236]
            D.C: Advice about the magic potion
            F: Composite Bogen (shortened Rp)
Period 6:   B-flat major (56/2/2–61/3/6) [237–345]
            D.C: Expectation, arrival and greeting of Siegfried
            F: Successive forms (half-unified)
Großer Übergang: (61/4/1–63/4/3) [346–387]
            F: Simple Bar
Period 7:   B-flat major (63/4/4–68/1/5) [388–465]
            D.C: Siegfried's bond with Gunther
            F: Composite Reprisenbar

---

15. Lorenz numbers the measures of the prelude separately from those of the first act
proper.

[*Götterdämmerung* I]
Period 8:   G major (end in *S*) (68/2/1–72/2/3) [466–566]
D.C: Gutrune ensnares Siegfried
F: Simple rondo
Period 9:   B minor (beg. in *Ltwk*. of *S*; half cadence in °*Dp*) (72/2/4–73/
4/6) [567–597]
D.C: Gunther tells of Brünnhilde
F: Composite Bogen
Period 10: B-flat major (74/1/1–84/1/6) [598–869]
D.C: Blood-brotherhood
F: Composite double Bogen
Period 11: E-flat minor (half cadence) (84/2/1–87/1/3) [870–923]
D.C: Hagen's watch
F: Potentiated Bar
Nachspiel: E-flat minor (87/1/4–88/2/7) [924–966]
F: Potentiated Bar
Übergang: 10 measures
Vorspiel to Brünnhilde scene: (88/3/8–89/5/3) [977–1019]
F: Simple Reprisenbar
Period 12: B minor (89/5/4–93/2/5) [1020–1090]
D.C: Waltraute's arrival
F: Successive forms (un-unified)[16]
Period 13: E-flat major (beg. in minor) (93/3/1–97/5/3) [1091–1170]
D.C: Brünnhilde's stormy welcome of Waltraute
F: Composite Bar
Überleitung to F-sharp minor: (97/5/4–99/2/2) [1171–1199]
F: Simple Bogen
Einleitung to narration: (99/2/3–100/2/2) [1200–1221]
F: Simple Bar
Period 14: F-sharp minor (100/2/3–109/4/4) [1222–1428]
D.C: Waltraute's narration
F: Composite Bar
Period 15: F-sharp minor (end in major) (109/4/4–115/2/1) [1428–1547]
D.C: Brünnhilde's reluctance to give up the Ring
F: Successive forms (coda-like)
Übergang: (115/2/2–119/2/2) [1547–1608]
F: Simple Bogen
Period 16: B minor (119/2/3–128/5/5) [1609–1844]
D.C: Siegfried's betrayal
F: Successive forms (coda-like)

16. This period actually conforms to the Gegenbar form which Lorenz did not acknowledge until *Geheimnis* II.

[*Götterdämmerung* II]
Act II
Period 1: B minor (end in major) (129/1/1–141/2/8) [1–202]
           D.C: Prelude and Alberich scene
           F: Composite refrain

Period 2: B-flat major (141/2/9–143/1/2) [203–256]
           D.C: News of Gunther's approach
           F: Composite expanded Bar (together with P.3)
Period 3: G major (beg. in *D*) (143/1/3–150/2/4) [256–383]
           D.C: Gutrune receives Siegfried
           F: Composite expanded Bar (together with P.2)

Period 4: C major (minor) (150/3/1–170/2/4) [384–679]
           D.C: Assembly of the vassals
           F: Potentiated Bogen
Period 5: B-flat major (171/1/1–175/3/4) [680–749]
           D.C: Waiting for Gunther
           F: Simple Bar
Period 6: B-flat major (175/3/5–178/2/3) [750–787]
           D.C: Reception of Gunther
           F: Composite Bogen

Übergang: Dominant introduction (G major) to Wedding celebration,
           abruptly interrupted by Brünnhilde's actions until the C-major
           conclusion of the act (179/1/1–180/1/4) [788–813]
           F: Simple Bogen
Period 7: B-flat minor (beg. in *Ltwk.* of *S*; half cadence in *S*) (180/1/5–
           182/2/4) [814–859]
           D.C: Brünnhilde sees Siegfried
           F: Simple expanded Bogen
Period 8: D minor (F major) (182/3/1–185/2/5) [860–906]
           D.C: Brünnhilde sees the Ring
           F: Simple expanded Bogen
Period 9: C minor (185/3/1–192/2/3) [907–1009]
           D.C: Brünnhilde's outburst of rage
           F: Bar
Period 10: E-flat minor (end in *Tp*) (192/2/4–193/3/7) [1010–1038]
           D.C: Brünnhilde announces her shame
           F: Composite Bogen
Period 11: C major (beg. in *(D)D*) (194/1/1–198/2/1) [1039–1118]
           D.C: Siegfried's justification
           F: Composite Bar
Period 12: E-flat major (beg. in *Tp*) (198/2/2–203/1/1) [1119–1213]
           D.C: Oath and counter oath
           F: Composite strophic

[*Götterdämmerung* II]
Period 13: C major (beg. in *(D)D*) (203/1/1–207/4/1) [1213–1285]
        D.C: Siegfried's high spirits
        F: Composite Bogen
Nachspiel & Übergang: (207/4/2–209/3/2) [1286–1333]
        F: Successive forms (coda-like)
Period 14: C minor (end in major) (209/3/3–230/5/5) [1334–1704]
        D.C: Conspiracy for vengeance and conclusion of wedding
        celebrations
        F: Refrain
                Period is divided into six musical sections by the sound-
                ing of the Rachebundmotiv
        A.   Brünnhilde's wretchedness (209/3/3–211/3/1) [1334–
                1376] (Simple Bar)
                        [Lorenz omits the next six measures, but includes
                        them in his measure counts]
                        Refrain (211/4/3–212/1/2) [1383–1387]
        B.   Brünnhilde joins with Hagen (212/1/3–216/3/1) [1388–
                1461] (simple strophic)
                        Refrain (216/3/1–216/4/1) [1462–1465]
        C.   Gunther's doubt (216/4/2–219/4/5) [1466–1516]
                (Potentiated Bogen)[17]
                        Refrain (220/1/1–220/2/3) [1517–1524]
        D.   Gunther agrees to the murder (220/2/4–223/2/4) [1525–
                1580] (Successive forms (half-unified))
                        Refrain (223/2/5–223/3/3) [1581–1584]
        E.   Thoughts of Gutrune (223/2/5–225/3/2) [1585–1616]
                (Successive forms (half-unified))
                        Refrain (225/3/3–226/1/1) [1617–1623]
        F.   Oath trio, mixed with wedding music (226/1/2–230/5/5)
                [1624–1704] (Composite Bar)

Act III

Vorspiel: F major (231/1/1–232/5/4) [1–38]
        F: Simple Bogen
Period 1:   F major (232/5/5–251/2/3) [39–260]
        D.C: The Rhine maidens in their merriment
        F: Composite Bar
Überleitung: (251/2/4–252/3/3) [261–279]
        F: Potentiated Bar

17. The HS. of P.14.C begins with the previous refrain.

[*Götterdämmerung* III]
Period 2: F minor (beg. in *D*; end in major) (252/3/4–272/2/1) [280–477]
            D.C: The Rhine maidens in their seriousness
            F: Composite Bar
Nachspiel, and Abrundung of scene 1 in F major (272/2/2–273/4/5) [478–511]
Period 3: A major (273/4/6–276/5/2) [511–553]
            D.C: Hunting party
            F: Potentiated Bar
Period 4: D major (potentiated half cadence) (276/5/3–282/3/1) [554–633]
            D.C: Introductory dialogue
            F: Composite strophic
Übergang: (282/3/2–283/2/4) [634–653]
Period 5: G minor (half cadence) (283/2/5–290/3/1) [654–757]
            D.C: Siegfried's narrative about Mime and Fafner
            F: Composite Bogen (shortened Rp)
Übergang: G major to B minor (290/3/2–291/2/1) [758–767]
Period 6: A major (developing from *(D)D*) (291/2/2–301/1/2) [768–912]
            D.C: Siegfried's memory of Brünnhilde and death
            F: Composite expanded Bogen
Period 7: C minor (301/2/3–305/2/4) [913–988]
            D.C: Siegfried's Funeral March
            F: Simple refrain
Period 8: C minor (305/2/5–307/3/5) [989–1032]
            D.C: Gutrune's alarm
            F: Simple perfect Bogen
Period 9: C minor (end in *D⁺*) (307/4/1–314/3/2 and 315/4/2–317/3/4) [1033–1157 and 1186–1219][18]
            D.C: Resolution of the Gibichungen plot
            F: Composite Bar
Period 10: D-flat major (314/3/3–336/2/1 [with interruption 315/4/2–317/3/4]) [1158–1501 (with interruption from mm. 1186–1219)]
            D.C: Brünnhilde's Immolation scene
            F: Composite perfect Bogen
Period 11: D-flat major (336/2/2–340/5/3) [1502–1580][19]
            D.C: Götterdämmerung
            F: Potentiated Bar

---

18. This overlapping is discussed in chapter 5 of the present work.
19. Mistakenly given as [1502–1562] in *Geheimnis* I.

Bibliography

The following bibliography is organized according to the following outline. Works are not listed more than once, although they may overlap categories.

Lorenz

Lorenz's Writings

Monographs

Alessandro Scarlattis Jugendoper: Ein Beitrag zur Geschichte der italienische Oper. 2 vols. Ausburg: Benno Filsner, 1927.

*Abendländische Musikgeschichte im Rhythmus der Generationen: Eine
   Anregung.* Berlin: Max Hesse, 1928.
Das Geheimnis der Form bei Richard Wagner. Vol. 1: *Der musikalische
   Aufbau des Bühnenfestspieles 'Der Ring des Nibelungen'*; Vol. 2: *Der
   musikalische Aufbau von Richard Wagners 'Tristan und Isolde'*; Vol. 3:
   *Der musikalische Aufbau von Richard Wagners 'Die Meistersinger von
   Nürnburg'*; Vol. 4: *Der musikalische Aufbau von Richard Wagners
   'Parsifal'.* Berlin: Max Hesse, 1924–1933. Reprint, Tutzing: Hans
   Schneider, 1966.
"Gedanken und Studien zur musikalischen Formgebung in Richard Wagner's
   Ring des Nibelungen." Ph.D. diss., Frankfurt-am-Main, 1922.

Articles[1]

"Die Abstammung Richard Wagners." *Allgemeine Musikzeitung* 65 (1938):
   311–13.
"Die Ahnentafel in der Musikerbiographie." *Allgemeine Musikzeitung* 65
   (1938): 782.
"Alessandro Scarlattis Opern und Wien." *Zeitschrift für Musikwissenschaft*
   9 (1926–27): 86–89.
"Arnold Scherings 'Welle der Klangstile'." *Rheinische Musik- und
   Theaterzeitung* 30 (1929): 325–26.
"Atonale Strebungen im Jahre 1300." *Der Auftakt* 9 (1929): 8–11.
"Auf und ab in Bruckners Schaffenskraft." *Der Auftakt* 13 (1933): 128–31.
"Der Begriff der 'Tonalitäts-Auflösung'." *Rheinische Musik- und
   Theaterzeitung* 28 (1927): 43–44.
"Betrachtungen über Beethovens Eroica-Skizzen: Ein Beitrag zur Psychologie
   des Schaffens." *Zeitschrift für Musikwissenschaft* 7 (1924–25): 409–22.
"Ein alter Bach-Stammbaum." *Neue Zeitschrift für Musik* 82 (1915): 281–82.
"Ein unbekannter Beethoven-Brief." *Süddeutsche Monatshefte* 27 (1929):
   47–49.

---

1. A glance at the many diverse journals in which Lorenz published articles suggests that
this bibliography may not be comprehensive, despite my best efforts. Indeed, there are several
other articles which I have been unable to track down:
    a. The prospectus published along with the first issue of *Die Musik* in 1901 lists as
forthcoming two articles by Lorenz which never appeared: "Richard Strauss's Polyphonie,"
and "Deklamationsfehler bei Wagner."
    b. In addition to the several articles listed in the biliography from the *Münchener Neueste
Nachrichten*, I have found references to two more: one on Mozart's *Die Zauberflöte* (28 May
1923), and one on Bruckner's "Lebenswellen" (May 1929). It seems likely that this newspaper
contains more articles by Lorenz, whose home was in Munich.
    c. Two citations from secondary sources proved elusive; the articles are nowhere in the
volumes cited: "Das Bühnenbild in Wagners Dramen." *Hellweg: Wochenschrift für Deutsche
Kunst* (1927); "Bedeutung der Periodisierung für den Unterricht in der Musikgeschichte."
Halbmonatsschrift für Schulmusikpflege 24 (1939): 90.

"Eine Verbesserung in den Rhythmisierungsversuchen neumierter und choraliter notierter Gesänge." *Zeitschrift für Musikwissenschaft* 10 (1927–28): 321–26.

"Die Festspiele in Bayreuth." *Die Musik* 22 (1930): 578–83.

"Das Finale in Mozarts Meisteropern." *Die Musik* 19 (1927): 621–32.

"'Der fliegende Holländer'—Oper oder Worttondrama?" *Bayreuther Festspielführer* (1939): 102–108.

"Die formale Gestaltung des Vorspiels zu Tristan und Isolde." *Zeitschrift für Musikwissenschaft* 5 (1923): 546–57.

"Der formale Schwung in Richard Strauss' 'Till Eulenspiegel'." *Die Musik* 17 (1925): 658–69.

"Der gefilmte Kapellmeister." *Neue Zeitschrift für Musik* 81 (1914): 377–78.

"Das Generationsproblem in der Musikgeschichte." *Allgemeine Musik-Zeitung* 55 (1928): 490–91.

"Das 'Gruppenprinzip' in der Instrumentation des 'Ring'." *Bayreuther Festspielführer* (1937): 112–16.

"Das Heldische in Richard Wagners Parsifal." *Bayreuther Festspielführer* (1931): 102–109.

"Homophone Großrhythmik in Bachs Polyphonie." *Die Musik* 22 (1930): 245–53.

"Klangmischung in Anton Bruckners Orchester." *Allgemeine Musik-Zeitung* 63 (1936): 717–20.

"Kunstform—Kunstgeist." *Bayreuther Blätter* 50 (1927): 123–28.

"Ludwig Schnorr von Carolsfeld: Zur 100. Wiederkehr seines Geburtstages 2. Juli 1836." *Die Musik* 28 (1936): 736–55; *Allgemeine Musik-Zeitung* 63 (1936): 465f.

"Der musikalische Aufbau von Wagners 'Lohengrin'." *Bayreuther Festspielführer* (1936): 189–98. Translated by Stewart Spencer in *Wagner* 2 (April 1981): 40–44.

"Der musikalische Aufbau von Wagners 'Parsifal'." *Bayreuther Festspielführer* (1933): 161–68. Translated by Stewart Spencer in *Wagner* 2 (January 1981): 21–25.

"Der musikalische Aufbau von Wagners 'Tristan und Isolde'." *Bayreuther Festspielführer* (1938): 139–45. Reprinted in *Hundert Jahre Tristan*, edited by Wieland Wagner. Emsdetten: Lechte, 1965. Translated by Stewart Spencer in *Wagner* 2 (July 1981): 74–77.

"Musikalische Form bei Wagner." In *Deutsches Musikjahrbuch* 1, ed. Rolf Cunz, 198–210. Essen: Schlingloff, 1923.

"Musikwissenschaft im Aufbau." *Zeitschrift für Musik* 106 (1939): 367–70.

"Musikwissenschaft und Ahnenforschung." *Zeitschrift für Musik* 105 (1938): 1372–73.

"Musikwissenschaft und Erbbiologie." *Deutsche Militär-Musiker-Zeitung* 62 (1940): 165–66.

"Musikwissenschaft und Judenfrage." *Die Musik* 31 (1938): 177–79.

"Musikwissenschaft und Schallplatte." *Skizzen* 12 (1938): 3–4, 20.

"Neue Anschauungen auf dem Gebiete der musikalischen Formenlehre." *Forschungen und Fortschritte* 6 (1933): 287–88.

"Neue Formerkenntnisse, angewandt auf Richard Straußens 'Don Juan'." *Archiv für Musikforschung* 1 (1936): 452–66.

"Neue Gedanken zur Klangspaltung und Klangverschmelzung." In *Festschrift Arnold Schering zum sechzigsten Geburtstag*, edited by Helmut Osthoff, Walter Serauky, and Adam Adrio, 137–50. Berlin: A. Glas, 1937. Reprint, Hildesheim: Georg Olms, 1973.

"Die Oper als formal-konstruktives Experiment." *Musik im Leben* 5 (1929): 80–81.

"Die Orchestereinleitungen der Festspiel-Werke 1934." *Bayreuther Festspielführer* (1934): 171–76.

"Parsifal als Übermensch." *Die Musik* 1 (1902): 1876–82.

"Periodizität in der Musikgeschichte." *Die Musik* 21 (1929): 644–50.

"Die Pflege der deutschen Musik und die Entstehung der Schülerkapellen in Deutsch-Ostafrika." *Afrika-Nachrichten* 17 (1936): 229–31.

"Das Relativitätsprinzip in der musikalischen Form." In *Studien zur Musikgeschichte: Festschrift für Guido Adler zum 75. Geburtstag*, 179–86. Vienna: Universal Edition, 1930. Reprint, Vienna: Universal Edition, 1971.

"Die Religion des Parsifal." *Die Musik* 25 (1933): 342–47.

"Richard Wagner als Musiker." *Wille und Macht* 1 (1 November 1933): 24–28.

"Richard Wagner, ein Meister des musikalischen Aufbaues." *Die Sonne* 10 (1933): 63–69.

"Richard Wagners 'neue Religion'." *Allgemeine Musikzeitung* 66 (1939): 459–62.

"Richard Wagners 'Parsifal' und der Nationalsozialismus." *Deutsches Wesen* (July 1933): 6–8.

"Striche in genialen Meisterwerken." *Die Musik* 28 (1936): 597–600.

"Der Tannhäuser-Ouvertüre historische Sendung." *Bayreuther Festspielführer* (1930): 58–62.

"Theatermusik oder dramatische Sinfonie?" In *Deutsches Musikjahrbuch* 2/3, edited by Rolf Cunz, 186–93. Essen: Th. Reismann-Grone, 1925.

"Die Tonalität in Wagners 'Tristan und Isolde'." *Bayreuther Festspielführer* (1927): 177–86.

"Tonalitäts-Spannung." *Münchener Neueste Nachrichten*, 13 November 1927, 18.

"Die Tonkunst grüßt den Führer!" *Zeitschrift für Musik* 106 (1939): 355.

"Über die musikalische Form von Richard Wagners Meisterwerken." *Bayreuther Festspielführer* (1924): 138–49. Reprinted in *Richard Wagner: Das Betroffensein der Nachwelt: Beiträge zur Wirkungsgeschichte*, edited by Dietrich Mach, 75–87. Darmstadt: Wissenschaftliche Buchgesellschaft, 1984.

"Der verräterische Pausentakt in Bruckners 'Fünfter'." *Die Musik* 29 (1937): 274–75.

"Der Wechsel der Klangstile in Arnold Scherings Betrachtungsweise." *Münchener Neueste Nachrichten*, 9 December 1928, 13.

"Wege zur Erkenntnis von Richard Wagners Kunstwerk." *Bayreuther Blätter* 56 (1933): 109–14.

"Die Wellenlinie in Bruckners Schaffenskraft." *Kirchenmusikalisches Jahrbuch* 25 (1930): 122–27.

"Worauf beruht die bekannte Wirkung der Durchführung im 1. Eroicasatze?" *Neues Beethoven-Jahrbuch* 1 (1924): 159–83.

"Wort-Ton-Dramatiker und Text-Dichtende Komponisten." *Bayreuther Festspielführer* (1928): 117–22.

"Wotans Abschied und Feuerzauber: Eine Formuntersuchung." *Hellweg: Wochenschrift für Deutsche Kunst* (10 October 1923): 710–13.

"Zum musikalischen Aufbau der Meistersinger von Nürnberg." *Bayreuther Festpielführer* (1925): 131–35. Translated by Stewart Spencer in *Wagner* 4 (January 1983): 9–13.

"Zur Bach Pflege: Eine Anregung." *Neue Zeitschrift für Musik* 82 (1915): 170.

"Zur Instrumentation von Anton Bruckners Symphonien." *Zeitschrift für Musik* 103 (1936): 1318–25.

Book Reviews

Review of *Melodielehre als Einführung in die Musiktheorie*, by Karl Blessinger. *Die Musik* 24 (1932): 538–39.

Review of *Zeitstil und Persönlichkeitsstil in den Variationenswerken der musikalischen Romantik*, by Martin Friedland. *Die Musik* 24 (1932): 380.

"Ernst Kurth: Romantische Harmonik und ihre Krise in Wagners 'Tristan'." *Die Musik* 16 (1924): 255–62.

"Ernst Kurths 'Musikpsychologie'." *Die Musik* 23 (1930): 182–87.

Review of *Bach-Probleme*, by Roderich von Mojsisovics. *Die Musik* 23 (1931): 933.

Review of *Alessandro Scarlatti 'il Palermitano'* by Ulisse Prota-Guirleo. *Zeitschrift für Musikwissenschaft* 9 (1926–27): 505–507.

Obituaries and Letters

"Zur Scarlatti-Forschung." *Zeitschrift für Musik* 94 (1927): 34–35.

"Otto Baensch." *Zeitschrift für Musik* 103 (1936): 1227.

"José Viana da Motta." *Zeitschrift für Musik* 105 (1938): 1318.

"Nachwort" to "Die Tonalität des 'Tristan'" by Eugen Schmitz. *Zeitschrift für Musik* 106 (1939): 141–42.

Editions

Wagner, Richard. *Ausgewählte Schriften und Briefe*. 2 vols. Berlin: B.
  Hahnefeld, 1938. Excerpts published by Lorenz as "Worte des Sehers,"
  Zeitschrift für Musik 105 (1938): 721–28.
Weber, Carl Maria von. *Jugendopern*. [*Das stumme Waldmädchen, Peter
  Schmoll und seine Nachbarn*]. Carl Maria von Weber Musikalische
  Werke, Reihe 2, Bd. 1. Augsburg: Benno Filser, 1926. Reprint, New York:
  Broude International Editions, 1977.
Edition of the basso continuo in J.E. Kindermann, *Ausgewählte Werke des
  Nürnberger Organisten*, edited by Felix Schreiber. In *Denkmäler der
  Tonkunst Bayern*, vols. 21–4. Leipzig: Breitkopf & Härtel, 1924.

Courses Taught at the University of Munich 1924–1939

Allgemeine Übersicht über die abendländische Musikgeschichte
Anton Bruckner
Anton Bruckners Symphonien
Der musikalische Aufbau von Richard Wagners *Meistersinger von Nürnberg*
Der musikalische Aufbau von Richard Wagners *Parsifal*
Der musikalische Aufbau von Richard Wagners *Ring des Nibelungen*
Der musikalische Aufbau von Richard Wagners *Tristan und Isolde*
Einfluß der Rasse auf die Musikentwicklung
Einführung in die Musikwissenschaft
Entwicklung der Opernform von 1700 bis zur neuesten Gegenwart
Entwicklungsgeschichte der Opernform von 1600
Geschichte der Instrumentalmusik I (1600–1750)
Geschichte der Instrumentalmusik II (von 1750 bis zur Gegenwart)
Geschichte der Oper (Übersicht)
Harmonielehre I
Harmonielehre II
Harmonielehre III (Chromatik und Enharmonik) mit Übungen in
  harmonischer Analyse
Harmonielehre für Anfänger
Harmonielehre für Fortgeschrittene
Instrumentenkunde mit Führungen durch die Musikabteilung des Deutschen
  Museums
Kontrapunkt
Kontrapunkt II
Kontrapunkt für Anfänger
Musik und Rasse
Musikalische Formenlehre
[Praktische] Übungen in der Ausführung historischer Kammermusik
Richard Strauß

Richard Strauß und seine Instrumental-Werke
Richard Strauß und seine Symphonischen Dichtungen
Richard Wagners *Meistersinger von Nürnberg*
Richard Wagners Nationale Sendung
Übersicht über die gesamte abendländische Musikgeschichte nach den
    Grundsätzen der Generationenlehre
Übungen im Analysieren von Musikstücken
Übungen im doppelte Kontrapunkt und der Formenlehre
Übungen im Zergliedern von Musikstücken
Übungen in der Ausführung historischer Vokal- und Instrumentalmusik
Übungen in der harmonischen Analyse für Fortgeschrittene
Übungen in der innermusikalische Deutung von Tonwerken (Harmonik,
    Rhythmik und Form)
Übungen in der musikalischen Analyse

Reviews of Lorenz's Work

Baensch, Otto. Review of *Das Geheimnis der Form bei Richard Wagner*.
    Vol. 2: *Der musikalische Aufbau von Richard Wagners 'Tristan und
    Isolde'*, by Alfred Lorenz. *Zeitschrift für Musikwissenschaft* 9 (1927):
    597–600.

Berten, Walter. Review of *Richard Wagner: Ausgewählte Schriften und Briefe*,
    edited by Alfred Lorenz. *Die Musik* 31 (1938): 121–22.

Golther, W. Review of *Richard Wagner: Ausgewählte Schriften und Briefe*,
    edited by Alfred Lorenz. Zeitschrift für Musik 105 (1938): 758.

Grunsky, Hans Alfred. "Der musikalische Aufbau von Wagners Tristan und
    Isolde nach Alfred Lorenz." [Review of *Das Geheimnis der Form bei
    Richard Wagner*. Vol. 2: *Der musikalische Aufbau von Richard Wagners
    'Tristan und Isolde'*, by Alfred Lorenz.] *Die Musik* 20 (1927): 93–103.

———. "Über Alfred Lorenz's "Der musikalische Aufbau von Wagners
    Tristan und Isolde." [Review of *Das Geheimnis der Form bei Richard
    Wagner*. Vol. 2: *Der musikalische Aufbau von Richard Wagners 'Tristan
    und Isolde'*, by Alfred Lorenz.] *Zeitschrift für Musik* 94 (1927): 559–
    61.

Grunsky, Karl. "Alfred Lorenz: Das Geheimnis der Form bei Richard Wagner,
    Band IV, Parsifal." [Review of *Das Geheimnis der Form bei Richard
    Wagner*. Vol. 4: *Der musikalische Aufbau von Richard Wagners 'Parsifal'*,
    by Alfred Lorenz.] *Die Musik* 25 (1933): 754–58.

———. "Ein Buch der Vorbereitung auf den Tristan." [Review of *Das
    Geheimnis der Form bei Richard Wagner*. Vol. 2: *Der musikalische Aufbau
    von Richard Wagners 'Tristan und Isolde'*, by Alfred Lorenz.] *Bayreuther
    Blätter* 50 (1927): 33–35.

———. "Ein Meisterbuch über ein Meisterwerk." [Review of *Das Geheimnis
    der Form bei Richard Wagner*. Vol. 3: *Der musikalische Aufbau von*

Richard Wagners 'Die Meistersinger von Nürnberg', by Alfred Lorenz.] *Die Musik* 23 (1930): 190–93.

———. Review of *Das Geheimnis der Form bei Richard Wagner*. Vol. 1: *Der musikalische Aufbau des Bühnenfestspieles 'Der Ring des Nibelungen'*, by Alfred Lorenz. *Bayreuther Blätter* 47 (1924): 119–21.

———. "Vom Geheimnis der musikalischen Form bei Wagner." [Review of *Das Geheimnis der Form bei Richard Wagner*. Vol. 1: *Der musikalische Aufbau des Bühnenfestspieles 'Der Ring des Nibelungen'*, by Alfred Lorenz.] *Neue Musik-Zeitung* 46 (1925): 309–10.

———. Review of *Das Geheimnis der Form bei Richard Wagner*. Vol. 2: *Der musikalische Aufbau von Richard Wagners 'Tristan und Isolde'*, by Alfred Lorenz. *Neue Musik-Zeitung* 48 (1927): 537–38.

Günther, Siegfried. Review of *Das Geheimnis der Form bei Richard Wagner*. Vol. 1: *Der musikalische Aufbau des Bühnenfestspieles 'Der Ring des Nibelungen'*, by Alfred Lorenz. *Zeitschrift für Musikwissenschaft* 8 (1925): 50–51.

Mies, Paul. Review of reprint of *Das Geheimnis der Form bei Richard Wagner*. *Musikhandel* 19 (1968): 246.

Millenkovich-Morold, Max von. Review of *Das Geheimnis der Form bei Richard Wagner*. Vol. 3: *Der musikalische Aufbau von Richard Wagners 'Die Meistersinger von Nürnberg'*, by Alfred Lorenz. *Zeitschrift für Musik* 99 (1932): 46–47.

[Millenkovich-]Morold, Max. Review of *Das Geheimnis der Form bei Richard Wagner*. Vol. 4: *Der musikalische Aufbau von Richard Wagners 'Parsifal'*, by Alfred Lorenz. *Zeitschrift für Musik* 101 (1934): 420–22.

Wagner Literature (Including Works about Lorenz)

Pre-1945

Adler, Guido. *Richard Wagner: Vorlesungen gehalten an der Universität zu Wien*. Leipzig: Breitkopf & Härtel, 1904.

Baensch, Otto. "Richard Wagners Werk: Ein kunstgeschichtliches Wunder." *Bayreuther Festspielführer* (1933): 167–80.

Bekker, Paul. *Richard Wagner: His Life in His Work*. Translated by M.M. Bozman. New York: Norton, 1931. Reprint, Westport: Greenwood Press, 1971. [first pub. 1924]

Chamberlain, Houston Stewart. "Richard Wagner und die musikalische Form: Ein unveröffentlicher Brief H.S. Chamberlains." *Bayreuther Festspielführer* (1930): 32–34.

Egert, Paul. "Alfred Lorenz 70 Jahre alt: Zum 11.Juli 1938." *Die Musik* 30 (1938): 652–56.

Egk, Werner. "Wege der Harmonik." *Völkische Kultur: Monatsschrift für die gesamte geistige Bewegung des neuen Deutschlands* 2 (1934): 139–41.

Ehrenfels, Christian von. "Die musikalische Architektonik." *Bayreuther Blätter* 19 (1896): 257–63.

―――. "Richard Wagner und seine Apostaten: Ein Beitrag zur Jahrhundertfeier" (1913). In *Philosophischen Schriften: Metaphysik*, edited by Reinhard Fabian, 382–418. Munich: Philosophia Verlag, 1990.

―――. "Zur Klärung der Wagnerkontroverse" (1896). In *Philosophischen Schriften: Ästhetik*, edited by Reinhard Fabian, 97–117. Munich: Philosophia Verlag, 1986.

Engelsmann, Walter. "Die 'Konstruktion' der Melodie in Wagners 'Tristan und Isolde'." *Bayreuther Festspielführer* (1938): 145–56.

―――. *Wagners Klingendes Universum*. Potsdam: Müller & Kiepenheuer, 1933.

"Der Entdecker der Wagnersche Formprinzipien: Zum 70. Geburtstag von Universitätsprofessor Alfred Lorenz." *Völkischer Beobachter*, 11 July 1938.

Ficker, Rudolf von. "Alfred Lorenz" [obituary]. *Archiv für Musikforschung* 5 (1940): 64.

Gerigk, Herbert. "Alfred Lorenz" [obituary]. *Die Musik* 32 (1939): 105.

Grunsky, Hans Alfred. "Einer der uns fehlt: Dem Gedanken von Alfred Lorenz." In *Neue Wagner-Forschungen: Erste Folge*, edited by Otto Strobel, 35–42. Karlsruhe: G. Braun, 1943.

―――. "Neues zur Formenlehre." *Zeitschrift für Musikwissenschaft* 16 (1934): 84–91.

Grunsky, Karl. "Die Formfrage bei Richard Wagner." *Die Musik* 15 (1923): 436–40.

―――. "Ein letzter Streifzug." *Bayreuther Blätter* 61 (1938): 231–37.

―――. "Reim und musikalische Form in den Meistersingern." *Richard-Wagner Jahrbuch* 5 (1913): 138–87.

―――. "Das Vorspiel und der erste Akt von 'Tristan und Isolde'." *Richard-Wagner Jahrbuch* 2 (1907): 207–84.

―――. "Wagner als Sinfoniker." *Richard Wagner-Jahrbuch* 1 (1906): 227–44.

―――. "Wege zu Wagner." *Bayreuther Festspielführer* (1934): 124–30.

Hanslick, Eduard. "Die Meistersinger von Richard Wagner." In *Die moderne Oper: Kritiken und Studien*, 292–305. Berlin: Allgemeiner Verein für Deutsche Literatur, 1885.

Herzfeld, Friedrich. "Alfred Lorenz, der Wagner-Forscher." *Allgemeine Musikzeitung* 63 (1936): 481–82.

Krohn, Ilmari. "Lohengrins Formbyggnad [formal structure]." *Svensk tidskrift för musikforskning* 4 (1922): 1–25.

Mann, Thomas. *Pro and Contra Wagner*. Translated by Allan Blunden. London: Faber & Faber, 1985.

Mey, Curt. *Die Meistergesang in Geschichte und Kunst: ausführliche Erklärung der Tabulaturen, Schulregeln, Sitten und Gebräuche der Meistersinger, sowie deren Anwendung in Richard Wagners 'Die Meistersinger von Nürnberg'.* Leipzig: Hermann Seemann, 1901.

———. "Richard Wagner als Ästhetiker." *Richard Wagner-Jahrbuch* 1 (1906): 152–69.

Millenkovich-Morold, Max von. "Alfred Lorenz: Zu seinem 70. Geburtstage." *Zeitschrift für Musik* 105 (1938): 719–21.

Newman, Ernest. *The Life of Richard Wagner.* 4 vols. New York: Knopf, 1933–46. Reprint, Cambridge: Cambridge University Press, 1976.

Schmitz, Eugen. "Die Tonalität des 'Tristan'." *Zeitschrift für Musik* 106 (1939): 138–41; "Nachwort," by Alfred Lorenz, 141–42.

Seidl, Arthur. "Ist Richard Wagner 'Romantik' oder bedeutet er vielmehr 'Klassik'—'Form-Auflösung' oder 'Gesetzes-Erfüllung'?" In *Deutsches Musikjahrbuch* 2/3, edited by Rolf Cunz, 126–30. Essen: Th. Reismann-Grone, 1925.

Strobel, Otto. *Richard Wagner über sein Schaffen: Ein Beitrag zur "Künstlerästhetik."* Munich: Bayerische Druckerei & Verlagsanstalt, 1924.

———. "Ziele und Wege der Wagnerforschung." In *Neue Wagner-Forschungen: Erste Folge,* edited by Otto Strobel, 15–32. Karlsruhe: G. Braun, 1943.

Veidl, Theodor. "Die formale Gestaltung des Tristan-Vorspiels." *Die Musik* 34 (1942): 127–30; response by Herbert von Stein, *Die Musik* 35 (1942): 78–79.

Wagner, Richard. *Gesammelte Schriften und Dichtungen.* Leipzig: Walter Tiemann, 1907.

———. *Richard Wagner an Mathilde Wesendonck: Tagebuchblätter und Briefe 1853–1871.* Edited by Wolfgang Golther. Leipzig: Breitkopf & Härtel, 1914.

———. *Selected Letters of Richard Wagner.* Edited and translated by Barry Millington and Stewart Spencer. New York: Norton, 1987.

Wolzogen, Hans von. "Leitmotive." *Bayreuther Blätter* 20 (1897): 313–30.

———. *Musikalisch-dramatische Parallelen: Beiträge zur Erkenntnis von der Musik als Ausdruck.* Leipzig: Breitkopf & Härtel, 1906. [First pub. serially in the *Bayreuther Blätter* between 1894 and 1903]

———. *Thematischer Leitfaden durch die Musik zu Rich. Wagners Festspiel 'Der Ring des Nibelungen'.* 2nd "verbesserte" edition. Leipzig: Schloemp, 1876.

———. *Wagneriana: Gesammelte Aufsätze über R. Wagner's Werke vom Ring bis zum Gral.* Leipzig: F. Freund, 1888.

Würz, Richard. "Alfred Lorenz 70 Jahre alt." *Münchener Neueste Nachrichten,* 19 July 1938.

Zentner, Wilhelm. "Alfred Lorenz" [obituary]. *Zeitschrift für Musik* 106 (1939): 1171.

———. "Musiker und Musikgelehrter: Zum 70.Geburtstag von Alfred Lorenz am 11.Juli 1938." *Neues Münchener Tagblatt*, 8 July 1938.

Post-1945

Abbate, Carolyn. "Opera as Symphony: A Wagnerian Myth." In *Analyzing Opera: Verdi and Wagner*, edited by Carolyn Abbate and Roger Parker, 92–124. Berkeley and Los Angeles: University of California Press, 1989.

———. "Wagner, 'On Modulation,' and *Tristan.*" *Cambridge Opera Journal* 1 (1989): 33–58.

Adorno, Theodore W. *In Search of Wagner*. Translated by Rodney Livingstone. London: Verso, 1991. [First pub. 1952]

Bailey, Robert. "The Genesis of Wagner's *Tristan und Isolde* and a Study of Wagner's Sketches and Drafts for the First Act." Ph.D. dissertation, Princeton University, 1969.

———. "The Structure of the Ring and its Evolution." *19th-Century Music* 1 (1977): 48–61.

———, ed. *Prelude and Transfiguration from* Tristan und Isolde. Norton Critical Score. New York: Norton, 1985.

Brinkmann, Reinhold. "'Drei der Fragen stell' ich mir frei': Zur Wanderer-Szene im 1. Akt von Wagners 'Siegfried'." *Jahrbuch der Staatlichen Instituts für Musikforschung Preußischer Kulturbesitz* 5 (1972): 120–62.

Cooke, Deryck. *I Saw the World End: A Study of Wagner's Ring*. Oxford: Oxford University Press, 1979.

Coren, Daniel. "Inspiration and Calculation in the Genesis of Wagner's *Siegfried.*" In *Studies in Musicology in Honor of Otto E. Albrecht*, edited by John W. Hill, 266–87. Kassel: Bärenreiter, 1980.

Dahlhaus, Carl, ed. *Das Drama Richard Wagners als musikalisches Kunstwerk*. Vol. 23 of *Studien zur Musikgeschichte des 19. Jahrhunderts*. Regensburg: Gustav Bosse, 1970.

———. "Formprinzipien in Wagner's 'Ring des Nibelungen'." In *Beiträge zur Geschichte der Oper*, edited by Heinz Becker, 95–129. Regensburg: Gustav Bosse, 1969.

———. "The Music." In *Wagner Handbook*, edited by Ulrich Müller and Peter Wapnewski, translated and edited by John Deathridge, 297–14. Cambridge, MA: Harvard University Press, 1992. [First pub. 1986]

———. *Richard Wagner's Music Dramas*. Translated by Mary Whittall. Cambridge: Cambridge University Press, 1979. [First pub. 1971]

———. "Tonalität und Form in Wagners 'Ring des Nibelungen'." *Archiv für Musikwissenschaft* 40 (1983): 165–73.

———. "Wagners Begriff der 'dichterisch-musikalischen Periode'." In

Beiträge zur Geschichte der Musikanschauung im 19. Jahrhunderts, edited by Walter Salmen, 179–94. Vol. 1 of *Studien zur Musikgeschichte des 19. Jahrhunderts*. Regensburg: Gustav Bosse, 1965.

—. "Wagners dramatisch-musikalischer Formbegriff." In *Colloquium 'Verdi-Wagner' Rom 1969*, edited by Friedrich Lippmann, 290–303. Vol. 11 of *Analecta Musicologica*. Cologne: Böhlau, 1972.

Darcy, Warren Jay. "Formal and Rhythmic Problems in Wagner's "Ring" Cycle." D.Mus.A. dissertation, University of Illinois at Urbana-Champaign, 1973.

—. *Wagner's* Das Rheingold. Studies in Musical Genesis and Structure. Oxford: Clarendon Press, 1993.

Deathridge, John, Martin Geck and Egon Voss. *Wagner Werk-Verzeichnis: Verzeichnis der musikalischen Werke Richard Wagners und ihrer Quellen.* Mainz: Schott, 1986.

Deathridge, John. "A Brief History of Wagner Research." In *Wagner Handbook*, translated and edited by John Deathridge, 202–23. Cambridge, MA: Harvard University Press, 1992. [First pub. 1986]

Deathridge, John, and Carl Dahlhaus. *The New Grove Wagner.* New York: Norton, 1984.

Dickinson, A[lan] E[dgar] F[rederic]. "The Structural Methods of the 'Ring': I. The Word and the Orchestra." *Monthly Musical Record* 84 (May 1954): 87–92.

—. "The Structural Methods of the 'Ring': II. Wider Impressions." *Monthly Musical Record* 84 (June 1954): 124–29.

Gozzi, Susanna. "Nuovi orientamenti della critica wagneriana." *Rivista italiana di musicologia* 19 (1984): 147–77.

Grasberger, Franz. "Zur Geschichte der Musikforschung: Alfred Ottokar Lorenz." *Österreichische Musikzeitschrift* 23 (1968): 555–56.

Grey, Thomas Spencer. "Richard Wagner and the Aesthetics of Musical Form in the Mid-Nineteenth Century (1840–1860)." Ph.D. dissertation, University of California, Berkeley, 1988.

—. *Wagner's Musical Prose: Texts and Contexts.* Cambridge: Cambridge University Press, 1995.

—. ". . . *wie ein rother Faden*: On the Origins of 'Leitmotif' as a Critical Construct and Musical Practice." In *Music Theory in the Age of Romanticism*, edited by Ian Bent, 187–210. Cambridge: Cambridge University Press, 1996.

Grunsky, Hans [Alfred]. "'Tristan und Isolde': Der symphonische Aufbau des dritten Aufzugs." *Zeitschrift für Musik* 113 (1952): 390–94.

Gutman, Robert W. *Richard Wagner: The Man, his Mind, and his Music.* New York: Harcourt, Brace, Jovanovich, 1968.

Hanisch, Ernst. "The Political Influence and Appropriation of Wagner." In *Wagner Handbook*, translated and edited by John Deathridge, 186–201. Cambridge, MA: Harvard University Press, 1992. [First pub. 1986]

Hess, Willy. "'Die Meistersinger von Nürnberg': Ihre dichterisch-musikalische Gesamtform." *Zeitschrift für Musik* 113 (1952): 394–97.

Kinderman, William. "Dramatic Recapitulation in Wagner's *Götterdämmerung.*" *19th-Century Music* 4 (Fall 1980): 101–12.

Knepler, Georg. "Richard Wagners musikalische Gestaltungsprinzipien." *Beiträge zur Musikwissenschaft* 5 (1963): 33–43.

Kropfinger, Klaus. *Wagner and Beethoven: Richard Wagner's Reception of Beethoven.* Translated by Peter Palmer. Cambridge: Cambridge University Press, 1991. [First pub. 1974]

Lacoue-Labarthe, Philippe. *Musica Ficta (Figures of Wagner).* Translated by Felicia McCarren. Stanford: Stanford University Press, 1994.

Lippmann, Friedrich. "Ein neuentdecktes Autograph Richard Wagners: Rezension der Königsberger 'Norma'-Aufführung von 1837." In *Musicæ scientiæ collectanea: Festschrift Karl Gustav Fellerer zum siebzigsten Geburtstag am 7. Juli 1972,* edited by Heinrich Hüschen, 373–79. Cologne: Volk, 1975.

McClatchie, Stephen. "Bruckner and the Bayreuthians; or, *Das Geheimnis der Form bei Anton Bruckner.*" In *Bruckner Studies,* edited by Timothy L. Jackson and Paul Hawkshaw, 110–21. Cambridge: Cambridge University Press, 1997.

———. "The Magic Wand of the Wagnerians: *Musik als Ausdruck.*" *Canadian University Music Review* 13 (1993): 71–92.

———. Review of Fredric Spotts, *Bayreuth: A History of the Wagner Festival. Cambridge Opera Journal* 7 (1995): 277–84; and correction, *Cambridge Opera Journal* 9 (1997): 97.

———. "Towards a Post-Modern Wagner." *Wagner* 13 (1992): 108–21.

McCreless, Patrick. "Schenker and the Norns." In *Analyzing Opera: Verdi and Wagner,* edited by Carolyn Abbate and Roger Parker, 276–97. Berkeley and Los Angeles: University of California Press, 1989.

———. *Wagner's "Siegfried": Its Drama, History and Music.* Ann Arbor: UMI Research Press, 1982.

Millington, Barry. *Wagner.* Rev. ed. London: Dent, 1992.

Müller, Ulrich and Peter Wapnewski, eds. *Wagner Handbook,* translated and edited by John Deathridge. Cambridge, MA: Harvard University Press, 1992. [First pub. 1986]

Murray, David R. "Major Analytical Approaches to Wagner's Musical Style: A Critique." *Music Review* 39 (1978): 211–22.

Die Musik in Geschichte und Gegenwart. S.v. "Wagner, Richard" by Curt von Westernhagen; "Lorenz, Alfred," by Richard Schaal.

New Grove Dictionary of Music and Musicians, 1980. S.v. "Lorenz, Alfred," no author given.

New Grove Dictionary of Opera, 1992. S.v. "Wagner, Richard," by Barry Millington.

Newcomb, Anthony. "The Birth of Music Out of the Spirit of Drama: An

Essay in Wagnerian Formal Analysis." *19th-Century Music* 5 (1981): 38–66.

———. "*Ritornello Ritornato*: A Variety of Wagnerian Refrain Form." In *Analyzing Opera: Verdi and Wagner*, edited by Carolyn Abbate and Roger Parker, 202–21. Berkeley and Los Angeles: University of California Press, 1989.

———. "Those Images That Yet Fresh Images Beget." *Journal of Musicology* 2 (1983): 227–45.

Schüler, Winfried. *Der Bayreuther Kreis von seiner Entstehung bis zum Ausgang der Wilhelminischen Ära: Wagnerkult und Kulturreform im Geiste völkischer Weltanschauung*. Vol. 12: *Neue Münstersche Beiträge zur Geschichtsforschung*. Edited by Heinz Gollwitzer. Münster: Aschendorff, 1971.

Spotts, Fredric. *Bayreuth: A History of the Wagner Festival*. New Haven and London: Yale University Press, 1994.

Stein, Herbert von. *Dichtung und Musik im Werk Richard Wagners*. Berlin: Gruyler, 1962.

———. "Richard Wagners Begriff der dichterisch-musikalischen Periode." *Die Musikforschung* 35 (1982): 162–65.

Stephan, Rudolf. "Gibt es ein Geheimnis der Form bei Richard Wagner?" In *Das Drama Richard Wagner als musikalische Kunstwerk*, ed. Carl Dahlhaus, 9–16. Vol. 23 of *Studien zur Musikgeschichte des 19. Jahrhunderts*. Regensburg: Gustav Bosse, 1970.

Stokes, Jeffrey L. "Contour and Motive: A Study of "Flight" and "Love" in Wagner's "Ring," "Tristan," and "Meistersinger." Ph.D. dissertation, State University of New York at Buffalo, 1984.

Van der Lek, Robbert. "Zum Begriff Übergang und zu seiner Anwendung durch Alfred Lorenz auf die Musik von Wagners 'Ring'." *Die Musikforschung* 35 (1982): 129–47.

Voss, Egon. "Noch einmal: Das Geheimnis der Form bei Richard Wagner." In *Theaterarbeit an Wagners 'Ring'*, edited by Dietrich Mach, 251–67. Munich: R. Piper, 1978. Translated by Stewart Spencer as "Once Again: the Secret of Form in Wagner's Works" in *Wagner* 4 (June 1983): 66–79.

Westernhagen, Curt von. *The Forging of the "Ring"*. Translated by Arnold and Mary Whittall. Cambridge: Cambridge University Press, 1976.

———. *Richard Wagner: Sein Werk, sein Wesen, seine Welt*. Zurich: Atlantis, 1956.

———. *Wagner: A Biography*. Translated by Mary Whittall. Cambridge: Cambridge University Press, 1981. [First pub. 1968]

Whittall, Arnold. "Wagner's Later Stage Works." In *New Oxford History of Music*, vol. 9: *Romanticism*, edited by Gerald Abraham, 257–321. Oxford: Oxford University Press, 1990.

Wildgruber, Jens. "Das Geheimnis der 'Barform' in R. Wagners *Die Meistersinger von Nürnberg*: Plädoyer für eine neue Art der

Formbetrachtung." In *Festschrift Heinz Becker*, edited by Jürgen Schläder and Reinhold Quandt, 205–13. Laaber: Laaber Verlag, 1982.

Zelinsky, Hartmut. *Richard Wagner: Ein deutsches Thema*. Frankfurt-am-Main: Zweitausendeins, 1976.

Philosophy and Aesthetics

Pre-1945

Benjamin, Walter. "The Work of Art in the Age of Mechanical Reproduction." In *Illuminations*, edited and with an introduction by Hannah Arendt, translated by Harry Zohn, 219–53. New York: Harcourt, Brace & World, 1968. [First pub. 1936]

Blessinger, Karl. "Musik als Ausdruck und als Form." *Neue Musik-Zeitung* 44 (1923): 97–98, 151–54.

Croce, Benedetto. *Aesthetic as Science of Expression and General Linguistic*. Rev. ed., translated by Douglas Ainslie. New York: Noonday Press, 1962. [First pub. 1902]

Dessoir, Max. *Ästhetik und allgemeine Kunstwissenschaft: In den Grundzügen dargestellt*. Stuttgart: Ferdinand Enke, 1906. Translated by S.A. Emery as *Aesthetics and Theory of Art*. Detroit: Wayne State University Press, 1970.

———. "Richard Wagner als Ästhetiker." *Bayreuther Blätter* 14 (1891): 97–110, 132–41.

Ehrenfels, Christian von. *Philosophischen Schriften*. 4 vols. Edited by Reinhard Fabian. Munich: Philosophia Verlag, 1982–90.

Grunsky, Hans Alfred. "Form und Erlebnis." *Bayreuther Festspielführer* (1934): 165–70.

Grunsky, Karl. *Musikästhetik*. Leipzig: G.F. Göschen, 1907.

Hanslick, Eduard. *On the Musically Beautiful: A Contribution towards the Revision of the Aesthetics of Music*. Translated and edited by Geoffrey Payzant. Indianapolis: Hackett, 1986.

Hausegger, Friedrich von. "Aesthetik von Innen." *Bayreuther Blätter* 16 (1893): 327–38; 18 (1895): 337–47.

———. *Die Musik als Ausdruck*. 2nd ed. Vienna: Konegen, 1887. First edition published serially in the *Bayreuther Blätter* 7 (1884) and as a book in 1885.

Heidegger, Martin. *Being and Time*. Translated by John Macquarrie and Edward Robinson. New York: Harper & Row, 1962.

———. "The Origin of the Work of Art." In *Poetry, Language, Thought*, 15–87. Translated by Albert Hofstadter. New York: Harper Colophon Books, 1971.

Mey, Curt. *Die Musik als tönende Weltidee: Versuch einer Metaphysik der*

Musik. Erster Teil: Die metaphysichen Urgesetze der Melodik. Leipzig: Hermann Seemann, 1901.

Moos, Paul. *Die Philosophie der Musik von Kant bis Eduard von Hartmann.* 2nd rev. edition Stuttgart: Deutsche Verlags-Anstalt, 1922 [orig. pub. as *Moderne Musikästhetik in Deutschland*, 1902.]

Nietzsche, Friedrich. *The Birth of Tragedy.* In *Basic Writings of Nietzsche*, edited and translated by Walter Kaufmann. New York: Modern Library, 1968.

Schopenhauer, Arthur. *The World as Will and Idea.* 3 vols. Translated by R.B. Haldane and J. Kemp. London: Routledge & Kegan Paul, 1883.

Spengler, Oswald. *The Decline of the West.* 2 vols. Translated by Charles Francis Atkinson. New York: Knopf, 1926, 1928.

Wolzogen, Hans von. "Von der Musik als Form und als Ausdruck." *Die Musik* 1 (1902): 1923–32.

Worringer, Wilhelm. *Abstraction and Empathy: A Contribution to the Psychology of Style.* Translated by Michael Bullock. New York: International Universities Press, 1953. [First pub. 1908]

———. *Form in Gothic.* Edited and translated by Herbert Read. New York: Schocken Books, 1967. [First pub. 1910]

Post-1945

Adorno, Theodor W. *The Jargon of Authenticity.* Translated by Knut Tarnowski and Frederic Will. Evanston: Northwestern University Press, 1973.

Almén, Byron. "Prophets of the Decline: The Worldviews of Heinrich Schenker and Oswald Spengler." *Indiana Theory Review* 17 (Spring 1996): 1–24.

Bujić, Bojan, ed. *Music in European Thought 1851–1912.* Cambridge: Cambridge University Press, 1988.

Danz, Ernst-Joachim. *Die Objektlose Kunst: Untersuchungen zur Musikästhetik Friedrich von Hauseggers.* Regensburg: Gustav Bosse, 1981.

———. "Richard Wagner und Friedrich von Hausegger: Der Meister und sein Ästhetiker in Graz." In *Richard Wagner 1813–1883: Die Rezeption im 19. und 20. Jahrhundert. Gesammelte Beiträge des Salzburger Symposiums*, edited by Ullrich Müller, Franz Hundsnurscher, and Cornelius Sommer, 249–75. Stuttgart: Hans Dieter Heinz, 1984.

Dahlhaus, Carl. *The Idea of Absolute Music.* Translated by Roger Lustig. Chicago: University of Chicago Press, 1989.

Horkheimer, Max and Theodore W. Adorno. *Dialectic of Enlightenment.* Translated by John Cumming. New York: Continuum, 1986.

Kockelmans, Joseph J. *Heidegger on Art and Art Works.* Dordrecht: Martinus Nijhoff, 1985.

Lacoue-Labarthe, Philippe. *Heidegger, Art and Politics.* Translated by Chris Turner. Oxford: Blackwell, 1990.

Levarie, Siegmund, and Ernst Levy. *Musical Morphology: A Discourse and a Dictionary.* Kent: Kent State University Press, 1983.

Lippman, Edward, ed. *Musical Aesthetics: A Historical Reader.* Vol. 2: *The Nineteenth Century.* Stuyvesant: Pendragon Press, 1988.

Paddison, Max. *Adorno's Aesthetics of Music.* Cambridge: Cambridge University Press, 1993.

Rajan, Tilottama. "Language, Music, and the Body: Nietzsche and Deconstruction." In *Intersections: Nineteenth-Century Philosophy and Contemporary Theory,* edited by Tilottama Rajan and David Clark, 147–69. Albany: SUNY Press, 1995.

Stollmann, Rainer. "Fascist Politics as a Total Work of Art: Tendencies of the Aestheticization of Political Life in National Socialism." Translated by Ronald L. Smith. *New German Critique* 14 (1978): 41–60.

Wolin, Richard, ed. *The Heidegger Controversy: A Critical Reader.* Cambridge, MA: MIT Press, 1993.

Theory and Analysis

Pre-1945

Baensch, Otto. "Der Aufbau des 2. Satzes in Beethovens IX. Symphonie." *Bayreuther Festspielführer* (1925): 238–46.

———. *Aufbau und Sinn des Chorfinales in Beethovens neunter Symphonie.* Berlin and Leipzig: Gruyter, 1930.

Bekker, Paul. *Musikgeschichte als Geschichte der musikalischen Formwandlungen.* Stuttgart, Berlin, and Leipzig: Deutsche Verlags-Anstalt, 1926. Reprint, Hildesheim: Georg Olms, 1976.

Bergfeld, Joachim. *Die formale Struktur der symphonischen Dichtungen Franz Liszts.* Inaugural Dissertation, Berlin, 1931. Eisenach: Philipp Kühner, 1931.

Braunstein, Josef. *Beethovens Leonore-Ouvertüren: Eine historisch-stilkritische Untersuchung.* Leipzig: Breitkopf & Härtel, 1927.

Eichenauer, Richard. *Von den Formen der Musik.* Wolfenbüttel: Georg Kallmeyer, 1943.

Erpf, Hermann. "Der Begriff der musikalischen Form." *Zeitschrift für Ästhetik und allgemeine Kunstwissenschaft* 9 (1914): 355–86.

Grunsky, Hans Alfred. "Der erste Satz von Bruckners Neunter: Ein Bild höchster Formvollendung." *Die Musik* 18 (1925): 21–34, 104–12.

———. "Form und Erlebnis." *Bayreuther Festspielführer* (1934): 165–70.

Halm, August. "Musikdrama und Sonatenform." In *Von Grenzen und Ländern der Musik: Gesammelte Aufsätze,* 47–57. Munich: Georg Müller, 1916.

————. *Von Form und Sinn der Musik: Gesammelte Aufsätze.* Edited, with an introductory essay, by Siegfried Schmalzriedt. Wiesbaden: Breitkopf & Härtel, 1978.

Karthaus, Werner. "Die musikalische Analyse." *Die Musik* 21 (1929): 264–71.

Kretzschmar, Hermann. "Anregungen zur Förderung musikalischer Hermeneutik." *Jahrbuch der Musikbibliothek Peters* 9 (1902): 45–66.

————. "Neue Anregungen zur Förderung musikalischer Hermeneutik." *Jahrbuch der Musikbibliothek Peters* 12 (1905): 75–86.

Krohn, Ilmari. *Der Formbau in den Symphonien von Jean Sibelius.* Helsinki: Finnische Literaturgesellschaft, 1942.

————. *Anton Bruckners Symphonien: Untersuchung über Formenbau und Stimmungsgehalt.* Helsinki: Finnische Literaturgesellschaft, 1955–57.

Kurth, Ernst. *Bruckner.* 2 vols. Berlin: Max Hesse, 1925. Reprint, Hildesheim: Georg Olms, 1971.

————. *Romantische Harmonik und ihre Kreis in Wagners 'Tristan'.* 3rd ed. Berlin: Max Hesse, 1923. Reprint, Hildesheim: Georg Olms, 1968. [First pub. 1920]

————. *Selected Writings.* Edited and translated by Lee Rothfarb. Cambridge: Cambridge University Press, 1991.

Luetger, Wilhelm. "Bachs Motette Jesu meine Freude." *Musik und Kirche* 4 (1932): 97–113.

Maisch, Walter. *Puccinis musikalische Formgebung untersucht an der Oper 'La Bohème'."* Neustadt a.d. Aisch: P.C.W. Schmidt'sche Buchdr., 1934.

Riemann, Hugo. *Große Kompositionslehre.* Bd. I: *Der homophone Satz (Melodielehre und Harmonielehre)*; Bd. 2: *Der polyphone Satz (Kontrapunkt, Fuge, und Kanon).* Berlin and Stuttgart: Spemann, 1902.

————. *Grundriß der Kompositionslehre (Musikalische Formenlehre).* 6th ed. Berlin: Max Hesse, 1920.

————. *Harmony Simplified; Or, the Theory of the Tonal Functions of Chords.* Translated by Henry Bewerunge. London: Augener & Co., [1895].

Röttger, Heinz. "Das Formproblem bei Richard Strauss, gezeigt an der Oper 'Die Frau ohne Schatten' mit Einschluß von 'Guntram' und 'Intermezzo'." Ph.D. dissertation, Munich, 1937. Berlin: Junker und Dünnhaupt, 1937.

Schenker, Heinrich. *Free Composition.* Vol. 3: *New Musical Theories and Fantasies.* Translated and edited by Ernst Oster. New York: Longman, 1979. [First pub. 1935]

Schering, Arnold. "Historische und Nationale Klangstile." *Jahrbuch der Musikbibliothek Peters* 33 (1927): 31–43.

————. "Musikalische Analyse und Wertidee." *Jahrbuch der Musikbibliothek Peters* 35 (1929): 9–20.

Schoenberg, Arnold. *The Musical Idea and the Logic, Technique, and Art of Its Presentation.* Edited, translated, and with a commentary by Patricia

Carpenter and Severine Neff. New York: Columbia University Press, 1995.

Schütze, Erich. "Zur Frage der musikalischen Analyse." *Die Musik* 31 (1939): 225–31.

Schuh, Willi. *Formprobleme bei Heinrich Schütz.* Leipzig: Breitkopf & Härtel, 1928. Reprint, Niedeln, Liechtenstein: Kraus Reprint, 1976.

Tobel, Rudolf von. *Die Formwelt der klassischen Instrumentalmusik.* Bern and Leipzig: Paul Haupt, 1935.

Wachten, Edmund. "Der einheitliche Grundzug der Straußschen Formgestaltung." *Zeitschrift für Musikwissenschaft* 16 (1934): 257–74.

Werker, Wilhelm. *Studien über die Symmetrie im Bau der Fugen und die motivische Zusammengehörigkeit der Präludien und Fugen des 'Wohltemperierten Klaviers' von Johann Sebastian Bach.* Leipzig: Breitkopf & Härtel, 1922. Reprint, Wiesbaden: Martin Sändig, 1969.

Post-1945

Abbate, Carolyn, and Roger Parker. "Dismembering Mozart." *Cambridge Opera Journal* 2 (1990): 187–95.

———. "Introduction: On Analyzing Opera." In *Analyzing Opera: Verdi and Wagner*, edited by Carolyn Abbate and Roger Parker, 1–24. Berkeley and Los Angeles: University of California Press, 1989.

Bent, Ian. *Analysis.* New York: Norton, 1987.

———, ed. *Music Analysis in the Nineteenth Century.* Vol. 1: *Fugue, Form and Style.* Vol. 2: *Hermeneutic Approaches.* Cambridge: Cambridge University Press, 1994.

Chew, Geoffrey. "Ernst Kurth, Music as Psychic Motion and *Tristan und Isolde*: Towards a Model for Analysing Musical Instability." *Music Analysis* 10 (1991): 171–93.

Chusid, Martin. "The Tonality of *Rigoletto*." In *Analyzing Opera: Verdi and Wagner*, edited by Carolyn Abbate and Roger Parker, 241–61. Berkeley and Los Angeles: University of California Press, 1989.

Cooper, Grosvenor, and Leonard Meyer. *The Rhythmic Structure of Music.* Chicago: University of Chicago Press, 1960.

Damschroder, David, and David Russell Williams. *Music Theory from Zarlino to Schenker: A Bibliography and Guide.* Stuyvesant: Pendragon, 1990.

Federhofer, Hellmut. *Beiträge zur musikalischen Gestaltanalyse.* Graz: Akademische Druck- und Verlagsanstalt, 1950.

Lawton, David. "Tonal Systems in *Aida*, Act III." In *Analyzing Opera: Verdi and Wagner*, edited by Carolyn Abbate and Roger Parker, 262–75. Berkeley and Los Angeles: University of California Press, 1989.

Levarie, Siegmund. *Mozart's "Le Nozze di Figaro": A Critical Analysis.* Chicago: University of Chicago Press, 1952.

Mickelsen, William Cooper. *Hugo Riemann's Theory of Harmony, with a Translation of Riemann's "History of Music Theory," Book 3*. Lincoln: University of Nebraska Press, 1977.

Moyer, Birgitte. "Concepts of Musical Form in the Nineteenth Century with Special Reference to A.B. Marx and Sonata Form." Ph.D. dissertation, Stanford University, 1969.

Neff, Severine. "Schoenberg and Goethe: Organicism and Analysis." In *Music Theory and the Exploration of the Past*, edited by Christopher Hatch and David W. Bernstein, 409–33. Chicago: University of Chicago Press, 1993.

New Grove Dictionary of Opera, 1992. S.v. "Analysis," by Carolyn Abbate; "Tonality (2)," by Arnold Whittall.

Parkanay, Stephen. "Ernst Kurth's *Bruckner* and the Adagio of the Seventh Symphony." *19th-Century Music* 11 (1988): 262–81.

Pastille, William. "Music and Morphology: Goethe's Influence on Schenker's Thought." In *Schenker Studies*, edited by Hedi Siegel, 29–44. Cambridge: Cambridge University Press, 1990.

Platoff, John. "Myths and Realities about Tonal Planning in Mozart's Operas." *Cambridge Opera Journal* 8 (1996): 3–15.

Powers, Harold. "One Halfstep at a Time: Tonal Transposition and 'Split Association' in Italian Opera." *Cambridge Opera Journal* 7 (1995): 135–64.

Rothfarb, Lee. "Beethoven's Formal Dynamics: August Halm's Phenomenological Perspective." In *Beethoven Forum 5*, edited by Lewis Lockwood, 65–84. Lincoln: University of Nebraska Press, 1996.

———. "Ernst Kurth's *Die Voraussetzungen der theoretischen Harmonik* and the Beginnings of Music Psychology." *Theoria* 4 (1989): 10–33.

———. *Ernst Kurth as Theorist and Analyst*. Philadelphia: University of Pennsylvania Press, 1988.

———. "Ernst Kurth in Historical Perspective: His Intellectual Inheritance and Music-Theoretical Legacy." *Schweizer Jahrbuch für Musikwissenschaft* 6–7 (1986–87): 23–42.

———. "Hermeneutics and Energetics: Analytical Alternatives in the Early 1900s." *Journal of Music Theory* 36.1 (1992): 43–68.

———. "Music Analysis, Cultural Morality, and Sociology in the Writings of August Halm." *Indiana Theory Review* 16 (1995): 171–96.

———. "The 'New Education' and Music Theory, 1900–1925." In *Music Theory and the Exploration of the Past*, edited by Christopher Hatch and David W. Bernstein, 449–71. Chicago: University of Chicago Press, 1993.

Solie, Ruth. "The Living Work: Organicism and Musical Analysis." *19th-Century Music* 4 (1980): 147–56.

Thaler, Lotte. *Organische Form in der Musiktheorie des 19. und beginnenden 20. Jahrhunderts*. Munich and Salzburg: Emil Katzbichler, 1984.

Webster, James. "Mozart's Operas and the Myth of Musical Unity." *Cambridge Opera Journal* 2 (1990): 197–218.

Whittall, Arnold. "'Twisted Relations': Method and Meaning in Britten's *Billy Budd*." *Cambridge Opera Journal* 2 (1990): 145–71.

Wintle, Christopher. "Issues in Dahlhaus." *Music Analysis* 1 (1982): 341–55.

Wuensch, Gerhard. "Hugo Riemann's Musical Theory." *Studies in Music from the University of Western Ontario* 2 (1977): 108–24.

General

Abbate, Carolyn. *Unsung Voices: Opera and Musical Narrative in the Nineteenth Century*. Princeton: Princeton University Press, 1991.

Abraham, Gerald. *A Hundred Years of Music*. 3rd ed. Chicago: Aldine, 1964. [First pub. 1938]

Allen, Warren Dwight. *Philosophies of Music History: A Study of General Histories of Music, 1600–1960*. New York: Dover, 1962.

Althusser, Louis. "Ideology and Ideological State Apparatuses." In *Essays on Ideology*, 1–60. London: Verso, 1984.

Botstein, Leon. "Listening through Reading: Musical Literacy and the Concert Audience." *19th-Century Music* 16 (Fall 1992): 129–45.

———. "Music and Its Public: Habits of Listening and the Crisis of Musical Modernism in Vienna, 1870–1914." Ph.D. dissertation, Harvard University, 1985.

Dahlhaus, Carl. *Between Romanticism and Modernism: Four Studies in the Music of the Later Nineteenth Century*. Translated by Mary Whittall. Berkeley: University of California Press, 1980. [First pub. 1974]

Eagleton, Terry. *Ideology: An Introduction*. London and New York: Verso, 1991.

Eksteins, Modris. *Rites of Spring: The Great War and the Birth of the Modern Age*. Toronto: Lester & Orpen Dennys, 1989.

Elsner, Andreas. "Zur Geschichte des musikwissenschaftlichen Lehrstuhls an der Universität München." Inaugural-Dissertation, Ludwig-Maximilians-Universität Munich, 1982.

———. "Zur Geschichte des musikwissenschaftlichen Lehrstuhls an der Universität München vom 19. zum 20. Jahrhundert." In *Die Ludwig-Maximilians-Universität in ihren Fakultäten*, edited by Laetitia Boehm and Johannes Spörl, Bd.2, 281–301. Berlin: Duncker & Humbolt, 1980.

Encyclopedia of the Third Reich. Edited by Christian Zentner and Friedmann Bedürstig. Translated and edited by Amy Hackett. New York: Macmillan, 1991.

Fallon, Daniel. *The German University: A Heroic Ideal in Conflict with the Modern World*. Boulder: Colorado Associated University Press, 1980.

Field, Geoffrey G. *Evangelist of Race: The Germanic Vision of Houston Stewart Chamberlain*. New York: Columbia University Press, 1981.

Grunsky, Karl. *Fragen der Bruckner-Auffassung*. Stuttgart: Heyder, 1936.

————. *Kampf um deutsche Musik!* Stuttgart: Erhard Walther, 1933.

————. *Volkstum und Musik*. Eßlingen a.N: Wilh. Langguith, 1934.

Handwörterbuch der musikalischen Terminologie. S.v. "Unendliche Melodie," by Fritz Reckow; "Leitmotive," by Christoph von Blumröder.

Handschin, Jacques. *Musikgeschichte im Überblick*. 2nd ed. Lucerne: Räber, 1964. [First pub. 1948]

Heiber, Helmut. *Walter Frank und sein Reichsinstitut für Geschichte des neuen Deutschlands*. Stuttgart: Deutsche Verlags-Anstalt, 1966.

Hepokoski, James. "The Dahlhaus Project and Its Extra-Musicological Sources." *19th-Century Music* 14 (1991): 221–46.

Herf, Jeffrey. *Reactionary Modernism: Technology, Culture, and Politics in Weimar and the Third Reich*. Cambridge: Cambridge University Press, 1984.

Herzfeld, Friedrich. "Das Problem der Generation in der Musik." *Die Musik* 26 (1934): 267–74.

Hohendahl, Peter Uwe. *Building a National Literature: The Case of Germany 1830–1870*. Translated by Renate Baron Franciscono. Ithaca and London: Cornell University Press, 1989.

————, ed. *A History of German Literary Criticism, 1730–1980*. Lincoln: University of Nebraska Press, 1988.

Jaeger, Hans. "Generations in History: Reflections on a Controversial Concept." *History and Theory* 24 (1985): 273–93.

Kater, Michael H. *The Twisted Muse: Musicians and Their Music in the Third Reich*. New York: Oxford, 1997.

Kerman, Joseph. *Opera as Drama*. New York: Alfred A. Knopf, 1956; rev. ed., Berkeley: University of California Press, 1988.

Kristeva, Julia. "Word, Dialogue, and Novel." In *The Kristeva Reader*, edited by Toril Moi, 34–61. New York: Columbia University Press, 1986.

Levi, Erik. *Music in the Third Reich*. New York: St. Martin's, 1994.

McGrath, William. *Dionysian Art and Populist Politics in Austria*. New Haven: Yale University Press, 1974.

Mercer-Taylor, Peter. "Unification and Tonal Absolution in *Der Freischütz*." *Music & Letters* 78 (1997): 220–32.

Meyer, Michael. "Musicology in the Third Reich: A Gap in Historical Studies." *European Studies Review* 8 (1978): 349–64.

————. "The Nazi Musicologist as Myth Maker in the Third Reich." *Journal of Contemporary History* 10 (1975): 649–55.

————. *The Politics of Music in the Third Reich*. New York: Peter Lang, 1991.

Montrose, Louis. "Renaissance Literary Studies and the Subject of History." *English Literary Renaissance* 16 (1986): 5–12.

Moser, Hans Joachim. *Geschichte der deutschen Musik*. Vol. 3: *Vom*

Auftreten Beethovens bis zur Gegenwart. 2nd ed. Stuttgart: Lokay, 1928. Reprint, Hildesheim: Georg Olms, 1968.

Mosse, George. *Mass and Man: Nationalist and Fascist Perceptions of Reality.* New York: Howard Fertig, 1980.

Mosse, George. *The Nationalization of the Masses: Political Symbolism and Mass Movements in Germany from the Napoleonic War through the Third Reich.* New York: Howard Fertig, 1975.

Noakes, Jeremy and Geoffrey Pridham. *Documents on Nazism, 1919–1945.* London: Jonathan Cape, 1974.

Neue Deutsche Biographie, edited by the Historische Kommission bei der Bayerischen Akademie der Wissenschaften. S.v. "Lorenz," by Silvia Backs (Ottokar), Claus Priesner (Richard), and Reinhold Schlötterer (Alfred).

Potter, Pamela. "The Deutsche Musikgesellschaft, 1918–1938," *Journal of Musicological Research* 11 (1991): 151–76.

———. "Did Himmler *Really* Like Gregorian Chant? The SS and Musicology." *Modernism/Modernity* 2.3 (1995): 45–68.

———. "Musicology Under Hitler: New Sources in Context." *Journal of the American Musicological Society* 49 (1996): 70–113.

———. "Trends in German Musicology, 1918–1945: The Effects of Methodological, Ideological, and Institutional Change on the Writing of Music History." Ph.D. dissertation, Yale University, 1991.

Potyra, Rudolf. *Die Theatermusikalien der Landesbibliothek Coburg: Katalog, mit einer Abhandlung zur Geschichte des Herzoglichen Hoftheaters Coburg-Gotha und seiner Notensammlung von Jürgen Erdmann.* 2 Vols. Munich: Henle, 1995.

Ringer, Fritz K. *The Decline of the German Mandarins: The German Academic Community, 1890–1933.* Cambridge, MA: Harvard University Press, 1969.

Roberge, Marc-André. "Le périodique *Die Musik* (1901–1944) et sa transformation à travers trois périodes de l'histoire allemande." *Revue de musicologie* 78 (1992): 109–44.

Rosenberg, Alfred. *Der Mythus des 20. Jahrhunderts: Eine Wertung der seelisch-geistigen Gestaltenkämpfe unserer Zeit.* 35–36th ed. Munich: Hoheneichen, 1934.

Saussure, Ferdinand de. *Course in General Linguistics.* Translated by Wade Baskin. New York: Philosophical Library, 1959. [First pub. 1916]

Smith, Barry, ed. *Foundations of Gestalt Theory.* Munich: Philosophia Verlag, 1988.

Stern, Fritz. *The Politics of Cultural Despair: A Study in the Rise of the Germanic Ideology.* New York: Anchor, 1965.

Tomlinson, Gary. *Music in Renaissance Magic: Toward a Historiography of Others.* Chicago: University of Chicago Press, 1993.

———. "The Web of Culture: A Context for Musicology." *19th-Century Music* 7 (1984): 350–62.

Treitler, Leo. *Music and the Historical Imagination*. Cambridge, MA: Harvard University Press, 1989.

———. "The Politics of Reception: Tailoring the Present as Fulfilment of a Desired Past." *Journal of the Royal Musical Association* 116 (1991): 280–98.

Viereck, Peter. *Metapolitics: The Roots of the Nazi Mind*. New York: Capricorn Books, 1961.

Index